The Kings of Wessex

FROM CERDIC TO ALFRED

The Kings of Wessex

FROM CERDIC TO ALFRED

MICHAEL JOHN KEY

AMBERLEY

First published 2025

Amberley Publishing
The Hill, Stroud
Gloucestershire, GL5 4EP

www.amberley-books.com

British Library Cataloguing in Publication Data.
A catalogue record for this book is available from the British Library.

ISBN 978 1 4456 9412 2 (hardback)
ISBN 978 1 4456 9413 9 (ebook)

1 2 3 4 5 6 7 8 9 10

Typesetting by SJmagic DESIGN SERVICES, India.
Printed in the UK.

Appointed GPSR EU Representative: Easy Access System Europe Oü, 16879218
Address: Mustamäe tee 50, 10621, Tallinn, Estonia
Contact Details: gpsr.requests@easproject.com, +358 40 500 3575

Contents

Acknowledgements

As with my earlier books, *Edward the Elder: King of the Anglo-Saxons*, and *House of Godwin: The Rise and Fall of an Anglo-Saxon Dynasty*, I am indebted during the completion of this latest work to those academics and scholars who have previously devoted their time and energy into translating and editing the key primary source texts, all of which I have found invaluable when conducting my research. They form a vital part of the resource material, and the completion of this book would not have been possible without their earlier endeavours. Thanks also go to the compilers and keepers of the *Prosopography of Anglo-Saxon England* database for its invaluable detail on the royal charters. Along with all the other primary and secondary sources consulted during my research, they are fully acknowledged within the enclosed bibliography.

The period covered by this history has been challenging in terms of the resources available to historians. I am grateful for the secondary source material and comments provided by the whole community of historians who have majored in or been involved in discussing or writing about Anglo-Saxon history over the last half-century or more. They have provided me with many additional insights, details, and lines of research well beyond the primary texts. In terms of the specific period covered by this book (*circa* 500 to the 880s), I am grateful for the library of secondary work and research provided by David Dumville, Nick Higham, Simon Keynes, D. P. Kirby, Michael Lapidge, and Barbara Yorke.

I would also like to recognise the work of everyone at Amberley Publishing, and especially Alex Bennett, in bringing this book to completion. Finally, I would once again give a special mention to my partner, Alice, for her continued patience.

List of Maps and Tables

Introduction

This book explores the history of the Anglo-Saxon kingdom of Wessex, spanning nearly four centuries from the sixth century to the ninth. More than twenty kings ruled the kingdom throughout its history, starting with its founder, the legendary warrior king Cerdic, and culminating with the most famous of them, Alfred the Great. We will follow the rise of Wessex from its early days, when the two Saxon Germanic tribes, the West Saxons from Hampshire and the Gewisse from the Upper Thames Valley, united to form the future kingdom and expand under a series of strong kings, eventually forging the most dominant Anglo-Saxon kingdom in England.

To understand the history of Wessex, medieval historians heavily rely on recorded dates and regnal timeframes, which are valuable tools given the limited data available. Our history begins with the Roman retreat from Britain in the fifth century and the subsequent arrival of the first Anglo-Saxons. It will end during the 880s, mid-way through the reign of Alfred the Great, when as the incumbent king of Wessex he would proclaim himself to be 'King of the Anglo-Saxons', thus ending the kingdom's distinct regnal period. Eventually, Alfred's descendants became the first kings of a united England.

As something of a surprise during my research, it became clear that a text devoted to the kingdom's chronology via its full regnal line of kings had not previously been addressed in detail. Hence, *The Kings of Wessex* may help fill some of that void. The book discusses some aspects of cultural and societal development, encompassing the early development of Christianity in Wessex. Nevertheless, the primary aim of the book is a consideration of Wessex's political and military history through its kingships, and they are the key elements around which the text functions.

It is problematic to label early Anglo-Saxon leaders like Cerdic and his son Cynric as kings in the traditional sense. The title is often given subjectively and maybe too quickly to them and their contemporaries from the fifth and sixth centuries. Although they were unquestionably warlords who exerted authority over significant territories, the idea of a lone ruler or king may have been misleading before the seventh century. The issue of British leadership during this period raises a similar question, and it's worth noting that power was divided among territorial regions to maintain stability. With Wessex, during the seventh century, men such as Cynegils, Cenwealh, and Caedwalla more closely resembled what we now recognise as kings, ruling their lands and administration in a monarchical fashion.

In general, I have endeavoured to keep the text running along chronological lines as much as possible. The depth of detail is very much reliant on when and where, and from which origin, primary source detail has been available. Unfortunately, much of the period covered by this book suffers from a paucity of primary source material. This is especially relevant to certain events occurring from the mid-fifth to early eighth centuries. In situations where reliable sources are lacking in detail, some speculation and supposition have been employed to supplement the known information, while avoiding tenuous or excessively intricate conjecture. My assumptions or theories on any particular incident are based on an assessment of the evidence, and ultimately readers are free to agree or disagree with the conclusions.

The Germanic origins of the West Saxons are discussed in more detail in the next chapter. However, to describe Cerdic and his immediate successors as 'West Saxon', and to similarly designate the Gewisse leadership under the same label, comes with a heavy literary licence. They did not refer to themselves by those designations, and it was not until the seventh century, after several generations of settlement by Germanic tribes in England, that they identified as West Saxon. Similarly, Wessex, the name of the kingdom which is derived from 'West Seaxe' or West Saxon, was a later accreditation used by later chroniclers.

Early ongoing references to the West Saxons and the Gewisse, particularly the latter, have hopefully limited any potential confusion as to their eventual connection. As will be seen in the early chapters, it was the Gewisse that took the first steps to develop much of what would later be claimed as Wessex's western territory. Historians may disagree on timescales regarding their eventual union of shared interest, and the significance or otherwise of the Gewisse. However, whether they were allies with joint kings or with a primary king and sub-king, I have adopted the principle that the two groups (Gewisse and West Saxon) should be defined as separate entities up to the reign of Ceawlin in the late seventh century. Thereafter, within the main text, both are jointly referred to as being West Saxon. To limit potential issues on regional names I have also used the terms 'Wessex', 'Anglo-Saxon' and 'England' throughout the text, alongside the names of the various separate kingdoms and shires as are recognised today, even though these derivations are all later constructs and were not applied during most of the period covered by this history.

The initial chapters hold to the principle of describing the native British population as either Celtic British or Romano-British, a description which applied following the end of Roman control within Britain. Some British tribes, primarily those in the south-east quadrant of the country, which had stronger, more enduring exposure to Roman culture, kept Roman influences for longer. Having generally reverted to their tribal regional divisions ahead of the arrival of the Anglo-Saxons, all British Celtic tribal kingdoms are identified specifically, such as the Atrebates, Belgae, Durotriges, Catuvellauni, etc. This rule equally applies to the Anglo-Saxons, with the original Germanic settlers identified separately within their new regional kingdoms, namely the West Saxons/Gewisse, South Saxons, East Saxons, Kentish, East Anglians, Mercians, etc.

On the subject of definitions, 'England', and for that matter Wales and Scotland, did not exist as recognised nations during the period covered by this book. The Anglo-Saxon kingdoms would not unite to create what we would identify as a single nation-state until the mid-tenth century, and wherever England is named for identification purposes in the text this should be borne in mind. Changes in the territories held by specific groups, within both the British tribal regions and later the Anglo-Saxon kingdoms, may often be difficult to follow in terms of geography. To avoid unnecessary complications, I have found it useful to describc some regions and tribal locations in the main text in terms of their present-day geographical settings and boundaries using modern-day regional names. Similarly, and more relevant in terms of the development of Wessex, all present-day county regional names – for example, Berkshire, Wiltshire and Dorset – are used throughout to help identify geographical regions more easily, even though they are later creations beyond most of the period covered in this book. The rule also applies to current towns and settlements, many of which did not exist before the ninth century. They are named in the text to help locate specific places.

Much of the historical period covered by this book was once simply identified by historians as the 'Dark Ages', so named to denote a decline in Western culture across Britain and northern Europe after the collapse of the Western Roman Empire.[1] The term therefore seemed appropriate to describe what was perceived as a suspension or interruption of learning and knowledge and societal development, evidenced by the recognised paucity of surviving texts from the period following population shifts and upheavals.[2] Nevertheless, in recent decades, use of the term has fallen from favour and it is now seen as a misnomer. Advancements in archaeology and extended knowledge, awareness, and understanding of everyday early medieval lives and cultural development, not forgetting the expansion of Christian ideology over that same period, have largely replaced earlier assumptions and enabled a re-evaluation. The re-assessed evidence shows that the pre-existing cultural and social foundations that had flourished during the Roman period were not permanently lost, but remained suspended during this period of significant upheaval and were able to resurface when greater political stability returned. As a consequence, most historians now prefer to label these centuries with the more nuanced and neutral title of 'Early Middle Ages'.[3]

We are still nonetheless faced with a lack of textual evidence to support the political, military, and social developments alongside specific events. It cannot be denied that the reduced library of written primary sources for this period remains slim. This is most relevant for the period pre-700, as evidenced in the chapters devoted to the West Saxon kings who ruled before Ine (late seventh century). The causes which led to this shortage of surviving primary sources may be complicated. However, it is undeniable the upheavals across Europe in the post-Roman world certainly impacted knowledge and destroyed much of the contemporary historical record. In England, the earliest Anglo-Saxon pagan invaders were little interested in textual records and probably were involved, alongside the inter-tribal warfare between the British, in the destruction of texts that had been amassed beforehand.

Turning our attention to the primary sources at our disposal, the combination of archaeological evidence and landscape studies offers valuable clues for evaluating trends in British and Anglo-Saxon society. We now have greater knowledge of the lives, deaths and burial rituals of the various ethnic groups. For example, the late fifth century saw the introduction of radically different burial practices across much of lowland England.[4] Discovered grave goods and cultural artefacts help to understand the timescales involved in the Anglo-Saxon settlement of England, their assimilation and levels of integration, and what impact these newcomers had on the native post-Roman British population.

Geographical and topographical research, coupled with landscape studies, helps us understand the timing and location of West Saxon expansion and their settlement patterns in southern England. This enables a more accurate assessment of settlement sites, army movements, and potential battlefields. Nonetheless, there remains disagreement among historians on how the archaeological evidence should be interpreted, particularly regarding the scale and character of Anglo-Saxon settlements.[5]

Concerning ideology, the rise of Christianity gives us an example of how belief systems impacted the interplay between the British and the Anglo-Saxons, and how it influenced and became an important aspect of the political and military choices made by the West Saxon kings.

When it comes to the written record, we can examine the main primary texts that form the basis for this text and other Anglo-Saxon historiographies. However, all the sources noted below will have diverse levels of reliability. Whereas writers such as Gildas and Bede (see below) seem to provide a broadly accurate outline of events, historians are now more prone to question what was previously unchallenged. Early medieval writers did not always maintain a distinction between history and legend and the religious scribes who provide much of our known detail for the period between 500 and 900 occasionally had agendas that went beyond a simple recording of the facts. The first principle is to accept what primary texts we have, although this comes with a substantial proviso that we simply cannot be certain that everything within these sources can be and should be taken verbatim. Arguably, this acknowledgement applies to any primary source text about the Early Middle Ages due to the scarcity of information available to historians.

The most comprehensive surviving records we have are the various versions of the *Anglo-Saxon Chronicle* (abbreviated hereafter as ASC).[6] They chronicle events from the first century onwards, but they first compiled and recorded their detail from the late ninth century. There are several editions, usually identified as versions A through F, compiled at the religious houses in Winchester, Abingdon, Canterbury, Worcester and Peterborough. Individual entries are usually succinct, and much of their content is identical and was copied from similar contemporary documents. The efficacy of the entries is mixed, with one historian describing the ASC as being 'largely worthless as history'.[7] This view has some credence but is a little ungenerous. Some content may have been passed down by word of mouth for generations, as an oral tradition existed in the Anglo-Saxon period. Other content was presumably taken from earlier source documents that have not survived. In any case, the ASC is the main supporter of Cerdic's backstory and the traditional founding of Wessex.

Concerning early references to the West Saxon kings in the ASC, there is a list known as the *West Saxon Genealogical Regnal List* (hereafter abbreviated as WSGRL) that appears as a preface within versions B, C and D of the chronicle but differs from the chronology given in versions A and E.[8] The WSGRL creates a second regnal strand for the West Saxon kings which contradicts some of the ASC detail. The two do not align precisely on the chronology of the kings until the succession of Cynegils in 611.

Within the other primary source material, one notable contemporary work is the *Historia ecclesiastica gentis Anglorum* (The Ecclesiastical History of the English People), written by the Venerable Bede, a monk from Monkwearmouth–Jarrow Abbey in Northumbria who lived during the late seventh and early eighth centuries.[9] It focuses on the history of early Christianity in England, shaped by his didactic codes, but it also gives us much detail of political events, including within Wessex. Bede communicated with scholars throughout the Anglo-Saxon kingdoms, although he did not travel widely himself, and much of his information came from his communications with his contemporary Abbot Albinus of St Augustine's in Canterbury, using detail gathered by the more widely travelled London priest Notthelm.[10]

The oldest direct reference for the post-Roman period comes from the writings of the Celtic monk Gildas, in particular his tract *De Excidio et Conquestu Britanniae* (The Ruin and Conquest of Britain), which has been described as a highly personal and stylised diatribe.[11] We do not know where Gildas was based in Britain, and his text was not intended to be a historic chronicle. It remains the only near-contemporary source concerning the immediate post-Roman British era, written sometime within the years *c.* 490–530.[12] The text recounts the Roman withdrawal and the Romano-British vainly requesting help from Rome against expanding barbarian threats. He lauds the later heroic actions of Ambrosius Aurelianus, one of the Romano-British leaders who resisted Anglo-Saxon expansion, and was the first to refer to the famous British victory over the Anglo-Saxons at Mount Badon (Mons Badonicus).

Along similar lines but with perhaps less factual credibility is the *Historia Brittonum* (History of the Britons), a later work of the ninth-century Welsh monk Nennius.[13] It chronicles the Celtic British before the arrival of the Germanic tribes. Its accuracy is debatable, and it contains references to old British legends and superstitions, but it remains a useful source of detail. A more famous work is the *Historia Regum Britanniae* (The History of the Kings of Britain) by Geoffrey of Monmouth, written during the 1130s and originally called *De gestis Britonum* (*On the Deeds of the Britons*).[14] This work is inextricably linked with the legendary figure of King Arthur, and chronicles the lives of British kings through to the seventh century. Once seen by historians as a valuable contribution to our combined history, it is now generally acknowledged as primarily a work of fiction, with a smattering of facts thrown in. Another primary work of Welsh-British origin that contributes some useful information towards the early British historical record is the *Annales Cambriae* (Annals of Wales), a work derived from Welsh sources gathered in St David's in Dyfed. The annal covers events from the mid-fifth century onwards, but invariably offers only single-line entries.[15]

The late ninth-century work *Life of King Alfred* by the monk Asser, the biographer of Alfred, provides much important and invaluable detail of not only Alfred's reign but also those of his father Æthelwulf and his brothers Æthelwald and Æthelred, along with a few insights into Ecgberht's reign.[16] A century after Asser comes the *Chronicon Æthelweardi*, a Latin translation of a claimed lost copy of the ASC written between the 970s and 980s by Æthelweard, a writer and ealdorman claimed to be a descendant of Æthelred I. It contains some details not included in any of the extant versions of the chronicle.[17]

More detached from the period being discussed, but providing useful detail when verifying other earlier or near-contemporary source material, are the works of the three early twelfth-century Anglo-Norman chroniclers: William of Malmesbury's *Gesta Regum Anglorum* (History of the English Kings) and *Gesta Pontificum Anglorum* (History of the English Bishops), John of Worcester's *Chronicon*, and Henry of Huntingdon's *Historia Anglorum* (History of the English People).[18] Their works contain entries addressing the post-Roman period, although many of these are simply updated versions of the ASC record. However, they also contain to a varying degree content from earlier centuries which must have been gathered from other documentary sources which have since been lost or destroyed. Two other primary sources are invaluable for at least part of this period. The first is the accessible database *Prosopography of Anglo-Saxon England*, wherein all extant charters and other documents issued during the Anglo-Saxon period are preserved, and the other is *English Historical Documents*, a compilation of key extant documents for the period.[19]

It has been frequently necessary for the chapters that follow to resort to assumption and speculation where primary source detail is in short supply. Likewise, at other times we should question the reliability and accuracy of what detail we do have. Some conjecture has been necessary to form a meaningful narrative, but I have tried to use this cautiously. Where extended discussion has been required on particular events I have been, relying on the forbearance of the readership, hopefully, able in the majority of instances to arrive at plausible conclusions to support my arguments, but I would also encourage readers to draw their own conclusions where debate and evidence remain open.

While still on the subject of primary sources, a brief mention of calendar dating is necessary. Different dates were used on occasion for the start of the twelve-month cycle, primarily within some entries of the ASC through to the ninth century, including 1 September, 24 September, 25 December, and 25 March. Some events occurring between September and the end of December were dated as if in the following year, and contrarily some pre-25 March events were pulled back into the previous year. Where these anomalous date entries have been identified, they have been adjusted to the calendar year beginning 1 January.

In terms of the scope of the main text and in summary, chapters one and two consider the first arrival of the Germanic tribes onto British shores and, concerning Wessex, the specific origins and background of Cerdic's West Saxons who first settled in Hampshire. Also covered are the evident connection with their allied tribe the Gewisse, which settled the Upper Thames Valley, and their contact with the native Celtic British. The Gewisse played a significant role in the early development of Wessex, as will be seen in the upcoming chapters. Chapter three delves into the traditional history of Cerdic in the sixth century and the parallel role played by the Gewisse, and chapter four looks at the reign of Cerdic's son Cynric. Subsequent territorial gains made by Ceawlin and Ceol are considered in chapter five, along with the notion of the Gewisse being the dominant factor in ongoing expansion during the late sixth century.

Chapter six discusses the further progress and growth made during the reigns of Ceolwulf, Cynegils and Cwichelm (597–642), alongside a consideration of the West Saxon/Gewisse conversion from paganism to

Christianity. Chapter seven follows further territorial advancements made by Cenwealh for Wessex in the mid-seventh century, and chapter eight assesses the internal divisions highlighted during the reigns of Æscwine and Centwine and the military successes of Caedwalla in the late seventh century. Chapter nine focuses on the consolidation made during the reign of Ine (688–726), perhaps the first king of Wessex to establish a recognised stable administration, and chapter ten looks at the reigns of Æthelheard and Cuthred (726–756) and their efforts to maintain the autonomy of the kingdom in the face of Mercian aggression.

Following on, chapter eleven assesses the internal factional divide between the dynasties of Sigeberht and Cynewulf, and chapter twelve considers the reign of Beorhtric and his subservient relationship with Mercia's king Offa in the late ninth century. The next two chapters are devoted to Beorhtric's successor Ecgberht, such was his impact on the advancement of Wessex in the early decades of the ninth century. The first of these, chapter thirteen, despite limited primary source material to work with, considers Ecgberht's reign from his seizure of the throne to his important victory over Mercia in 825, and chapter fourteen looks at the reinforcement of Wessex's position during the second half of his reign to 839. Chapter fifteen assesses the further expansion of West Saxon authority under Æthelwulf, this time eastwards into Kent, and chapter sixteen reviews the political events surrounding the brief reigns of Æthelbald and Æthelberht. The reign of their brother Æthelred from 865 is discussed in chapter seventeen, with his war against the Great Danish Army front and centre, leading to the succession of Alfred, the youngest of Æthelwulf's sons, in 871. The penultimate chapter follows Alfred's struggles against the Danes and his exile in the Somerset Levels ahead of his return to defeat the Danes at Edington in 878. The final chapter follows the subsequent division of England into two spheres, Anglo-Saxon and Danish (the Danelaw), wherein Alfred assumed control of all remaining independent Anglo-Saxon territory. Consequently, he was the last person to be titled King of Wessex, as he later proclaimed himself King of the Anglo-Saxons in 886. From this, the roots of the kingdom of England and its future line of kings emerged through his son, grandson and great-grandson.

Archaeology has allowed us to open windows into the lives of the British tribes and their Germanic conquerors. However, as expected, there is very little evidence above the ground that has survived from this period. In terms of Wessex, hillforts, which pre-date the arrival of the Saxons, are an obvious exception, as are the surviving sections of earthwork defences such as the Wansdyke or Bokerley Dyke. Some Anglo-Saxon work has survived in a few early churches, although most have been altered by subsequent Norman modifications or later Victorian architects. The Old Minster in Winchester was destroyed by the Normans, and other important West Saxon religious sites, such as at Wimborne or Dorchester-on-Thames, bear no resemblance to their original buildings. I have visited many of the important sites and locations referred to in the main text. Few remain completely unchanged over the centuries, with the exception of some hillforts, but some other sites mentioned in the book can still evoke some sense of the period.

Lastly, mention must be made of the personal names of the kings and other important individuals noted throughout the text. Their names are Brythonic or Germanic in origin, or sometimes a combination of both. Where two individuals have identical names, I have differentiated them as best as possible. However, readers familiar with the Early Middle Ages are aware that this era is characterised by individuals having similar or cyclic names. It is a problem that is unavoidable, so may I apologise in advance to readers and assure them I have done my best to minimise any discomfort.

1
The Germanic Migrations

Between the first and fifth centuries, lowland Britain was part of the Roman Empire. During this extended period, the Romans developed the regions we would later identify as England and Wales into an important outpost of empire. The conquered native Celtic British tribes adopted Roman ways and became citizens of the empire, leading to the Celtic aristocracy of this time being described as Romano-British. They embraced Roman systems and lifestyles, the infrastructure of towns (*civitates*) and roads, and the economic and administrative benefits, with many abandoning their pagan ideology to adopt early forms of Christian practice. The Roman imperial legions made this possible, but their withdrawal from Britain led to the door being opened to the 'Germanic migrations' of the fifth century.

First, we must go back a couple of centuries. Raids upon lowland Roman Britain were already commonplace. In response to incursions by Germanic groups from continental Europe, by the Irish and by the Picts of Scotland, the Romans reinforced London, its legionary bases, and other primary settlements. They also built a sequence of coastal forts at strategic points in East Anglia and the south-east, later known as the 'Saxon Shore'. These forts included Portchester, Pevensey, Richborough and Caister/Burgh. Nevertheless, by the mid-fourth century, coordinated attacks from British and Germanic tribes saw Roman *civitates* plundered and Rome was forced to send a large military force to restore control. In 383, Magnus Maximus, the commander of Roman forces in Britain, withdrew troops from northern and western Britain to support his failed bid for emperor. By 396, large-scale attacks resumed from the North Sea and northern Britain.[1]

Matters elsewhere across the empire compounded the situation. In 401, the Goths under Alaric I (from the Balkans region) invaded central Europe and Italy, and Rome was forced to reduce the supply of reinforcements to

Britain. This coincides with the last known Roman coinage to be minted in significant numbers in Britain, dated to 402, although these would continue to circulate for a period.[2] In 407, the remaining Roman garrisons in Britain declared self-autonomy under their general Constantine, who then proclaimed himself emperor and invaded Gaul (present-day France), taking most of the remaining troops with him.

Left to their own devices, the Romano-British leaders threw off their allegiance to Constantine and, by 409, expelled all remnants of Roman authority from Britain. Barbarian raids naturally increased, and in less than a year the British pleaded unsuccessfully for military aid from Emperor Honorius.[3] Honorius had greater concerns. In 410 it was recorded that, as part of a general barbarian expansion into western Europe, 'the Goths destroyed the stronghold of Rome, and afterwards the Romans never ruled in Britain'.[4] That event has been seen by historians as the demise of Rome's direct involvement in the affairs of the British Isles, but it was not quite the end. The ASC scribe makes an interesting entry for 418 when noting, 'Here the Romans assembled all the gold-hoards which were in Britain ... and took some with them into Gaul' – proof, perhaps, of the final withdrawal.[5] While Roman military control of Britain had ended, mercenary military aid may have continued into the 430s.[6] Meanwhile, raiding continued, with the writer Nennius recording that the first significant Germanic raid occurred in 429.[7]

Contrary to earlier assumptions, the final withdrawal of the Roman military did not lead to an immediate collapse of the British administration. Limited details suggest that individuals fully assimilated into the Roman system maintained a military presence along an imaginary line from Dorset to the Wash, and archaeological research conducted over recent decades shows that Romano-British lifestyles continued in one shape or form beyond the mid-fifth century. While a few leaders attempted to maintain civil society along Roman lines, many reverted to regional tribal leadership along the old Celtic hierarchical model. Nonetheless, emerging Celtic tribal centres appear in many cases to have remained within the former functioning *civitates*. Known tribal boundaries in the post-Roman period correspond closely to the former regional *civitas* areas of authority. These included, among others, important old Roman centres beyond London such as Canterbury, Colchester, St Albans, Dorchester, Exeter, Winchester, Cirencester, Silchester, Bath and Gloucester.

In a wider context, trends from the continent took longer to become established, although, as seen in the early adoption of Christianity in Ireland, this did not prevent ongoing cultural exchange in the post-Roman era. Increasingly challenged by external influences as the fifth century progressed, regional British leaders differed in how they responded to fluctuating developments. The Roman model unravelled, with the old Romano-British way of life increasingly becoming untenable. This is seen in the abandonment of villa complexes, disruption to trade, the failure of infrastructure, and a decline in agricultural production. The regions that had been more closely tied to the Roman system seem to have suffered a greater socio-economic collapse following Roman withdrawal, those on the margins of Roman authority less so. Inter-tribal cooperation within Britain was slow to advance, and ongoing contact with the continent was intermittent. However, evidence of eastern Mediterranean pottery in Cornwall and other western sites dating from the late fifth to mid-sixth centuries acknowledges external trade remained vibrant in some regions during periods of major transition.[8]

Historians debate if the Romano-British leadership resisted or embraced the shifts. New leaders surfaced, seemingly in a hybrid form. They may have continued to operate their administrations along Romano-British lines, but in terms of their military leadership and hierarchy we can recognise them as warlords or sub-kings, a prequel to the Anglo-Saxon tribal kings that were to emerge across England by the sixth century. Two such individuals mentioned in Bede's *Ecclesiastical History* were Ambrosius Aurelianus and Vortigern (the name in Brittonic meaning 'Great King' or 'Overlord)', who rose to prominence in the mid-fifth century.[9] They would clash over military control of central southern England before the Germanic migrations gained full traction. Vortigern is named by the writer Gildas and by Geoffrey of Monmouth, with references to his area of operation stretching from Kent to Wales. Ambrosius is a little easier to pin down, being the named leader of the British tribe known as the Atrebates that prospered in Hampshire and Berkshire, with a primary base at the Roman *civitas* of Silchester.

By the 440s, a final collapse of the remnants of Romano-British society was considered to be imminent. This period heralded the start of the Germanic migrations into Britain, the Anglo-Saxon invasion and the ensuing settlement of England. Proof of that comes in the ASC entry for 443, in which the scribe records that the British once again wrote to Rome requesting help against the Picts.[10] Much like in 410, the timing was bad. The Roman Empire had by then permanently divided into two, with the eastern empire centred at Byzantium (later known as Constantinople, and now Istanbul) busy defending itself against an invasion by the Hun, Ostrogoth and Alan tribes of eastern Europe led by Attila. These peoples would continue westward to invade Italy and Gaul.

Having failed to get help from Rome, the British leaders turned to mercenary aid from a Germanic tribe, which the sources generically describe as 'Angles'.[11] Gildas, a near contemporary, refers to the decision being made after a vote by a council of leaders, with the first mercenaries arriving in 443, the same year as the unanswered plea to Rome.[12] This would have been a last resort, so the situation must already have been desperate. The consensus among historians is that this decision opened lowland Britain to the later Germanic invasion and ushered in the eventual downfall of the Romano-British/Celtic tribal leadership. Gildas condemned the decision to summon mercenary help, as did later chroniclers such as the Venerable Bede, because of the results.[13] However, at the time it was by no means clear what door this decision would open. Bede's criticism seems paradoxical, as he was the seventh-century descendant of a Germanic migrant.

According to Bede, the British leader Vortigern was the man responsible for summoning the first group of mercenaries.[14] Gildas calls these German mercenaries 'the fierce and impious Saxons', and the British would name them '*laeti*', a Roman term akin to 'Barbarian'.[15] Ironically perhaps, many of these mercenary groups were made up of the same pirates who had conducted raids on England, that had prompted the British call for help in the first place. Essentially, Germanic mercenaries were given land by British leaders in exchange for fighting against Scottish, Irish and other Germanic raiders.

It is clear from early archaeological evidence of Anglo-Saxon settlement patterns that Vortigern and others did not summon mercenary help solely to fight raiders; they were quick to divert many towards their own inter-tribal matters, and this is perhaps the reason the Saxon Gewisse tribe settled in the Thames Valley. Proof of renewed internal warfare taking place comes from Nennius's *Historia Brittonum*, which records a battle known as Guoloph in 437 between the forces of Vortigern, probably leading an alliance of the Cantiaci of Kent and the Regnenses (Regni) of Sussex, against the Atrebates of Hampshire/Berkshire, possibly led by Ambrosius Aurelianus. Guoloph has been suggested as being near Nether Wallop, close to or around Danebury Hill Fort, a mile west of Stockbridge in Hampshire.[16] The victor is unclear, but it is possible that Vortigern employed Germanic mercenaries as Ambrosius is praised by Gildas for fighting against Germanic expansion whereas Vortigern is seen as the villain of the piece, suggesting he was the prime mover in recruiting mercenaries against rival British tribes.[17]

Beyond the middle of the fifth century there was an acceleration in the numbers arriving, many bringing their warrior vassals and families, and intent on settlement. The first migrants had been accepted without challenge, but that was when their numbers were still relatively few. Archaeological artefact evidence of Germanic origin from this early period has been found near to Roman *civitas* centres, showing that small groups of Germanic settlers had already established themselves peacefully, even ahead of the call for mercenaries.[18] Although the primary record is limited, we can imagine that, within a generation, not just fighting men but full families were settling in numbers across much of southern and eastern England in the second half of the fifth century.

However, the period from the early fifth century to the mid-sixth century holds a paradox. It clarifies why the migrations cannot be solely explained in terms of the collapse of Roman authority, and allows an added insight into why tribes from north-western Europe were willing to leave their homes and cross the North Sea. Over this period, particularly during the fifth century, much of Europe had suffered an above-normal series of serious crop failures combined with severe winters. This had resulted in more frequent famine, outbreaks of disease among humans and animals, and social disorder. Whole populations were forced to move home.

Britain was no exception. One estimate is that between 400 and 550 the population of the British Isles fell from around 6 million to nearer 3 million.[19] This is a staggering statistic, especially when we factor in the anomaly that the population was significantly bolstered by the arrival of new migrants. One notable event recorded in 442, just one of several such events across these decades, was a reported pestilence that was part of a worldwide pandemic.[20] As for the climate, tree rings and ice-core studies show evidence of a marked drop in temperatures across Europe around 535.[21] Such impactful events over an extended period have been largely ignored when debating the whys and wherefores of the Germanic migrations.

The number of Germanic Anglo-Saxon immigrants was relatively few in present-day terms, but the factors at play combined to give the settlers who had established themselves in eastern England greater and much earlier representation across the full population than one would expect. It would have taken centuries for population levels to recover. Germanic migrants therefore had room to expand across England as native populations declined, which gives us our paradox. The high death rate allowed newcomers to settle on vacant land without needing to fight the native British for the privilege.

Research recently conducted on whole-genome sequences from individuals excavated near Cambridge in 2016, with burials ranging from late Iron Age Britain to the middle Anglo-Saxon period, has offered significant new insight. After analysing shared fine-scale genetic ancestry from rare variants with hundreds of modern samples from Britain and Europe, scientists have estimated that on average the contemporary eastern English population derives 38 per cent of its ancestry from Anglo-Saxon migrations.[22] Given the wide period of the burials, this finding is remarkable. It would suggest that by the seventh or eighth century the Anglo-Saxon settlers in eastern England comprised a much higher percentage of the regional population than previously thought, wholly traceable to the events in the fifth and sixth centuries.

Further genetic studies have suggested up to a maximum of 30 per cent of the male lineage across the southern and eastern regions of England today is descended from the Germanic migrations and mixed Germanic–British unions between the fifth and eighth centuries, with a few specific areas giving much higher figures. Female lineage shows a lower figure, ranging from 5 to 25 per cent. The variation between genders is easily explained if we acknowledge that most Anglo-Saxon arrivals were young men of fighting age who mixed with the native British. These findings are not applicable to all of England, and were less pronounced in the west. Nevertheless, what it does support is the likelihood that the ratio of natives to migrants was impacted by the drop in overall population levels, as discussed above, that occurred in the fifth and sixth centuries.

Many of the earliest migrants would settle in or near the places where they first arrived, next to the North Sea and the eastern stretches of the English Channel. These were regions occupied by British tribes such as the Cantiaci and the Regnenses in the south-east, the Trinovantes in East Anglia, and the Brigantes in what would later become Yorkshire and Northumberland. There was, therefore, an uneven societal and economic impact for the Celtic British tribes across Britain. Those familiar with Roman lifestyles and their benefits would be most affected by the arrival of the Germanic tribes, for the earliest signs of Anglo-Saxon momentum would first appear in those areas, with warfare against the native British starting in earnest in the 470s. From this period would be formed in due course the Anglo-Saxon kingdoms of Kent, Sussex, East Anglia and Northumbria. This is reflected in the archaeological record, with the majority of finds of Germanic military gear dating from the period 450–480 occurring in Kent, East Anglia, Lincolnshire and the Humber.[23] In these regions, the Jutes and Saxons of Kent would be the trailblazers. In contrast, emerging Anglo-Saxon influence in what would become Wessex, and for that matter Mercia, would take a generation longer.

The popular image of the Germanic migrations portrayed by some historians in previous generations is of a violent and destructive military invasion against the native British that spread rapidly westward across England from the eastern and southern coasts. The virtual disappearance of Celtic place-name evidence across most of England led previous historians to believe that the process had also involved a replacement of the resident native population. From what we now know, the term 'invasion' is ill advised, and theories of displacement have been satisfactorily disproved. While some Celts moved westward as the Germanic settlers expanded their territories, archaeological finds provide conclusive evidence that most stayed where they were across eastern and central England, and the two cultures gradually assimilated. Irrefutably, the leadership changed hands from Romano-Celtic bloodstock to Germanic or Germanic–British bloodstock, but daily life continued as societal differences between the two groups gradually dissolved, different ethnic groups intermarried, and their cultures became one.

In subsequent decades and centuries, territory would change hands from the British to the Anglo-Saxons through warfare, as seen in the following chapters. However, the initial Germanic arrivals did not fight their way into the country but were invited. The shift of power was gradual, and the population demographics discussed above were undoubtedly a factor. As considered in subsequent chapters, there is strong evidence many Anglo-Saxons and British integrated well. Archaeological evidence from burial sites has found changes in social and cultural patterns between the early sixth to late seventh centuries among the newcomers and the native Romano-British populations, pointing to a more peaceful and lengthy assimilation process than earlier historians would argue.

In the late fifth century, migration shifted from raiding and mercenary work to permanent settlement. The Germanic Anglo-Saxon arrivals soon demanded more land, or, as Gildas calls it, increases to 'their monthly allotments'. When these were refused, they seized territory from the British by force. Gildas's prose, in keeping with the title of his work, noted that 'they (the Anglo-Saxons) first sank their claws into the eastern side of the island, pretending that they had come to defend the country, when really they were going to attack it'.[24] The influx would continue for generations, putting pressure on land and resources. In theory, each additional newcomer would place a strain on the original British population but also on those Germanic migrants who had already settled. Estimates for the number of Germanic migrants in the south and east towards the end of the fifth century begin at around 15 per cent of the regional population.[25]

The group known as the Gewisse, the tribe with origins in the Upper Thames Valley that would become a key component within the history and development of the later kingdom of Wessex, can be viewed as an obvious exception. They are proof of early Germanic settlement far from the eastern or southern coasts, supporting the argument that some groups were welcomed and given land by specific British tribes to help defend or bolster regional boundaries or territorial claims against rivals.[26]

Distinct Romano-British tribal boundaries were invariably unstable.[27] By the early sixth century and concerning more particularly what would become the territory first associated with the future kingdom of Wessex, the Atrebates dominated in Berkshire, north Hampshire, east Wilshire and west Surrey; the Belgae in south Hampshire and east Dorset; the Durotriges in Dorset, west Wiltshire and east Somerset; the Dumnonii in west Somerset and Devon; and the Dobunni in south Gloucestershire.

In reverting to their tribal regions after the withdrawal of the Romans, the boundary lines sometimes did not correspond with the pre-Roman first-century divisions. In terms of southern England, the Belgae appear to have lost a considerable part of their former western region to a mix of Atrebates, Durotriges and Dobunni. Limited knowledge exists on the durability of British tribal groups in the south-east, those first affected by the Germanic migrations, including the Cantiaci of Kent, Regnenses of Sussex, and Trinovantes of Essex and Suffolk. These regions would be the first to succumb to new leadership and cultural changes. In Kent, for example, archaeological finds indicate that native Britons had culturally adopted Anglo-Saxon ways by the early sixth century to the degree that it is almost impossible to differentiate the two.[28] Similarities exist in the adoption of the old Romano-British *civitas* centres by the Anglo-Saxons as their new seats of authority, such as Canterbury, Colchester and Chichester, and the much later formation of the first shires and their sub-divisions into the 'hundreds' (administrative divisions), many of which can be traced back to the original Roman division of administration.[29]

British resistance to ongoing Anglo-Saxon incursions was fragmented. In areas where British control gave way to Anglo-Saxon control, the native British population appears to have been treated prejudicially. Some suggest this would have led to the economic impoverishment of those still classed as 'Britons'.[30] Through acculturation many British were still able to prosper under their new conquerors, particularly those more determined to keep their wealth or status.[31] Consequently, this encouraged the ready adoption of Anglo-Saxon cultural traits, and this is supported by evidence that Saxon burial rites were spreading westward among the mixed British-Saxon populace, and that many British readily adopted Germanic early English speech to balance out their social inequality.[32] Where the Romano-British held influence, however, the use of Latin continued to be spoken and written by their elite,[33] and in the west the Brythonic (Brittonic) language survived as a practical language for much longer. Brythonic was still spoken in Wiltshire, for example, in the seventh century, and Brythonic Welsh and Cornish continued to be spoken further west by the British even after Anglo-Saxons had assumed authority there. As for the Anglo-Saxons, it would appear they were not interested in learning the native language as it would have marked them down as belonging to a defeated people. Some Brythonic terms survived or adapted, such as '*afon*' or '*avon*' for river, but only a few Welsh words were fully adopted into Old English.

Archaeological finds of British grave goods across Berkshire, Wiltshire, Dorset and Somerset dated to the early sixth century indicate the widespread presence of Anglo-Saxon jewellery, implying that the adoption of Germanic practices moved ahead of full Anglo-Saxon settlement and control.[34] In time, the Anglo-Saxons would absorb some British traits themselves, particularly after generations of intermarriage, and as discussed in a later chapter, their conversion to Christianity may have had influences from the original practices of the British. Many Romano-British had adopted Christianity, while the Germanic arrivals followed pagan practices. Nevertheless, there is no evidence of widespread persecution of Christian practices before the Anglo-Saxons' conversion to Christianity. In fact, the speed with which the Anglo-Saxons were later to adopt Christianity during the early decades of the seventh century implies that the earlier British Christian practices had remained vibrant within a significant percentage of the population.

To summarise, this brief insight explores the causes and time limits of migrations into England, while also introducing themes on the initial interactions between Germanic migrants and the British. Several factors led to the Anglo-Saxons establishing themselves as the dominant force across much of the country less than a century from their first arrival. To reiterate an important facet considered earlier, the population decline that was experienced in Britain between the fifth and sixth centuries looks to have played an important but overlooked part in the success of the migrants in establishing themselves across the eastern and south-eastern regions of England. Moving on, let us now consider more specifically the arrival and establishment of the West Saxons and their compatriots, the Gewisse, who later founded the kingdom of Wessex.

Fig. 1. Map of Celtic Tribal Regions across southern Britain, *c.* 450.

2
West Saxon Origins and the Gewisse

The Germanic tribes that arrived in England from the mid-fifth century onwards, as mercenaries, invaders, or settlers, were the forerunners of a people with shared cultural similarities that we now familiarly identify collectively as 'Anglo-Saxon'. They were an amalgam of dozens of individual tribes formed from three main cultural and social groupings: the Angles, Saxons and Jutes. When contemporary sources first referred to them as such remains unclear, but the term Anglo-Saxon was already in use by the early seventh century.

The early eighth-century text *Ecclesiastical History*, written by the Northumbrian monk Bede, is perhaps the earliest surviving work to name the Germanic tribal divisions across England.[1] On arrival they would coalesce into regional tribal groups. In terms of present-day regional identification, the Angles settled in East Anglia, the East Midlands, Yorkshire and Northumberland; the Saxons in Essex, Kent, Sussex and Hampshire; and the Jutes in Kent and Hampshire and on the Isle of Wight. In time these tribal divisions would transmogrify, and, looking well ahead, would divide into what would become several Anglo-Saxon kingdoms known as the 'Heptarchy', comprising Kent, Essex, Sussex, Wessex, East Anglia, Mercia and Northumbria.

The name 'Saxon' is thought to have originated from the Germanic word '*sax*' and later from the Old English '*seaxan*' and its derivatives '*seaxe*' and '*seax*'. It was the name for a long-bladed utilitarian knife of various designs, often curved, in common usage. It was a weapon somewhere between a short sword and a knife, with blades varying between 20 to 50 centimetres in length.[2] Evidently, the seax had symbolic meaning to the Saxons, and in the eyes of the native British was something that distinguished the Saxon newcomers. Images of the seax still appear in the present-day county emblems of both Essex (meaning East Saxons) and Middlesex (Middle Saxons).

West Saxons, and perhaps here we should also include the Gewisse, were an amalgam of several tribal groups whose homeland was first identified by Bede as 'Old Saxony', a region lying across north and north-west Germany.[3] Old Saxony equates in present-day terms to the German states of Lower Saxony and Westphalia, which include the sites of modern-day Hamburg, Bremen, Minden and Paderborn. The West Saxons were so named because they were to become the most westerly of the Saxon tribal groupings across southern England, and by extension 'Wessex' was a combination and derivation of the name 'West Seaxe'. The Gewisse's origin is complex and, as mentioned later, the name may have been given to them by native British people in their settled region.

The arrival of the warlords Cerdic and Cynric in Hampshire is recorded in the primary sources, and this traditionally marks the initial West Saxon presence. However, in recent times, archaeology has provided evidence of fifth-century Anglo-Saxon settlement in the Upper Thames Valley, supporting the claims made for the earlier establishment of the tribal group known as the Gewisse predating the archaeological evidence for Saxons in Hampshire. Romano-Saxon pottery found at Abingdon and Oxford dating from the mid-fifth century confirms Saxons had already settled in that region.[4] Excavation projects since the millennium have confirmed that the Upper Thames Valley contains one of the densest concentrations of early Anglo-Saxon archaeology in the country, particularly the region around Abingdon and Dorchester-on-Thames.[5] Furthermore, the 2018–20 excavation of an early sixth-century Anglo-Saxon warrior-chieftain's grave site near Marlow may further indicate a widening of the Gewisse area of influence eastward, although it could be argued this individual could have been an early British ally.[6]

It is not clear when contemporaries first used the labels of West Saxon and Wessex. The former must have preceded the latter. They were not used before the seventh century and possibly not in common use until the eighth. We have therefore used literary licence in early chapters when referring to the kingdom of Wessex. Before proceeding further, we need to clarify why the Gewisse should be linked to the West Saxons and Wessex, because the traditional history of Wessex revolves around origins in Hampshire. Departing from the history we were once led to accept, historians, academics and archaeologists have in recent decades turned tradition on its head. As seen in later chapters, the Gewisse that settled in the Upper Thames Valley are integral to the history of Wessex and its line of regnal kings.

What the warlord kings Cerdic, Cynric, Ceawlin and others called their domain during their own time is unknown. Writing in the early eighth century, Bede refers to the West Saxons in his *Ecclesiastical History,* but he is also one of the first sources to refer to the Gewisse, although he gives no territorial clues as to where they were primarily located.[7] Should we interpret Bede as instinctively telling us that for the origins of the West Saxons also read Gewisse, as he considered the use of the names 'Gewisse' and 'West Saxon' interchangeable? As his information came from sources in the south of England, it is a safe assumption that the term was in wide circulation across England in his lifetime before later falling into abeyance.[8] The ASC, which was produced by scribes in the late ninth century, does not use the name Gewisse even once when describing the history of events in Wessex. Only after the Thames Valley/Berkshire region was lost to the Mercians during the 660s did Bede cease using the name Gewisse in his text, thereafter describing them instead as West Saxons.[9]

The ASC minimises or disregards the Gewisse's role and relevance, which possibly requires some further explanation. As seen within its pages, the ASC would successfully transfer the achievements of the Gewisse to Cerdic's descendants, seemingly by design and then later by ignorance. This perhaps was an initiative prompted by Alfred the Great in the late ninth century to promote the undisputed genealogy of himself and his bloodline back beyond his grandfather Ecgberht – in short, to reposition his dynastic legacy squarely within Hampshire as the heart of his Wessex, after a period in which the kingdom had nearly been lost to Danish invaders before becoming, in the last decade of his reign, the dominant Anglo-Saxon kingdom in England. This naturally casts doubt on the historical accuracy of Cerdic and his heirs, which we will discuss in due course. Linking their lineage to Cerdic, as opposed to Ceawlin and the Gewisse, became a central issue for successive kings of Wessex irrespective of the reality.

At face value, there is no logical geographical reason to connect the two groups. The Gewisse were based on the northern edge of the British Atrebates, centred in Berkshire south of present-day Oxford, and Cerdic's West Saxons first settled in the British Belgae kingdom south of Winchester. But without doubt, the Gewisse and their early leaders were to play a central role in the development of Wessex. They were, based on the known military achievements of the kings of the seventh and eighth centuries, the chief force behind the initial expansion of the kingdom westward into north Wiltshire and Somerset. The evidence is so strong that surprisingly some historians still relate the traditional Wessex and Cerdic story without acknowledging their Gewisse allies.

We have concluded that the origins of the Gewisse predate the arrival of Cerdic's West Saxons. They formed part of the early Germanic influx, even though their emergence in the Upper Thames Valley appears to be at odds with the coastal locations of most other Germanic arrivals. This can be explained if we accept they were among the first mercenary groups the British called upon to fight for them against other rivals, perhaps in this location acting for the Atrebates against either the Catuvellauni or the Dobunni.[10] It is perhaps speculative, but the earliest connection between the Gewisse to the north of the Atrebates and the West Saxons to their south may have been instigated and prompted by their later alliances with the British. The regional tribes, the Atrebates and Belgae, were assumed to have remained dominant at this stage. After this period, the former Roman *civitas* of Silchester, which had become an important centre for the Atrebates, shows archaeological signs of being abandoned by its occupants, not just temporarily but permanently. The reason is unclear, but it seems to go beyond just West Saxon expansion into the region.[11]

Certainly, the Gewisse seem to have been able to establish themselves by the early sixth century in a region removed from other significant Saxon or Angle groupings. As seen in interpreting maps in subsequent decades, they had become fully independent. It cannot be discounted that this early assimilation may have led to closer union with the localised British, primarily the Atrebates, which enabled greater intermarriage here between Saxon and British. Hence the Gewisse links to British ancestry as claimed by some historians, which forms part of the ongoing discussions in later chapters. Before Cerdic, there are also archaeological indications in Hampshire that resemble Gewisse finds in the late fifth century. There were not only Jutish activities but, despite no references in primary texts, a West Saxon presence indicated by grave goods and other archaeological discoveries found in a few locations around Winchester, the capital of the Belgae.[12]

By the time the ASC informs us of Cerdic's arrival in Hampshire, the Gewisse had seemingly already integrated well with the local British while preserving their original ideology and practices.[13] To further support the archaeological evidence, finds linked to German Anglo-Saxon settlement also appear towards the end of the fifth century in the Upper Thames Valley around present-day Wallingford and Abingdon. Discovery in the nineteenth century of late fifth-century burial sites at nearby Dorchester-on-Thames reveals more evidence. There are grave artefact examples of a male wearing a Roman belt, denoting his rank, but being buried in the German tradition. Another example from the same site is a Roman belt buckle within a female grave that contained Germanic brooches. These imply a settled Germanic community (we assume the Gewisse), one already established among the local Romano-British but nonetheless keen to signify itself as being both Romano-British and Germanic Saxon.

In later centuries, scribes were keen to record the ancestry of the West Saxon kings. In one such genealogy list, given in the ASC version A in the year 597, the scribe refers to Cerdic as the great-grandson of a man named Gewis.[14] The similarity between 'Gewisse' and 'Gewis' cannot be accidental, and possibilities arise. By this entry, the scribe acknowledges the individual named Gewis preceded Cerdic by three generations, proving as best we can that the Saxon presence in the Upper Thames Valley began many years ahead of Cerdic's arrival. Simultaneously, this is the best evidence we have that the origin of the name Gewisse came from the man named Gewis, perhaps their founder or warlord leader. Furthermore, the chronicle entry appears to give us a connection via Cerdic between the West Saxons and the Gewisse.

Compelling as this connection is, historians have examined other possibilities. The Old English name Gewisse could originate from the German '*gewiss*', meaning 'certain' or 'sure'.[15] A looser translation of the meaning is 'confederate', which makes more sense in terms of them having acted first as mercenaries for the British. Finally, there is a body of thought that goes beyond the Gewisse having intermarried with native British and claims that, contrary to being Anglo-Saxon, they were predominantly of Welsh British extraction. One suggestion is that the name Gewisse originates and is linked to the former Welsh kingdom of Gwent, but this contention goes beyond the nucleus of the argument debated within the following chapters.[16]

Union between the two tribal regions that would eventually combine to form the kingdom of Wessex did not materialise until the Anglo-Saxon leadership had superseded the British. The Hampshire and Thames Valley groupings were separate factions and quite independent of one another during the sixth century.[17] The later connection is not in doubt, but the primary consideration is when should we consider them as a single entity, a united kingdom. Many historians would argue that the Gewisse were not just a key factor but have a reasonable claim to be identified as the tribal group from which the kingdom first emerged. Their relevance can be seen by the line of direction of most of the territorial gains westward made by the early kings during the latter period of the sixth century onwards. Furthermore, the first centre of Christian worship within the fledgling kingdom would be founded not in Winchester but in Dorchester-on-Thames in the Upper Thames Valley, in the centre of the original Gewisse settlement 3 miles north of Wallingford in Berkshire. Several early kings, such as Ceawlin, Cynegils and Cenwealh, are directly traceable to their centre of operations in that region. Further analysis of their names again points to ties with the British, or at least a mixed Saxon–British bloodstock, as hinted at earlier.

Gains over the British during the early sixth century were slow and measured. While still outnumbered by the native population, there appears to have been a major influx of further settlers throughout the sixth century into the southern and eastern regions of England. The distribution of all known Anglo-Saxon burial sites in southern England from the sixth and seventh centuries shows there was already significant settlement east of an imaginary line from east Dorset northwards but that it was still limited west of this. Artefacts dated as early as roughly 475 have been found in areas as disparate as Abingdon, Andover, Maidenhead and Winchester.[18]

Expanding the previous discussion on integration, these advances did not involve the replacement of the native British. There was plenty of uncultivated land in Wessex for new settlers and conquerors. Contrary to previous theories, recent evidence shows that after their tribal leaders conceded military defeat most of the British populace remained *in situ* under new Anglo-Saxon rulers. There was no mass movement westward, as once proffered by earlier historians. However, the West Saxons, in common with advances by other Anglo-Saxon kingdoms, seem to have replaced the hierarchy within the native societies with their own leadership class, despite being outnumbered by a much larger native populace. Localised studies have suggested that the male migrant population in the region that would become Wessex was still only about 10 per cent compared to figures of 20 per cent or more in East Anglia.[19]

In terms of the development of Wessex in later centuries, like its nearest Anglo-Saxon neighbours it would see its fortunes ebb and flow. The best we can estimate is that Wessex as a unified entity with a defined territory that we would recognise today emerged sometime during the late seventh century, much later than the neighbouring Angles of Mercia, the South Saxons of Sussex and the Jutes in Kent. Furthermore, Wessex's borders changed dramatically many times within the timeframe covered by this book. Major advances in west Dorset, Wiltshire, Somerset and Devon in the late seventh and eighth centuries did not bring with them immediate new West Saxon settlements in significant numbers. The process was much more protracted. Wessex's borders under Ceawlin or Ine bear no comparison with those under Ecgberht or Alfred in later centuries. Indeed, it took the West Saxons (and the Gewisse) around 300 years to seize full control of all the territory up to the River Tamar (between Devon and Cornwall) from their original starting points in Hampshire and Berkshire, roughly 150 miles away. This implies, or confirms, that West Saxon expansion was both slow and intermittent, with borders at times remaining fixed for decades.

By the time of Alfred's coronation, however, the king of Wessex would control the modern shires of Hampshire, Berkshire, Essex, Middlesex (London), Kent, Sussex, Dorset, Wiltshire, Somerset and Devon.

3
Cerdic and Cynric
c. 500–534

Faced with minimal primary source data and a lack of credible alternative textual evidence, historians generally acknowledge that the Saxon warlord Cerdic was the founder and first king of the West Saxons. He is certainly the man accredited with that honour by West Saxon scribes in later centuries, and a significant figure in the history of Wessex. Those less convinced have suggested that Cerdic is purely legendary, in the same vein as the Celtic British myth of Arthur. There is much room for debate. Unlike the West Saxons of Hampshire, the Gewisse, so relevant to the founding of Wessex, did not have their own named contemporary equivalent of Cerdic. He therefore remains, together with his son Cynric, our only named connection to the first Germanic tribal settlers who can be later identified as the founders of the West Saxon kingdom of Wessex.

Later scribes were keen to connect the royal West Saxon bloodline to Cerdic, indicating a clear intent among the late ninth-century compilers of the ASC to ensure that Cerdic's formative roots were linked to Hampshire, not to the Thames Valley Gewisse. The calculation behind this may stem from Alfred the Great, who was directly involved in promoting the chronicle during the 890s, linking his West Saxon heritage back to Wessex's early founders. A link to Cerdic was an affirmation of heritage and entitlement. All rulers who claimed bloodlines back to Cerdic and Cynric (Cerdicings) were also claiming descent from the pagan god Woden himself.[1] The late tenth-century scribe Æthelweard, in his work *Chronicon Æthelweardi,* extended this mythical link beyond Woden to a figure in Germanic mythology named Sceaf.[2] For whatever reason, their Germanic pagan origins remained an important factor for the West Saxons for centuries – a strange concept when we consider that every king of Wessex from the late seventh century onwards had converted to Christianity.

When delving further into Cerdic's background, affirmation of his Germanic origin becomes ambiguous. In a conclusion that contradicts West Saxon tradition, onomasticians have argued that the names Cerdic and Cynric are not Germanic but can be associated more closely with British origins. Cerdic's name is a variant of the Welsh Ceredig or Caradoc, which means 'caring' or 'protecting'. Perhaps this is a clue to his relevance in the power balance between the Britons and the Saxons, an indication he may have been employed at the head of a mercenary group.[3] As we will see, several of their successors had similar British-linked names, not Anglo-Saxon German ones, which casts doubt on much of the early historiography surrounding the origins of the West Saxon kings. Inversely, it perhaps links them more closely to their tribal allies, the Gewisse. However, accepting the hypothetical argument that Cerdic is only a legendary figure, it seems bizarre the West Saxons adopted a British name for their prime mythical hero and founder. Paradoxically, Cerdic and Cynric having names of potential British origins support them as real people within the historical record. If they were part of a later West Saxon propaganda exercise, they would surely have been given more obvious Saxon names to support the traditional version of events.

An ASC entry – version A only – in 552 during the reign of his son Cynric throws further light on Cerdic's claimed ancestry, listing nine generations between him and Woden.[4] Interestingly, within this list his great-grandfather is named Gewis, which is surely where the name Gewisse originates, therefore perhaps confirming that Cerdic's Brythonic name originates from a kinship background based in the Upper Thames Valley Saxon settlement, not the traditional Hampshire one. Within this list his father is named as Elesa, which perhaps comes from Elisa, a name which has been translated as 'wanderer' in Phoenician. Maybe the Celtic British had given this name to Cerdic's father to denote someone who had freshly settled in the region. The apparent adoption of British name elements may indicate that alliances and intermarriage by the West Saxons/Gewisse with important British families helped Germanic assimilation among the native Britons.[5] This origin hypothesis may well be the best explanation for the tribal link between the Upper Thames Valley and south-west Hampshire. Certainly, Bede, as noted earlier, considered the Gewisse and the West Saxons the same people. It may explain why the later West Saxon scribes were keen to associate Cerdic with their heritage if he perhaps was, after all, a legitimate descendant of the Gewisse in the Thames Valley.

The debate over Cerdic's ancestral link to the Gewisse gives much food for thought. He may have appeared in Hampshire as the leader of Germanic mercenaries sent by the Gewisse. Alternately, he may have arrived directly from the continent having been employed by the local Belgae tribe in Hampshire to defend them from other Germanic pirates or neighbouring British tribes. There is evidence that the neighbouring Durotriges had made gains in Belgae territory in the late fifth century. Expanding upon that premise, he could also have been employed to protect their eastern border against incursions by the Meonwara Jutes or the stronger threat imposed by Ælle and his South Saxons.[6] This would be as we see the associated presence of the Gewisse in the Thames Valley. Cerdic may therefore have received his Brythonic name from his British employers, replacing over time his original Germanic name.[7]

In acknowledging Cerdic, we are essentially accepting he was a real Germanic warlord, not just a figurehead that later kings of Wessex and their scribes found convenient to package within their ancestry. In the end we must either accept the only detail we have on record or treat it with a large dose of scepticism. Accepting him as a historical figure does not get easier when assessing his arrival on the shores of the Solent. Our main source for much of this early history is the entries gathered within the ASC, but these are also inconsistent. The chronicler names the chieftains Cerdic and Cynric as arriving together in Britain in 495 'with five ships at the place which is called Cerdic's Shore ... and the same day fought against the Welsh'.[8] To describe the native British here as 'Welsh' is misleading. Later writers would often refer to the British as 'Welsh' to differentiate them from the Saxons, irrespective of where in the country they were encountered, and seldom identified them as British or by their British tribal names. An alternate name for Cerdic's Shore has been given as Natanleaga, named after the local British Belgae chieftain Natanleod. This covers the region around the New Forest, but specifically refers to Netley Marsh, just west of Totton and next to the Solent.[9]

It is not acknowledged until 519 that Cerdic and Cynric 'succeeded to the kingdom of the West Saxons'.[10] Between these two dates, they are named only once. In an entry for 508 they again fought the British, as discussed below, but we are left pondering what else was occurring in the twenty-four years between their arrival and their succession as kings of the West Saxons. Perhaps more puzzling is that Bede, writing in his *Ecclesiastical History* almost two centuries before the ASC scribe, much closer to sixth-century events, makes not a single mention of either Cerdic or Cynric.

Doubt over the reliability of the chronological timetable must remain. To unravel a realistic timeline throughout this period of history with the evidence that is available presents us with many potential hurdles. For example, as seen in due course, Cynric allegedly lived until the year 560, which contradicts him fighting alongside his father in 495 unless we accept he lived well into his eighties. The reliability of the recorded dates for this early period in Wessex's history remains suspect, and the dating of events, at least up until the 540s, must be treated with caution. Neither Cerdic's activities nor Cynric's can be cast in stone. Compared to the ASC date of 495, Æthelweard dates Cerdic and Cynric's first landing five years later, and this conflict between the dating of events is a regular theme among the primary sources.[11]

An ASC entry for 501 refers to another landing at Portsmouth, although whether this was Saxon or Jute is unclear. In 514 two more West Saxon chiefs, Stuf and Wihtgar, whom the twelfth-century chronicler Henry of Huntingdon calls Cerdic's nephews, landed in the Solent with three shiploads of warriors and fought a successful encounter against a contingent of Britons.[12] However, the next entry relating to Cerdic and Cynric comes in 508, six years ahead of Stuf and Wihtgar's arrival, when they are recorded defeating a British army of 5,000 men in battle, killing their leader Natanleod, 'after whom the land as far as Cerdic's Ford was named Netley'. As for the accuracy, that number of British being involved appears fanciful; a fifth of that figure seems more realistic.

In terms of location, Cerdic's Ford has been suggested as being Chandlers Ford or Charford. Chandlers Ford is several miles north of modern-day Southampton, next to the watercourse known as Monk's Brook, which suggests that the West Saxons were making their first steps northward.[13] Charford lies 3 miles north of present-day Fordingbridge on the east bank of the River Avon, 10 miles north-west of Netley Marsh, with the Avon here marking the natural boundary between what would later become the shires of Dorset and Hampshire.[14] The river perhaps also marked the boundary between the Belgae and their western neighbours, the Durotriges.

Henry of Huntingdon expanded on the battle, describing Cerdic being joined by Saxon allies Æsc from Kent and Ælle from Sussex, and also a warlord named Port, who may have been a Jute. The victory was gained by Cynric attacking the Britons from the rear after his father's contingent had suffered an initial setback.[15] Help from Saxon and Jutish allies is plausible, in particular from the Meonwara Jutes near the Hampshire–Sussex border and from the South Saxon king Ælle, who had made greater and faster progress against the British Regnenses in the Sussex (South Saxon) region. The Jutes in the Meon Valley and on the Isle of Wight had probably arrived ahead of the West Saxon presence in the region. The South Saxons in Sussex and the Jutes in Kent had been there longer, possibly negotiating for land with the Regnenses and Cantiaci before taking control.

The identified boundaries within the British tribal system raise the question of how far the British lapsed into their original regional territories after the Roman withdrawal. How many of the Romano-British citizenry reverted to their previous tribal divisions? The native pre-Roman tribal territories had not wholly disappeared but had changed after centuries of Roman control. Beyond ongoing cultural differences, the former British tribes in the south-east, such as the Cantiaci, did not adopt their earlier identities to any extent between the Roman withdrawal and the beginning of the Germanic settlements. The situation is less clear for the Belgae and Atrebates, the tribes in the regions settled by Cerdic and the Gewisse. Before the Roman occupation, they had held much greater swathes of territory to their west compared to the late fifth century. Territory had been taken from them by tribes like the Durotriges and Dobunni.

The extent of their remaining authority is nuanced. We can see them by this period as principally Romano-British, but still preserving more of their Celtic British traditions than their British contemporaries further east. Some level of organised resistance was initially encountered from the Belgae, as evidenced by the entries in the ASC, but it looks to have been relatively basic. The muted military response Cerdic and the Gewisse encountered from the Belgae and the Atrebates reflects their earlier status within the Roman system which had diluted their tribal identities. It also explains why their territory would be more easily absorbed without recourse to protracted warfare in the Saxon seizures across Hampshire and west Berkshire, with one example being the peaceful capitulation of the Belgae *civitas* of Venta Belgarum (Winchester).

Elsewhere, having apparently suffered little immediate impact from the Germanic migrations, the British in the west more readily adopted old regional divisions based on their previous warrior-king cultures. The West Saxon advances westward during the sixth and seventh centuries came up against organised resistance based on the old British tribal boundaries and divisions, but not a defence in the shape of a united Romano-British coalition.

During 519, Cerdic and Cynric 'fought against the Britons at a place they now name Cerdic's Ford'.[16] We have discovered Cerdic's Ford already, as considered above, but whether this was the same location as the encounter from eleven years previously is open to debate. Possibly there was a battle at each of the two sites. Historians fall into two camps, but based on the earlier references to Netley Marsh and Charford, controlled by the Belgae leader Natanleod, the River Avon location at Charford has more to recommend it. However, Cerdic was still fighting for control of the same land in 519 that he had in 508, which poses the question why the West Saxon expansion was so slow. Possibly the Saxons had negotiated a peace treaty with the Belgae after their gains from the first battle, and by the second battle had already accepted that additional territory must be secured to accommodate new West Saxon arrivals.

Henry of Huntingdon once again provides the most detail for this second major battle, and his text dismisses any possibility that he conflated the two. Huntingdon describes the battle lasting for hours 'until as daylight faded into evening, the Saxons gained victory'. Betraying his twelfth-century clerical background but pursuing one of the themes propounded earlier by the writer Gildas and then repeated by Bede, Huntingdon adds that 'a great plague was inflicted that day upon the natives of Albion' (i.e. the British).[17] In his text he refers to five such plagues or invasions – the Romans, the Picts/Scots, the Angles/Saxons, the Danes and the Normans – that God had inflicted upon the British, whom he describes as a 'faithless people'.[18]

Cerdic and Cynric, so it is said, became 'kings' of the West Saxons in 519, suggesting the battle that year had improved their status within the Belgae region. They may have thereafter mutually ruled and divided the settled area in Hampshire. A later addendum to the chronicle in another hand adds '... and the royal family of the West Saxons ruled from that day on', which suggests someone was keen to emphasise they were not just warlords but kings and the ancestors of, among others, Alfred the Great.[19] Cerdic and Cynric, if we concur they ruled jointly at some stage, can reliably be credited as warlord leaders, but describing them as kings in this period is perhaps conceptual. The terms 'king' and 'kingdom' in this early period were applied too readily by later medieval writers, perhaps based on their own perceptions of authority.

In contrast to their more powerful Germanic contemporaries from Sussex and Kent, Cerdic and Cynric had still barely established themselves.[20] Unlike these fully fledged neighbouring kingdoms, the West Saxons in Hampshire during the early decades of the sixth century had not yet forged anything resembling a kingdom. The concept of Wessex was still in the future. However, as discussed elsewhere, the evidence supports the concept that their allies in the Upper Thames Valley, the Gewisse, may have the greater claim as progenitors of the kingdom of Wessex.

The chronology discussed above is taken primarily from the ASC record. But as touched upon in the introduction, a sign of the fog pervading Wessex's early history is clear in the chronology of the *West Saxon Genealogical Regnal List* (WSGRL). The WSGRL appears in the preface to three versions of the ASC (B, C and D) but not the two that provide the most detail behind Cerdic (A and E). As evidenced in the full list given below, there are major departures from the ASC chronology.

West Saxon Genealogical Regnal List

King	Reign		King	Reign
Cerdic	538–554		Aethelheard	726–740
Cynric	554–581		Cuthred	740–756
Ceawlin	581–588		Sigebert	756–757
Ceol	588–594		Cynewulf	757–786
Ceolwulf	594–611		Beorhtric	786–802
Cynegils	611–642		Egbert	802–839
Cenwalh	642–673		Aethelwulf	839–855(8)
Seaxburh	673–674		Aethelbald	855(8)–860
Aescwine	674–676		Aethelbert	860–866
Centwine	676–685/6		Aethelred	866–871
Caedwalla	685/6–688		Alfred	871–899
Ine	688–726			

(Note: The ASC and the WSGRL regnal dates do not align until Cynegils in 611.)

The list gives a different timeline for the activities of Cerdic and Cynric and sweeps away any resemblance to the ASC detail. They are so divergent that historians are left confounded, scrambling to find a rationale. The WSGRL records Cerdic ruled Wessex from 538 to 554 and that Cynric ruled from 554 to 581.[21] The contradiction is clear if we accept the ASC detail for Cerdic's arrival in England in 495, as the WSGRL date for his death means that Cerdic must have been a very old man when he died. Equally, if Cynric arrived in 495 and died in 581, he would have been in his mid-nineties, which is incongruous. The two documents align only after listing the transfer of the throne of Wessex from Ceolwulf to Cynegils in 611. In explaining this sixth-century deviation of dates, more than one historian has posited that the various ASC entries were artificially extended backwards along the chronological timetable to make it appear for obvious reasons that the kingdom of Wessex was founded at an earlier date than it was.[22] However, another explanation for the wide variation has been put down to basic miscalculation. The argument is that later medieval annalists counted back nineteen years from 519 (Cerdic's succession as per the ASC) to 500 (Cerdic's first arrival according to *Æthelweard's Chronicon*), instead of counting forward by nineteen years, which gives the year 538 (Cerdic's succession as per the WSGRL).[23]

One other suggestion, to be explored in the next chapter, may also explain part of the timeline differences. Versions A and F of the ASC directly list the line of descent from Cerdic to Cynric. However, versions B, C and D include a generation between them, with a man named Creoda being named as Cerdic's son and Cynric's father.[24] How these variations came about is unclear, but Creoda's inclusion in the genealogy could explain the unusual longevity of Cynric's lifetime if we work on the ASC dates.

Whatever we choose to accept among these explanations, the foundation of the West Saxon dynastic line, and Cerdic's place in it, still cannot be substantiated with any confidence, leaving us with what one historian has described as a period of 'political fiction'.[25] To find some order from the chaos we shall work in terms of Cerdic and Cynric using the ASC dating given in versions A and E, with Cerdic ruling in Wessex until he died in 534, which is more logical in terms of the other military events described elsewhere in this chapter.

Before Cerdic's West Saxons established themselves, the most powerful Anglo-Saxon king in this period across the south of England was Ælle, king of Sussex.[26] However, Ælle's timeline is also confusing. Although we must treat the dates if not the events with caution, he is recorded in the ASC defeating the British soon after his first arrival in 477, and having further success at battles in 485 and 491.[27] Bede later named Ælle as the first in the line of what would later be defined by the ASC as 'Bretwalda'. This was an Old English term combining *Bryten* (Britain) and *walda* or *wealda* (meaning 'to rule'), and it was said to denote the strongest Anglo-Saxon ruler, implying overlordship across all of England south of the Humber.[28] Praiseworthy as this title sounds, it is a false perception. A better definition would be 'Britain Ruler' or 'wide ruler'.[29] No Anglo-Saxon leader had anything resembling the overlordship of England during that time, particularly from a base in Sussex. Nevertheless, it implies that Ælle's reputation was significant enough to be remembered two hundred years after his death. Some suggest that Ælle's activity has also been shifted too far back and that the period of South Saxon expansion was later, perhaps in the mid-sixth century.[30]

The South Saxons had settled successfully, with the critical factor being population density in relation to arable land. Research of settlement patterns in Kent and Sussex shows small areas of mixed British-Germanic high-density population, demonstrating that both regions were constrained by geographical features.[31] For Ælle, expansion east was not an option.

To move north from Sussex beyond the Andredsweald forest was also fraught with unknown difficulties, bringing the South Saxons into possible variance with the East and Middle Saxons or Mercians. For Ælle, expanding westward was the best option, perhaps along the coast past the Meonwara Jutes, the fledgling West Saxons and the already overcome British Belgae in south Hampshire into the British-held territory of the Durotriges in Dorset. We are in the realm of speculation; we have no written primary evidence. However, as the sources only record a handful of references to conflict between the British and Cerdic/Cynric in thirty years, we can surmise that there was perhaps an agreement whereby the Belgae accepted unchallenged movement across their territory in exchange for a wider peace with all Anglo-Saxons.

The fortunes of Sussex were to collapse during the 520s. A Frankish primary source acknowledged that from the 520s onwards, Germanics across the south-east of England were undergoing a period of reverse migration back to the continent in large numbers, and most of them were South Saxons.[32] This coincides with a known period of stagnation, whereby the Anglo-Saxon advance westward, impacting the West Saxon leadership, appears to have stalled for almost two generations. The ASC records that in 527, to add to the Cerdic 'shore' and 'ford' references previously considered, Cerdic and Cynric fought against the Britons at Cerdic's Wood (Cerdiceslea). Although this encounter is repeated by Henry of Huntingdon, neither source provides any clue as to its location.[33] The identity of Cerdiceslea/Cerdic's Wood remains elusive. One suggestion is that it refers to the village of Chearsley, a few miles north of present-day Thame close to the river of that name. This looks too distant from West Saxon or Gewisse activity, until we see Chearsley lies on the then border between the Atrebates and the Catuvellauni tribes. The Belgae and Atrebates are believed to have cooperated occasionally, so we might argue that Cerdic, in his role as a mercenary for the Belgae, led his forces to support the Gewisse mercenaries acting for the Atrebates against the Catuvellauni. This remains speculative, but the Domesday survey of 1086 records that Chearsley was once called Cerdeslai, a name very similar to Cerdiceslea (Cerdic's Wood).[34]

In 530, Cerdic and Cynric are next recorded crossing the Solent to the Isle of Wight and fighting and defeating the Jutes at Wihtgar's stronghold (Wihtwarabyrg). This has been suggested as possibly on the site of present-day Carisbrooke Castle. Wihtgar's identity as a Saxon, not a Jute, causes confusion here. However, the ASC scribe clarifies matters in his entry for 534 when confirming that 'they gave all Wight to their two nephews Stuf and Wihtgar', which acknowledges that Saxons held control of at least part of the island at this period. The fight in 530 was not against Wihtgar himself, but merely refers to his later control there, and it is believed the island is named after him.[35]

As previously indicated, Cerdic was recorded as dying in 534, whereupon Cynric succeeded him. However, our concern here is the sequence of events during the long period of unrecorded activity between the West Saxons and the British. Between Cerdic's Wood in 527 and the recorded battle of 552 in which Cynric defeated the British at Old Sarum hillfort (more of which in the next chapter), there are no other primary source entries throughout those twenty-five years detailing any conflict whatsoever. Some historians have proposed that successful British resistance by the Durotriges along a defensive line of earthworks and hillforts in eastern Dorset may have seen the West Saxon advance brought to a halt.[36] This may have coincided with a period of natural realignment and territorial consolidation in which military actions ceased, or perhaps many Anglo-Saxons returned to mainland Europe because of serious famine or disease. The primary sources are silent. But there may be another important reason for this.

Several historians have proposed that the suspension of West Saxon advances may be explained by an unrecorded but significant defeat at the hands of the British, one so serious it took them a quarter of a century to recover. In searching for potential clues around this period, the only serious candidate of such magnitude would be the battle of Mount Badon (Mons Badonicus), which has legendary status among Celtic British texts but is absent from most Anglo-Saxon texts. However, it does seem to be the case that sustained British resistance under a strong leader prevented further Saxon advances across Dorset around this time.[37]

British tradition has it that the legendary figure of King Arthur commanded the British forces at Mount Badon. His association with this battle is based on the *Historia Brittonum* by the ninth-century Welsh monk Nennius and repeated by the *Annales Cambriae* in the tenth century. Geoffrey of Monmouth's twelfth-century *History of the Kings of Britain* did more than any other text to expand upon the legend of Arthur, although he placed him out of context with any real-life sixth-century warlord and provides no serious help to our potential chronology.[38] However, accumulated recent research has concluded that if Arthur was more than just a legend his involvement at Badon was still unlikely. He probably never fought the Saxons, and he should be placed not in England but firmly in Wales.[39] Instead, some historians have proposed the Britons were more likely led by the more real and less legendary Romano-British leader Ambrosius Aurelianus.

It is difficult to pin down when and where the battle took place. Those sources that attempt to position it in the historical record give a very wide range of dates, from the mid-fifth century to the mid-sixth century. Bede, for example, using Gildas's text *De Excidio et Conquestu Britanniae* (On the Ruin and Conquest of Britain) and calculating his own timetable of events, dates it reasonably precisely between 494 and 500, telling us it involved a siege.[40] Gildas's work is dated to the middle of the sixth century, so we know the battle was before 550. An entry in the *Annales Cambriae* gives the year as early as 516.[41]

Other sources give other dates. It is entirely possible the battle of Mount Badon could have been a fifth-century clash wherein the British were attempting to stop a westward Saxon advance. If Ælle of Sussex had launched such a campaign, as hinted at earlier, it may have stalled at Mount Badon. However, the timing is confusing. It is unclear if Cerdic was involved in the battle, as it happened before his proposed arrival and initial encounters with the British. The apparent severity of the Saxon defeat argues against an earlier date, because there was no other period of inactivity along the British-Saxon border in the south on a par with that seen during the 520s and 530s. If we accept the earlier date scenario, it is difficult to support the argument that the British were defeated by a weak and newly arrived West Saxon presence in Hampshire given they may have recently defeated Ælle at the height of his power.

To reiterate, potential economic and social causes may have led to the battle. Recent archaeological evidence from Kent highlights a break in the sequence of Germanic ceramic finds which seems to show a downturn in Jutish fortunes in the early decades of the sixth century. Likewise, according to burial details, the South Saxons soon experienced a substantial decline which was not arrested until the late sixth century.[42] Readers can perceptibly draw their own conclusions from the available primary source detail, but a date sometime during the 520s for the battle is convincing when we combine two of the facts we have. First, the pressures noted above caused a relocation of South Saxon and Kentish peoples in the south, and possibly West Saxons too, beginning in the 520s; perhaps this was precipitated by some natural disaster, feasibly crop failure and food shortages. The response could have been to seek new land to settle further west, which required defeating the incumbent British. Second, the extended period of military inactivity among the West Saxons from the 520s onwards, in parallel with their Germanic neighbours to their east, implies a serious setback had taken place at this time as a consequence of the relocation. Nevertheless, in placing the battle at a later date, during the rule of Cerdic, we are by implication acknowledging the involvement of West Saxons alongside other Saxon and Jutish allies.

Mount Badon implies a hillfort, which supports Bede's acknowledgement that the battle involved a siege. Archaeological investigation of several potential sites has not revealed a clear favourite, although excavations have identified that several Iron Age hillfort across southern England were reinforced and recommissioned for a restricted period during the fifth, sixth and seventh centuries by both Britons and Saxons. Let us first acknowledge we cannot confirm beyond doubt where the battle of Mount Badon took place.

Just as historians cannot agree on the date, they cannot agree on the location. Several candidates have been proposed with place-name links to 'Badon'. These include the hillfort of Liddington Castle, adjacent to the Ridgeway 4 miles south-east of Swindon near the village of Baydon, and the hillfort of Little Solsbury Hill near Bath, which was previously known as Badanceaster.[43] Other suggestions have been Ringsbury Camp, 5 miles west of Swindon, near the village of Braydon; Badbury Camp, 2 miles west of Faringdon in Oxfordshire); and Badbury Rings near Wimborne.[44]

Each of the above locations is possible, along with several others not named here. The location of Liddington Castle gives it perhaps more credibility, as it was closer to the existing boundary of any Saxon advance westward. However, this battle was significant in terms of the combatants involved, and the Liddington site was only about 8 acres in area, which seems too small to accommodate the British in sufficient numbers. Ringsbury Camp is of a similar size. In contrast, the inner embankments of Badbury Rings in Dorset enclose an area of 18 acres, and including the outermost ring of embankments gives us an area of 41 acres.

The question, perhaps, is how far west we consider the Anglo-Saxon tribes to have been able to advance by the late fifth and early sixth centuries along a staggered north-to-south frontline between modern-day Oxfordshire and Dorset. Except for Badbury Rings, all the above-named sites are within the corridor between the Thames and the Bristol Avon/Severn, which implies the battle involved the Gewisse from the Upper Thames Valley, not Cerdic's West Saxons. However, the ongoing frontline fighting between the British and Anglo-Saxon tribes does not support these more northerly locations. The advances by the Gewisse did not begin until the second half of the sixth century. West of the Gewisse, the Dobunni tribe held control over the area near Cirencester and likely connected with the Atrebates to the east. In turn, the Atrebates and their Belgae neighbours to the south still separated Cerdic from the Gewisse.

It seems unlikely, then, that there was sufficient Anglo-Saxon momentum from the Thames Valley and Cotswold region at this time for the battle of Mount Badon to have taken place in the above-mentioned corridor. In contrast, for the eco-political reasons already discussed in this chapter, an Anglo-Saxon advance westward into Dorset below the Belgae and

Atrebates seems to represent the more likely chain of events. The Durotriges of Dorset look to have had a series of defences along a line from the coast north and north-west from the edge of Hampshire through Dorset into Wiltshire, utilising the earthworks of Grim's Ditch and Bokerley Dyke and the hillforts of, among others, Badbury Rings, Hambledon Hill, Hod Hill, and Spetisbury Rings.[45] Some of these earthworks were old Iron Age defences, reinforced in the post-Roman period as a border defence by the Durotriges.[46] Badbury Rings therefore looks to be possibly the most logical choice for Mount Badon, although this must come with caveats and can only be speculative due to the dearth of primary source information.

Cerdic is recorded as dying in 534.[47] An Anglo-Saxon charter of Edward the Elder *circa* 900, gifting lands to Winchester's Old Minster, refers to 'Ceardices Beorg' (Cerdic's Barrow) and suggests that Cerdic's burial mound lay in the countryside to the north-east of modern-day Andover in Hampshire, between the two important routes of the Harrow Way and the Portway.[48] If this was the burial site of Cerdic, it confirms not only how far north-westward the Hampshire West Saxons had advanced and settled by the 540s, but also that this barrow had remained a significant feature in the landscape for centuries.

From the minimal textual evidence we have, the Anglo-Saxon setback at Mount Badon suggests that the West Saxons had barely advanced beyond the River Avon during Cerdic's lifetime. However, although the primary sources are a little confused, some control appears to have been gained after 530 on the Isle of Wight, as hinted at earlier. Primary sources suggest Cerdic and Cynric acted as joint kings, possibly dividing authority across the fledgling kingdom of Wessex. That Cerdic's death took place in the same year that Cynric transferred control of the island to his nephew Wihtgar nevertheless suggests that consolidation was required at that point and that Cynric's primary concern was to reinforce his control over West Saxon territory on the mainland.

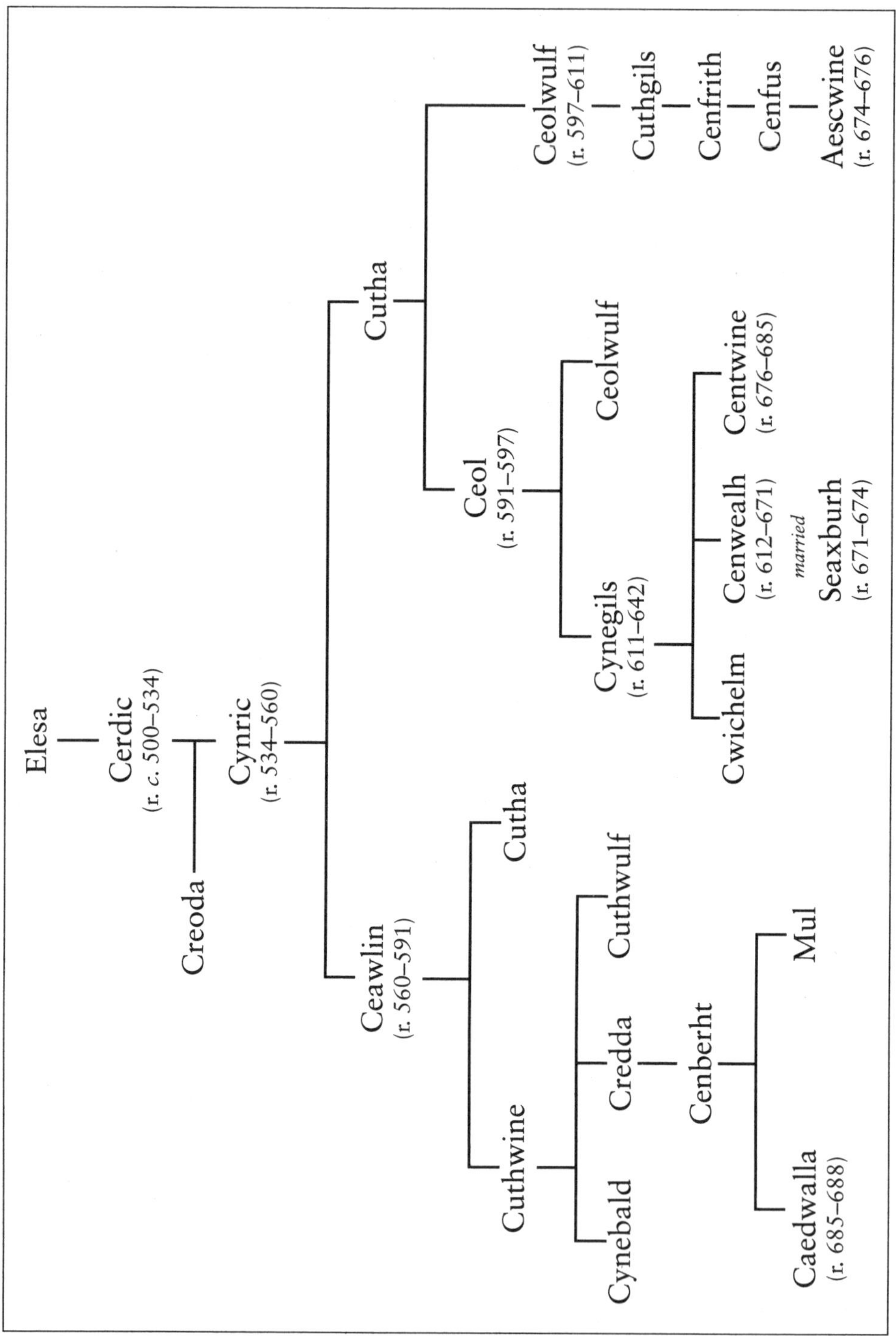

Fig. 2. West Saxon/Gewisse genealogy: Cerdic to Caedwalla.

4
Cerdic, Cynric and Creoda
534–560

Based on the ASC entries in the early decades of the sixth century, the reigns of Cerdic and Cynric look to have significantly overlapped. They may well have acted as joint kings for a period after Cynric had reached his majority and was able to enforce his own personal authority. The reliability of these entries, particularly regarding Cynric's first appearance alongside Cerdic, is a whole debate on its own, and despite the ASC's keenness to convince later generations that they acted together in the early days of West Saxon settlement, most historians consider this narrative spurious.[1]

While their kinship connection may be questionable, the theme surrounding Cynric's ancestry runs parallel with Cerdic's. The possible bloodline ties to the Gewisse and British have been reviewed and do not necessitate additional discussion. However, the considerable divergence in the regnal dates between the ASC and the WSGRL, as listed in the previous chapter, remains a major difficulty for historians piecing together sixth-century West Saxon developments.

We can compare the timelines of the ASC and WSGRL from Cerdic to 611, the year when the two sources align at Ceolwulf's death.

ASC (version A)	West Saxon Genealogical Regnal List
Arrival of Cerdic & Cynric: 495	
Cerdic: 519–534	Cerdic: 538–554
Cynric: 534–560	Cynric: 554–581
Ceawlin: 560–591	Ceawlin: 581–588
Ceol: 591–597	Ceol: 588–594
Ceolwulf: 597–611	Ceolwulf: 594–611

(Note: ASC versions B, C & D name Creoda between Cerdic and Cynric but exclude any dates for him.)

Opinion remains divided among historians as to the correct calendar alignment.[2] Neither of the given early timeframes within the two main primary sources can be relied on totally, and they are so far apart that some form of compromise between them looks difficult. There is one possible suggestion that may at least close the gap between them, however, and it concerns the figure of Creoda, who will be discussed later. Creoda aside, we will proceed as we did when debating Cerdic's career and defer to the ASC timeline if only because it avoids additional confusion.

In terms of etymology, the origin of the name Cynric has potential Celtic British links. It is said to derive from the Latin 'Cunorix' and translated by the Welsh into 'Cinir' or 'Kynyr', hence Cynric.[3] However, his name also has an Old English etymology meaning 'kin-ruler', which we could speculate relates to him superseding his father before his father's death.[4]

Before moving on to consider Cynric's rule and Creoda's involvement, we might address the topic of when men such as Cerdic and Cynric become recognised not only as warlords but as higher-status kings of their respective territories. At what period did this not-so-subtle transformation take place? For the Anglo-Saxons in England, it seems that a late fifth-century development gradually became universal by the sixth century. It seems to have received some influence from the interaction of the Anglo-Saxon newcomers with the resident British tribes that were already operating their tribal regions through monarchies. In addition, the conquering and subsequent occupation of territory by Germanic tribal leaders necessitated a more organised structure to hold and preserve claimed land for settlement beyond the more rudimentary methods formerly employed by warlords. We see the first kings among the Angles, Saxons and Jutes being recognised first in the eastern regions nearest to mainland Europe, which supports an argument that influences from the continent were the biggest factor. For a leader to hold the title of 'king' meant that they had garnered not just localised support but more widespread backing from combined separate tribal groups and individual warlords into a cohesive single entity, a permanent marker displaying a tribe's presence and permanence in a particular region or territory.

A major environmental event that began around the moment Cynric replaced Cerdic looks to have sped up this process. As already addressed, approaching the mid-sixth century the British Isles, along with much of Europe, experienced what has been called a 'climatic downturn'.[5] The trigger for this appears to have been a volcanic eruption in Iceland in 536, followed and reinforced in quick succession by two further eruptions in 540 and 547. Based on original contemporary sources, Bede's *Ecclesiastical History* and the ASC later referred to the sun going dark until 9.00 a.m. on 1 March 538 and the same being repeated on 20 June 540.[6] The Icelandic eruptions, combined with at least one other recorded eruption in the eastern Mediterranean, unloaded vast quantities of ash into the atmosphere, which obscured the sun for significant periods across much of the northern hemisphere.[7]

In England, perhaps due to its proximity to Iceland, there was a greater and more dramatic drop in temperatures than elsewhere, with the period 536–545 calculated to have been the coldest decade recorded throughout the past two millennia.[8] The result was several years of crop failure and famine, followed during the 540s by a particularly virulent period of plague (bubonic). Unconnected as these events may seem in relation to political developments, they look to be the primary cause for the reversal of migration from Britain to Europe and for Anglo-Saxon advances westward being suspended over this same period. This sequence of events promoted the further development of the privileged classes, bringing about the final development that underscored the shift from warlords to kings.

This period of upheaval and movement of peoples may also have prompted further work to reinforce the major defensive construction known as the Wansdyke, a long ditch-and-bank earthwork that crossed east to west through Wiltshire and Somerset. Various dates have been given for its construction, but it was probably started by the Atrebates, Durotriges or Belgae, beginning at the Roman withdrawal. The post-Roman dating can be verified when looking at the section at Morgan's Hill north of the village of Bishops Cannings near Devizes, which was constructed over and through the previously built Roman road between London and Bath. It comprised two sections separated by a 20-mile stretch of lower ground between Bath to the west and Mildenhall near Marlborough to the east.[9] The western end of the west section rested at Maes Knoll, an Iron Age hillfort south of modern Bristol. The east section's eastern end can be traced near the A345 Marlborough–Pewsey road, formerly the edge of Savernake Forest.

Both sections had a defensive structure facing north, which suggests the British tribes to its south had been keen to defend against more aggressive tribes to the north of the Wansdyke, possibly the Dobunni.[10] Some archaeologists have suggested that earthworks around Inkpen Beacon, south-east of Hungerford, point to the eastern end of the Wansdyke being several more miles to the east. The section running across the Wiltshire Downs is the best preserved, and some sections have surviving banks over 10 feet high and ditches several feet deep in parts.

Some historians argue that Cynric's son Ceawlin or others may have reinforced the earthwork in a later period along some sections. The archaeological evidence accepts that some modifications and reinforcements were made, although these alterations confuse the evidence for dating its first stage of construction.[11] There were further phases in the seventh century, perhaps under Cenwealh, and then later in the ninth century. However, the Wansdyke merely delayed and impeded invading forces. Unlike Offa's Dyke, it was not meant as a lasting barrier.

As for Cynric's kingship, the ASC makes no reference to him whatsoever between 534 and 552. Though disappointing for historians and academics, it is not an exceptional omission. Within that same eighteen-year period the ASC scribes added only four other entries: two related to the climatic events of 538 and 540 noted above, another to Cynric's relative Wihtgar's death in 544, and an elongated entry in 547 that inexplicably details thirteen generations of the royal line of the kings of Bamburgh (Bernicia in Northumbria).[12] Cynric resurfaces in the ASC in an entry for 552, but before considering that further we might look at the potential association of the West Saxon royal line with the man named Creoda at this time. He has but a single entry throughout the pages of the ASC, and even then only in versions B, C and D.[13] That entry comes in 855, over three hundred years after his lifetime, in another repeated genealogical ancestral list for the West Saxon royal house. In it, the three versions of the ASC name him as 'Cerdic's offspring', lying between Cerdic and Cynric.

The monk Asser in his *Life of King Alfred*, which is contemporary with the first compilation of the ASC, confirms that Creoda was Cynric's father and Ceawlin's grandfather, thus highlighting that an awareness of Creoda was promoted during Alfred's reign.[14] As further acknowledgement, Creoda is listed as the father of Cynric in a manuscript known as the 'Anglian collection', which itself may have been a copy of a much older document.[15] The inference is that Creoda had the potential to have been the king of the West Saxons between Cerdic and Cynric, but circumstances may have prevented him from succeeding. Nevertheless, he was also a recognised ancestor of the late seventh-century kings Caedwalla and Ine, who were centred in Hampshire. Clearly, it was important for Creoda's name to be inserted into the Cerdicing line within some primary sources, even if his name does not appear in others. Although further detail about Creoda is unlikely to emerge, references to him may suggest an attempt to forge a connection between the Cerdicing line, which developed in Hampshire, and the Gewisse in the Thames Valley.

This potentially throws much of the accepted chronology for both Cerdic and Cynric into greater uncertainty. Many secondary sources omit any reference to Creoda, preferring instead to overlook this reference to a man that may lie mid-generation between Cerdic and Cynric, thereby avoiding as best they can further muddling of the debated timelines. However, let us try and build an argument for Creoda's existence, which may resolve some of the dilemmas we find in the ASC whereby Cynric is named in entries between 495 to 560 and in the WSGRL between 554 and 581.

There may be an argument for a compromise suggestion, one that supports including Creoda in the timeframes of the early sixth century. Readers are urged to remain open-minded as various scenarios deviate from the regnal dates of primary sources. Let us propose Cerdic arrived in England post-500 with his young son Creoda. Cerdic became de facto king of Wessex sometime around or after 519, while Creoda, not Cerdic, had a son named Cynric born sometime between 515 and 520. At a later point in the 530s (it is suggested around 534), it was agreed that Creoda could share the throne with Cerdic. Creoda then predeceased his father, who died sometime around 538–540, and so when Cerdic died his grandson Cynric became sole ruler, thus explaining why Creoda is not recorded as having the kingship of Wessex at any stage by the WSGRL.

The potential timeframe for Cynric's active years is supported by him and his son Ceawlin being recorded in the ASC fighting a battle in 556.[16] This would allow an age for Ceawlin of at least sixteen to eighteen in that year (i.e. born no later than 540), and likewise give some substance to the record of Cynric's death and Ceawlin's succession taking place in 560 (as per the ASC). The WSGRL date of 581 for Cynric's death contradicts Ceawlin's other recorded activities as king, as most of his actions, as detailed in the ASC, happened prior to that date. Interestingly, Creoda's omission from the WSGRL may paradoxically explain why it employed later sequencing for both Cynric and Ceawlin.

Finally, we can approach the Cerdic, Creoda and Cynric relationship from one more angle. Aside from their potential kinship connections, they may have shared the kingship between them for a certain period in some combination. This may have followed on through into Ceawlin's reign. As seen in examples from other periods and places, and for much of the next century, sometimes two or perhaps three leaders may have ruled in parallel over various regions within either West Saxon or Gewisse-controlled territory, sharing the throne and responsibilities. One potential configuration is that Cerdic's last years and Cynric's early years in control of south-west Hampshire coincided with Creoda ruling in parallel for a time over the Gewisse Saxons in the Upper Thames Valley.[17]

It is plausible that while there was a blood alliance between the two groupings, based on the ancestry connection of Cerdic to his purported father Elesa, each group had its king in place. Our missing detail is that at no stage do the primary sources acknowledge parallel rule, let alone that the Gewisse were such an important factor in the story of Wessex's development. Certainly, the ASC records that Cynric and Ceawlin fought together against the British at 'Bera's stronghold' in 556, which suggests that the West Saxons of Hampshire and the Gewisse of Berkshire were acting together, and under the arrangement noted above, somewhere on a border with the British in north Wiltshire.[18] This association may have transformed or changed itself by 560 or soon after. At some stage, they formed a union under a single king and a sub-king, with the nominated king contradicting the tradition expounded by later chroniclers by forming his main court not at Winchester but possibly at Dorchester-on-Thames or Abingdon or somewhere else in the Upper Thames Valley. This goes against the traditional West Saxon version of events but ideally explains why the next phase of expansion beyond 560, during the reign of Ceawlin, looks to have come not from Hampshire but from Berkshire.

Returning to safer ground, much of Cynric's period as king overlapped with the period of uncertainty involving some Anglo-Saxon migrations back to the continent, successive crop failures, and episodes of the bubonic plague. The period from 540 to 550 is perhaps an opportune time to reassess the power balance between the tribes across the south of England, both British and Anglo-Saxon. The inference from the concise primary source detail we have is that among the British tribes the Durotriges to the west still held a line centred on Bokerley Dyke in east Dorset, the Belgae still held Winchester and central Hampshire, and the Atrebates northern Hampshire and part of Berkshire stretching into Wiltshire. We can extrapolate that much based on Cynric's later seizure of Old Sarum in 552. In the 540s, then, he was not powerful enough to expand West Saxon territory significantly in any direction. The Meonwara Jutes still held sway in south-east Hampshire, and at this stage held most of the Isle of Wight.

Beyond the Meonwara Jutes, the South Saxons of Sussex and the Jutes of Kent had already defeated and subdued the regional British Regnenses and Cantiaci tribes, a consequence of their closeness to the continent, which had led to their earlier settlement combined with a probable greater number of fighting men arriving from the late fifth century onwards to compete against the native British. In terms of the archaeology relating to this period, both Sussex and Kent hold more evidence of earlier Germanic settlements than can be seen across southern Hampshire.[19] For the Saxon Gewisse the situation is clouded. There are hints they were trying to gain territory from the Catuvellauni to their north-east, primarily unsuccessfully up to that point, but would soon be poised to make significant advances westward from their base in the Upper Thames Valley against the Dobunni during the reign of Ceawlin. Beyond Cynric, it would be the Gewisse and Ceawlin who would lead the drive for territorial expansion within the West Saxon–Gewisse alliance.

Either after piecemeal gains throughout the late 540s and early 550s, or in one well-planned thrust into Wiltshire, in 552 Cynric's army seized the important British hillfort of Searo Byrig, more commonly known today as Old Sarum, and 'put the Britons to flight'.[20] Its archaeology shows that Old Sarum had been important before the Roman period, and although it may have been abandoned during Roman rule it had been occupied and reinforced again by the Durotriges in their conflict with the adjacent Belgae. Cynric was possibly still allied with the Belgae. There is no primary source detail anywhere in the historiography after 527 describing the West Saxons fighting the Belgae in Hampshire, or at a later stage seizing the former Roman *civitas* and by then the Belgae capital at Winchester by force. There is a variation in the surviving archaeology from this period which supports an argument for suspended activity further westward beyond the Hampshire Avon. Equally, there is no hard archaeology so far to confirm serious evidence of major West Saxon activity south of Winchester during this period, which would be necessary to support the chronological record of West Saxon settlement in significant numbers.[21] This may be explained by a greater level of Saxon assimilation with the original British population of southern Hampshire than was previously considered, and several historians have argued that the lack of archaeology supports this contention.[22]

Archaeological digs around Winchester have connected the Belgae with nearby Jutish settlements that were outliers from the Meonwara.[23] The inference is that by the mid-sixth century, Cynric's West Saxons were on friendly terms with both the Belgae and the Meonwara, and what would lead in due course to full assimilation with the Belgae had already developed. In the absence of later recorded military activity, the West Saxons would at an unspecified period, possibly in the seventh century, be permitted to settle in and around the former *civitas* of Winchester peacefully. In due course, they would first develop a large trading port at Hamwic/Hamtun, on the site of present-day Southampton, near the estuary of the River Itchen, and would not develop Winchester until the reign of Ecgberht in the ninth century.

Reasonable proof that Cynric was sharing the throne with his son Ceawlin by 556 is found in the ASC entry of that year, when they both 'fought against the Britons at Bera's stronghold'.[24] If we further accept the premise that they each controlled separate regions – which, based on similar instances in Kent and Northumbria, seems to have been an acceptable way of dividing power – then we might also argue that this battle recognises that tribes in Hampshire and the Thames Valley were now working together militarily and presumably politically. This idea of military cooperation is supported by the *Chronicon* of John of Worcester in his attempt at locating Bera's stronghold. He notes that 'Cynric and Ceawlin did battle ...

at Barbury and put them to flight', which relates to the hillfort known as Barbury Castle, 5 miles directly south of modern-day Swindon.[25]

In common with several other Iron Age hillforts across Wiltshire, Barbury Castle lies on the Ridgeway, which passes through the centre of the hillfort. Considering known ancient trackways, and working on the basis that Cynric had advanced north from the region around captured Old Sarum, he probably crossed the River Kennet near Marlborough as the track followed a line along what is now called Kingsbury Street north-west out of the modern town. The road changes to Free's Avenue as it heads north and becomes a minor track that continues to Barbury.[26] We can speculate that Ceawlin's Gewisse contingent had followed the east-to-west track from the direction of Ashbourne, where it joins the aforementioned north-to-south route just south of Barbury, and at that point their forces joined ahead of launching their assault on the hillfort.

As in other examples of these early encounters, the twelfth-century chronicler Henry of Huntingdon provides the most detailed version of events. Presumably, he had access to earlier texts that his contemporaries did not. Huntingdon writes of the British at Barbury forming a defensive formation in nine lines, including cavalry and archers, while the Saxons charged them in a single formation. However, contrary to the summary given by the ASC and John of Worcester, Huntingdon does not proclaim a West Saxon–Gewisse victory, writing instead that 'the issue was still unresolved', which implies that Cynric and Ceawlin were repulsed.[27]

Roughly following the geographical alignment of Old Sarum and Barbury, it appears they lay along or close to the likely southern and south-western border between the Atrebates and their rivals the Durotriges. Some suggest that we can perhaps also associate this with the original western margin of the area controlled previously by the Romano-British leader Ambrosius Aurelianus.[28] Likewise, Barbury was close to a point where the boundaries between three British tribes – the Belgae, the Atrebates and the Dobunni – are thought to have met. It would seem this former British tribal boundary was now forming the boundary protecting the sixth-century British from further Anglo-Saxon advances into the south-west. Working on Huntingdon's claim that the 556 battle at Barbury was indecisive, this impacted further immediate advances into central Wiltshire, and Cynric's death four years later may have further delayed inroads into Dorset.

The primary sources do not inform us of Cynric's death, but the inference is that he died in 560, the year that the ASC records Ceawlin's succession to what the scribe describes as 'the kingdom in Wessex'.[29] It is from Ceawlin's succession, as recorded by the ASC, that we can acknowledge that the different sixth-century timeline of the regnal list within the WSGRL looks most exposed. The WSGRL has Cynric ruling until 581 and Ceawlin ruling thereafter from 581 until 588.[30] This cannot be accurate. No other primary source mentions Cynric after 560. Moreover, the majority of references to Ceawlin in the next chapter are about events pre-dating the mid-580s. From widespread research, there is negligible support among secondary sources and historians for Ceawlin's alternate timeline. Based on this reasoning, we will stick with the more logical ASC regnal timeline after Cynric.

Cynric's demise and disappearance from the sources also marks a major change in how later ASC scribes recorded matters relating to the West Saxons and Ceawlin's kingship that may at first seem insignificant. Ceawlin is referred to as the 'king of Wessex', but any reference to the activities of the Hampshire-based West Saxons now ceases. It is not until well into the seventh century that further recorded events originate from that region. In contrast, from 560 the ASC seamlessly records events during Ceawlin's reign that overwhelmingly concern not matters relating to Dorset or south Wiltshire but events ranging from the Thames Valley to the Chilterns and across to the Severn Estuary. In other words, the centre of recorded West Saxon activity transfers to the region formerly settled by the Gewisse. It is through them that the next important phase of territorial expansion takes place, creating a challenge to historians who do not wish to go beyond the traditional rhetoric surrounding Wessex and the West Saxons.

As touched on earlier, the Gewisse's role in the region's expansion and formation into what was later known as the kingdom of Wessex was profound. In the early eighth century Bede used the terms West Saxon and Gewisse interchangeably, noting that 'the West Saxons, who in early days were called the Gewisse' were the same, whether he was describing events along the south coast or along the Thames.[31] For us perhaps the question is when to stop using the term 'Gewisse' when describing events relating to an evolving Wessex. Ceawlin's kingship might be a sounder period than any in which to make the change, even if his military activity suggests he based himself in Gewisse territory, not West Saxon Hampshire territory. We have already established the premise that Wessex resulted from the union of the two groups, even if the agreed timeframe for that remains fluid, and even though the kingdom's name was derived from the West Saxons. Let us agree therefore to avoid the need to keep differentiating between them. Henceforth, with immediate effect, whichever of the two groups it concerns, we will refer to either or both for the remaining chapters as the 'West Saxons'.

5
Ceawlin and Ceol
560–597

Regardless of whether Ceawlin shared the throne with Cynric or acted as a sub-king during the latter's final years, it was Ceawlin who succeeded to the whole of the kingdom. We have a scenario where he may have already been operating from inside the Gewisse region, either ahead of the 556 encounter at Barbury Castle or as a consequence of that victory. It is plausible and in keeping with both Anglo-Saxon and British practices that Cynric appointed a sub-king or even more than one to act on his behalf across some or part of the designated regions he controlled, and appointing his son in such a role – in this case over Gewisse territory – would not have been unusual.

Assuming Ceawlin was already sub-king, it is no surprise that he was named king after Cynric's death. Both the ASC and John of Worcester state that this happened in 560, the latter adding that Ceawlin was to reign for thirty-three years.[1] The discrepancies between the ASC and WSGRL timelines have been addressed already, but they are at their most obvious here. There is a difference of twenty-one years between them, with the WSGRL listing Ceawlin's succession as late as 581.[2]

An explanation for this continued variation in dates is hard to find. It is possible that later scribes misinterpreted earlier entries in documents that have not survived, and concerning Ceawlin specifically one possible answer for his reign being brought forward may be Alfred the Great's desire for the ASC to help integrate him more closely into the Cerdicing lineage.[3] The WSGRL seems to have Ceawlin's reign beginning much too late, even to the point of contradicting other primary source details of his exploits pre-581, such as his famous victory over the British at Dyrham in 577.[4] If we accept he did not become king until 581, then all his major military achievements were carried out while he was heir to an incredibly old Cynric.

Most historians assume that Cynric's overriding military objective was to expand West Saxon territory westward from a base in Hampshire. What remains hidden is whether Ceawlin came to prominence in the Gewisse region prior to 556 and whether he was of Gewisse blood. In accepting his career relates overwhelmingly to events emanating from the Thames Valley and not Hampshire, we are automatically questioning his bloodline connection to Cynric. This is not an ideal situation if we intend to follow the traditional West Saxon genealogy trail. Primary source texts during the 560s are again less than ideal, with Ceawlin going unrecorded for the first eight years of his reign. This lack of detail could suggest a period of deeper assimilation and consolidation along the Thames Valley with the Berkshire Atrebates and other adjacent British tribes. A similar period of stabilisation with the Belgae and Atrebates may also have been taking place around the West Saxon presence in Hampshire.

During this interval in the sources it would seem Ceawlin was making plans to expand his authority beyond the original Gewisse settlement area. When the sources do provide details their attention switches to events circulating in the Thames Valley, which we can postulate was Ceawlin's main area of influence from the beginning. The military advances made in the late sixth century and the initial foundations of Christianity in Wessex in the seventh century were driven from the Gewisse heartland, not from the West Saxon settlements across Hampshire, and Ceawlin would in due course be associated with westward advances against the British in Somerset and around the Severn Estuary.

Until the latter part of the sixth century, the various Germanic Angle, Saxon and Jute tribes limited their military activity primarily to fighting the native British. Alliances were negotiated between the Germanic tribes and with the British. However, the ASC entry for 568 comes as a surprise as it refers to conflict not with one of the British tribes but with other Anglo-Saxons.[5] The clash chronicled in 568 was distinct, marking the first encounter between Anglo-Saxons to be chronologically recorded within a primary source.

A warlord named Cutha is named prominently alongside Ceawlin in the encounter, which was fought against a man named Æthelberht of Kent. However, there are complications. Both version F of the ASC and Henry of Huntingdon name Cutha as Ceawlin's brother, presumably with Cutha the younger of the two.[6] William of Malmesbury's *Gesta Regum Anglorum* similarly names Cutha as Ceawlin's brother but mentions Ceawlin having a son with the same name.[7] Huntingdon and Malmesbury's contemporary John of Worcester refers only to a son named Cutha and does not mention a brother.[8] Several entries in versions A and E of the ASC between 568 and 584, and then later in genealogy lists from 685 and 855, also confuse the issue, describing Cutha as a son of Cynric but also as the offspring of either Ceawlin or Cuthwine, at times also referring to Cuthwulf, which was possibly the full name of this later Cutha.[9] To best resolve what is a difficult situation we should perhaps accept Malmesbury's text but add that there were three men named Cutha: one the brother of Ceawlin; another his son, who has alternately been named Cuthwine; and another who was Cuthwine's son with the alternate name of Cuthwulf. Hereafter, we shall name this third Cutha as Cuthwulf to keep our confusion within limits. Cuthwulf was Cuthwine's son, so he was also Ceawlin's grandson.

As with his two predecessors, there is sufficient evidence to show that the designated name of Ceawlin may link him by blood to the Celtic British. Perhaps his mother was British, from the Atrebates, or from the nearby Dobunni who held territory in Gloucestershire and the south-west Midlands. Within the *Welsh Genealogies* Ceawlin is recorded as Collen or Kollen. The Welsh scribes refer to him as being the son of Gwynoc and grandson of Kydeboc, which translated from the Brythonic gives us Cerdic and Cynric.[10] In contrast, Cutha is a Saxon name. What should be emphasised here is that some primary sources during this period frequently described those of Celtic British ethnicity as being Welsh rather than British. This 'Welshness' should not be taken to refer to what we now identify as Wales but rather the Celtic British in the general sense of the sixth century.

The Welsh chroniclers state that Ceawlin's wife was Ethinen, the daughter of an Irish chieftain.[11] It is credible there were marital agreements between the Welsh and Irish, and we know there had been intermarriage between Anglo-Saxons and Britons, but whether Ceawlin's wife was Welsh cannot be confirmed. Perhaps Ceawlin negotiated his marriage as part of an ongoing alliance with the Atrebate leadership in the Thames Valley, by this point from a position of strength. In terms of alliances, evidence suggests the West Saxons had no warfare with the Atrebates or Belgae from 540 onwards. It is fair to argue there was significant ongoing peaceful integration between the Anglo-Saxons and the native British in the areas the West Saxons had settled.

When looking at Ceawlin's sphere of activity during his reign, it appears that he operated primarily if not solely from a base in Berkshire and the Upper Thames Valley. We should assume he visited Hampshire and the Solent in his role as king, but there is no source detail which points to him having masterminded a military campaign from Hampshire, confirming what looks to be a lack of major West Saxon progress beyond the River Avon during this period. This may have lasted a few decades, as the ASC remains silent regarding any military activity in Dorset during Ceawlin's reign. It is not until Cynegils' West Saxon victory in 614 at Bea's Mount (Beandun) on the Dorset–Devon border against an alliance of the British Dumnonii tribe of Devon and the Durotriges of West Dorset that we have acknowledgement of further military advances in that region.[12] It is perhaps significant that there is no further entry in the ASC relating to Hampshire until it notes the building of the church at Winchester in 643, which might imply that the various British, Saxon and Jute groupings in the region were on peaceful terms.[13]

In terms of administration, some historians have suggested that the Roman model of *civitas* centres was still valid, although managed on a more rudimentary level, with trade based on bartering of goods replacing a rigid fiscal tax system. With this in mind, there may have been more than one sub-king, or warlord if that title sits more easily, each with governing control centred perhaps on former *civitates* or at one of the larger newly formed Anglo-Saxon settlements. Nonetheless, Ceawlin may have held full authority for a period, and we see him then as perhaps the first West Saxon king to do so while a seamless connection between the West Saxons and the Gewisse was still forming.

Ceawlin's mention in the ASC is sparse, but it still holds valuable information. His period as king witnessed a major expansion of territory, both to his west and to his east, with successful battles against British tribes and at least one against a Germanic contemporary, Æthelberht of Kent, which will be explored below. Such would be the legacy of Ceawlin's influence that Bede would name him as the second Bretwalda. Interestingly, Bede names him 'Caelin' and 'king of the West Saxons, known in their language as Ceawlin', which implies that Caelin was his Brythonic name and that 'Ceawlin' is in fact of Anglo-Saxon derivation, not British.[14]

Ceawlin's case as the first great warlord and military leader of Wessex is compelling. He is certainly in the pantheon of outstanding West Saxon kings. Whether or not we acknowledge the possibility of his half-British bloodstock, it is no wonder that Alfred and the chronicle scribes wished to link Ceawlin to the bloodline of Cerdic, and by the late ninth century he was regarded unquestionably as Cynric's son in the primary sources.[15]

In his first major military action as king, Ceawlin moved north-east of present-day Reading to conquer the neighbouring region occupied by the Cilternsaete tribe, from which the Chiltern Hills would take their name. It is unclear if they were British or Anglo-Saxon. The etymology of 'Chiltern' has been linked to the word 'celt'. This could imply the tribe were Romano-British with links to the adjacent Catuvellauni, and there is an argument they could be connected to the Middle Saxons who had settled to the west of London.[16] It cannot be discounted that Ceawlin acted together or in concert with the British Atrebates, as the continuity between the Atrebates as a political entity and the development of Wessex from Ceawlin's reign into the seventh century suggests they held mutual interests. On a wider scale the Catuvellauni, whose kingdom had once stretched east to west from Cambridge to Oxford and north to south from Peterborough to London, had been under immense pressure from several directions. They had already lost significant territory to a combination of various Anglian tribes that had also allied themselves with smaller British tribes.

Ceawlin's movement against the Cilternsaete would bring him into direct conflict with the Catuvellauni, but his immediate attention was drawn towards the expansion of the Jutish-Saxon kingdom of Kent under their young king Æthelberht. The result was a major battle between them, known as Wibba's Mount or Wibbandun, which ended in victory for Ceawlin and his brother during 568. The ASC recorded, 'Here Ceawlin and Cutha fought against Æthelberht and drove him into Kent ... and they killed two ealdormen, Oslaf and Cnebba, on Wibba's Mount.'[17] Despite the triumph, version F of the ASC records that Cutha was killed, with William of Malmesbury noting that he had 'an untimely death'.[18]

There are various options for the battle site, and its dating is a topic of discussion. Historians cannot be clear whether Æthelberht's forces had already campaigned well into Catuvellauni territory and clashed with Ceawlin there, or whether the encounter came nearer to home in present-day Surrey. Apart from being, as noted earlier, the first direct clash of Anglo-Saxon factions to be recorded in the ASC, it is also the first dated instance in the chronicle of the title 'ealdorman'.[19] Use of the term in 568 may be a little premature. We can perhaps relate it to how the late tenth-century chronicle scribes saw the equivalent position, for what might previously have been a sub-king or warlord chieftain. To be an ealdorman was to swear an oath and be tied to the king's fate. In general, ealdormen were appointed by the king to act in all matters on his behalf within a designated region or territory, providing support and men-at-arms in times of war in exchange for royal favours, including the awarding of land.

We can reasonably argue that Ceawlin's army at Wibbandun had a British contingent of allies. For Wibbandun itself there are several proposed sites. Perhaps the least favoured in geographical terms is Wyboston, lying on the west bank of the Great Ouse, 8 miles north-east of Bedford.[20] This location, a derivative of 'Wibba's Dun', suggests Æthelberht of Kent was campaigning well beyond London, while Ceawlin may have been continuing his Chilterns campaign in Catuvellauni territory. Given that Ceawlin's next recorded battle three years later was apparently near Bedford, as considered below, the argument for Wyboston has much to support it, with Ceawlin perhaps looking to establish a defensive boundary along the Great Ouse.

Henry of Huntingdon records that the West Saxons 'were compelled' to fight the Kentish since the latter 'had arrogantly entered their kingdom with troops'.[21] Meanwhile, the *Chronicon Æthelweardi* considers that it was Ceawlin and his brother that 'stirred up a civil war'.[22] Two nearby place names may support the Wyboston option. Just south of it is the village of Chawton, which may be derived from Ceawston or Ceawlinston (i.e. Ceawlin's town), and Cnebba, one of the two Kentish ealdormen killed in the battle, has been associated with Knebworth, 20 miles to the south.[23]

The other potential sites, all in Surrey, are more favoured given the geography and juxtaposition of Kent and Wessex in the late sixth century. The first option is Wimbledon, a site which was first proposed in the sixteenth century; more precisely, some historians suggest Wimbledon Common.[24] On the western edge of the Common to the east of the modern A3 road there is a sports ground named Wibbandune, but it is unclear whether the ground was named in respect of the earlier battle or whether the area was already named as such beforehand.

Another option is Chobham Heath or Common, located one mile north of the village. The argument for Chobham is based on place-name similarity, as a charter of Chertsey Abbey, founded in the seventh century, refers to a site named 'Wipseden' (the hill/dun of Wippa) on Chobham Heath.[25] A final and more popular option for Wibbandun is the village of Worplesdon, or more precisely Whitmoor Common a mile to its east and 2 miles north of modern Guildford. Several historians support this location, not only by place-name association but by its proximity to an ancient east–west trackway. Worplesdon is purportedly linked to Wibbandune via the name 'Wibsden', which it is claimed is what the local inhabitants of Worplesdon up to recent times called their village.[26] There is no conclusive evidence that raises any of these possibilities above any of the others. However, any one of the Surrey locations seem to sit more easily than the Wyboston site as a point of contact and conflict.

Bede was later to write that Æthelberht of Kent's suzerainty 'stretched as far as the great river Humber'.[27] We can imagine Bede's Christianity influencing his writing. He is perhaps implying that Æthelberht's later patronage of Christianity in the 590s – he was still a pagan when he fought Ceawlin in 568 – gave him an ideological authority beyond the boundaries of his kingdom. It was certainly an embellishment in terms of

Æthelberht's military achievements, although there is evidence that the Kentish kings were already overlords of the East Anglians and the British Trinovantes north of the River Thames.[28]

The year 568 looks to be too early for Æthelberht to have already assumed the Kentish throne. There is some disagreement among the primary sources as to when he became king and for how long he reigned.[29] The recorded king of Kent up until 580, perhaps even 590, was his father Eormenric. Æthelberht's alleged birth in 550 would make him a potential heir to Kent at just eighteen in 568. Consequently, some historians have claimed the battle was post-580, in effect accepting the WSGRL chronology for Ceawlin, which is inconsistent with the chronology of both the ASC and Bede's *Ecclesiastical History*.

It has been suggested by some that the conflict involved ideology. Ceawlin, it is said, was already a Christian convert, suggesting that his victory over Æthelberht was symbolic of Christianity defeating paganism.[30] It is true that Æthelberht was pagan; he would not convert to Christianity until the missionary monk Augustine's arrival from Rome in the mid-590s.[31] However, Ceawlin's ideology is difficult to distinguish. The logical view for this period is that he was still pagan in 568 and would possibly remain so throughout his lifetime, and explaining Wibbandun as being a clash of ideologies therefore seems overly elaborate.

Mention should be made at this point of the position of the South Saxons, located as they were between the West Saxons and the Kentish Jutes/Saxons. The only known king of Sussex between Ælle and the late seventh century was Ælle's son Cissa. This man had likely died by 568, but in any case he left no direct descendant. However, Roger of Wendover's *Flores Historiarum* informs us that by this stage the throne of Sussex had passed to the bloodline of Cerdic, which tells us by indirect reference that Ceawlin already held authority over all of Hampshire and West Sussex.[32] It is unclear how Wendover obtained this information, and the notion of Ceawlin having already conquered the South Saxons is not supported by any other primary source.

Ceawlin's next move after Wibbandun was beyond the Chilterns into Catuvellauni territory during 571, in a battle against the British named as Bedcanford. However, he may have been absent from this action as he is not named by the ASC scribes. We can perhaps assume Ceawlin appointed a sub-king for this campaign, but nonetheless, the scribes contradict each other. Whereas version A describes Cuthwulf as fighting the action, version E states it was Cutha.[33] We should probably accept version E as being more credible, with Ceawlin's son Cutha leading the army, as version A's reference to Cuthwulf in an action in 571 seems premature when working on our earlier conclusion that he was probably Ceawlin's grandson.

The campaign invalidates the early writer Gildas's assumption that the Anglo-Saxons (primarily the East Angles and Middle Saxons) had generations earlier already assumed authority much further west than modern Bedfordshire. The Catuvellauni were slow to cede control to Angle and Saxon invaders, and the south-east Midlands was riven by factions, with Anglo-Saxon tribes contesting land with the established British tribes and among themselves. If we accept Henry of Huntingdon assertion that Bedcanford 'is now called Bedford', then the territory gained did not include Bedford itself.[34] The victory at Bedcanford not only weakened the Catuvellauni but also their allies the Trinovantes, who had been helping repel various Anglo-Saxon advances.

The primary sources record Bedcanford secured the townships of Limbury, Aylesbury, Bensington and Eynsham.[35] At first glance these settlements do not have any logical connection. Limbury is now a suburb of modern-day Luton, and Eynsham is 5 miles north-west of Oxford, 40 miles distant. This has caused some historians to question the veracity of the chronicle entry in the context of sixth-century territorial disputes.[36] There is the possibility that they are listed specifically to denote the full extent of the territory gained by this single victory, presumably a crushing defeat for the Catuvellauni leadership. Alternately, they were perhaps named because they were all important settlements controlled by British warlords.[37]

When the map is studied more carefully, these locations appear to form a logical boundary, each lying along an important route, at least three of them occupying former fortified sites. The River Lea passes Limbury, the location of a former Roman fort, and 3 miles to the west is the source of the Lea, next to the Roman Icknield Way and the route from Towcester to St Albans.[38] The Icknield Way connects with the Ridgeway at Ivinghoe Beacon, and near Tring the Ridgeway passes just to the south of the source of the River Thame, which in turn passes just to the north of Aylesbury, where a ford once stood close to a former Iron Age hillfort. Flowing generally westward, the Thame eventually joins the River Thames, which then passes through Benson a few miles to the north and flows on through Oxford northward and then west before passing just to the south of Eynsham. By joining these points, we have a delineated boundary defined by the Lea, the Icknield Way, the Ridgeway, the Thame and the Thames, passing through Aylesbury and Benson between Limbury and Eynsham.

After this border readjustment, lack of entries from the primary sources implies there was again a brief period of peace. Six years later, in 577,

Ceawlin moved west to confront the Dobunni tribe that had earlier taken the region around the Severn Estuary, north Somerset and north-west Wiltshire from either the Belgae or the Atrebates. The conclusion of this campaign was to see Ceawlin achieve perhaps his greatest military victory, the decisive battle at Dyrham (Deorham), 7 miles north of Bath. He was joined there by his second son, Cuthwine, with the ASC noting that 'here Cuthwine and Ceawlin fought against the Britons'.[39] This initial push west was the prelude to a much further advance westwards and south-westwards from Berkshire and north Wiltshire into Somerset in later decades. Perhaps there was already a realisation during the 570s that the greatest opportunity for expansion lay in that direction into territory still controlled by British tribes rather than the more volatile situation of the contested territories around the Chilterns and towards London.

The British Dobunni had formed an alliance of tribal groups in the region around Gloucestershire, north Somerset and north-west Wiltshire, comprising the Caer Baddan under King Farinmael, the Caer Ceri under King Condidan and the Caer Gloui under King Conmail (Commagil). They are identified in the sources as holding in turn the three former Roman *civitates* of Bath, Cirencester and Gloucester, although the belief that all *civitates* still served as major British settlements in the late sixth century is not clearly supported by the archaeology. Bath and Gloucester were minimally populated during this period, for instance, and only Cirencester seems to have kept its position as an important population centre.[40]

We have minimal detail about the battle itself. Henry of Huntingdon, perhaps with literary licence, tells us the British forces were 'densely packed and magnificent', and 'the fighting was extremely hard' before the British were put to flight.[41] Historians favour the battle site being adjacent to the Iron Age hillfort of Hinton Hill, less than a mile north of present-day Dyrham village. The assumption must be that the British had early warning of Ceawlin's advance westward and had assembled their troops inside the hillfort. It was the last high ground before the Severn Estuary, so a good point at which to combine their forces, although it is equally accepted that Hinton was not in contemporary use, with the fortifications insufficient to resist a mass assault. Worse still, its ramparts were better at repelling attacks from the south or west whereas Ceawlin's army was advancing from the east. Because of this, perhaps fearing entrapment, the consensus is that the British vacated the hillfort, forming their men along two low ridges, about 300 and 800 metres to the east, the remnants of which can barely be made out in today's landscape.[42] The furthest advanced of these was to the west of the crossroads of the modern

A46 road and the minor road to Hinton, near to the adjacent Crown Inn pub today.

Ceawlin likely expected the British to be behind the ramparts, so seeing them east of the hillfort was possibly a pleasant surprise. Rather than hit the first of the British lines head on, he diverted some – perhaps most – of his troops around their flanks, causing confusion. After initial contact the Saxons began to roll up both flanks, causing a withdrawal wherein the two British lines impeded each other as they retreated to regroup.[43] Initial confusion among the British ranks turned into a rout and the Saxons were able to pursue the surviving British into and beyond the hillfort, with kings Farinmael, Condidan and Conmail all killed.[44] We can only guess at the number of combatants. Possibly, there were only a few thousand warriors on each side, or maybe even fewer.

Victory at Dyrham theoretically opened an unchallenged route to the Severn Estuary, less than 15 miles away. It had effectively forged a wedge between the British tribes in Devon and Cornwall and those within the south-west midlands and Wales. However, Ceawlin may not have been able to fully exploit his newly gained advantage. There was no opportunity at this stage for a permanent West Saxon settlement alongside the Severn. Archaeological evidence would suggest that while such a presence is noted soon after 577 around Cirencester, settlement in the more westerly sites at Bath and Gloucester does not seem to have occurred for some time.[45] The number of Brythonic place names that have survived to the present day within this area points to a surviving British presence well beyond Ceawlin's reign. Similarly, several sites in north-west Wiltshire and the Gloucestershire–Somerset border have produced grave goods showing that British culture still flourished in this region well into the seventh century.[46] A strong Anglo-Saxon presence along the Severn Estuary cannot be confirmed until perhaps a century after the battle of Dyrham, and it was not Ceawlin's successors but the Anglian Hwicce tribe, from what would be Gloucestershire and Worcestershire (later part of Mercia), that appear to have first settled this former Dobunni territory.[47]

A hiatus in the primary record after 577 may indicate a West Saxon consolidation around Cirencester. However, the next ASC entry concerning Ceawlin's reign, dated to 584, suggests there had been developments along the north-eastern border that he and Cutha had established after Bedcanford. Which British were still holding territory – or which Anglo-Saxons had gained authority – along the northern fringes of London and those regions that would later form the shires of Buckinghamshire, Bedfordshire and Hertfordshire is almost impossible to fathom. It is a mixed picture which historians rarely discuss. The impression is that regions quickly changed from British to Anglo-Saxon overnight, but the reality was more nuanced, with the borders between rival British and Anglo-Saxon groups having a degree of movement. There is a level of fluidity here, suggesting that the Catuvellauni, the tribe that had occupied this key region for centuries, did not cede ground easily. Various mixed Angle and Saxon tribal groups that had gained control of parcels of land formerly controlled by the Catuvellauni were consolidating rather than pushing for further expansion.

Based on the reported location of the battle, Ceawlin's next action in 584 was against the Catuvellauni. The ASC records that Ceawlin and Cutha 'fought against the Britons at a place called Battle Wood and Cutha was killed'.[48] John of Worcester names the 584 battle Fethanleag, as does Henry of Huntingdon, but there remains a dispute over which of Ceawlin's sons was killed in it. Worcester agrees with the ASC and names Cutha, while Huntingdon names the younger son, Cuthwine, seemingly incorrectly.[49] Cutha is not referenced again in any primary source beyond the year 584.

Identifying the exact location for Fethanleag has proved difficult. On the basis that the battle took place somewhere near or inside Catuvellauni territory, one favoured suggestion is near the village of Stoke Lyne, about 4 miles north of present-day Bicester. Support for this site comes from the Fethanleag place-name connection to an ancient wood named 'Fethelee' which is mentioned in a twelfth-century document relating to Stoke Lyne.[50] Further speculation based on the topography around Stoke Lyne suggests the battlefield was more specifically south of an east–west watercourse, just west of the modern B4100 road near Stoke Woods, which are possibly the remains of the Fethelee wood.[51]

As for the outcome of the battle, Ceawlin was reportedly victorious and took many towns and much war loot thereafter. However, the same chronicle entry intriguingly adds that Ceawlin 'in anger ... turned back to his own (territory)'.[52] This has been interpreted as a rather odd addition.[53] Why come home in 'anger' after a successful campaign? Let us presume it relates to the death of Cutha. It is reasonable to expect that he wished to escort the corpse back into home territory for formal burial. However, other matters may have been at play. He may have been angry at the manner of Cutha's death during the battle, but perhaps more importantly news of the death might have subtly altered the political situation within the kingdom, which necessitated a response from Ceawlin. It is known that Cuthwine was forced into exile after 590, and he was never to become king after his father's death. As discussed below, Ceawlin himself was later removed from power in 591 by his nephew Ceol (aka Ceolric), son of the king's deceased brother Cutha. Is it possible that while Ceawlin and his son were on the Fethanleag campaign Ceol had tried to seize the throne of Wessex? He would make a more successful attempt in 591, so perhaps a failed attempt in 584 would explain Ceawlin's 'anger'.

This may have been the beginning of a fight for control within the West Saxon leadership. There are no further entries among the primary sources concerning Ceawlin's rule until we hear of him being ousted in 591, and it is likely that the seven-year silence signifies not peace but a prolonged period of challenges for the kingship. The version A entry of the ASC for 591 simply states that 'Here Ceol ruled for five years', and version E that 'Here Ceolric ruled for six years'.[54] However, Ceawlin was not dead; he had been removed from power, so it is unclear if or why he became unpopular. It may be just a case of a younger man seeking greater power, with Ceol aggrieved that, as a blood relative with his own potential claim to the throne, he had not received sufficient reward from Ceawlin. There could even have been a clash between the West Saxons of Hampshire and the Gewisse of the Thames Valley.

Despite lacking desired detail, we have knowledge of Ceawlin's dethronement in 591. It was possibly the result of a successful surprise coup by Ceol at a chosen moment that is hidden from us, which is perhaps unsurprising if we accept he had potentially made a previous attempt in 584. Cuthwine presumably sought exile alongside his deposed father. Nevertheless, although Ceol had been proclaimed king, Ceawlin and his bloodline remained a threat into the following year. Maybe Ceawlin initiated moves to recover the throne, or perhaps Ceol realised that his own position was not secure while his predecessor lived.

Ceawlin still had much support behind him, and in 592 he challenged his usurper at the battle recorded as Woden's Barrow (named after the pagan god). It was a fight both sides had probably sought, for until matters were resolved between them the kingdom would remain unstable; indeed, it was perhaps the culmination of a brief period of civil war.[55] Ceol is not named directly, but we might presume he led his forces, and we certainly know Ceawlin was involved as the ASC noted that 'there was great slaughter at Woden's Barrow and Ceawlin was driven out'.[56] William of Malmesbury's *Gesta Regum Anglorum* refers to Ceol having British military support, with the 'English and Britons conspiring together' as they 'cut his (Ceawlin's) army to pieces at Wodnesdic (Woden's Barrow)', although it should be mentioned that no other primary source follows this line.[57] Nonetheless, it is plausible both leaders had British allies within their ranks, as we should acknowledge that the regional British would have been equally concerned about who held power.

There is a suggestion that Woden's Barrow may refer to the village of Wanborough on the eastern edge of present-day Swindon, although this is based on dubious charter evidence from much later and appears unlikely. The site of Woden's Barrow is more securely identified as the tumulus also known as Adam's Grave, a Neolithic long barrow which lies on Walker's Hill just north of the village of Alton Priors in the Vale of Pewsey in Wiltshire.[58] The Alton Barnes White Horse on nearby Milk Hill is a nineteenth-century addition to the landscape, but the Wiltshire branch of the Great Ridgeway follows a line across Walker's Hill and then down through Alton Priors heading south.[59] Evidently, the two opposing forces had used this Ridgeway track to march towards the battle, with one side perhaps forming a defensive line on Walker's Hill, thereby forcing an engagement. The landscape here remains essentially unchanged since the sixth century. Adam's Grave gives us sweeping views of the line of the Marlborough Downs and across the Vale of Pewsey. As indicated by its name, the site itself had some mystical significance to the pagan Anglo-Saxons. This location would be the setting for another battle in 715, when the West Saxon king Ine fought the Mercian king Ceolred.

Woden's Barrow was Ceol's victory, but Ceawlin managed to escape and his son Cuthwine might have done too. Ceawlin's removal marked a shift in the royal genealogy towards the bloodline of his brother Cutha, who had predeceased him, although Cuthwine's grandchildren would re-merge in the regnal lists in the shape of Caedwalla (Ceawlin's great-great-grandson) ninety-five years later. However, Ceawlin still remained a potential threat so he was hunted down and killed the following year, along with his chief supporters Cwichelm and Crida.[60] Cuthwine, meanwhile, seems to have avoided capture and could have led opposition to Ceol and to Ceol's successor, Ceolwulf, for several years. Debate surrounds his re-emergence during Ceolwulf's reign, as we will see.

Before we proceed, Ceawlin requires some further discussion. The second of seven Anglo-Saxon leaders to be given the title of Bretwalda by Bede,[61] he is described as one of the key figures in the final Anglo-Saxon conquest of southern Britain.[62] At the height of his power, he and his vassal warlords ruled a territory of about 2,500 to 3,000 square miles. His reputation seems to have remained strong for many generations. Other primary texts that extolled him, since lost, existed during the twelfth century, as William of Malmesbury remarked that 'Ceawlin's famous might in battle is lauded by the annals in excess, an object of wonder to the English and of hatred to the Britons', with a pointed observation that 'he was the ruin of them both'.[63]

John of Worcester is clear that Ceol was Ceawlin's nephew, noting that he was the son of Cutha, Ceawlin's brother.[64] We have no evidence, in this case, other than the sources that support Ceol's heritage, but it has also been proposed that Ceol was purely a usurper who took his chance and bore no relation to Ceawlin.[65] In most cases the maternal bloodline is ignored, which does not help us trace branches of the genealogical tree. Beyond Ceol, for the next hundred years the regnal line would remain with the bloodline of Cutha and not Ceawlin, at least as recorded by the primary sources.[66]

The upheavals of 592–593 began a period of military decline, perhaps until the succession of Cynegils in 611. Wessex's influence on its neighbours may have declined, even though it faced no immediate threat to its borders. The localised British may have been subjugated, but the conglomeration of Anglo-Saxon tribes uniting under the all-encompassing and ever-expanding kingdom of Mercia, to the north of Oxford and the River Thames, would pose a major threat in the decades to come. In addition, the power of Ceawlin's erstwhile foe Æthelberht of Kent had grown after his marriage to a Frankish princess drew support from the continent.

Nothing is known of Ceol's reign. Apart from the ASC recording his brief duration as king, there are no further entries bearing his name. Even his death goes unmentioned. There is no primary text detailing any conflict with neighbouring tribes during his tenure, although the suspicion is that further headway was made in absorbing the remaining leadership of the Atrebates of Silchester. It is believed Silchester was in use until about the turn of the seventh century, when for reasons unknown it was abandoned by the Atrebates. Whether this signified the final symbolic relinquishing of Atrebate influence within the area controlled by Wessex is unclear.

As with all his predecessors, there is no surviving evidence that Ceol produced any charter proclamations. In later periods charters would prove invaluable sources of detail and information for historians. They were the formal royal written edicts issued by kings, conferring land rights or other benefits on the nobility, or in due course on the Church and its officials. The earliest identified extant West Saxon charter does not appear until the reign of Cenwealh around 670.[67]

Based on the dates of his successor, his brother Ceolwulf, we must assume Ceol died relatively young in 597. We could speculate that his end was dramatic. Perhaps he was assassinated by Cuthwine or one of Ceawlin's former supporters; perhaps, in a move closer to home, he was ousted by his own brother. We simply do not know. He might have briefly shared authority with Ceolwulf beforehand. His son, Cynegils, was perhaps still too young to succeed him in 597, although he would replace his uncle fourteen years later.[68]

6
Ceolwulf, Cynegils and Cwichelm
597–642

The ASC informs us that Ceolwulf became the king of Wessex in 597, possibly in June, with the scribe noting that 'he continually fought and strove either against the Angle race, or against the Welsh, or against the Picts, or against the Scots'.[1] Ceolwulf succeeded his brother Ceol at a time when the borders of Wessex were under threat from several directions. Determining the exact situation north of the River Thames during this period is difficult. The 'Welsh' most likely relates to the British Catuvellauni or the Dobunni in the south Midlands, although the late sixth century was also a period when the Anglo-Saxon Hwicce were establishing themselves in the region around Gloucestershire and Worcestershire.

The Hwicce's roots were perhaps a blend of Saxon and Angle, and in time they would be merged into the expanding Anglian kingdom of Mercia. Mercia itself was a seventh-century construct, a union of several Anglian tribes such as the South and Middle Mercians, the South and Middle Angles, the Magonsaete, the Hwicce and the Wreocansaete. The chronicle's reference to the 'Angle race' is therefore not easy to interpret, as it may refer to the Hwicce or Mercia more directly. In Mercia, its king Pybba (r. 593–616) was beginning to extend his authority, potentially challenging the remnants of the British Dobunni or possibly the Hwicce, and therefore the northern border of Wessex.

The year of Ceolwulf's succession also saw a much more significant event that would ultimately change the Anglo-Saxon way of life beyond recognition. During 597, the Roman monk Augustine arrived on the shores of Kent with a remit from Pope Gregory I to preach Roman Christianity across England. Æthelberht of Kent readily accepted conversion – his Frankish wife Bertha was already a Christian – and in 601 Augustine was given his pallium by the pope for a bishopric to be based at Canterbury. At the same time, Bishop Paulinus was sent north to convert and baptise the Northumbrian king Edwin.[2] However, there was no immediate widespread adoption of this new ideology across the other Anglo-Saxon kingdoms. Essex would follow Kent in due course, and then East Anglia, but most of the populace in those areas proved slow to convert. A large percentage of the Anglo-Saxons remained practising pagans, even some in Kent as late as the 640s given that Bede writes of a law being brought in by the Kentish king Eorcenberht (640–664) ordering that '(pagan) idols be abandoned and destroyed throughout the whole kingdom'.[3] The last Anglo-Saxon kingdoms to accept conversion later in the seventh century were Mercia and, surprisingly given its proximity to the new hub of Christianity, Sussex. Wessex's initial conversions took place years after Augustine's arrival, and Cynegils, the first West Saxon king to convert, was not baptised until 635 at Dorchester-on-Thames.

Lack of primary source detail during Ceolwulf's reign suggests that the period of instability beginning in his predecessor Ceol's reign continued. His authority was not only threatened from beyond his borders, but potentially from within. Cuthwine, the son of Ceawlin, remained in exile as a threat to the dynasty that had violently deposed his father.[4] However, if Ceolwulf attempted to eradicate Cuthwine and his bloodline, he was unsuccessful. Cuthwine's three sons, Cynebald, Cedda and Cuthwulf, would go on to pose a threat to Ceolwulf's successors. The ASC makes no further mention of Cuthwine himself other than in later genealogy listings, such as the entry for 688.[5]

Historians speculate that around 605 Ceolwulf may have made a power-sharing deal with Cuthwine's third son, Cuthwulf, to secure Wessex's northern borders along the Upper Thames Valley against the expanding threat from Mercia. The extent of Cuthwulf's role is unclear, and there is no evidence he acted as a sub-king, but it appears Ceolwulf was able to turn his attention elsewhere. John of Worcester claims Ceolwulf looked instead towards Sussex, noting that he 'waged war against the South Saxons'.[6] He could have been defending Hampshire against the South Saxons, or he could have been attempting to expand into Sussex himself.

As per Ceol before him, the ASC fails to mention Ceolwulf's death, but the later text the *Annals of St Neots* acknowledges a reign of fourteen years (597–611).[7] The ASC records the succession in 611 of Cynegils, whom the WSGRL confirms was the son of Ceol and therefore Ceolwulf's nephew.[8] However, if there was any connection between the dynasties represented by Cuthwine and Ceolwulf – a claim made by later chroniclers to maintain an unbroken link to the Cerdicings after Caedwalla became king in 685 – then it could only have been through the female line.[9] Cynegils' name is interesting, because while it can be argued that Ceol and Ceolwulf's names are more Germanic than Celtic British, Cynegils' name returns us to the British-Welsh etymology seen previously with Cerdic and Cynric. 'Cyne' is Celtic for 'royal', but Cynegils' full name has been best translated to mean literally 'grey dog'.[10]

It is at Cynegils' succession that the two main primary sources, the WSGRL and the ASC version A, finally and principally align on their regnal dates.[11] Hereafter, with small exceptions within version E, we can rely more readily on the published chronology. While version A aligns with the WSGRL in recording a continuous reign of thirty-one years for Cynegils, version E refers in its entry of 626 to a certain Cwichelm being 'king of the West Saxons'.[12] This may just be a case of semantics. From other primary source details, it is clear that during this period Cynegils and Cwichelm cooperated militarily against their joint enemies and later closely followed each other into converting to Christianity.

The WSGRL does not acknowledge any royal status for Cwichelm, whereas Henry of Huntingdon claims he shared the throne as joint king from as early as 614.[13] Evidence is lacking, but it is probable that Cwichelm was Cynegils' son. Huntingdon's dating may be a little premature, but assessing all available textual evidence gives the impression that Cynegils and Cwichelm, irrespective of any blood relationship, shared power for a period before Cwichelm's death in 636.[14] This may have been as joint kings or as king and sub-king, with each holding a specific region, perhaps centred on the old divisions with bases in Hampshire and the Upper Thames Valley, or with Cwichelm acting as a forerunner in the role of ealdorman.[15]

The mutual division of power may denote a kinship connection, possibly father and son. A later ASC entry during Cenwealh's time as king in 648, further supported by John of Worcester, is clear that Cenwealh's relation Cuthred was Cwichelm's son, and Cwichelm was in turn 'Cynegils' offspring'.[16] However, the reliability of this entry is cast into question when validating the exact blood connection. Opinion among historians remains divided, because the ASC scribe used the Latin term for relation/kinsman (*propinquus*) when describing Cenwealh and Cuthred's relationship rather than the term for grandson (*nepos*).[17]

Cynegils and Cwichelm first acted together in a battle of 614, when the ASC notes they 'fought on Bea's Mount, and killed two thousand and sixty-five Welsh'.[18] For 'Welsh' (the name given by later Anglo-Saxon chroniclers to describe 'strangers'), we can read 'British'. 'Bea's Mount' is more commonly now referred to as 'Beandun', but the stated number of deaths seems bizarrely precise and therefore suspect. The campaign against the British that led to the battle of Beandun was probably the most significant West Saxon military operation since Ceawlin's victory at Dyrham in 577. Historians have offered several potential locations for this important encounter, with three contenders in Dorset and two in Somerset.

Let us deal first with the Somerset locations. An argument has been made for Beandun being Brean Down or Bleadon Hill, both sites implying the West Saxons had already breached the western Wansdyke defences near Bath. Jutting out into the Bristol Channel, Brean Down is a promontory a couple of miles south-west of modern Weston-super-Mare that may have held a British fortification. Bleadon Hill, meanwhile, lies 4 miles inland, just south of Weston. Either site could have been the consequence of a plan which one historian has seen as a prelude to seizing the hillfort at Cadbury Hill near Congresbury.[19] Brean Down's coastal position also implies many ships were required, which is probably beyond the capabilities of early seventh-century West Saxons, and therefore Bleadon Hill seems the more plausible. Equally, the battle being a prelude to seizing Cadbury Hill is difficult to support as surely Cynegils would have attacked that position directly from the east, not from the west.

Of the three locations in Dorset, two lie close to the Hampshire border – perhaps too close. The first is Badbury Rings, already mentioned as a contender for the location of Mount Badon. Nevertheless, the argument for Beandun being at Badbury is weak, as it suggests the West Saxons had barely advanced more than 12 miles west of the Hampshire Avon in four generations. The second Dorset option, by place-name association, is Bindon Hill close to the village of Wool, lying on the River Frome 4 miles west of Wareham.[20] Again, the proximity to Wareham suggests it lies too far east to be a viable option in 614; knowledge of later West Saxon advances into the West Country tells us that the Durotriges of east Dorset had already been subsumed under West Saxon authority by this period. A consistent argument is that the early seventh-century border with the British lay further west, with the remaining Durotriges and their allies the Dumnonii perhaps holding a line nearer to the Dorset–Devon border.

With that rationale, the most favoured location for the battle of Beandun among historians is a third site, also called Bindon, lying close to the River Axe near the likely border between the West Saxons and the British at that time. Extensive landscape research by local historians has provided us with a strong case for the battle being adjacent to this site, just to the east of Axmouth and the River Axe.[21] The consensus is that Cynegils and Cwichelm were planning on expanding control into East

Devon, but the Dumnonii and the surviving leadership of the Durotriges were in turn keen to confront the West Saxons as part of a British stratagem to remove or at least delay the threat to Devon.

Research by local historians suggests that Cynegils and Cwichelm had assembled their army close to Bindon, on either side of what are now the minor roads of Coombe Terrace and Higher Lane, in the valley to the east of the River Axe and present-day Axmouth. In the seventh century, this was the direct road east towards Dorchester. Just to the north was the imposing Hawkesdown Hill. Presumably, the West Saxons had intended to cross the River Axe but before doing so had received critical information that the British planned to advance and cross the river. It would seem Cynegils chose the ground tactically. Then as now, the combe formed a natural route moving eastward to the higher ground beyond, effectively funnelling the unsuspecting British troops up the valley. The British were ambushed, their substantial force increasingly confined and prevented from forming a defensive line. Hemmed in by the valley slopes, the British vanguard was forced back onto the rearguard.

In terms of numbers involved at Beandun, the ASC scribe's claim of 2,065 British losses implies not just a significantly large army but also that it was routed as men tried to flee back across the tidal river.[22] The chroniclers John of Worcester and Henry of Huntingdon are similarly precise as to the British casualties, with Worcester recording 2,046 deaths and Henry 2,062.[23] The source for these numbers is unclear, but all three are bizarrely but separately precise. In reality, both armies were certainly smaller than inferred. One estimate for the total fighting strength available to Cynegils across early seventh-century Wessex is in the region of 8,000 men.[24] To gather a third of this count for one battle would have been exceptional. Perhaps we can estimate the Saxon numbers would not have exceeded 2,000 men. The British army may have been slightly larger, but not large enough to meet the casualty figures given in the above sources.

Questions about the British leadership arise, even if Cynegils and/or Cwichelm were skilled in military strategy. To be unaware that a large Saxon army was in the vicinity seems negligent, allowing the British to be ambushed, but having crossed the Axe while still being unaware seems doubly inept, forcing them to fight with their backs to the river once they had been pushed back down the valley.

Though Beandun was a significant victory, it was not decisive for territorial expansion. What it did possibly achieve was a consolidation east of the River Axe. After Beandun the West Saxon advance westward took a long pause. There was no more recorded military activity along that border for the next forty years, and it would be several decades before the West Saxons attempted to gain permanent new territory within eastern Devon. We can imagine Saxon settlers were imported into the newly won territory alongside the original British population under new regional Saxon leadership, but another logical reason for the long-term suspension of ongoing military activity is that there was simply no urgency to gain additional territory when the requirements of new settlers had already been met. When warfare against the Dumnonii resumed it would bear the hallmarks of the West Saxon leadership wishing to expand their territorial power and wealth rather than occurring as a response to market forces and demands.

In contrast to what used to be a long-held viewpoint, the Anglo-Saxon advances – and in this aspect the West Saxon advance across Dorset and south Somerset – did not involve a wholesale relocation of the settled British population. There is nothing to support the argument that within the British regions under West Saxon authority there was a movement to replace or remove the native populace. From the archaeological evidence, most British did not choose to exile themselves further west but instead remained living and working on their home soil, accepting vassalage under new Anglo-Saxon leaders.

It appears the native populations and the newcomers assimilated well, with the victors absorbing much of the local social structures already in place and the native British adopting Germanic cultures. British readiness to adopt new cultures has already been considered. Germanic-derived culture was already widespread across all the Anglo-Saxon territories by around 570, so by the early seventh century it was already deeply established.[25] As the seventh century progresses, the chronicles speak not of the kings of Wessex fighting British tribes north of the Thames or in the Chilterns, but of their struggles against the rival Anglo-Saxon kingdoms that had replaced the British leadership.

While focus shifted away from Wessex, political developments in the south-east and East Anglia and then Northumbria were to impact West Saxon policy. The first event was the death of the successful and powerful Kentish king Æthelberht on 24 February 616, the first Anglo-Saxon king to have converted to Roman Catholicism. His successor, his son Eadbald, had first refused to convert but was later baptised by Archbishop Laurentius, Augustine's successor at Canterbury, before 619. This transition came parallel with new developments in both East Anglia and Northumbria. The East Angles under Raedwald, who had himself converted to Christianity and whom Bede names as his third Bretwalda, had already superseded Kent as the dominant kingdom,[26] and

Raedwald had already helped establish Edwin (aka Eadwine) as king in Northumbria in 616 in favour of the previous incumbent Æthelfrith, whom he had defeated in battle that year.[27] However, Raedwald, whom most historians now agree was the occupant of the famous ship burial mound discovered at Sutton Hoo in Suffolk in 1939, was to die in 625. An alliance between Northumbria and Kent followed when Edwin married Eadbald's sister Æthelburg in 625 on the proviso that Edwin accepted baptism.[28]

Although this development seemed insignificant to Wessex, it was not. We learn from Bede's notes, taken from his contacts in the south-east, that in 623 the East Saxons 'went out to fight the Gewisse and they and all their army perished', possibly somewhere in present-day Surrey.[29] We might speculate that the East Saxons had come under pressure from their stronger neighbours in Kent and East Anglia, particularly after the death of their King Saeberht in 617, and East Saxon plans to expand beyond London clashed with West Saxon plans to expand eastward along the Thames Valley. Three of Saeberht's sons – his successors Sexred and Saeward, and an unnamed third brother – were all killed in the battle.[30] For Wessex, this victory, possibly led by Cwichelm, secured the eastern border. Certainly, the South Saxons had already ceased to be a threat; their kingdom had been under Kentish control since Ceolwulf fought them in 607, and in the immediate future it would be enveloped by the growing authority of first Northumbria and then Mercia later in the seventh century.

By 626 Edwin of Northumbria had assumed a dominant position beyond the Humber, although it would prove brief. However, there is no hint of a Northumbrian military expedition southwards at this time, and Penda of Mercia would soon challenge Edwin's dominance. After his marriage alliance with Kent, Edwin had offered his protection to other lesser leaders in the south, including the Jutes on the Isle of Wight and possibly also the South Saxons. Despite lacking direct involvement, the West Saxon leaders had to respond to this new development. Their response, spearheaded by Cwichelm, was both curious and abstruse, although understandable on another level. We can assume that the Northumbrian king's involvement in southern affairs impacted West Saxon plans, none more so than the new Northumbrian interest in the Isle of Wight.

At Easter 626, Cwichelm took measures. Cynegils is not named as being involved, which probably allows us to conclude that matters relating to the Isle of Wight and Sussex were within Cwichelm's remit. As recorded by Bede and other primary sources, some of them in great detail, the West Saxon joint king despatched a man named Eomer to the

Northumbrian court with specific instructions to gain access to the king's court and to assassinate Edwin.[31] John of Worcester and Bede provide the most detail of what took place, with Worcester writing that 'Eomer ... came to King Edwin on Easter Sunday and unsheathing his dagger ... attacked him. Lilla, the king's most trusted thegn, at once threw himself before the attacker's blow, but the enemy thrust his weapon with such force that he wounded the king as well through the body of the slain warrior.'[32] The ASC adds that a second thegn named Forthhere was also killed or wounded in the attack, but ultimately Eomer failed in his task. Edwin, though wounded, survived.[33]

Cwichelm presumably expected Edwin's assassination to throw Northumbria into political turmoil and cause it to drop its interest in the regions around Wessex. Northumbria seems to have posed a bigger threat to Wessex than the primary sources show, as evidenced by the extreme nature of Cwichelm's plot to assassinate Edwin. It was a puzzling gamble that failed. The lack of any reference to Cynegils in the plot implies it had been planned without his involvement. Wessex was about to pay a heavy price for Cwichelm's rashness.

Bede tells us that as soon as he had recovered from his wounds Edwin 'marched against the West Saxons' and 'slew all whom he discovered to have plotted his death or forced them to surrender'.[34] Possibly his brother-in-law, Eadbald of Kent, sent men to aid the campaign against Wessex. Version E of the ASC adds that Edwin felled 'five kings' and 'killed a great number of people'.[35] To make some sense of these texts, we should perhaps understand that this acknowledges that Northumbria during the first half of the seventh century was more influential beyond its borders than previously considered. Furthermore, Edwin must have sent a substantial army southward during 626–627, with or without additional support from Kent and Sussex. The ASC reference to 'kings' presumably relates to regional ealdormen, as both Cynegils and Cwichelm lived to fight another day. However, to lose five of these senior nobles acknowledges the West Saxons were hit hard.

Compensation and tribute would have been demanded from Wessex. Some clue as to what this involved may be gleaned from the seventh-century document the Tribal Hidage, drawn up to assess and record the territory each Anglo-Saxon tribe held south of the River Humber. The Hidage would be revised in later centuries, and there is an argument that the original version was compiled during the height of the Mercian king Wulfhere's reign later in the seventh century. However, that the original version excluded Northumbrian territory (land north of the Humber) gives us a clue that it probably first originated during the peak of Northumbrian power, pointing to Edwin's period of dominance south of the Humber during the 620s.[36] The Hidage land assessment, used for tax and tribute purposes on productive land, was based on the number of hides. One hide equated to between 60 and 120 acres, depending on its level of productivity. The clue within the Hidage, based on one historian's recent reassessment, is that Wessex may have had to transfer an enormous tribute of 100,000 hides of land to Northumbrian authority during this period.[37] This land was probably in Berkshire, Buckinghamshire and the Chilterns, which Wessex had gained after the battles of Bedcanford in 571 and Fethanleag in 584.

It is unclear how these land transfers may have impacted Mercia and their new king Penda, who had emerged from an Angle power base in former Dobunni territory in the central west Midlands, with connections to the Magonsaete, or possibly the Hwicce. However, the damage Northumbria had inflicted on Wessex was not lost on Penda. Exploiting the situation along the Mercian–Wessex border, he pillaged through Hwicce territory towards Cirencester in 628. The ASC records that 'Cynegils and Cwichelm fought against Penda ... and then came to an agreement', while the chronicler Æthelweard writes that they fought 'near a town that is Cirencester'.[38] Henry of Huntingdon and John of Worcester tell us that the two sides fought until sunset, and then made peace and separated.[39] This downplays what may have been a West Saxon defeat, as it is unclear what is meant by 'agreement'. Possibly it concerned tribute payments or some land concessions near Cirencester whereby recognised Hwicce land moved from West Saxon to Mercian control. Their contemporary William of Malmesbury took the incompatible opposite view in his *Gesta Regum Anglorum*, noting that Penda 'had crossed his own frontiers in an attempt to win Cirencester ... but unable to bear the onslaught of these united princes (Cynegils and Cwichelm) he fled with few companions'.[40]

The region around Gloucester and Cirencester formed part of the southern area of the Hwicce, the Anglian tribe that would attach itself to Mercia. Excavated burials from south-eastern Gloucestershire show archaeological evidence of their presence there in the late sixth century, but by the 620s Mercia controlled the northern territory of the Hwicce and it is believed, despite Malmesbury's claims, that the battle of 628 was probably the point when the southern region of the Hwicce became part of the sphere associated with Mercia.[41]

The border between Mercian and West Saxon interests in this region would henceforth be along the Bristol Avon. Wessex was excluded from any influence next to the Severn Valley. The loss of such a large swathe of territory in three years to the Northumbrians and the Mercians perhaps marks the period when more of the Gewisse began a movement into east Somerset, an area that had already seen gains over the British. Some historians have seen this as a major displacement from the Thames region at this period, although this conclusion seems unwarranted. It is known that the kings of Wessex kept control around Oxford and Abingdon, albeit by paying tribute.[42]

Edwin of Northumbria had meanwhile subdued Mercia's allies in the north and had led a successful campaign into the Welsh kingdom of Gwynedd. The stage was being set for a clash between Edwin and Penda, with Cynegils and Cwichelm reduced to bystanders. Penda of Mercia was able to ally himself with Cadwallon ap Cadfan, king of Gwynedd, and launch a campaign northwards in 633 intending to end continued Northumbrian authority south of the Humber. The two armies would meet decisively that year at the battle of Hatfield Chase, within a marshy region east of the River Don about 8 miles north-east of present-day Doncaster. The ASC dates it to 12 October 633, Bede two days later.[43] Hatfield Chase was a famous victory for the pagan Penda over the baptised Edwin, with both Edwin and his son Osfrith killed in the fighting. Penda followed this with a disruptive campaign north of the Humber, leading to a collapse of Northumbrian power. Edwin's widow Æthelburg escaped back to her Kentish homeland as the various dynasties in Northumbria reacted to events.

Bede and his contemporary ecclesiastics and chroniclers saw this period not only as warfare between Anglo-Saxon kingdoms but from their standpoint as a struggle between Christianity and paganism. This is an opportune moment therefore to review how far Christianity had spread since the arrival of Augustine's delegation in Kent during the 590s. In general, the spread of Christianity among the Anglo-Saxons was slower than the Roman Church wished it to be. The next four archbishops at Canterbury after Augustine (Laurentius, Mellitus, Justus and Honorius) were former members of Augustine's original mission. Not until 655 did Deusdedit, an Anglo-Saxon by birth, succeed to the position. More widely, it would take nearly ninety years for all the Anglo-Saxon tribes to abandon paganism. Eadbald of Kent only accepted baptism at his accession on his father Æthelberht's death in 616. Rædwald of East Anglia continued to practise paganism and Christianity in parallel, keeping a pagan shrine alongside his Christian altar.[44] Edwin of Northumbria had received baptism in 627, and Penda of Mercia would continue to practice paganism throughout his life until his death on 15 November 655, at the battle of Winwaed, when fighting the already converted Oswiu of Northumbria.[45] According to both the ASC and Bede, it was only after Penda's death that Mercia became Christian.[46] Meanwhile, the West Saxon kings would not receive baptism until the 630s, the first South Saxon Christian king was Æthelwealh as late as the 670s, and the Meonwara and Isle of Wight Jutes would be the outliers, delaying conversion until the 680s or 690s.[47]

However, there is a wider picture that is often overlooked. Before the Germanic invasions, most of the native Celtic or Romano-British had already abandoned paganism in favour of Christianity – not all Roman religious doctrine, but Christian practices nevertheless. Defining the impact pagan conquerors had on the practices of British Christians is challenging. Anglo-Saxons may have been slow to adopt the new ideology, but British natives did not abandon their beliefs. In fact, the British themselves may have influenced Anglo-Saxon conversion rates within newly assimilated societies. In the northern and western districts Roman Catholicism came up against the pre-existing Celtic Christian community, particularly prevalent in Northumbria, which had already been visited by missionaries from Ireland and Scotland. Their differences were minor, based on the interpretation of doctrine and semantics, but these small variances would not be resolved until the mid-seventh century.[48]

Although Penda had beaten the Northumbrians at Hatfield Chase in 633 he was not able to take further advantage. Furthermore, Edwin's successor in Northumbria, Oswald, would soon play his part in the conversion of Cynegils and Cwichelm in the aftermath of the events of 627 between Wessex and Northumbria. It is likely the outcome at Hatfield Chase changed how Northumbria's new king approached his connection with Wessex, and it looks to have served both Northumbria and Wessex well at this stage to reconfigure their political alignment as a way of counteracting further Mercian aggression. It is even possible they arranged a new alliance to support each other militarily.

It was at this moment in 634, the year after Hatfield Chase, that Pope Honorius I commissioned a monk named Birinus to convert the West Saxons to Christianity.[49] Birinus would later be known as the 'Apostle to the West Saxons'.[50] He is said to have arrived at the port of Hamwic, now part of modern Southampton, lying on the west bank of the River Itchen. The area of St Mary's in Southampton and the church of that name was reputedly originally named and founded by him.[51] However, some historians dispute this claim, and if the first church at Hamwic was founded by Birinus it was probably at a later date. His first known uncontested foundation – what would become the first major church in Wessex – was at Dorchester-on-Thames, in the heartland of original Gewisse territory. That he chose there rather than Hamwic or elsewhere suggests that the Upper Thames Valley region still had greater significance for the West Saxon/Gewisse kings in the 630s than any other location in their kingdom. The church of St Mary's at Reading, only 20 miles downstream of Dorchester, was also later founded by Birinus.

Birinus's arrival into Wessex just as Oswald of Northumbria sought a renewal of friendship with Cynegils and Cwichelm has been considered coincidental. However, is this plausible? Perhaps instead we can see Oswald as a facilitator, encouraging the Christian Church to send a missionary to convert the West Saxon kings at a time when they were exposed militarily and open to committing to a new alliance with his kingdom, one that may have been conditional on them converting. As soon as Birinus's rudimentary church at Dorchester-on-Thames was completed in 635, Cynegils was baptised there by Birinus. It was a spiritual ceremony designed to show his ideological conversion from paganism, and his selection suggests that he either held more authority than Cwichelm or was more willing to convert.[52] In any case, Cynegils thus became the first West Saxon Christian king.

Oswald of Northumbria not only attended the service but acted as godfather in the ceremony, demonstrating that he was fulfilling a role as Cynegils' sponsor.[53] The term godfather, as used by Bede here, appears to have had particular relevance for the Anglo-Saxons.[54] As detailed later in the laws of Ine in the early eighth century, the godfather and godson relationship was tied to *wergild*, a Germanic system of compensation to victims of crime with values set upon individuals in accordance to their social rank. In acting here in the role of godfather, Oswald was staking his right to receive compensation should anything happen to Cynegils. Cynegils confirmed the significance of this gathering by marrying his daughter Cyneburh to Oswald on the same day. However, Oswald was not yet willing to hand back the territory that Wessex had surrendered to Oswald's predecessor several years earlier, although perhaps the marriage arrangement had come with other concessions for Cynegils and Wessex.

It is noticeable that Cwichelm, who was almost certainly Cynegils' son, was not baptised alongside his father. Perhaps he was less willing to deny his pagan roots, or possibly Oswald may have influenced matters. It could imply the Northumbrian king was reluctant to sponsor Cwichelm due to his involvement in the plot to assassinate his Northumbrian predecessor several years earlier. However, within twelve months Cwichelm too received baptism from Birinus at Dorchester-on-Thames.[55] Perhaps in the interim he had been persuaded to change his faith. However, as noted by the ASC scribe, Cwichelm 'passed away the same year', which more plausibly suggests he was only persuaded to convert, possibly by his father, when it became clear he was dying.

Unlike many of the West Saxon kings and leaders that have no known burial site, there is some speculation that Cwichelm was buried at Cuckamsley Knob (aka Cuckhamsley Hill or Scutchamer Knob), originally an Iron Age round barrow on the Wiltshire Downs, sitting alongside a section of the Ridgeway track 2 miles west of Chilton and the modern A34 road.[56] This remained an important site, and would become a meeting place of the shire moot. Several recent excavations of the mound have failed to reveal any confirmed evidence of a seventh-century burial chamber, however.

The decision by Birinus to locate his primary religious house in the Thames Valley and not at Winchester or Hamwic/Hamtun is perhaps an opportunity to consider whether there was still a clear delineation between the West Saxons and the Gewisse. Historians responsible for older secondary source texts have underplayed the relevance of the Gewisse in the story of Wessex. Some have overlooked them completely, sticking to the traditional story of Cerdic and the West Saxon regnal list. Later historians have seen this as ill-judged, and recent works on this period have largely redressed the balance. The initial geographical separation aside, it seems that during the seventh century their tribal and cultural connections became more evident. Joint military cooperation against common enemies may have sped up some form of formal political union. By the time of Cynegils and Cwichelm, with one operating from Hampshire and the other from the Thames Valley, the two regional groupings had perhaps metamorphosed into a single kingdom, albeit with joint kings for the moment. This would have been further accelerated if, as suspected, the Belgae and the Atrebates had already conceded peacefully the region that lay between southern Hampshire and the Upper Thames Valley.

It is plausible Ceol and Cynegils were themselves West Saxon (i.e. from Hampshire) rather than Gewisse (i.e. Thames Valley) judging by regional sphere of influence. This would date the final melding of the two tribal groups approximately sometime before the third decade of the seventh century, during the period of Cynegils and Cwichelm. Some historians alternately argue for a later date. They see the union between the two allied groups taking place during the 690s or 700s under the reign of Ine, pointing to his centre of operations as confirmation that the union of Wessex would have its hub in Hampshire, not the Thames Valley.[57]

Debate continues as to when most of the old British tribes surrendered to Anglo-Saxon rule. This is a topic that in general cannot be readily defined, and of course different regions transferred leadership sooner than others based primarily on their geographical locations. The Cantiaci of Kent, Regnenses of Sussex and Trinovantes of Essex, for example, had already been under full Anglo-Saxon overlordship almost two centuries before their British compatriots in the west, such as the Durotriges and Dumnonii, would eventually succumb. Anglicisation in England was a lengthy process, varying by region. What seems striking in the middle ground, the area later dominated by Mercia, is that the sources seem to cease referring to the Catuvellauni and Dobunni almost overnight when chronicling Anglo-Saxon advances. Clearly, this does not represent the actual situation. However, in terms of Wessex, we are more fortunate. Although there are periods when timelines are difficult to configure, it is much easier to speculate upon the shifting 'front line' between the British and the West Saxons. Awareness of the precise point of geographical division between them in the south and south-west is easier to define than it is for any developments further north.

The debate on the timeframe and transference from British to Anglo-Saxon control across England will no doubt continue. In terms of Wessex and its two regional groups, the Gewisse and the West Saxons, they seem to have absorbed or been absorbed by the original British regional tribes, the Atrebates and the Belgae, no later than Cynegils' reign. Use of the names Atrebates and Belgae when describing regional divisions within the Upper Thames Valley and Hampshire therefore becomes a redundant concept by the mid-seventh century, when they are better labelled with Anglo-Saxon definitions. Likewise, it is by the mid-seventh century that we can view the creation of the kingdom of Wessex in more definitive terms. It identifies the territory and people who shaped it, not just the abstract kingdom represented by Cynric or Ceawlin.

Cynegils would rule on the throne of Wessex for another seven years. He was probably assisted by Cuthred, who was either Cwichelm's son or nephew. Versions B, C and F of the ASC describe Cuthred during this period as 'king' and he may have shared the throne following Cwichelm's demise.[58] In 639, Cuthred was also baptised at Dorchester-on-Thames by Birinus as his godson, and in later years he would act alongside Cynegils' successor Cenwealh.

In 641, the power balance shifted in Mercia's favour when Penda and his Welsh allies from Gwynedd heavily defeated Oswald on 5 August at the battle of Maserfield.[59] Oswald was killed during the defeat, alongside, according to the *Annales Cambriae*, Penda's brother Eowa.[60] We would naturally assume Eowa fought alongside his brother, but a few historians have opened up a debate that Eowa, based in northern Mercia, had already taken vassalage to Oswald and was fighting alongside the Northumbrians against Penda's Mercians.[61] The precise location of Maserfield is unknown, but historians favour it having been near present-day Oswestry on either side of the modern English–Welsh border.[62] The place-name etymology translates as 'Oswald's Tree', and from the Welsh Croesoswald, meaning 'Oswald's Cross'.[63] As things stood, Oswestry was then inside the Welsh kingdom of Powys. This suggests that the Northumbrians had crossed northern Mercia and were preparing to raid Wales.

Cynegils' life ended before he could worry about Penda and the rise of Mercia. All versions of the ASC fail to record his death, but his successor Cenwealh is invariably recorded as succeeding to the kingdom in 643.[64] The implication is that Cynegils was of advanced age upon his death. His remains were reputedly buried in Winchester, again acknowledging that the West Saxons already controlled the former *civitas*, but it would not be until the 660s that his successor founded the Old Minster church there and Cynegils' remains were reinterred in the new church. Along with other, later Anglo-Saxon kings and senior bishops who were buried in the Old Minster, Cynegils' remains were moved again in the late eleventh century into the present Norman cathedral. His remains, along with others, would be moved once more. In the twelfth century the bishop of Winchester, Henry of Blois, gathered up the ancient burials and moved them into specially commissioned lead boxes. The problem was the bishop was unsure who he was moving, so the bones may already have been in disarray. Perhaps the remains of two- or three-dozen individuals, including Cynegils, were muddled and condensed together in ten cartulary chests, and of these Cynegils and his successor Cenwealh are recorded as the oldest among them.

During the seventeenth-century English Civil War, the cartularies were vandalised by Parliamentarian troops and the bones scattered. The collected remains were placed haphazardly into six surviving cartularies. These chests remained on display in the Norman cathedral, but in 2012 a team of scientists and osteologists were granted permission to open the chests and examine the contents. After several years of work, involving forensic radiocarbon dating and the study of ancient DNA, the chests were announced in 2019 to have contained over 1,300 fragments from a minimum of twenty-three individuals. In total, there were fifteen more individuals than those named on the chests, including two adolescent boys.[65] Cynegils is presumed to be among them, but the bones of any specific individual were impossible to define apart from one. Among them, the team identified the remains of a single female. Since she is the lone woman listed on the chests, it's clear that these are the remains of Queen Emma. She was the queen of two English kings, Æthelred II and Cnut, in the early eleventh century.

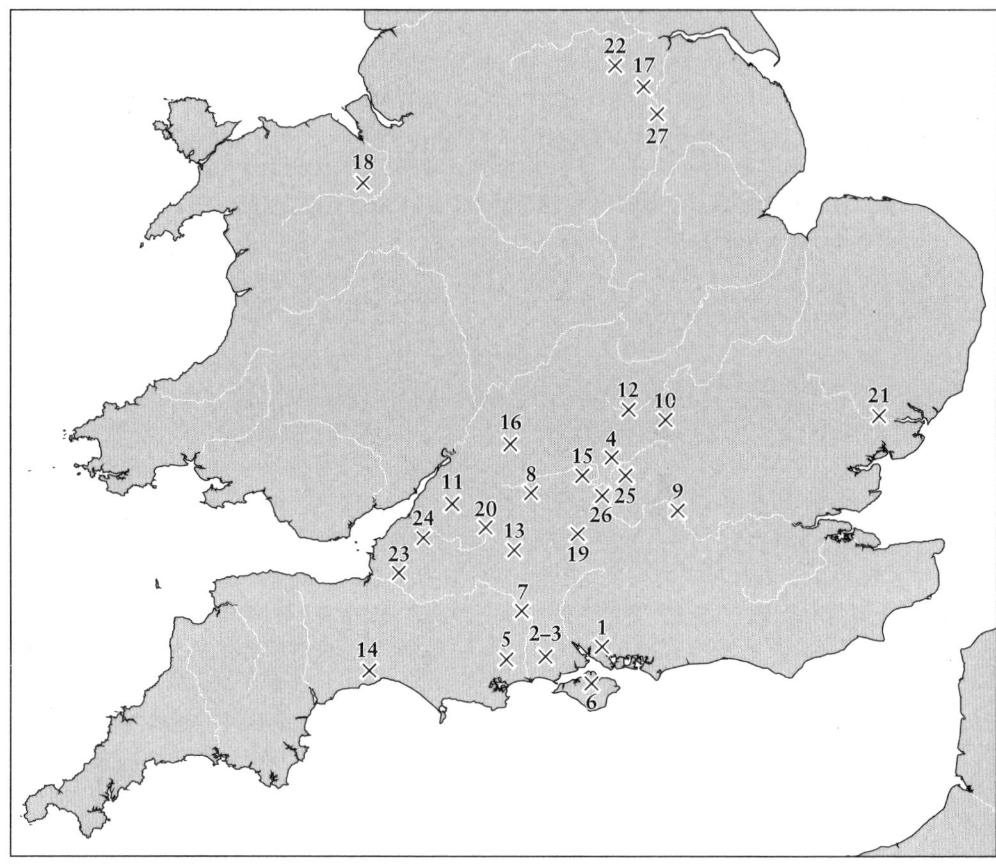

Fig. 3. Map of important battles, c. 500–679.

1 Natanleaga, 495 (West Saxons v. British)
2 Cerdic's Ford 1, 508 (WS v. British)
3 Cerdic's Ford 2, 519 (WS v. British)
4 Cerdiceslea, 527 (WS v. British)
5 Mount Badon, 520s (Saxons v. British)
6 Wihtwarabyrg, 530 (WS v. Jutes)
7 Old Sarum, 552 (WS v. British)
8 Bera's Stronghold, 556 (WS v. British)
9 Wibbandun, 568 (WS v. Saxon Kent)
10 Bedcanford, 571 (WS v. British)
11 Dyrham, 577 (WS v. British)
12 Fethalnleag, 584 (WS v. British)
13 Woden's Barrow, 592 (WS v. WS)
14 Beandun, 614 (WS v. British)
15 Berkshire?, 627 (WS v. Northumbrians)
16 Cirencester, 628 (WS v. Mercians)
17 Hatfield Chase, 633 (Mercians v. Northumbrians)
18 Maserfield, 641 (Mercians v. Northumbrians)
19 Hampshire?, 645 (WS v. Mercians)
20 Bradford-on-Avon, 653 (WS v. British)
21 Bulcamp Forest, 653 (Mercians v. East Anglians)
22 Winwaed, 655 (Mercians v. Northumbrians)
23 Peonnum, 658 (WS v. British)
24 Posentesbyrig, 661 (WS v. British)
25 Ashdown, 661 (WS v. Mercians)
26 Bedanheaford, 675 (WS v. Mercians)
27 Gainsborough, 679 (Mercians v. Northumbrians)

7
Cenwealh and Seaxburh
642–674

According to versions A and E of the ASC, Cynegils was succeeded by his second son, Cenwealh, in 643.[1] Versions B and C record his succession as being two years earlier, while the WSGRL splits the difference and places it in 642. While there was as yet no rule of royal primogeniture within Wessex, and this remained the case throughout the Anglo-Saxon period until the Norman Conquest, it would seem that Cenwealh was the natural choice to succeed his father. There was, however, another blood candidate in the person of Cuthred. Working on the basis considered in the previous chapter, Cuthred was Cwichelm's son, thereby making him Cenwealh's nephew. Despite this, he didn't make a claim for the throne, possibly due to his youth.

Cenwealh's name, supporting his roots through the Gewisse, is of British Celtic etymology, '*cene*' meaning 'bold' or 'keen'.[2] His British or part-British heritage is acknowledged when we see that '*wahl*' or '*walh*' was the Anglo-Saxon word for Celt or Welsh.[3] The implication is there was still significant British DNA within the royal house, and so dominant are British names during the formation of Wessex that his nephew's name Cuthred, being of Anglo-Saxon origin, stands out as one of the few exceptions during this period. In terms of Cenwealh's given name, the implication is that his mother was at the very least part Anglo-Saxon, or more likely a full-blooded Anglo-Saxon.

Cenwealh was not as convinced as his father had been about Christianity. Although his brother and nephew converted, he was still a pagan when he became king. This was highlighted by Bede, who noted in his *Ecclesiastical History* that Cenwealh 'refused to receive the faith' when replacing his father.[4] That he remained a pagan upon taking the throne tells us that converting to Christianity was not yet seen as a critical ideological or philosophical necessity for the West Saxon witan (literally 'wise men', a sort of king's council) when choosing their new king. Seemingly in contrast to Cenwealh's paganism, the ASC version A records that in his first year as king (643) he 'ordered the church at Winchester to be built'. Still, there is disagreement regarding the dating. Version E dates the commencement of building work to 641, and versions B and C have it beginning in 642, all three of which precede Cenwealh's recognised succession.[5]

However, on the basis Cenwealh is recorded as being baptised during 646 by versions A and E of the ASC, we should probably accept version F's account that the church at Winchester was commissioned in 648, and not earlier.[6] Logic suggests Cenwealh was likely to commission the building after he had been baptised, and not before. Even 648 may be too early a date for reasons we will soon outline. The church would be commonly known as the Old Minster, but it bore the official name St Peter and St Paul. These references to Winchester are the first times the settlement is named within the ASC. Known as Wintanceaster in Old English, it had been a Roman *civitas* and, as noted beforehand, an important site for the Belgae, when it was known as Venta Belgarum.

On first taking the throne of Wessex, Cenwealh faced a renewed threat from Penda of Mercia. This was perhaps no surprise after Penda's victory over Oswald at Maserfield. The Northumbrian leadership had been seriously weakened, and the internal divisions that followed Oswald's death would lead to a temporary split in the kingdom, which would divide and revert to its two former allied Anglian regions: Bernicia, the region north of the River Tees centred at Bamburgh; and Deira, the region between the Tees and the River Humber centred at York. Cenwealh therefore inherited the throne just as the West Saxon detente with Northumbria became irrelevant in deterring Mercian aggression towards Wessex.

Perhaps slow to acquire full power across all the kingdom, Cenwealh was unable to defend the borders of Wessex against Penda. To stall a potential invasion, he offered vassalage to the Mercian king, and presumably tribute payments. However, the key to any arrangement was for the still pagan Cenwealh to agree to the Mercian king's request that he marry one of his daughters. Penda had two known daughters, Cyneburh and Cyneswitha. Cyneburh in due course marred Ealhfrith, the king of Deira, so although the sources do not name her the implication is that Cenwealh's betrothal was to Cyneswitha, and took place around 643–4. Although Penda remained pagan, he had allowed his daughters to convert and practise Christianity. Both sisters would eventually become nuns.

The marriage to Cyneswitha placed Cenwealh and his kingdom for a brief period into what one historian has called the 'Mercian orbit'.[7] However, for reasons unknown, the marriage failed. Perhaps their spiritual beliefs were incompatible; after all, Cenwealh remained a pagan until 646. John of Worcester avoids mention of the marriage itself but refers to its fallout when he describes Cenwealh repudiating his Mercian wife in 645.[8] Bede writes that this was done so Cenwealh could marry another, presumably his second wife, Seaxburh.[9] In hindsight, it looks peculiar for Cenwealh to agree to a union to help avoid a war with Mercia only to then reject his Mercian wife soon afterwards to marry another. This was an obvious slur towards Penda and was taken as one, and we assume Cenwealh knew fully that his decision to repudiate Cyneswitha could lead to war.

So, not unexpectedly, John of Worcester informs us that in 645 'Penda attacked him (Cenwealh) and deprived him of his kingdom'.[10] The ASC adds Cenwealh was 'driven out by King Penda', and Henry of Huntingdon refers to Cenwealh being defeated in battle at an unknown location before seeking self-exile at the court of King Anna of East Anglia, a nephew of Raedwald and an enemy of Penda.[11] The West Saxon king would convert to Christianity in 646 while in exile, with John of Worcester recording that it was the already Christianised and devout Anna who persuaded Cenwealh to convert. Cenwealh was baptised while in exile by Bishop Felix, the man who had previously converted the East Anglian leadership.[12]

Cenwealh's return to Wessex came no earlier than 648, but certainly before Penda's death in 655. Suggestions that he may not have been able to return to his kingdom until Penda's death seem an exaggeration,[13] with available evidence pointing to the contrary. Immediately on his return, enthused by Anna and his recent conversion to Christianity, Cenwealh put in motion plans to begin the building of the church of St Peter and St Paul at Winchester, later known as the Old Minster. Winchester was also by now the site of the main royal palace of Wessex. The extent of Penda's influence in Wessex during Cenwealh's absence is unclear. His main concern seems to have been pillaging the area, with no mention of him sacking Winchester or Hamtun or seizing territory permanently.

Who governed the West Saxons during Cenwealh's absence is debatable. Maybe an unnamed noble acted on behalf of Penda across Wessex. There is one individual whose naming is consistent on either side of the period of Cenwealh's exile, and that is his nephew Cuthred. If he did not take exile alongside his uncle, it is plausible he led resistance against the Mercians between 645 and 648. Cenwealh is recorded awarding 3,000 hides of land by 'Ashdown' to Cuthred in 648, no small gift, an area identified in western Berkshire from east of present-day Swindon across to Wantage. Henry of Huntingdon's *Historia Anglorum* adds that the 648 gift to Cuthred was 'in return for his aid'.[14] This might imply Cuthred was a designated sub-king who had acted for Wessex during Cenwealh's absence, or if we take it further his 'aid' may have involved ongoing resistance to Penda. Cenwealh's absence may also have allowed a certain Cenberht to rise to prominence. This Cenberht is recognised as the father of the later king Caedwalla (r. 685–688), and he may have acted as another sub-king under Cenwealh after the latter's return.[15]

Penda's attention would be diverted away from Wessex towards first East Anglia and then Bernician Northumbria. In 651 a Mercian campaign into East Anglia forced its king, Anna, into temporary exile, and upon his return another Mercian campaign was launched against him in 653. Penda was accompanied by his son Peada, whom Bede describes as 'king of the Middle Angles', which acknowledges the still evident tribal regions that had come together to form the union of 'Mercia'.[16] Anna's East Anglian army was forced into battle at Bulcamp Forest, just 5 miles from the Suffolk coast, and Anna and his son Jurmin were killed. Anna's brother Æthelhere succeeded him, but in vassalage to Penda.[17]

Penda had also involved himself in the ongoing Northumbrian dynastic struggle between Deira and Bernicia. After Oswiu of Bernicia gained the throne of Northumbria in 654, Penda allowed his daughter Cyneburh to marry Oswiu's son Ealhfrith; and his son Peada, who had converted to Christianity, married Oswiu's daughter Ealhflaed. However, the fickleness of the age is demonstrated the following year when Penda switched his allegiance to Oswiu's factional rival Æthelwald and invaded Oswiu's kingdom. However, as his army returned south, his forces were ambushed by the Northumbrians on 15 November 655 and Penda was killed next to a river which Bede names as the Winwaed.[18] The location has been speculated to be somewhere between present-day Leeds and Doncaster, the stretch of river referred to by Bede being along either the Aire, Calder or Don. One recent more specific suggestion has been a location next to the River Went, a tributary of the River Don a few miles south of Pontefract.[19] East Anglians had formed part of Penda's Mercian army, as it was recorded that Æthelhere of East Anglia also died in the battle.[20] Oswiu's victory gave him temporary control of northern Mercia as far south as Nottingham. Peada held southern Mercia, but only briefly. Perhaps as revenge for Penda's betrayal of the alliance with her father Oswiu, Ealhflaed, according to Bede, poisoned her husband Peada at Easter 656.[21] Peada's younger brother Wulfhere assumed the throne of

Mercia. Like Peada, Wulfhere had opposed his father's ideology and had already accepted baptism in 653.

The earlier dominance of the pagan Penda raises the question of how his control of the Upper Thames Valley impacted Birinus's church at Dorchester-on-Thames. Evidently, it made little difference. More relevant was the death of its founder on 3 December 649.[22] Birinus was buried at his foundation, and was canonised as a saint soon afterwards. Penda allowed both church and grave to go undisturbed, but Birinus's slumber would be interrupted instead by the Catholic Church during the 680s when a bishop named Haeddi had the saint's remains translated to Winchester.[23] They would be moved again within the Old Minster in the tenth century, and again in the twelfth century to the new Norman cathedral, along with the remains of other Anglo-Saxon monarchs and clergy.

Birinus's replacement at Dorchester was the already consecrated Frankish bishop Agilbert. His appointment may have been suggested by Archbishop Honorius at Canterbury, and according to Bede Cenwealh had been impressed by Agilbert's 'learning and industry'.[24] A cult later developed around Birinus and a shrine dedicated to him containing relics was built in the updated church at Dorchester-on-Thames. This shrine was destroyed and the relics were lost in 1536. However, fragments of the vaulting were rediscovered during the 1870s and were incorporated during the 1960s into a reconstructed shrine that stands today in the south aisle of the present-day building at Dorchester.

The Mercian warfare against first East Anglia and then Northumbria had given Cenwealh an extended break from any serious external Anglo-Saxon interference.[25] It had afforded him time to re-establish himself during the 650s, so much so that the ASC records him fighting the British, presumably the Durotriges, at Bradford-on-Avon in 652.[26] The late tenth-century chronicler Æthelweard in his *Chronicon* recalls in contrast that Cenwealh 'waged civil war', perhaps against a rival unknown claimant.[27] However, William of Malmesbury writes of Cenwealh 'crushing' the British 'at a place called Wirtgeornesburh', which probably refers to the same encounter, although we cannot be certain.[28]

Primary sources fall silent once more during a period of peace. Yet in 658, the West Saxons record an extensive campaign by Cenwealh for territorial expansion following their triumph at Bradford-on-Avon. The first battle that year was named Peonnum, which William of Malmesbury describes as 'the hill called Penne', where Cenwealh 'drove them (the British) in flight as far as the (River) Parret'.[29] Henry of Huntingdon writes that the British initiated the encounter to force Cenwealh out of central

Somerset, which if correct leads us to assume that he had already taken much British territory across Somerset without noticeable bloodshed.[30]

In trying to locate the battlefield, Peonnum is translated as 'at the Penns', with '*penn*' the Celtic word for 'head' or 'top'. This confirms it was a hill site, leading to several possible options. Accepting the reference to the River Parrett as a starting point, some suggestions for Peonnum look too far removed from known West Saxon activity during the 650s. This includes the suggestion of Pinhoe (aka Pen Beacon), 3 miles north-east of the modern centre of Exeter.[31] Another site with potential is Penselwood (Pen Selwood), specifically the site of a former hillfort earthwork known as Kenwalch's Castle. The earthwork is now under tree cover, a mile to the north of the village of Penselwood several miles east of Wincanton. In the medieval period, Penselwood lay on the edge of the large forest of Selwood, and in 658 the hillfort was possibly temporarily occupied by the British. The name Kenwalch is believed to derive from Cenwealh, further supporting Penselwood. However, this may refer to another event, as Kenwalch's Castle seems too far south for a possible connection to the 658 campaign, being as it is 25 miles from the Parrett at its closest point.

With Cenwealh's Somerset centre of operations in mind, a more favoured location for Peonnum suggested in recent times is Pen Hill in the Mendips, a couple of miles north of Wells and only 15 miles from the Parrett.[32] Pen Hill is one of the highest points on the Mendips. If the British were already gone from the Wansdyke, it would have been the logical direction for Cenwealh to advance. After Peonnum, Cenwealh looks to have consolidated his position across eastern Somerset. He is recorded fighting and defeating the British again around Easter 661 at a site named Posent's Stronghold (aka Posentesbyrig).[33] We are hampered by a lack of information about how far Cenwealh managed to penetrate the region. Of the suggested battle sites for Posentesbyrig, a favoured location which tallies with an advance into the Mendips could be Ponter's Ball, a rampart-and-ditch site 2 miles east of Glastonbury. The name derives from the Latin '*pontis vallum*' (meaning 'the bridge over the ditch').[34] The modern A361 road bisects the former line of the embankment, the best surviving section lying north of the road. Local archaeologists have proposed this was an earthwork designed to form part of the defences around Glastonbury, a site already important to the British. However, excavations during the 1970s suggest it was a much later construction, although this, by itself, does not exclude a West Saxon attack on Glastonbury in 661.

Accepting Ponter's Ball presents a challenge because it implies Cenwealh made no westward progress in three years if Peonnum was indeed Pen Hill in the Mendips. Another option is the hillfort at Posbury in Devon, lying between the converging headwaters of tributaries of the rivers Yeo and Culvery, a couple of miles south-west of Crediton.[35] Strategically, Posbury was ideally placed to guard what was one of the primary routes into Devon. In that respect, it could be a candidate for Posentesbyrig, but Posbury sits 50 miles from the Mendips and Glastonbury, seemingly too far beyond what we have identified as secured West Saxon territory at this period.

Nonetheless, there is a final point worth discussing. If we accept Posbury was the site for Posentesbyrig, it is only 10 miles from the suggested site for the battle of Peonnum at Pinhoe. When looked at separately the arguments for Posbury and Pinhoe are not convincing, but when assessed together their geographical proximity gives pause for thought. There is a compelling case Cenwealh may have fought the battles of 658 and 661 in the same vicinity north of Exeter, not in Somerset. If we consider this a valid argument, it suggests West Saxon advances westward during the 660s were more significant than previously assumed.

West Saxon military commitments possibly impacted the construction plans for the church of St Peter and St Paul (the Old Minster) at Winchester, and rather than the year 648 as previously proposed, a later date close to 660 for its completion has been suggested by some historians. This was also the year its first bishop took up residence, and as a further clue, Dorchester-on-Thames would lose its resident bishop that same year.[36] The Old Minster is believed to have been built on the site of an earlier, much smaller Christian church, perhaps one founded by Cynegils. Its location in Winchester would mark the site of the upgraded minster in later centuries and eventually the site of the Norman cathedral. Winchester was of course a walled settlement, having been an important Roman *civitas*. Perhaps the more intriguing question is why the diocese was moved to Winchester from Dorchester at this time. It could be that Cenwealh considered Dorchester too near to the border with his aggressive Mercian neighbour, or that it was during this period that the leadership of Wessex wished to establish their primary religious house alongside their main seat of political power.

However, Winchester was not yet the administrative hub, or the major important royal centre it would later become. It was overshadowed in terms of population by the port of Hamwic and nearby Hamtun alongside the River Itchen on the Solent. The name 'Hampshire' originates from the major settlement of Hamwic-Hamtun, which tells us how important Hamtun's early foundation was for the West Saxons within the development of Winchester. The commercial importance of Hamwic-Hamtun would exceed that of Winchester until the ninth century, but Hamwic was still important for trade into Winchester beyond that due to the limitations and restrictions of the River Itchen upriver north of Bishopstoke.

The transfer of the bishopric in 660 was not without further incident. The bishopric at Winchester was first given to a Frankish cleric named Wine. Bede describes him as being given 'half of a divided see', and this appointment meant that Agilbert, the resident bishop at Dorchester-on-Thames, the man who replaced Birinus, was overlooked. Disappointed at not being awarded the bishopric at the Old Minster, Agilbert took exception. The decision had been Cenwealh's, with Bede writing that the king had 'tired of his (Agilbert's) barbarous speech'.[37] This comment is perhaps a little mystifying until we discover that Wine could converse in Old English while Agilbert could not, so Cenwealh simply preferred the new bishop to be someone he could easily understand.[38] Agilbert duly resigned, transferring himself to Northumbria where he was present to ordain Wilfrid as the abbot at the newly founded abbey at Ripon. Thereafter, he would partake in the important synod at Whitby held in 664 (of which more later), which would decide whether the divided Church across all the Anglo-Saxon kingdoms would follow the Christian doctrine and Catholic practices of Rome or those of the older, established Celtic Irish Christian community.

The appointment of bishops would soon fade into irrelevance for Cenwealh when Wulfhere, the new Mercian king and son of Penda, having resolved his dispute with Northumbria, suddenly launched an invasion. Wulfhere crossed the border into Wessex with a large army in 661. It was perfectly timed, coinciding with Cenwealh's West Country campaign in which he fought the British in 661 at Posent's Stronghold (aka Posentesbyrig). In the king's absence, the West Saxon border with Mercia had been left under the leadership of Cuthred, the nephew to whom the king had awarded 3,000 hides of land in 648. It was precisely against this region – the area known as Ashdown in Berkshire – that Wulfhere directed his invasion.

We know that Wulfhere was thereafter able to move further into Wessex. There is no record of any battle, but the presumption is that Cuthred attempted to resist him, as the ASC notes that Cuthred 'passed away'. It is here, also in the same entry, that the aforementioned Cenberht, the father of the future king Caedwalla, reappears once more in the sources: 'King Cenberht passed away.'[39] We can speculate Cenberht also died in the fighting as the Mercian army then pushed into Hampshire. However, we cannot ignore that Cenberht is referred to as 'king'. It is possible that the scribe, knowing that Cenberht's son Caedwalla would become king during the 680s, exaggerated Cenberht's position. Even so, it implies that he was more relevant than we have perhaps previously recognised during Cenwealh's reign, and that he held a significant position of power, possibly centred in Hampshire.

Too late to help Cuthred, but before Wulfhere had marched deeper into Wessex, the *Chronicon Æthelweardi* tells us that Cenwealh 'led Wulfhere, son of Penda, captive to Ashdown, after defeating his army'.[40] This sounds impressive, but as hinted at in Cenberht's subsequent demise and Wulfhere's continued march south, Æthelweard could not have been more wrong. Where he gathered his information in this instance is unclear. Henry of Huntingdon, providing detail from a primary source no longer extant, confirms that 'Cenwealh fought elsewhere against Wulfhere' but was 'driven from the field of war', with Wulfhere's army then marching right across Hampshire to the Solent before he 'subdued and captured the Isle of Wight' from the Jutes.[41]

The inference is that there was a full West Saxon capitulation. Mention of Wulfhere's subjugation of the Isle of Wight, and specifically the Jutes, raises the question of how much power Cenwealh and his immediate predecessors held over the island. It is plausible the Jutes had regained full control from the West Saxons during Cenwealh's period of exile. Allied to this is the parallel fate of the Meonwara Jutes along the Hampshire–Sussex border. Wulfhere promptly received, in what looks to have been a bloodless operation, the vassalage of the South Saxon king Æthelwealh (aka Æthelwald), and then negotiated an agreement that would keep Sussex within the Mercian sphere of control for the next two decades. More relevant, at least in the immediate term, was the conversion of Æthelwealh to Christianity, with the ASC noting that 'Wulfhere ... received him as godson at baptism'.[42] This tallies with the godfather role that Oswald of Northumbria had played at Cynegils' baptism, a relationship which had great symbolic as well as ideological and political significance for the Anglo-Saxons.

The Sussex king's conversion was seemingly not as impulsive as it might appear. We know from the ASC that Wulfhere had sent a missionary monk named Eoppa into Sussex several years earlier, soon after his own conversion. As a sign of the new Mercian king's enthusiasm for his adopted ideology, he would also donate funds to complete the building of the new monastery at Medeshamstede (the foundation of what would later become St Peter's minster at Peterborough) that his brother Peada had begun. The ceremony in 664 was attended by many senior clergy and nobility.[43] These reputedly included Wulfhere's former adversary King Oswiu of Northumbria, King Sigehere of Essex, several bishops including the Mercian bishop Jaruman and the bishops of London and Rochester, and the first Anglo-Saxon-born archbishop of Canterbury, Deusdedit, just months before his death from plague.[44]

After the baptism of the South Saxon king in 661, Wulfhere transferred to his new vassal direct authority for the Jutish regions of the Isle of Wight and the Meonwara in south-east Hampshire. A generation later, this would lead to conflict between Wessex and Sussex. The further absorption of the South Saxon king Æthelwealh into the Mercian sphere, confirming that Wulfhere planned to exploit the situation to its fullest, is acknowledged by Æthelwealh's arranged marriage soon afterwards to a Hwicce Mercian noblewoman named Eafe.[45] In effect, under his aegis, Sussex would be used as a rival power to deter West Saxon expansion in that direction.

Beyond Sussex, Wulfhere then orchestrated an equally important alliance with King Eorcenberht of Kent, sealed by his own marriage within twelve months to Eorcenberht's daughter Eormenhild.[46] At Eorcenberht's death in 664 his son Ecgberht maintained the alliance with Wulfhere, and Mercia would hold a position of domination over the south-east up to Wulfhere's death in 675. Further to these developments the Mercian king, although withdrawing himself and most of his forces north across the River Thames no later than 662, additionally assigned the Mercian nobleman Frithuwold to act as military governor and sub-king over Berkshire and Surrey.

How Cenwealh's position stood during and immediately after his defeat to Wulfhere is unclear. We can safely assume that he had given vassalage to the Mercian king while remaining nominally king of Wessex. There is no hint he was expelled again. Neither did Wulfhere place a client king or Mercian ealdorman inside central Wessex in the same manner that Frithuwold had been given authority in Berkshire and Surrey. Seemingly, there was also no agreement in line with those made beforehand with Sussex and Kent. Maybe Wulfhere believed the measures he had put in place sufficed to keep Cenwealh in check, and we know from the primary sources Cenwealh remained markedly passive militarily after 661. From 664 through to 670, version A of the chronicle has only three entries and version E just four, and they are largely concerned with ecclesiastic appointments or deaths.[47]

It would seem that Cenwealh was a pragmatist. Assuming he was required to give annual tribute to Mercia thereafter, he devoted his time instead to matters of the Church. Bishops were becoming important figures even in this early period of Christianity, and this is seen in their relevance in the signature lists of the earliest surviving charters from Anglo-Saxon England. The first extant charters produced by a king of Wessex came from Cenwealh around 670, and they were witnessed only by senior ecclesiastics and not by any secular nobility.[48] Having already fallen out with Bishop Agilbert in 660, the West Saxon king soon fell out with Bishop Wine at Winchester, only a couple of years after the latter's appointment. Wine is recorded as briefly holding the bishoprics of Dorchester-on-Thames and Winchester in plurality after Agilbert's resignation.

Matters deteriorated quickly, with John of Worcester informing us that in 663, after barely three years in the role, Wine was 'driven from his bishopric (of Winchester) by King Cenwealh'.[49] Why he was removed is unclear, but historians point to his translation to Dorchester coming in 663 just before his removal.[50] We can speculate that his translation to Dorchester may have been a prelude to him being replaced at Winchester. The resultant fallout between Wine and Cenwealh, leading to the bishop's removal, would leave Wessex with no bishop at either Winchester or Dorchester.

As for Wine, Wulfhere of Mercia, perhaps taking him from what was then Mercian-controlled Dorchester, appointed him to the bishopric of London in 666, with Bede adding that the bishop had 'bought the see' from Wulfhere.[51] The importance of Dorchester declined on Wine's promotion to London, and even though Wessex would regain control of the district around Oxford twenty years later the bishopric had already fallen into abeyance.[52] After Wine's removal Cenwealh tried to persuade Agilbert to return to England. Bede states he had 'offered to make amends' if Agilbert would return to the Winchester bishopric.[53] However, Agilbert had moved on in 667 to become the bishop of Paris, so, perhaps as expected, Agilbert declined the offer. There was no bishop appointed to replace Wine at Winchester until Leuthere (Hlothhere in Old English) received the bishopric seven years later, and it was Agilbert who first recommended Leuthere, his nephew, for the appointment. With the aid of Theodore, the new archbishop of Canterbury, Leuthere was consecrated at Winchester during 670.[54] He would later ordain the celebrated monk Aldhelm in his first prominent position as the abbot at Malmesbury in 675.

The delay in appointing a new bishop in Wessex wasn't solely because of Cenwealh's relationship with the Church. A significant event was to unfold in 664, a wider quarrel that was taking place within the divided Christian community across the country – small differences, it is true, but ones that had festered as a consequence of the ever-increasing relevance of Christianity across the fully converted Anglo-Saxon kingdoms. The issues that required resolution resulted in a church synod held at Whitby in Northumbria in 664. In brief, the synod was called to resolve the ideological disunity between the practices of the Roman and Irish/Celtic forms of Christianity within the recently formed Anglo-Saxon Church.[55] The synod at Whitby has been portrayed by some historians as a balanced assembly of the leading contemporary churchmen across England. Nevertheless, it can be better described as a theological discussion primarily led, as précised by Bede, by followers of the Roman doctrine from Kent and Gaul as they attempted to convince their northern brethren, who followed the Irish tradition, to amend their practices in line with Canterbury.[56]

It appears at first glance to have been primarily about semantics. There was no formal division, as both groups were part of a larger unified organisation. However, there were subtle differences in their relationship with the papacy, the power of the bishops, and the daily practices of the priests, including wearing of the tonsure. One key issue concerned the dating of Easter, the moveable Christian feast, a topic called the 'Paschal Controversy'.[57] Basically, both groups followed different methods of calculating the observance of Easter Sunday. Bede writes the Roman followers declared 'the Irish observance' of that important date in the calendar 'was contrary to the custom of the universal church'.[58] Roman Christianity via Canterbury was based on a 532-year cycle for Easter, as per fifth-century papal calculation, whereas Irish/Celtic practices were based on an 84-year cycle using a fourth-century calculation issued by Rome.[59] The outcome, presided over by Oswiu of Northumbria, as detailed in Bede's *Ecclesiastical History*, was the pronouncement that all Christian groups within mainland Britain would follow the Easter calendar cycle as followed by Rome and Canterbury.

Nevertheless, the fallout may have dragged on. After Archbishop Deusdedit of Canterbury died in July during the 'great plague among men' of 664, the archbishopric remained unaccountably vacant.[60] It was two years before his replacement Wigheard (aka Wighard) was selected by the acting secular heads of Christianity in England, Oswiu of Northumbria and Ecgberht of Kent. However, en route to receive his pallium and consecration by the pope Wigheard unfortunately also died from the plague. It was another three years before a replacement, Theodore of Tarsus, consecrated by Pope Vitalian in Rome, was sent to Canterbury to assume the archbishopric on 27 May 669. Effectively, England had been without a consecrated archbishop from July 664 to May 669. This had impacted the appointment of other bishops, including the primary ecclesiastic position in Wessex.

Theodore was to rejuvenate the Christian doctrine, appointing new bishoprics, setting up schools of theology and learning in the major religious houses, and increasing the regularity of Church synods. It would be from his legacy that a generation of Anglo-Saxon missionaries would travel to the continent from England from the 680s onwards to preach to and convert pagans across much of Europe, particularly in Germany. That the subsequent spread of Christianity across much of northern mainland Europe should be indebted to Anglo-Saxon monks sounds extraordinary, but is nonetheless a fact. Among the first of these missionaries were Wihtberht, Willibrord, Willibald and Boniface.

The emergence of Boniface provides some clues as to the West Saxon advances into and beyond Exeter by the 690s. Boniface was born in Crediton in 675 and attended a former British monastery in Exeter. A Saxon monastery had replaced it while Boniface was still a young man, indicating the British had been pushed deeper into Devon during the reigns of Cenwealh's immediate successors.[61]

Wulfhere's reign has been suggested by some historians as the period when the Tribal Hidage document was first issued, coming soon after Wulfhere's successful campaign in the south.[62] We have discussed the potential origins of the Hidage document in some detail in the previous chapter. The existing document may have been copied from a later version, suggesting it could have been amended in Mercia. In terms of Wessex specifically, the Hidage lists its area as 100,000 hides (12 million acres), which does not relate to the size of the kingdom in the late seventh century but looks to include modifications to reflect the area of greater Wessex as it stood during the tenth or eleventh century.[63]

Elsewhere, an entry in the *Annales Cambriae* refers to a battle in 665 at Liddington Castle hillfort, 4 miles south-east of present-day Swindon. Its omission from the ASC implies it was a minor affair, but its appearance in the *Annales Cambriae* suggests a localised rebellion involving the British.[64] However, this was unlikely to have involved the West Saxons. We have other evidence that Wulfhere of Mercia had placed northern Somerset under an unnamed Mercian sub-king by that stage, and the encounter at Liddington might have some connection with that development.[65]

The rest of Cenwealh's reign passed under vassalage to Mercia. He goes unmentioned until 672, when the ASC noted his death.[66] In terms of his administration, as with many of his contemporaries, the governmental processes during his reign are hidden from us. However, the Tribal Hidage confirms that there was a fully functioning system of tax collection in operation so there must have been a network to process, administer, and distribute government and royal finances. Trade, particularly imports, was taxed. Some continental-produced coinage was already in distribution, primarily small gold coins known as *scillingas* or *thrymsas*, modelled on Frankish designs. Due to its proximity to Europe, Kent would be the first Anglo-Saxon kingdom to produce coinage, and Wessex would follow sometime around or just after Cenwealh's reign. Later in the century, English moneyers would begin producing small silver coins known as *sceattas*.[67]

As noted previously, Cenwealh is distinguished for being the first king of Wessex to pass down surviving charters, meaning we have some record of his administration. However, there are only three extant, all issued in 670–671. One donated land on the Hampshire–Wiltshire border to the Old Minster at Winchester, another a grant to the see at Sherborne. The Sherborne grant bears Wulfhere's signature, which recognises that Cenwealh held vassalage to Mercia in the last years of his reign.[68] In assessing Cenwealh's kingship, William of Malmesbury portrayed him as a poor ruler in his early years compared to his father, Cynegils,, noting that 'the royal splendour went to his head, and he paid little heed to what his father had done'.[69] This criticism looks to be perhaps an admonishment for Cenwealh divorcing his first wife and delaying his conversion to Christianity. Malmesbury would go on to praise Cenwealh for his conversion and his later kingship, remarking, 'So strong did he become, that he who before had not succeeded in defending even his own frontiers, now extended his sway in all directions.'[70]

Cenwealh's second marriage was to Seaxburh, a woman from the Gewisse. The marriage had remained childless, and on his death there was no obvious heir. His place of burial is not recorded. His death initiated a short period of adjustment and change within the West Saxon hierarchies, those bloodlines that had previously dominated the agenda, as they manoeuvred claimants into position for the throne. However, possibly due to the influence of Mercia, the question of who would emerge as king was deferred until 674. A serious claimant was the deceased king's younger brother Centwine, the third son of Cynegils, although his age in 672 is uncertain, and some historians, based on Aldhelm's impartial contemporary collected texts, have questioned Centwine's blood connection.[71] Therefore, with no agreement on the succession, the West Saxon council nominated Cenwealh's wife Seaxburh as monarch. She would likely have had the backing of Bishop Leuthere of Winchester, and possibly also that of archbishop Theodore. Presumably, Wulfhere of Mercia looked favourably on a woman being offered the throne of Wessex, however temporary it might be.

The ASC recorded Seaxburh was given leave to rule immediately after her husband, and recognition of her role as monarch is acknowledged by her entry in the WSGRL.[72] However, it would have been unusual, to say the least, for a woman to be placed permanently on the throne. Therefore Seaxburh may have always been considered a temporary fix. Furthermore, the democratic process of the witan was not as transparent as it would later become. The emergence of Æscwine, and then later Caedwalla, during this period demonstrates that the military backing garnered by an individual was equally relevant in gaining promotion to the throne.

However, not all later sources are clear that Seaxburh assumed the throne, even temporarily. Bede writes instead that 'sub-kings took upon themselves the government of the kingdom'.[73] The identities of these sub-kings and the regions they ruled remains a mystery; Bede provides no more detail. One such man who may have been a sub-king by any other name was an individual named Cenfus, although he is not listed in modern interpretations of the regnal lists.[74] Cenfus is referenced as being the father of Æscwine, who would, according to most sources, be recognised as the new king of Wessex in 674.[75] Some form of power sharing in the aftermath of Cenwealh's death was possible, although in addition to discounting Seaxburh Bede also dismissed as sub-kings the next two kings in the WSGRL, Æscwine and Centwine. This may say less about the facts and more about his source of information, Bishop Daniel of Winchester, a contemporary of Aldhelm and Boniface during the reign of Ine.[76] It is further suggested Bede deliberately omitted mention of Seaxburh because he viewed her marriage to Cenwealh as illegitimate and thus also her right to rule.

Meanwhile, William of Malmesbury recorded Cenwealh had nominated Seaxburh on his deathbed. He also writes in surprising detail in praise of Seaxburh and her qualities, noting that 'nor did she ... lack the energy to face the duties of the throne. She personally raised fresh troops, and kept the old in their allegiance; she ruled her subjects mercifully, and showed a threatening front to her enemies, did everything, in short, in such a way that there was no difference to be seen, except her sex.'[77] If this account is justified, Seaxburh lived up to her name, which combined the symbolic Saxon long knife with the Old English for 'fort'. Undoubtedly, she was a woman of substance in a male-dominated world. Malmesbury's entry extolls Seaxburh's leadership qualities, skills and virtues for a woman, which were uncommon or unrecognised by her contemporaries and therefore worth noting. However, her time on the throne was short-lived. The ASC notes she ruled for one year, although she may have ruled for nearly three, as the succession date of her replacement differs in the ASC and the WSGRL.[78] In the 670s we approach a period of confusion over who held power in Wessex, as will be seen in the following chapter.

Seaxburh as queen was conceivably always a temporary solution to a difficult problem. Her gender could have been seen as problematic by certain nobles, but the issue of her and Cenwealh's childlessness was always going to be prominent. Some historians support the idea she retired to become a nun at Winchester, whether by force or voluntarily. However, the consensus is her reign was probably cut short instead by death, as put by Malmesbury: 'She died, however, this woman of mettle more that womanly, after scarce a year in power.'[79]

8
Æscwine, Centwine and Caedwalla
676–688

During the 670s we enter a phase in the history of the West Saxon kings that suggests several potential future scenarios. Beyond Seaxburh, it is difficult to be precise about when Cenwealth's immediate recognised successors ruled, and for how long, in the late seventh century.[1] As already seen, Bede does not recognise the reign of Seaxburh in his texts, and is clear in recording that 'sub-kings took upon themselves the government of the kingdom, dividing it up and ruling for about ten years'.[2] Who Bede is referring to is unclear. Not only does he ignore Seaxburh throughout his *Ecclesiastical History*, but he also omits to name her immediate successors, Æscwine and Centwine, among these sub-kings. Their omissions give pause for thought, as Bede was writing only a few decades beyond this period. However, we should also remember that much of his information regarding southern events came from his contacts in Kent, and news of events that did not impact the south-east directly were potentially overlooked by Bede's correspondents. Nonetheless, beyond Æscwine there are grounds for acknowledging that the power within Wessex may have been divided in ways which we cannot determine.

The ASC and WSGRL contradict Bede and each other. The chronicle claims there was a two-year gap between the closure of Seaxburh's rule and the appointment of Æscwine as her replacement. In contrast, the WSGRL extends her reign from one year to three, with no vacant throne between 672 and 674.[3] Universal agreement among historians may never be achieved on this issue. Based on primary sources, and disregarding Bede's idea of a vacant throne for more than ten years, it is possible that during the period between Cenwealh's death in 671 and Caedwalla's rise in 685, Seaxburh ruled until 674, Æscwine succeeded her and ruled between 674 and 676, Centwine succeeded Aescwine and ruled between 676 and 685, and Caedwalla succeeded Centwine in 685.

The West Saxon witan may have seen Æscwine as the more mature and warlike candidate in 674, able to lead the defence of the kingdom against further Mercian interventions. This may have been the reason Seaxburh's reign was ended, as contrary to William of Malmesbury's text on her the early thirteenth-century writer Roger of Wendover noted she 'was expelled from the kingdom by the indignant nobles, who would not go to war under the conduct of a woman'.[4]

By 674, Cenwealh's surviving brother Centwine may have reached maturity and was able to stake a claim to the throne. There was also another young candidate named Caedwalla who claimed a bloodline back to Ceawlin, the king whose dynastic regnal line had been replaced by Centwine's predecessors. The bloodline of Ceawlin had been sidelined for a century following the internecine warfare of the late sixth century. Both Centwine and Caedwalla seem to have had valid claims, though Caedwalla's age may have made him unsuitable.

In 674, Æscwine emerged as the third and strongest contender. He was the son of Cenfus, who, as noted in the previous chapter, may have been one of the regional sub-kings who controlled Wessex, or part of Wessex, during Seaxburh's rule. Regarding Æscwine's bloodline, William of Malmesbury, the only chronicler to provide this detail, was to claim that the previously named Ceolwulf was indeed the brother of Cynegils, making Æscwine Cynegils' great-great-nephew.[5] For his claim Æscwine may have invoked his ancestral connection to Cynric, a reputed link recorded by the ASC, traceable through his father Cenfus via Cenfrith, Cuthgils, and Ceolwulf (not the king of the same name) and finally to Cynric himself.[6] He was not unique in this. In due course, both Centwine and Caedwalla would be given similar pedigrees back to Cerdic by the ASC scribes when they succeeded Æscwine. This link to Cerdic and Cynric was nothing new; ASC entries suggest a bloodline tracing back to them was a prerequisite for contenders for the throne. Its importance during Alfred the Great's time symbolised his need to have a shared Germanic and West Saxon heritage regardless of the reality.

Where Æscwine could claim to be unique compared to his predecessors was his name. He was the first named king who did not follow the pattern of personal names beginning with 'C', which we have previously associated with some possible British lineage. Taken by itself, that would imply that Æscwine was also the first king of Wessex to have had Anglo-Saxon parentage. However, if we accept his father was Cenfus – a Brythonic name – this contention cannot be supported. Perhaps it suggests that Cenfus was also of mixed Saxon and British blood and that Æscwine's mother was Saxon.

Some historians view Æscwine's succession as a simple usurpation, although there is no evidence he seized the throne by force. He appears to have had some major support from inside the witan, including the influential Cenred, a probable ally of Cenfus and the father of the future king Ine (r. 688–726). Cenred appears in one of the oldest surviving West Saxon charters, donating land in Dorset to the abbot of Tisbury in southern Wiltshire.[7]

Other possible supporters behind Æscwine, and by association Cenred, Centwine and later Ine, were two nobles named Baldred and Cissa. Although there are no extant charters that Æscwine directly issued, Baldred has two charters in his own name where he is titled 'king of part of Wessex'. Caedwalla and Centwine are included among the witnesses in these charters.[8] Cissa, meanwhile, signs another charter later in 682 as 'sub-king of Centwine'.[9] This detail supports Bede's premise that several individuals, including Baldred and Cissa, may have acted jointly to share power across the kingdom for an unspecified period, either with or alongside Æscwine and then later Centwine. That being the case, it is perhaps unusual the main chronicle sources during the 670s and 680s, including Bede, do not name these sub-kings.

Æscwine's appointment came as the pendulum of power shifted between Wessex and Mercia. Perhaps in response to the political situation in Wessex, which was possibly perceived as a period of anarchy, Wulfhere of Mercia again moved against his neighbour. He and Æscwine are recorded as fighting a battle at Beda's Head (Bedanheaford) in 675.[10] Henry of Huntingdon, with detail taken from an earlier text since lost, wrote that 'both armies suffered a terrible shattering'.[11] Some historians have suggested the battle occurred somewhere along the Oxfordshire–Berkshire section of the River Thames, and this seems a rational assumption.[12] One possible site by both place-name association and geographical location is Beedon Hill, close to the modern A34, 6 miles north of Newbury.[13]

Others have suggested a site further south near to Great Bedwyn on the Wiltshire–Hampshire border, with Beda's Head interpreted as 'the head of Bieda', a stream running through the Bedwyns. Great Bedwyn may already have been an important royal vill, and in later centuries the site even had its own mint. After the discovery of early medieval graves in the vicinity in the 1890s, local historians have argued for the battle being associated more specifically with Crofton, 2 miles south-west of Great Bedwyn, although the age of these remains has not yet been substantiated by further archaeology.[14] This latter suggestion presupposes the Mercians had again invaded deep into Wessex before being challenged. So little is known about Æscwine that this encounter, which we presume was a victory for Wessex although it is not clearly stated, is perhaps the highlight of his brief reign, and perhaps it was only after this battle that he secured full support as king.

From a Mercian perspective, Wulfhere looks to have been trying not only to reassert vassalage over Wessex but to regain internal support from his Mercian nobles. His dominance in the south was under duress, and he had already experienced a major setback when reinvading Northumbria in 674, as noted by the author of Wilfrid's *Vita Sancti Wilfrithi* (Life of St Wilfrid), wherein Ecgfrith of Northumbria had defeated Wulfhere's army, forcing the Mercians to concede the region of Lindsey (what would become Lincolnshire).[15]

Defeats to Northumbria and Wessex show that Wulfhere's authority was on the wane. Following these setbacks, coincidence or otherwise, Wulfhere would die months after the battle of Beda's Head, according to Henry of Huntingdon through disease.[16] He was replaced by his brother Æthelred (Æthelred I of Mercia), who would later be praised for his military campaign into Kent and for fending off an invasion by Ecgfrith of Northumbria. However, perhaps surprisingly given Wessex's position, Æthelred avoided confrontation with Wessex, William of Malmesbury noting that he 'spent the rest of his life enslaved to comfort'.[17] Malmesbury's slur on Æthelred was unfounded, but Mercia was undeniably militarily weaker than it had been throughout most of Wulfhere's reign (658–675). Mercia would not directly challenge Wessex again until the 710s. Nevertheless, territory which Wessex had previously lost remained in Mercian hands. Evidence from Centwine's reign only a few years later supports the fact that Mercia still held some former Gewisse/Hwicce territory in southern Gloucestershire and on the edge of northern Wiltshire.

The sources tell us virtually nothing about Æscwine. However, it was during his period in power that the important religious site at Malmesbury was expanded. According to William of Malmesbury, it was founded by the scholar and poet Aldhelm, who became the church's first abbot in 675.[18] Cenwealh's involvement in the project pre-672 looks likely, even though the main support for this is within an admittedly disputed charter from Bishop Leuthere of Winchester granting land for its construction.[19] By 705, during the reign of Ine, Aldhelm would be transferred to the bishopric at Sherborne. He and Ine were undoubtedly on good terms, although the claim that they were related is almost certainly false.

Æscwine's time in power was brief. He died in 676, although his age and the cause of his demise are not recorded, and there are no surviving charters issued under his kingship.[20] On his death the previously bypassed Centwine emerged, with the ASC recording his succession in 676.[21] Centwine's name translates from Old English as 'noble and wise' or 'noble friend'. The question of his lineage remains open, as while he is noted as being the son of Cynegils, an argument remains that he was a lesser relative, perhaps a cousin whom later scribes 'promoted' to preserve the regnal link to Cerdic.[22] The connection between Centwine and Cynegils was an issue even among their contemporaries. A poem by Aldhelm written sometime after 689 to Centwine's daughter Eadburga (aka Bugga), in honour of a church she had founded, praised her father but omitted mention of her grandfather Cynegils. This may not seem significant, but Cynegils had been the first Christian king of Wessex, so Aldhelm, some argue, would have surely referred to him in any letter to his granddaughter.[23]

Some historians see Centwine's rise to the throne as reuniting Wessex at a time when Bede refers to rule by sub-kings, but there is an important point to consider.[24] Contrary to the understanding that all West Saxon kings from Cynegils onwards were Christian, and despite the ongoing expansion of Christianity among the populace, it is probable that Æscwine had remained a pagan. Similarly, Centwine was also a pagan throughout most of his ten-year reign. Perhaps their continued paganism explains Bede's omission of their kingship within his texts. Bede was a direct contemporary of these kings, and their ideology was something he would not have wished to recognise within the Anglo-Saxon kingdoms as the end of the seventh century approached. In truth, this period of non-Christian kings in Wessex continued under Caedwalla, who only converted towards the end of his life. Thanks to this late conversion, however, Caedwalla is not overlooked in Bede's *Ecclesiastical History*.

There is some detail of Centwine's marriage. The *Life of St Wilfrid* records him marrying Eormengyth, a sister of Queen Eormenburh, the Kentish second wife of King Ecgfrith of Northumbria, but intriguingly, given Centwine's ongoing pagan ideological stance, Eormengyth was a practising Christian.[25] Their only child, their daughter Eadburga, would in time become the abbess at Minster-in-Thanet in Kent. Wulfhere of Mercia had previously cemented an alliance with Kent by marrying Eormenhild of Kent, and we can imagine Centwine was hoping to replace Mercia as a reliable ally to Kent. Centwine's marriage tie to the royal bloodline of Kent can therefore be seen as an opportunity for Wessex, but it is also plausible it was one of several reasons for the renewed aggression into Kent by the new Mercian king, Æthelred I, during 676.

King Hlothhere of Kent had been making moves to gain territory in both Essex and Surrey at Mercia's expense before Æthelred could fully establish himself. Æthelred's first act, possibly aided by the South Saxons, was therefore to invade Hlothhere's kingdom. Bede recorded that the new Mercian king 'devastated Kent, profaning churches and monasteries' and in 'the general devastation destroyed Rochester'.[26] The Mercian campaign against Kent also enabled the South Saxon king Æthelwealh to keep his authority over south-eastern Hampshire and the Isle of Wight, previously granted to him by Wulfhere. In terms of Centwine, peace looks to have held between himself and Æthelwealh of Sussex.

However, in 679 Æthelred turned his attention instead northward towards Northumbria in a campaign to recover the recently lost region of Lindsey (Lincolnshire). By doing so he was spurning the earlier alliance that had seen him marry Osthryth, daughter of Oswiu and sister of the incumbent Northumbrian king Ecgfrith. The two kingdoms clashed at an unspecified location near the River Trent, perhaps near Gainsborough, with Osthryth's young brother Ælfwine being killed during the Mercian victory.[27] Lindsey was recovered by Mercia and would remain under its aegis thereafter, with the defeat ending any further or future serious involvement or influence from the Northumbrian kings south of the River Humber. The West Saxons would be affected by this, as their earlier pact with the Northumbrians had somewhat slowed Mercian expansion.

Meanwhile, the squabbles between throne and clergy that would become a perennial issue were emerging. Cenwealh's disagreements with the bishops Agilbert and Wine were early examples, and during the 670s another such quarrel was played out in Northumbria and would later spread to impact the course of events across Wessex. Bishop Wilfrid had already been promoted from Ripon to York when Archbishop Theodore's changes to the size of the diocese in Northumbria led to his displacement and the involvement of Pope Agatho. Theodore had implemented these changes with Ecgfrith of Northumbria's agreement, so when Wilfrid objected he was expelled from Northumbria. Wilfrid travelled to Rome to plead with the Pope. However, on his return he was first imprisoned for his actions before being exiled for a second time. He then moved himself into Mercia, but Queen Osthryth, Ecgfrith's sister, refused to accept service from him. Wilfrid next turned to Wessex. However, he found a similar problem there. Centwine's Christian wife Eormengyth detested Wilfrid, and although the king was reputedly impressed by Wilfrid's preachings he was moved on quickly.

Finally, in 681, Wilfrid was invited by Æthelwealh to Sussex, which had been the last of the major Anglo-Saxon kingdoms to accept Christianity.[28] Æthelwealh donated land at Selsey for a new religious house with Wilfrid as its bishop, and it was built a couple of miles north of present-day Selsey on a site near a creek at Church Norton.[29] Wilfrid's remit included converting the Jutes on the Isle of Wight, although, as told in the *Life of Wilfrid*, some came at 'the king's command' rather than of their own free will.[30] The Selsey site today only contains the remains of the chancel of the thirteenth-century Norman church, but various earlier Saxon artefacts have been found there, including reputed remnants of Wilfrid's palm cross.[31]

The recent Mercian–South Saxon vassal alliance had affected Centwine's ambitions, particularly in nearby south-east Hampshire and the Isle of Wight, which may in turn have impacted further development at Winchester and further expansion at Hamwic/Hamtun. However, Centwine's alliance with Kent seems to have ensured warfare between Wessex and Sussex was avoided. Wessex, at yet another impasse with its neighbours, looked to the British on its western border. The West Saxons appear to have taken Taunton, and then Exeter, sometime before 680. We certainly know much of east Devon was in West Saxon hands by 680, as the famous missionary Boniface was born around that time in either Exeter or Crediton (7 miles north-west of Exeter) after it had already passed into West Saxon administration. The ASC scribe limited himself to recording that in 682 'Centwine put the Britons to flight as far as the sea', which is not particularly informative.[32]

Nonetheless, another extant letter from Aldhelm, by then the abbot of Malmesbury, provides some useful detail. Writing more than a decade later to Centwine's daughter Eadburga, Aldhelm refers to her father having won three major battles in the west during his time as king.[33] These must be references to victories during the 670s and early 680s over the Dumnonii, victories that had enabled the West Saxons to gain control of Taunton and Exeter, and a wide swath of territory across eastern Devon and west Somerset. William of Malmesbury puts a different slant on at least one of these successes by effectively calling it a British rebellion which Centwine crushed 'with a slaughter so horrific that their (the British) hopes were ended', which presupposes the West Saxons were holding recently gained territory in Devon.[34] Some historians have speculated that during Centwine's reign advances had been made as far as the River Tamar and perhaps beyond it, seizing most of Devon in the process.[35] However, such an all-encompassing advance seems highly unlikely in the late seventh century. If a West Saxon army had forged that far west during the 680s it would have been temporary; they were not ready or able to permanently secure or settle such distant territory. Knowledge of the warfare in the West Country between the West Saxons and the British through the eighth and ninth centuries makes a later push towards the Tamar more realistic.

Towards the end of his reign, and perhaps with his wife Eormengyth's involvement, Centwine converted to Christianity. He is recognised in 682 as the first patron of Glastonbury Abbey through his only surviving charter, in which he donated land near Taunton to the abbey.[36] Hædde, formerly the abbot at Glastonbury but appointed to the bishopric of Winchester when Centwine became king, was no doubt influential in this. Emphasising Centwine's late conversion, Aldhelm described him as a strong and 'just' king, but he also praised him for 'granting many estates to recently established churches'.[37] If these endowments were formalised within charters they have not survived.

Perhaps of even more interest about Aldhelm are charters from 681 showing him, on behalf of Malmesbury Abbey, receiving land in and around Tetbury from Æthelred of Mercia.[38] These charters are witnessed by Theodore, archbishop of Canterbury, which acknowledges the ongoing relationship between the Mercian throne and Canterbury irrespective of the political situation. Furthermore, Aldhelm receiving grants from both Wessex and Mercia within the same calendar year reveals the Church's neutrality. In addition to Tetbury, another Mercian charter from 680 giving land to Aldhelm near Wootton Bassett confirms beyond doubt that Wessex no longer had control of northern Wiltshire and south-east Gloucestershire.[39] This last point perhaps demonstrates that by moving into western Somerset and then Devon, the West Saxons had in turn ceded to Mercia land which had once been a central part of Gewisse territory.

On a wider issue, the whole of the British Isles was hit with a virulent outbreak of pneumonic plague in 684.[40] Plague was a recognised cyclical threat, and its appearance was frequently recorded by the church scribes. It had returned to Britain roughly twenty years earlier, devastating the monastery at Barking in 666 and the church community of Lichfield in 672 (killing its bishop), before resurfacing in 680. Perhaps surviving the pandemic of 684 explains Centwine's conversion, as he would in the following year receive formal baptism. However, in a move that probably confused all his supporters and most of the nobility, Centwine then promptly abdicated the throne of Wessex. His was the first known voluntary abdication. Maybe the ASC scribes were unimpressed, because his conversion, abdication and subsequent death all went without mention in the chronicle. Furthermore, he had abdicated without a recognised male heir to replace him.

Aldhelm, in writing of Centwine's decision to give up the throne, notes he 'gave up riches and the reins of government ... in the name of Christ'.[41] He is believed to have retired to lead a religious life, although whether this decision had been influenced by the pandemic, the sudden rise of Caedwalla or an epiphany is unclear. His withdrawal certainly enabled Caedwalla to make a rapid and successful bid for the throne. Centwine may have still been relatively young, even by the time he died. His widow Eormengyth provides a clue that her husband had died by 694, as she retired after his death to become the abbess at Minster-in-Thanet in her native Kent in 695, a role in which she was followed by her only daughter, Eadburga.

The transfer of power to Caedwalla during 685 has all the hallmarks of a peaceful arrangement, but there is some ambiguity within the various primary sources. The ASC version A notes that 'Caedwalla began to contend for the kingdom'.[42] Elsewhere, William of Malmesbury implies that there had been an earlier challenge for the throne but writes to support Caedwalla when adding that 'a faction of conspirators' had previously driven him into exile, but, 'whether through pity for his misfortunes or admiration for his valour, all the young and able-bodied followed the fugitive'.[43] We have no dates from Malmesbury to support this incident, but he seems to be referring to when Centwine first became king, naming his supporters, and not Caedwalla's, as the 'conspirators'. This narrative of Caedwalla having been exiled at some earlier stage during Centwine's reign appears to have some validity. Along the same lines is an alternate proposal that one of the battles noted above was an earlier, unsuccessful attempt by Caedwalla to seize the throne.[44]

This theme surrounding Caedwalla's early activities is bolstered by the *Vita Wilfridi*, which noted he spent a period of exile in either the Chilterns or the Andredsweald forest in Sussex.[45] As hinted at by Malmesbury, he may have gathered a strong army of followers in the process, and as confirmed by the ASC, he 'began to contend for the kingdom', which eventually led to Centwine's peaceful capitulation.[46] To substantiate Caedwalla's legitimate entitlement to Wessex, the ninth-century ASC scribes were keen to acknowledge a link to the Cerdicing heritage through his father Cenberht and grandfather Cedda (one of Cuthwine's sons). These two were confusingly linked back to Cerdic as the great-grandson of Cuthwine (Cutha) and great-great-grandson of Ceawlin. Similar ingenuity would be needed when the scribes were required to find a link between Caedwalla's successor Ine and the bloodline descendants of Cuthwine. Whatever the truth of it, William of Malmesbury adds his backing for Caedwalla being a 'noble offshoot of the royal stock' but overlooks Cenberht and the more direct blood link by declaring him to be the great-nephew of Ceawlin.[47]

If we accept the genealogy for Caedwalla (and in turn Ine), the year 685 marks the first return to power of Ceawlin's bloodline since Ceawlin was ousted by Ceol's faction in 591–2. However, in nominating Caedwalla the witan had limited alternatives. Neither Centwine nor Æscwine had a male heir, and both the male bloodlines of Cynegils' other sons, Centwine's brothers Cwichelm and Cenwealh, had failed. The only son to be born to either of them was Cwichelm's son Cuthred, and as observed in a previous chapter he had predeceased his father.

Caedwalla is not an Anglo-Saxon name but one of British derivation, the anglicised form of the Celtic name Cadwallon. As such, some historians have argued not only was he part British (Welsh) but he could even have been related to the Welsh king Cadwaladr ap Cadwallon of Gwynedd, possibly a son, and named after Cadwaladr's father Cadwallon ap Cadfan.[48] This is an intriguing idea, but possibly ambitious; there is no conclusive evidence either way. However, whereas some of his predecessors had closer links with the native British tribes, Caedwalla's origins may not be linked to them via the old Gewisse associations. He seems instead to have stronger ties with Hampshire and the south-east, and maybe he resulted from a marriage between a West Saxon and a Briton. Either way, it is difficult to substantiate his bloodline connections.

As it transpired, Caedwalla was to use the relative stability of Centwine's reign to extend the power of Wessex swiftly into the domain of its Anglo-Saxon neighbours to the east.[49] Perhaps only months into his reign, he launched a campaign against the South Saxons. This strongly suggests he knew the political situation there, and of course, one way of gaining deeper support for his fledgling rule was to offer his nobles the opportunity to gain pillaged riches on campaign. Sussex had already been weakened by renewed conflict with Kent. John of Worcester tells us that in February 685 there had been a clash of arms between the two kingdoms, during which the Kentish king Hlothhere received a fatal blow and died during treatment for his injury.[50] According to Bede, Hlothhere's nephew Eadric, the son of Ecgberht I, had led the South Saxons into battle, which opens up a whole new scenario in which Hlothhere had potentially robbed Eadric of his inheritance.[51]

Caedwalla's succession and his campaign into Sussex are so intertwined that some historians have questioned whether we have misread the limited chronology available. Given Caedwalla had already been in Sussex during his exile with strong support behind him, some have speculated that he had undertaken the Sussex campaign with Centwine's agreement, on the basis that if successful Centwine would abdicate and Caedwalla would assume the throne in his stead. Certainly, the timeline could support this hypothesis. Putting aside further speculation, sometime in 685 Caedwalla's army confronted a South Saxon army that was diminished after its recent encounter with Kent. Their king, Æthelwealh, appears to have challenged the West Saxons as close to his western border as he could manage. According to local tradition, the battle took place south-east of Stoughton, a village only 5 miles north-west of Chichester and therefore close to the Wessex–Sussex border which was originally occupied primarily by the Meonwara Jutes. It should be remembered there was an alliance between the South Saxons and Meonwara.

We have no clues whether the Meonwara helped fill the ranks of Æthelwealh's army, remained neutral, or fought alongside the West Saxons. For the encounter itself we have little detail, other than during the fighting the South Saxon king was killed. According to the same tradition that supports the location near Stoughton, Æthelwealh's body was reputedly buried within the southernmost of the group of barrows on the nearby downs known locally as the 'devil's humps'.[52] The barrows are Iron Age in origin but archaeologists acknowledge they show signs of additional usage during the late Anglo-Saxon period.

The battle appears to have been a West Saxon victory, although the sources are confusing. Henry of Huntingdon notes that the South Saxon ealdormen Berhthun and Andhun chased Caedwalla back across the Wessex border, although no further battle was recorded.[53] This withdrawal may have been forced, but it is equally possible Caedwalla was keen to return to Wessex to stabilise his position on the throne as part of some form of agreement with Centwine and the Wessex witan. Evidence he had assumed full control before later resuming his campaign into the south-east is seen in a charter of 685, one of only six accredited to him, in which he granted plots of land to Bishop Wilfrid across the former Jutish Meonwara territory in and around the region of Bognor.[54] It would appear that following Æthelwealh's death Caedwalla's reign saw the Meonwara region along the southern Hampshire–Sussex border come under West Saxon control as far as Selsey. Wilfrid was then based at Selsey, so this is presumably when Caedwalla first encountered him. In time, according to the writings of Aldhelm, the pagan Caedwalla would come to see Wilfrid as his 'spiritual father', and the brief relationship that developed between them was significant in Caedwalla's later conversion to Christianity and his pilgrimage to Rome in 688.[55]

The South Saxon ealdorman Berhthun claimed the vacant throne of Sussex, while Bede tells us that Hlothhere's nephew Eadric, who had fought alongside South Saxons against his uncle, was appointed sole king in Kent.[56] This is another example of Bede's ability, despite never leaving his native Northumbria, to gain details from the south of England through his correspondence with other clerics based in the south-east, including much about Caedwalla that other primary sources omit, which we suspect was from his correspondence with Bishop Daniel of Winchester, who had access after 705 to details on the West Saxon kings.[57]

One such entry by Bede in his *Ecclesiastical History* concerns the emergence of Caedwalla: 'After Caedwalla had gained possession of the kingdom of the Gewisse he also captured the Isle of Wight.'[58] Mention of the Gewisse is intriguing. It might suggest that Caedwalla's support had been centred in Hampshire and that he had needed to secure the Gewisse region before he could then conduct campaigns to the south and east. This may also again illuminate Bede's idea of a region divided under sub-kings. Perhaps the Saxons living in the former Gewisse region had been key supporters of Centwine, making it necessary for Caedwalla to ensure their allegiance at the earliest opportunity when establishing his authority throughout Wessex.

During 686, the West Saxon king would launch a series of campaigns. There was a second assault against Sussex, a push to control the Isle of Wight, and finally an invasion into Kent. His ambition was undeniable, and he mostly succeeded. However, the primary sources are a little confused as the region in which Caedwalla initially concentrated his efforts. The ASC tells us only that 'Caedwalla and Mul (his brother) ravaged Kent and Wight'.[59] In contrast, Bede, William of Malmesbury, Henry of Huntingdon and the later chronicler Stephen of Ripon in his *Life of Wilfrid* provide between them enough detail to enable us to follow Caedwalla's wars chronologically as they developed.

With the Meonwara Jutes already subdued, Caedwalla first moved to attack the Jutes on the Isle of Wight. They had been under the protection of the South Saxon king as part of the Mercian–South Saxon alliance, but that arrangement had ended with the defeat of Æthelwealh of Sussex. Bede writes that Caedwalla 'endeavoured to wipe out all the natives' on the island.[60] William of Malmesbury writes of the Jutes there 'rebelling', though against whom is not clear. He adds they were 'relying on Mercian support' that never came before they were 'nearly wiped out' by Caedwalla's forces.[61] Henry of Huntingdon viewed it as an ideological war, describing the inhabitants of the island as 'still idolatrous'.[62] This implies Caedwalla, previously accepted as being pagan, had already converted to Christianity, even if he was yet to be formally baptised. Foremost in motivating his attempted massacre of the Jutes on the island was the reputed encouragement of Bishop Wilfrid, who wished for the islanders to be punished.

The brutality of the campaign and Wilfrid's support for it was something later chroniclers such as Stephen of Ripon preferred to overlook.[63] Devout as Wilfrid may have been, there was more to his enthusiasm than religious fervour. The West Saxon king had vowed to give to the Church, or more specifically Wilfrid, a quarter of the island (about 300 hides) after it had been taken. During the fighting, the island's Jutish king Æthelwold (Bede names him Arwald) was killed, but his two sons – or two brothers, the sources vary – agreed to be baptised afterwards by Wilfrid. There is some confusion among the primary sources, but it would seem they did not wholeheartedly accept conversion. According to Henry of Huntingdon, they were immediately executed after being baptised, which sounds specious. The more reliable text comes from Bede, who writes instead of them breaking an oath and escaping to the mainland but being discovered near Swaything and then summarily killed.[64]

Having conquered the Isle of Wight, Caedwalla marched his army into Sussex. Its new king, Berhthun, was too weak to prevent the West Saxon invasion this time and he was soon killed, with Bede writing that the kingdom of Sussex was 'reduced to a worse state of slavery'.[65] Quickly moving on, Caedwalla saw an opportunity to exploit similar weakness in the Kentish leadership. Eadric, recently crowned king there, had not stabilised his position and was unpopular, with Henry of Huntingdon noting that Eadric reigned 'with neither the love nor the respect of the Kentish people'.[66] There were potentially large financial rewards for Wessex if it could control Kent. Through its trade with the continent, it was a rich kingdom. Hlothhere had revised the kingdom's legal codes, and among his rulings was a law imposing stricter tolls on trade passing through the ports of Kent. Considering London was one of those ports at this time, the royal Kentish exchequer had benefited greatly. Leading a rapid and decisive campaign, Caedwalla, with his brother Mul alongside him, conquered the kingdom with apparent ease.[67]

Within just eighteen months as king of Wessex, Caedwalla had achieved control of the Isle of Wight, Sussex and Kent, and apparently Surrey as well. Adding them to the authority he already held from Wessex's expansion westward, Caedwalla held a level of power in the south and a size of territory well beyond any of his West Saxon predecessors. In terms of Surrey, his influence there is seen both in his charter for a minster at Farnham, possibly the forerunner of Waverley Abbey, and also in his witnessing a charter for land at Battersea for the abbey at Barking alongside Eorcenwald, the bishop of the East Saxons.[68] This acknowledges the cooperation already garnered with Essex and more generally with the Church. An East Saxon charter from Saebbi of Essex, also for Barking, which included some West Saxon witnesses scattered within the East Saxon signatories, confirms there was a brief and new cooperation between Wessex and Essex.[69]

It was of course impossible for Caedwalla to conquer and settle both Sussex and Kent in the fullest sense. His military resources were limited. He therefore appointed his brother Mul to administer Kent, possibly organised around the garrisoning of major strategic settlements. At first there were no problems, as evidenced by Mul's reconfirmation of a Kentish royal grant to the church at Minster-in-Thanet, a site which already had previous association with the West Saxon royal line.[70] All seemed well, so much so Henry of Huntingdon describes Mul in Kent as being 'fearful in strength and noble in appearance' and 'universally loved'.[71]

Another outcome of this reconfiguration of power was Archbishop Theodore's intent to resolve his earlier dispute with Bishop Wilfrid at Selsey. This reconciliation seems to have Caedwalla's fingerprints on it, a sign of the archbishop's wish to align himself with the new power in Kent. Despite the benefits that had come to him from Caedwalla's campaign against the Jutes, Wilfrid still wanted to return to Northumbria, and with a new king recently appointed in the person of Aldfrith, the possibility of a return arose. Theodore therefore advocated successfully on Wilfrid's behalf, and he was reassigned back to York with additional authority in Ripon. This was also beneficial for Bishop Hædde at the Old Minster, as by the end of 686 Wilfrid's foundation diocese of Selsey was absorbed by Winchester.[72]

The East Saxon joint kings Sæbbi and Sigehere had taken advantage of Kent's weakness and supported Caedwalla's actions for their own reasons. An alliance with Essex concerning Kent is evident in Caedwalla's charter for land in Kent early in 687 being witnessed by Sigehere.[73] Nonetheless, political stability did not last long, and this perhaps shows the West Saxons were slow to appreciate the uniqueness of Kent in terms of its Frankish connections. The Kentish royal dynasty had strong blood ties with the Francia royal dynasty, and the recent kings Eorcenberht, Eormenred and Hlothhere all had names of Frankish origin. It is known that in the eighth and early ninth century Francia would involve itself more than once in the internal politics of the Anglo-Saxon kingdoms, and it is plausible that the Franks may also have helped undermine the West Saxons in Kent between 686 and 688.

During 687, Mul looks to have overreached himself. The sources are a little confusing, but it may be that he faced a rebellion. Henry of

Huntingdon writes that Mul, 'considering the enemy to be feeble ... rushed into a certain house in pursuit of plunder, taking only twelve soldiers with him'. Caedwalla's brother 'was unexpectedly surrounded', and 'would not surrender to arms and was burnt alive in that very house with his twelve soldiers'.[74] William of Malmesbury adds that 'Mul lacked the courage to break out and face the enemy'.[75] This points to a resurgence of the former Kentish royal dynasty, and Caedwalla's reaction to the news of his brother's assassination was no surprise. Sometime in 688, he launched what must have been a major assault into Kent, and without regard to any future political consequences he reduced the kingdom into what one historian has described as economic and political disarray before, 'sated with amazing slaughter and immense plunder', he returned home.[76]

If Caedwalla ruled over Kent directly, it was not for long. He was forced to withdraw his forces to Wessex soon after, the implication being that he had been seriously wounded during his violent campaign of revenge. The resultant power vacuum inside Kent was filled by a new Kentish–East Saxon alignment, with Oswine, a descendant of Eorcenberht, taking control of the eastern region of the kingdom and Sæbbi of Essex's son Swæfheard acting as sub-king for his father in the western region, dividing Kent again along a traditional partition. Frankish involvement in these developments is plausible. In Wessex, meanwhile, Caedwalla must have shocked contemporaries when he took the extraordinary step of abdicating the throne of Wessex.

Bede claims that Hædde, bishop of Winchester, helped persuade Caedwalla to seek baptism and go on a final pilgrimage, and towards the end of 688 he departed for Rome.[77] Caedwalla is the first Anglo-Saxon king known to have made the journey, and he did so aware that he did not have long to live, perhaps due to his battle wound. En route to Rome, he donated funds to construct a church at Saumur in Francia and was also recorded as stopping in Lombardy at the court of their king Cunincpert.[78] On 10 April 689, Easter Sunday, Caedwalla was baptised by Pope Sergius I and given the name Peter, with Bede writing that he 'was anxious to gain the special privilege of being washed in the fountain of baptism within the threshold of the apostles'.[79] Caedwalla only just made it. He died, aged about thirty, only ten days later and was buried in St Peter's Cathedral. His late conversion was seen by the clergy as significant and deserving of praise, so much so that a twenty-four-line epitaph playing on the theme of renunciation was placed on his tomb by order of the pope, and repeated by Bede in full in his *Ecclesiastical History*.[80]

In considering Caedwalla's brief reign, many historians support the argument that he first came to the fore in the Thames Valley or the Chilterns.[81] Others put forward suggestions that he already had connections in Sussex, while a few support the claim by the twelfth-century writer Geoffrey of Monmouth in his *Historia Regum Britannie* that Caedwalla was a misinterpretation of the name of Cadwaladr ap Cadwallon, the Welsh king of Gwynedd.[82] Nonetheless, Monmouth's claim is discredited as there is clear disparity between their periods of activity. Cadwaladr is understood to have ruled Gwynedd between 655 and 682 and was much older.

Of the six extant charters credited to Caedwalla, all bar one concern land in Surrey, Sussex and Kent – the regions he had gained in warfare, not the regions normally identified with seventh-century Wessex.[83] The exception was a charter to Aldhelm late in his reign in which he conferred estates at Somerford Keynes near Cricklade, at Bradon Forest, north-west of modern Swindon, and near the confluence of the rivers Nadder and Wylye at Wilton.[84] They all concerned donations to the Church.

When summarising Caedwalla's reign there is some discomfort and ambiguity among clerical chroniclers. Aldhelm described Caedwalla as 'renowned in war and arms ... a powerful occupant of the throne'.[85] William of Malmesbury refers obliquely to the destruction that took place in Kent. He says of Caedwalla that 'it is hard to do justice to his devotion to religion even before he was baptised, which led him to give God the tithes of all the spoils he had converted to his own use', adding that, 'while we approve of the intention, we must disapprove the action'.[86] Here Malmesbury welcomes a repentant sinner, from whose actions funds to the Church had come as a byproduct.

For a brief period, Caedwalla had forged Wessex into a power to rival Mercia. However, this was a period of neutrality between the two kingdoms during which Æthelred of Mercia steered clear of any conflict because he was aware of Caedwalla's military prowess. In abdicating so cleanly and swiftly, Caedwalla had potentially plunged Wessex into another period of uncertainty. But the long reign of his successor, Ine, would in time give Wessex a stronger foundation for survival and future advancement.

Fig. 4. Map of Anglo-Saxon and British kingdoms and tribal regions, early eighth century.

9

Ine
688–726

The year 688 saw Wessex beset by an old problem: there was no suitable heir from Caedwalla's marriage. The situation had been similar with his immediate predecessors Cenwealh, Æscwine and Centwine/Seaxburh. Faced with this, the West Saxon witan looked to find a successor who could claim majority support. One of Æscwine's primary supporters had been the nobleman Cenred, and it is plausible that he briefly filled the power vacuum before raising enough support for Ine, the eldest of his two sons, to be named as king. Ine was only about eighteen, and it is possible Cenred and his son may have shared the throne for a brief period.[1] The ASC acknowledges Ine's kingship beginning in 688, whereas the WSGRL dates it to the following year, which could reflect a brief period when Cenred and Ine acted together.[2]

The latest political reshuffle within Wessex allowed the East Saxon leadership to ally themselves more closely with Kent, demonstrated by five charters issued during 689–690. Power inside Kent was shared briefly between Oswine, a descendant of Eormenred of Kent, and Swæfberht and Swæfheard of Essex. However, matters were to change when Wihtred, the third son of the former Kentish king Ecgberht I, emerged in 691–692. Charter evidence shows that Wihtred temporarily shared the Kentish throne with the East Saxon Swæfheard but had taken full control by 694.[3] He brought long-term stability to Kent in the same way Ine would in Wessex, and the two men were to enjoy parallel reigns for more than thirty years.

Ine's father Cenred's long-standing importance, perhaps even as one of Bede's unnamed and unlisted sub-kings, is evidenced in an earlier charter issued under his name during the 670s. His continued importance during Ine's reign is seen in his witnessing of a charter in 692 alongside or perhaps in place of his son.[4] Cenred's longevity and influence is debated, but within Ine's law codes from 694 Ine himself acknowledges his father's help in compiling the codes.[5] Alongside kingship came the claimed links for Cenred going back to

Ceawlin, as acknowledged by John of Worcester, thereby lending additional legitimacy to Ine.[6] Worcester's contemporary William of Malmesbury is less certain when writing that Ine was called to the throne 'more for his acquired prowess and energy than for his blood link with the royal line'.[7]

The wide support base for Cenred and Ine seems to have been a deciding factor, with perhaps an agreement made to assign some authority among a few of their chief supporters. This surfaces within one of Ine's early charters of 693, wherein two men, Æthelbald and Baldred, both sign as 'king of part-Wessex'.[8] They are also seen issuing two charters each in their names with the same given title during the 690s, which acknowledges they had designated authority over two regional districts of Wessex for a period.

Ine became only the third in the West Saxon regnal list (after Æscwine and Seaxburh) whose personal name does not begin with a 'C'. However, this may be a misconception. While he is recognised as Ine by historians and primary texts, some suggest that his name is an affectionate diminutive of the longer name 'Centwine'.[9] Perhaps this also implies that a distinction was specifically made to separate him from the former king Centwine's rival dynasty. Whatever the case, Ine was a rare name, and he remains the only individual with that name to be listed throughout the *Prosopography of Anglo-Saxon England* database.

Cenred had four children. Ine had a brother named Ingeld and two sisters, Cuthburh and Cwenburh, both of whom were to receive sainthood during the eighth century. To reforge the broken political alliance with Northumbria, sometime before 690 Cenred arranged for Cuthburh to marry the Northumbrian king Aldfrith, brother of former king Ecgfrith and youngest son of Oswiu. Cuthburh and Aldfrith had a son named Osred, who would become the king of Northumbria in due course, but their marriage was later dissolved, with John of Worcester putting this down to their devoutness, both of them having 'renounced their carnal union for the love of God'.[10] Cuthburh would return south to become a nun and join her sister Cwenburh at Barking Abbey, and in 705, with the help of Ine, she would found the monastery at Wimborne that was later dedicated to her. Becoming its first abbess, she was soon joined there by her sister Cwenburh.[11]

During the early years of Ine's reign, Æthelred I of Mercia seized the opportunity to make small territorial gains from Wessex north of the River Thames. Elsewhere, the West Saxons were able to tighten their authority on the Isle of Wight and the former Jutish region along the Hampshire–West Sussex borderlands. Additionally, beyond Sussex they still held authority within much of Surrey. A brief South Saxon rebellion was ended with the support of a local West Saxon ally named Nothhelm (aka Nunna), who appears in a charter of 692 as a kinsman of Ine, perhaps linked by some marriage arrangement. He was still allied with Ine in 710 as a client king, as evidenced by his presence supporting the West Saxons in their campaign in Devon and Cornwall that year.[12]

However, Ine – and, if we accept the co-rulership, his father Cenred also – had not completely given up Caedwalla's earlier West Saxon foothold in Kent. Historians debate the evidence, but Ine probably launched a new military campaign into Kent around 690–1.[13] William of Malmesbury notes Kent was forced to sue for peace, with the *ASC* adding that 'the inhabitants of Kent came to terms with Ine and granted him 10,000 (pounds) because they burned Mul earlier'.[14] John of Worcester quotes a much lower figure of £3,750 taken from another earlier source.[15] However, Malmesbury's text is more illuminating. Reference to the earlier burning of Caedwalla's brother Mul and the monetary value given implies it may not have been a tribute payment to prevent further West Saxon invasion but was instead a much-delayed reparation payment of *wergild* for the life of Mul, who had royal blood. It would appear Ine and Wihtred of Kent came to terms, part of which was an acceptance that Ine held no influence in Kent thereafter. Wessex had to wait a whole century for Ecgberht, the grandfather of Alfred the Great, to regain a West Saxon influence in Kentish affairs.

Advances by Wessex in the west are more difficult to assess. There looks to have been little further development in establishing a greater West Saxon presence in western Devon until Ine's campaign of 710. Instead, during the 690s, Ine was more concerned with cementing earlier West Saxon control across Dorset and perhaps more significantly Somerset and eastern Devon. This included reinforcing at this time the known established settlements in the heartland of Wessex at South Petherton, 7 miles west of modern Yeovil, and at Somerton, and then further west at Taunton and Exeter. We know that new Anglo-Saxon place names in west Somerset beyond the River Parrett can be traced to Ine's reign around the late seventh or early eighth century.

Very little is known about Ine's activities in the late 690s and early 700s. His marriage to Æthelburh (aka Æthelburg) would seem to have been an internal political compromise and may have occurred as soon as he became king. She has been linked in kinship to Ine's successor Æthelheard (r. 726–740), who was possibly her brother.[16] However, this comes with the proviso that Æthelheard's own background remains open to speculation, casting doubt on Æthelburh's connections.

Ine's reign marks the point at which historians can pull together with greater reliability some of the concepts of kingship and government inside Wessex. The level of primary detail available from his period on the throne enables a wider discussion on law and order as seen through his notable set of law codes. Furthermore, the interaction between the king and the Church, and the wider expansion of the Christian message to other parts of northern Europe through Anglo-Saxon missionaries, shows additional developments of Christian ideology during Ine's reign. The dearth of primary source evidence before Ine does not imply the West Saxons controlled a completely lawless society. However, the evidence suggests that Ine was the first king to take law and order seriously in Wessex in the shape of his own law codes. The earliest extant examples of Anglo-Saxon law codes, albeit rudimentary, had come from Æthelberht of Kent around 600–605. They concerned levels of compensation and punishment according to social rank – something typical of Germanic-origin legal systems – and included influences from continental Europe and Kent's early adoption of Roman Christianity.[17]

Codes issued by Hlothhere and Eadric appeared in Kent just before Ine's codes, and Wihtred of Kent issued his own set of laws around 694–695. There are indications that Ine and Wihtred collaborated; for instance, Ine's law code number 20 appears as a direct word-for-word copy of one of Wihtred's codes. As noted by Ine himself, his father Cenred, alongside bishops Eorcenwald and Hædde, aided him in compiling his codes. It may be no coincidence that this followed an unpredictable political period, whereby Cenred may have understood that constructing such codes would assist in further securing his son's authority. Ine refers to Eorcenwald as 'my bishop', which may imply that Wessex shared some control of London, but more importantly it helps us pinpoint with greater accuracy when the laws were compiled. Eorcenwald died in 693, which suggests that the final law code texts were completed and distributed no later than 692–694.[18] Ine's codes would become so integral to the West Saxon establishment that two centuries later they formed an integral part of Alfred the Great's law codes (clauses 44 to 120 inclusive), designed to supplement existing West Saxon legislation rather than to supersede it.

There are seventy-six separate codes, many with sub-clauses.[19] The influence of the clergy is evident in the individual codes and their wording. Their selectivity may also suggest an intent to show Ine's legitimate authority, and some argue they form an ideological statement for a king who wanted to show himself as a lawgiver and a guarantor of peace and justice, not a warlord ruler like many of his predecessors.[20] The codes also acknowledge that by this period there was a governmental network operating on behalf of the king through appointed ealdormen and officials. We know Ine's administration includes the first references to a division of the kingdom into administrative sub-divisions that would in due course develop into shires with their own courts, presided over by royal representatives who were responsible for collecting tax and upholding the law.

Ine's law codes mark the importance to Anglo-Saxons of social hierarchy and societal obligations based around class status, covering a range of topics, including landownership, crime and the rights of women.[21] In contrast to some parallel social constructs across continental Europe, Ine's laws acknowledged women's rights to inherit property and to act as legal witnesses, but the laws also reinforced the idea as it stood in the Middle Ages that women had limited rights and were subordinate to men. Offences like property damage, trespassing and theft carried strict penalties, focused on deterrence and compensation. The codes on crime acknowledge the importance of status, with identical offences receiving different punishments and penalties depending on an individual's social standing. The nobility would be required to make *wergild* payments rather than physical punishment.. Until the wider circulation of coinage in later years, payments would take the form of goods or services. Those who could not make these payments would face punishment, depending on the severity of the crime, ranging from maiming to death.

In terms of how the laws interpreted the balance between Saxon and Briton, several clauses refer to the British.[22] Britons, however wealthy, were always identified in the codes as being of inferior rank to their Anglo-Saxon counterparts. That a two-tier division based on ethnic grounds was still a valid concept in Wessex approximately two centuries after the first Germanic settlements comes as a surprising revelation. For example, compared to Anglo-Saxons, Britons were required to pay double the specified *wergild* to the victim or kin for any crime they had committed, thereby disadvantaging the native British population economically, socially and legally. This discrimination shows that even by the late seventh century there remained strong societal divisions between Anglo-Saxon and Briton. This in turn led to increased efforts by native Britons, as hinted at in a previous chapter, to assimilate themselves into Anglo-Saxon culture by whatever means, whether learning to speak English or changing family burial practices.

Commercially, the law codes made it possible for merchants to operate within a controlled environment where trade could thrive. The port of Hamwic on the Solent was further developed in this period alongside the royal vill at Hamtun, and possibly witnessed there the first production of West Saxon coinage, although there are no surviving examples bearing Ine's name or image. Most numismatists remain unsure when coin production across England expanded significantly. Some coins produced in Europe had been in circulation since the withdrawal of Rome from Britain, and there is evidence Kentish mints were producing *sceattas* in the early seventh century.[23]

The codes also included means of assessing the goods owed by landowners to the king and/or the appointed royal administrator or local nobility. The usual goods-in-kind payment was based on the production value of an area and property measured in hides. Around this period a hide represented an area of about 80–100 acres, although by 1066 it would average nearer to 120 acres. It is illuminating, for example, to see that a typical 10-hide property had to raise annual tributes with various quantities of cows, geese, chickens and fish, and measures of ale, bread, honey, cheese and butter.

Further research into the codes highlights more unusual obligations. For example, clauses state how travellers or merchants entering Wessex should conduct themselves, keeping to the road while shouting or blowing a horn to signify their presence when arriving at a settlement.[24]

Ine's codes also give us some idea of the military structures adopted by Wessex and the other kingdoms. Defence was centred on the regional militia, the fyrd, the origin of which was Germanic. This system had worked successfully in various forms beforehand, the concept being that any free man aged over fifteen was subject to attend a summoning of the fyrd when called upon. By the mid-ninth century, it had been refined so that the number summoned depended upon the productivity of that local region, hence a general rule was stipulated that one man, complete with what arms and armour he could muster, was required for every 5 hides of land, effectively representing one man in every five of the adult male population.

The longevity of Ine's reign perhaps allows us a moment to assess the growth of the Church and the developments surrounding the rise of Christianity and its relationship with the monarchy since the first baptisms of the Anglo-Saxon kings. The more immediate and practical advantage to the king was ideological. Tying themselves close to the Church allowed kings a benefit given only to them, namely the entitlement to elevate themselves conceptually above their vassals and subjects. The Christian Church had given the secular nobility – the main landholders – certain levels of prestige, such as assurances of eternal life, safe havens for their offspring to be educated, and retirement homes for them or their widows in later life. It gave approval in the name of God for warfare against pagans, and warfare for territorial gains, but remarkably was not averse to occasionally allowing the Anglo-Saxon kings to raise arms against fellow Christians. In return, the nobility would give the clergy and their religious houses privileges in the shape of land donations or tributes in coins or goods.

Ine was a king intent on promoting his Christian ideology, and the religious devotions of his sisters Cuthburh and Cwenburh suggest that all the family were devout in their beliefs. However, his direct relationship with the papacy is difficult to assess. William of Malmesbury perhaps illuminates this point when writing about two letters sent in 693 by Pope Sergius I to Æthelred of Mercia, Aldfrith of Northumbria and Aldwulf of East Anglia, concerning Theodore's successor Berhtwald's appointment to the archbishopric at Canterbury.[25] Berhtwald was the first Anglo-Saxon-born man to hold the role, which he did for over thirty-three years. That Ine was not included among the recipients of this papal letter may indirectly show he had a lesser relationship with Rome than the other kingdoms.

For the lower classes, as expected, the choice between materialism and salvation was nuanced. By Ine's reign, the influence of Christianity among the general populace was probably still limited and it is unclear what percentage of the population were practising Christians.[26] Textual evidence shows that the Christian concept of heaven and hell and a belief in the sanctity of saints and their ability to intervene in everyday life played out alongside old beliefs such as a fear of Elves or the benefits of magical charms to cure illnesses or aid agricultural production. Such beliefs lingered for centuries, intertwining with the new religion.[27] Archaeological digs across England relating to this period have identified a steady decline in cremations, as practised by pagans, in favour of burials, as per Christianity.[28] But this fact alone is not conclusive. There was already a general trend of burials replacing cremations, and some discovered burial goods confirm a number of groups still practising paganism were choosing burial over cremation.

To relieve pressure on the Old Minster and divide the large diocese surrounding Winchester, a new foundation church with its bishopric was laid at Sherborne in Dorset in 705.[29] The church replaced a previous religious house built during Cenwealh's reign, which itself had been on the site of a former Dumnonii religious house. Ine's church would in turn be replaced in the eleventh century by the current abbey church on the site. Its first bishop was Aldhelm, who transferred from his role as abbot at Malmesbury.[30] The footprint of the eighth-century building lies to the east of the current building, with the present-day east wall likely aligned to the position of the former west wall, although nothing of Ine's original church survives above ground.

Bishop Hædde of Winchester died in 705. His replacement, Daniel, was already a close friend of Aldhelm, having been with him at Malmesbury Abbey.[31] Daniel would correspond with Bede, becoming one of his main sources of information for his *Ecclesiastical History* on events in the south. In his later work, *Gesta Pontificum Anglorum*, William of Malmesbury confirms the Old Minster and Winchester held responsibility for Hampshire and Surrey, and Sherborne assumed responsibility for Wiltshire, Dorset, Somerset, Berkshire, Devon and even Cornwall.[32] It was only after a synod at Brentford that same year that ecclesiastic control of Surrey was moved from East Saxon London to West Saxon Winchester.[33] Wilfrid's former foundation at Selsey was not assigned to Wessex or Winchester but was given its own bishopric. However, ecclesiastic responsibility did not mean political control in all cases. Ine could not claim in 705 that he had administrative or military control of much of Berkshire or Devon, let alone Cornwall.

In territorial terms, if not demographics, Aldhelm's ecclesiastic authority was much greater than Daniel's, a point highlighted by Malmesbury.[34] Within later academic circles Aldhelm's reputation as the most significant religious figure within Wessex during this period has persisted. He was reputedly the first native Anglo-Saxon to write verse in Latin.[35] There is certainly evidence that Ine and Aldhelm worked together in establishing several religious houses across Wessex throughout the 690s and 700s, including Malmesbury and Glastonbury, and the expansion at Glastonbury included Ine's agreement for it to be rebuilt in stone (completed in 712), with the original foundations believed to form the west end of the nave within the surviving ruins of the abbey. Aldhelm also has links to the houses at Bradford-on-Avon and Tetbury and another monastery alongside the River Frome, either near Frome or Wareham.[36] The Anglo-Saxon church of St Lawrence still stands in Bradford-on-Avon today, although the surviving building represents a later rebuild of Aldhelm's original church.

Aldhelm died on 25 May 709, aged about seventy, while visiting the church at Doulting, just to the east of Shepton Mallet.[37] At Sherborne he was succeeded by Forthhere. He was buried at Malmesbury Abbey, although William of Malmesbury later recorded that 'Aldhelm has always remained unhonoured, buried in undeserved obscurity'.[38] The omission was partially rectified in 2004 with the erection of a statue of Aldhelm, but at Sherborne Abbey, not Malmesbury.

Aside from the major religious houses already noted, Ine was involved in promoting sites at Wimborne, Wells, Muchelney and Bradfield. Historians generally accept he was the most effective supporter – and possibly the originator – of the process which led to the creation of an organised church across Wessex through a network of monasteries and mission stations.[39] In praising his devotion, William of Malmesbury noted that 'Ine was wisdom personified' and that 'you would never see anyone braver or know his equal in holiness'.[40] The mutual bargain between the king and Church is encapsulated within the text of Ine's charter of 704 addressed to all religious houses within Wessex, whereby he exempted them from secular burdens (primarily tax).[41] However, beyond Ine, ongoing commitments to the Church would have repercussions. It was perhaps not expected that granting increasing endowments to the Church would permanently deprive royal treasuries of some of their prospective income, limiting to varying degrees their ability to distribute land grants to their secular supporters.

As hinted at above, Ine's reign saw Anglo-Saxon missionaries beginning to journey to mainland northern Europe to convert the pagan populace. The mission would continue well beyond Ine's reign. Their more precise aim looks to have been to convert their fellow Angles and Saxons in the Germanic regions, notably but not exclusively east of the River Rhine, the region from which many of the Anglo-Saxon English had originated. There would be several notable individuals leading this crusade for Christianity. The first was Willibrord, who later became Utrecht's first bishop. Those who followed included two notable figures from Wessex, Willibald and Boniface. Willibald is believed to have been the son of a West Saxon warlord.[42] He first set out for Rome in 721, but would later become the bishop of Eichstatt in Bavaria.

Boniface was known originally as Wynfrith but was renamed by Pope Gregory III. As seen already, he was born in Devon, and first became a monk at Nursling, north-west of modern Southampton, a church which would be destroyed by Danes in 878. It was Ine, seeking to reinforce his relationship with Archbishop Berhtwald at Canterbury, who sent Boniface in 710 to be his envoy to the archbishop.[43] Boniface was later despatched to aid Willibrord but would become the most revered of the missionaries, working among the Frisian Saxons during Ine's reign. His greatest achievements would come after 725, converting pagans in Thuringia around Erfurt and Weimar in central Germany and establishing several bishoprics both there and in Bavaria before becoming archbishop of Mainz in 751. A native of Wessex he may have been, but Boniface is understandably more readily revered among German Christians, and when he died he was buried in the abbey at Fulda. Through his West Saxon roots in Exeter, Boniface was belatedly recognised and chosen as the patron saint of Devon in 2019.

Much of Ine's political and military fortunes are hidden from us. In the ASC entries between 694 and 710, the king of Wessex is given no mention. This silence from the primary sources could be viewed positively, presenting to historians the image of a period of peace, a theme touched on several times in this book. Perhaps for Ine's reign this could also be put down to economic development, the new law codes, a greater role for the Church and, importantly, similar peaceful interludes within the leadership of Wessex's near neighbours. There are twelve extant charters which Ine issued throughout his reign and a further half-dozen that bear his name as witness.[44] Even accepting the possibility of later forgeries, this amounts to more than any previous West Saxon monarch, and more than many of his successors. As might be expected, these charters mostly involved donations to religious houses rather than the secular nobility.

In 710, with the military support of his South Saxon client king Nothhelm (aka Nunna), Ine launched a new military campaign westward.[45] Some historians have suggested that this was to counteract a raid by the British Dumnonii under their warlord Geraint, whom Henry of Huntingdon titles misleadingly as the 'king of Wales'. Huntingdon describes the two forces clashing at an unnamed location, with the British 'turning their backs on the English ... abandoning their arms and spoils to their pursuers'.[46] Mention of spoils suggests a British raid across Devon, but one suggested scenario is that Ine mobilised his army in response to a Dumnonii initiative that could have advanced as far east as Langport in Somerset.[47]

Ine took full advantage of this resumption of British–West Saxon warfare. With the Dumnonii forced back towards Cornwall, he looks to have cemented the West Saxon dominance over Devon, controlling more territory across it than any king to that date. Debate remains, but the case is argued that following the victory of 710 Ine was even able to allocate to West Saxons some small parcels of land west of the River Tamar, although for how long and how successfully is unknown.[48] What seems beyond doubt is that, barring a few brief but largely unsuccessful raids by the Dumnonii, the latter period of Ine's reign saw an extensive movement of permanent West Saxon settlement along the Devon–Cornish border.

Returning to developments in Mercia, the lengthy reign of Æthelred had come to an end in 704 with his abdication to become a monk after twenty-nine years on the throne. His successor Cenred (aka Coenred), a son of Wulfhere, also abdicated and followed him into the clergy five years later.[49] Further north, Aldfrith of Northumbria, the former spouse of Ine's sister Cuthburh, had died in 704, and after a brief challenge for the throne Oswine, the son of Aldfrith and Cuthwine, became king of Northumbria. Ceolred of Mercia was poisoned in 716, but the year before he had taken a Mercian army into Wessex.[50]

Historians concur that his campaign of 715 against Wessex, breaking thirty years of peace between the two kingdoms, was initiated to redirect his internal troubles, hoping to garner support among the nobility by giving them the opportunity to gain wealth from plunder. This political strategy had been employed many times before by kings keen to preserve their popularity, including some West Saxon examples. Although numbers are unknown, Ceolred looks to have taken a substantial Mercian army south. The primary sources confirm Ine led his army to challenge the invader, and depending on how quickly we imagine his response to have been there are two favoured locations for the ensuing battle, which the ASC names as 'Woden's Barrow'.

The first, Wanborough, 2 miles east of present-day Swindon, is based on place-name association. However, this location is too far north, and would have meant Ine challenging the Mercians as soon as they had crossed the Wessex–Mercia border. It may be recalled that 'Woden's Barrow' was already the site of the battle of 592, in which Ceawlin was finally defeated and exiled by his rival and successor Ceol. Most historians favour this site for its plausibility and precedence in the debate regarding the 592 battle, and we could effectively call the 715 encounter the second battle of Woden's Barrow.

To recollect, Woden's Barrow was the former name given to the barrow/tumulus now more commonly known as Adams Grave on Walker's Hill, north of the village of Alton Priors in central Wiltshire.[51] Walker's Hill is equidistant between the Alton Barnes White Horse chalk figure and Knap Hill, lying less than a mile to the north of the village. The site aligns with a Wiltshire branch of the Great Ridgeway track, which leads towards Dorset. It is likely that large armies used this track to bypass river valleys and travel faster. If Ceolred had crossed the Wansdyke near Boreham, a few miles south-west of Marlborough, this would have been his probable route into the heart of Wessex.

Regardless of the placement, the ASC version A simply notes that 'here Ine and Ceolred fought', and secondary sources cannot agree on which army won the battle.[52] Henry of Huntingdon noted that 'the fighting was so dreadful on both sides that it is not to be known which of them suffered the more appalling slaughter'.[53] Logic suggests the Mercians came off worse; the lack of details on the Mercian campaign and Ceolred's murder by his own people the next year makes it hard to imagine otherwise. A letter from Boniface to his successor in Mercia, Aethelbald, hints at some level of Ceolred's unpopularity, describing as it does how 'after a sinful life Ceolred was struck mad by an evil spirit in the middle of a feast and so died, raging and distracted'.[54] This may have been some kind of seizure, but it could also suggest poisoning.

In 718, Ine's brother Ingeld died. The ASC notes that he 'passed away', and John of Worcester adds that he 'came to the end of his life', implying natural causes.[55] References in the ASC and in Æthelweard's *Chronicon* refer to Ingeld having a son named Eoppa, who was named as the great-grandfather of Ecgberht, a later king of Wessex.[56] As discussed in a later chapter, this bloodline connection is hard to justify. However, as Ine was to have no surviving legal heir when he died it is understandable that West Saxon chroniclers looked for a bloodline connection through Ingeld's offspring instead. Ecgberht's father has been identified as Ealhmund, who was for a brief time king of Kent during the 780s. The link at that time between Kent and Wessex is unclear. However, it was through this connection rather than through the childless Ine that Alfred the Great would later relate his ties to the Cerdicings.

In the last years of Ine's reign, two men described as æthelings, Ealdberht (aka Eadberht) and Cynewulf, made separate unsuccessful challenges for the throne. Perhaps both had connections to Ingeld, possibly through a maternal link or bloodlines of Centwine, Caedwalla or Æscwine. The possibility they were sons of Ingeld needs consideration, as Ine's relationship with his brother may have been strained. It is noticeable that within the witness lists of the charters issued by Ine his brother does not appear in a single document. The first known internal challenge came from Cynewulf in 721. Accumulated evidence suggests that West Saxon authority in Sussex had weakened, and alongside this, under their appointed new king Æthelbald (from 716), Mercia was resurgent. However, there is no reason to assume that Ine's reign had become unpopular. The sources merely record that Cynewulf was killed by Ine, but the E version of the ASC writes that 'they killed the ætheling', implying that Cynewulf's claim to the throne was based on a family connection to the West Saxon dynastic bloodline.[57]

The second challenge came from Ealdberht in 722. He looks to have exiled himself from court after denunciating Ine's rule from the apparent safety of Devon, probably hoping to raise not only West Saxon support in the region but, if the primary sources are to be accepted, from the Dumnonii and Cornovii British. Details are hazy, but the question remains: why would recently settled West Saxons in Devon choose to join Ealdberht's rebellion? The reasoning behind the Dumnonii aligning themselves behind Ealdberht is more straightforward, with the opportunity for plunder and revenge against Ine hard to resist. Ealdberht's rebel force moved quickly to seize control of the burh fort at Taunton, a fortification recently built as part of the overall military West Saxon strategy for Somerset. Archaeologists have confirmed the original burh at Taunton did not occupy the same location as the later Norman castle, the remains of which now form part of the Museum of Somerset. The burh's former location is therefore unclear, but it probably lay close to the River Tone.[58]

In response to Ealdberht, Ine sent an army westward in 722 to deal with the rebellion under the leadership of his wife, Queen Æthelburh. Historians have debated why Æthelburh was chosen. Maybe Ine was occupied elsewhere, or seriously ill, but this also reveals the confidence he had in his wife. On her arrival in Somerset, we are told she 'threw down Taunton (the fort), which Ine had built earlier', with John of Worcester adding that she 'completely destroyed' it.[59] Some historians have cast doubt on these entries. It is plausible that Ealdberht's force had already vacated Taunton before Æthelburh's arrival, and she was left, as the sources note, with the task of destroying the fort to prevent it being used as a stronghold for potential future rebellions. There is no doubt that Æthelburh had Ine's confidence, and the capability to lead a military campaign at Taunton, regardless of the fort's desertion. Specific mention of her within the primary sources, particularly the ASC, should not be underplayed. Historians acknowledge inadequacies in referencing women in primary texts. Consequently, where reference is made to women, particularly in a non-clerical context, there is greater credibility given. Æthelburh appears in the witness lists in only one of her husband's extant charters, one of the last he produced in 725 just before his abdication, but there is an argument for recognising the important standing she had in a world dominated by men.[60]

There are no other entries in the ASC regarding Ine's military operations, but we are indebted to the brief entries within the *Annales Cambriae,* which survives in three versions, with version A recording three battles between the West Saxons and the British during 721–722. The text writes of 'the battle of Hehil among the Cornish, the battle of Garth Maelog, and the battle of Pencon among the south Britons ... and the British were the victors in those three battles'.[61] Historians have concluded the last two named battles were probably encounters between the Welsh and the Mercians at unknown locations and did not involve the West Saxons. Furthermore, it is not beyond possibility that Garth Maelog and/or Pencon were direct encounters between two Welsh kingdoms or between the Welsh and the Cornish.

However, the third named battle, Hehil, is accepted as a clash between the West Saxons and the Cornish Dumnonii (as noted in the *Annales Cambriae*), and it was likely a setback for the West Saxons. The only question is identifying its location, but we lack the material evidence necessary to narrow down the options. The *Annales Cambriae* version A spells the site 'Hehil', while the others have the alternate spellings of 'Heyl' and 'Heil', all originating from the word *heyl*, the Cornish for 'estuary'.[62] The Anglo-Saxons would subsequently rename many places with original Brythonic names into Old English, so the battle site could be next to one of several estuaries across Cornwall or west Devon. There are three favoured locations for Hehil, but they are widely separated geographically.

The first of these is the village of Hele in the Culm Valley, 8 miles north-east of Exeter.[63] This site is a contender if we factor in that the encounter came soon after Æthelburh's siege at Taunton (only 20 miles north-east of Hele), perhaps including British elements that had been involved with Ealdberht's rebellion. The question remains whether Ine took command or if Æthelburh played a role in the battle. The second possible site is Hayle and the Hayle Estuary deep inside Cornwall, only 3 miles east of St Ives, a complete contradiction geographically to the Culm Valley. As a place name alone for Hehil or Heyl it is favoured by many historians, but it seems too far into the Cornish peninsula for the West Saxons to have ventured during this period.

The third potential site for Hehil is also some distance inside Cornwall, somewhere close to the River Camel, which by place-name association is a river believed to have been named the Heil.[64] From its estuary at Wadebridge the Camel (Heil) meanders across Cornwall to its source north of Bodmin Moor. However, the chosen battle location is much closer to the estuary. It is next to the river at Egloshayle, just east of Wadebridge. As the first bridge at Wadebridge was not constructed until the late Middle Ages, Egloshayle became the first secure crossing point of the Camel further inland. River crossing points such at Egloshayle were often good locations to entrap any enemy, and it could be that the West Saxon army were attacked while crossing the river there. The argument against this location, like the Hayle Estuary, it that is too far west. However, it is nearer to Devon, being less than 25 miles west of the nearest stretch of the River Tamar. The absence of any reference to Hehil in the ASC argues for a West Saxon defeat. Some historians further argue Hehil was such a major defeat it had serious repercussions for ongoing West Saxon advances in the south-west for decades. In terms of its aftermath, there were no new attempts by the kings of Wessex to launch a further full-scale assault into Cornwall until Ecgberht in the early ninth century, although possibly Cynewulf during the 760s came the closest before Ecgberht.

This also raises the question of the West Saxon occupation of western Devon and along the western fringes of the River Tamar. Place-name research has identified that the outcome of the battle impacted the varying levels of merged Saxon settlement between the north and south sections of the Cornish–Devonian border. In the northern section, 90 per cent of ongoing place names are Saxon English, while in the modern Cornish hundred bordering the Tamar in the south roughly half are still Celtic British in origin.[65] This statistic suggests that the depth and timeline of the Saxon advance across the south-west peninsula was irregular, with the number of surviving Celtic place names in the southern region inferring the British authority there lasted for much longer, This could arguably be explained by a British victory at Hehil.

Back on the eastern border of the kingdom, Ine's long-term ally Nothhelm of Sussex had died sometime after 717. He is last seen issuing a charter granting land to Selsey Abbey, a document witnessed by someone named Æthelstan who is designated as the 'King of the South Saxons'.[66] This Æthelstan seems to have acted for a while as joint king alongside Nothhelm and may have been Ine's client king thereafter. It was in Sussex that Ealdberht, the rebel from Taunton, was to suddenly resurface and raise a further rebellion after 722. Ine may have assumed direct control, but the insurrection in Sussex may have continued for the rest of his reign. The sign is that there were two or three years of difficulties in quelling rebellion in Sussex before Henry of Huntingdon and the ASC confirm that in 725 Ine defeated the South Saxons, at a battle somewhere near to Roman Stane Street between Chichester and Billingshurst, 'and there killed the ætheling Ealdberht whom he had earlier driven out'.[67]

We should perhaps consider Ealdberht's relationship with Ine more closely. Ealdberht's involvement in rebellions from the widely separate regions of Somerset and Sussex, both aimed against Ine's rule, suggests something beyond a regional insurrection. Furthermore, Æthelburh's involvement at Taunton may suggest Ealdberht was more than just a rebellious West Saxon noble. Was she first sent to act as an intermediary?[68] We might reasonably speculate that he had a kinship connection with Ine's dynastic line, perhaps a nephew of either Ine or Æthelburh through an unknown relative. His continued efforts to disrupt Ine's rule from inside Sussex using South Saxon allies between 722 and 725 implies a more personal grudge. To stretch conjecture further, maybe Ealdberht was Ine's illegitimate son, or perhaps even Æthelburh's son from an unknown earlier marriage.

That same year the long-term Kentish king Wihtred died on 23 April 725, and the throne of Kent would be shared between his three sons, primarily Eadberht I and Æthelberht II.[69] However, this transfer of Kentish power and Ine's victory over the South Saxons did not subsequently lead to any benefit for Wessex. In fact, in a sudden move reminiscent of his predecessors Centwine and Caedwalla, Ine was to abdicate the throne within the next twelve months. This choice was becoming a habit, with Ine, who was in his mid-fifties, the third consecutive king of Wessex to follow that path. Ine's abdication was accompanied by a decline in West Saxon influence due to the resurgence of Mercian involvement in the south-east that had been triggered by the Mercian king Æthelbald. The connection between the Mercian resurgence and Ine's action is unclear, but his abdication appears hasty. William of Malmesbury meanwhile relates that Æthelburh spent a lot of time persuading her husband to retire to Rome prior to his abdication.[70] They left for Rome together in the early months of 726, but Ine was to die there within the same calendar year.[71]

Perhaps Ine became ill during the journey, but a more likely reason for his death so soon after arriving in Rome, and the reason he had abdicated earlier, was that he was already terminally ill. John of Worcester confirms this when describing the trip as a 'pilgrimage ... so that he (Ine) might deserve to be received with greater friendship by the saints in heaven'.[72] In Rome, Ine lived long enough to start the first payments of 'Peter's pence', which was to become a regular tribute made by Anglo-Saxon kings to the papacy thereafter. He apparently lived long enough to found the Saxon school near St Peter's in the district of Borgo in Rome, which later became a hostelry for English visitors.[73]

Ine's lengthy reign of thirty-seven years positively impacted the development of Wessex as a kingdom, particularly in terms of state control and administration. Without demeaning the progress made by his worthy predecessors, Ine was perhaps the first in the line of West Saxon kings who can be seen as developing his kingdom in ways other than pure military success and accumulation of territory, most significantly through his promotion of his law codes and his support for a new generation of Christian mercenaries going back to Germany to convert the distant cousins of the Anglo-Saxons.

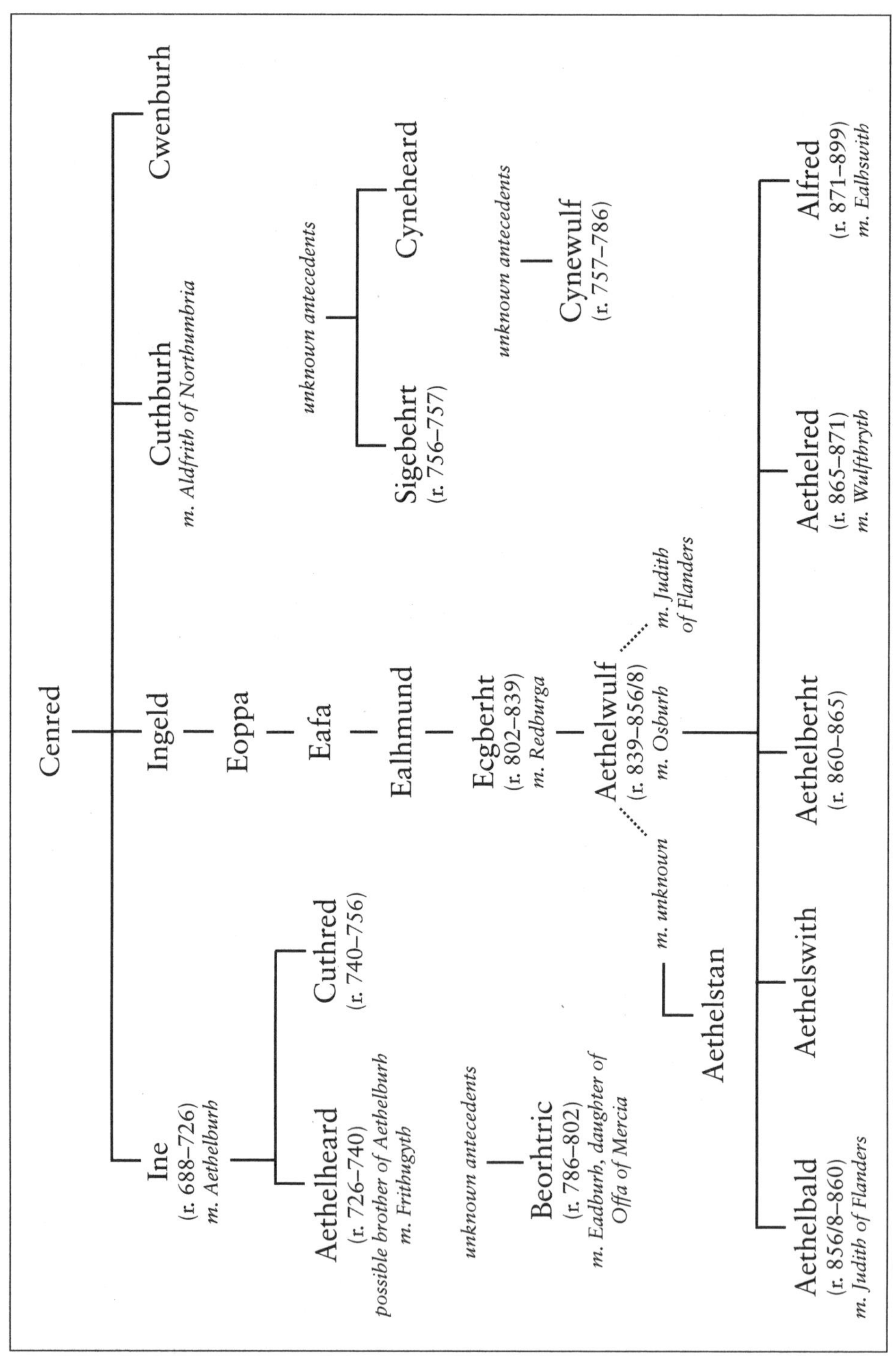

Fig. 5. West Saxon genealogy: Ine to Alfred.

10
Æthelheard and Cuthred
726–756

The heirless Ine was living out his last days in Rome while the West Saxon witan were again debating their next king. Two men, Æthelheard and Oswald, would emerge as candidates but neither of them appears to have had a convincing entitlement. Let us deal first with Æthelheard. In version E of the ASC, the scribe describes him as a 'relative' of Ine.[1] Both William of Malmesbury and Henry of Huntingdon write of him being Ine's relative, and of succeeding him by pre-arrangement on Ine's abdication.[2] Their contemporary John of Worcester simply refers to him as 'a descendant of King Cerdic'.[3] The root of this kinship connection is perhaps based on a spurious charter from Glastonbury stating that he was Queen Æthelburh's brother, making him Ine's brother-in-law, although this is not confirmed in any other contemporary document.[4] Æthelburh herself was alleged to have had a royal bloodline connection before her marriage, and if we accept Æthelheard was her brother, he did also. However, what cannot be ignored is Æthelheard's absence from the witness lists in all of Ine's extant charters; if he was a kinsman of the king, we would expect him to have signed a few.

Whatever Æthelheard's antecedents, the witan saw him as the best option to provide the smoothest transition of power, particularly if Ine's abdication had been unexpected. Various versions of the ASC differ on the timeline, but soon after his succession Æthelheard was challenged by Oswald, the other serious claimant. Interestingly, the ASC describes Oswald as an ætheling, a title the scribe did not extend to Æthelheard. Oswald is named as the son of Æthelbald, who it may be remembered from the previous chapter was one of Ine's right-hand men during his early reign. Evidence of this comes from three charters of Ine between 688 and 699 which Æthelbald witnessed with the title of 'king of part-Wessex'.[5] Furthermore, the chronicle scribe lists Oswald's antecedents through several generations, giving a bloodline chain not recognised in other primary sources but having a claimed link to the Cerdicings through Oswald's great-grandfather Cynebald, reputedly the third son of Cuthwine, who was in turn the son of Ceawlin.[6]

Despite Æthelheard's nomination, Oswald had a more rightful claim to the throne. Unlike their endeavours with other Wessex kings, later chroniclers did not try very hard to integrate Æthelheard into the West Saxon genealogical tree. Maybe Oswald was considered too young to be king; we do not know his age. But perhaps we are also looking here at a successful coup against the ætheling Oswald, whereby Æthelheard was able to seize the throne thanks to more powerful backing. We have, by the eighth century, arrived at a curious point in the West Saxon royal genealogical tree. The focus had long been on connecting the bloodline of kings to warrior kings Cerdic and Cynric. However, with that brittle connection being broken after Ine, the chroniclers somehow turned a temporary blind eye. After the ætheling Oswald's failure to succeed to the throne, and thereafter through to the accession of Alfred's grandfather Ecgberht in 802, the rulers of eighth-century Wessex were to emerge from other unknown or unidentifiable branches of the royal house.[7]

One interesting detail is that version A of the ASC conflicts with other versions, and with the WSGRL, in noting that Æthelheard assumed the throne of Wessex in 728, not 726.[8] This is a little puzzling, as version A, written at Winchester, should be more reliable on this matter than other versions. There is no obvious reason, but one possibility is that despite the witan ratifying Æthelheard's claim in 726 Oswald may have continued to challenge for the throne, and it took a further two years before his challenge ceased or was removed. The ASC version A recognises an internal power struggle, stating that Æthelheard and Oswald fought in 728, with Æthelheard winning. William of Malmesbury substantiates this scenario, describing it as Oswald's rebellion and noting that Æthelheard 'suffered much interference from Oswald, a young man of the royal blood'.[9] Oswald may therefore have hoped and waited for at least two years. He is recorded as 'passing away' in 730, perhaps during another failed attempt to seize the throne by force.[10]

Æthelheard's success against Oswald and his confirmation of the West Saxon throne may not have relied on internal support alone. Some historians have speculated instead upon the level of influence Æthelbald of Mercia may have had in the political affairs of Wessex during this period. The primary sources make no mention of his involvement, although it is a persuasive argument. The internal factional divide after Ine's abdication, whether or not it involved a clash of arms, appears to have considerably weakened Wessex militarily, allowing Mercian interference.[11] Whether this ultimately included military help for Æthelheard to have secured the throne from Oswald's challenge cannot be proven. However, Mercian involvement in the West Saxon succession at some level would remain a constant theme until the ninth century.

Æthelbald had been king of Mercia since 716, and it would appear he was determined by the mid-720s to bring Mercia back to its position of dominance over the other Anglo-Saxon kingdoms that it had held under Penda (r. 626–655), Wulfhere (r. 658–675) and Æthelred I (r. 675–704). Æthelbald would oversee a rapid surge in the political and military strength of Mercia, beginning a period of hegemony lasting through to the early ninth century that historians often label as the Mercian Supremacy. By the late 720s the position across Surrey, Sussex and Kent was ripe for Æthelbald to set out plans to expand Mercian influence back again into the south-east, something akin to the political influence the kingdom had held under Wulfhere.

In terms of the balance of power between Wessex and Mercia, we see during the late 720s a reversal in fortunes that developed quickly after Æthelheard's succession in Wessex. No direct warfare occurred between the kingdoms, but Æthelbald's expansionist plans were clear. Disrupting the West Saxon succession, and maybe militarily supporting Æthelheard, the candidate with the lesser claim to the throne, had perhaps been the first stage. In defence of Æthelheard, we might argue that he knew he could not withstand a more powerful Mercia and had sought peace and compromise. Nevertheless, Æthelbald looks to have been biding his time while he concentrated on recovering Mercian influence elsewhere.

That the new king of Wessex had accepted some form of agreement, or vassalage to the Mercian king, can be supported by confirmation of his marriage in 729 to Frithugyth, whose name denotes a Mercian background rather than a West Saxon one, suggesting a prudent political arrangement.[12] Frithugyth's name suggests dynastic links to Frithuwold, a Mercian who had acted as sub-king for Wulfhere of Mercia in Surrey, Berkshire and Buckinghamshire in the previous century, and it is possible she was the daughter of Frithuwold's son Frithuric.[13] Further confirmation of Frithugyth's relevance is that she appeared alongside her new husband that same year as a charter witness.[14] Indeed, she was to be a witness in all three of Æthelheard's extant charters, the last issued in 737, and is recorded in the ASC accompanying Bishop Forthhere of Sherborne on a pilgrimage to Rome.[15] For a queen to be so prominent within the charter lists was and would remain historically rare in the West Saxon royal court, and may indicate Mercian involvement inside Wessex.

By 730, Mercia had recovered all of Berkshire from Wessex. This was an apparently peaceful transfer of landownership with no recorded warfare, encompassing most if not all the land that had been traditionally disputed between the two kingdoms since the sixth century. This could well have been part of an arrangement or understanding between Æthelheard and Æthelbald relating to earlier Mercian support for Æthelheard's claim to the Wessex throne. Developments in the 730s would support the scenario of Mercia's dominant position, with some historians describing the king of Wessex as already a vassal to the king of Mercia.[16] To support this premise, Æthelweard appears as a witness to one of Æthelbald's charters, dated around 730, donating land to the church at Abingdon. They are the only two secular witnesses, and even though Æthelweard is given the title of 'king' in this charter, he appears below the four bishops who also witnessed the document.[17]

This charter detail acknowledges a pattern whereby over several years the Mercian king was appropriating border territories from all his neighbouring kingdoms, although Bede in his *Ecclesiastical History* perhaps excessively claims that by 731 all the kingdoms south of the Humber were 'subject to Æthelbald'.[18] There is little direct evidence of the dependency status of the other Anglo-Saxon kings at this point.[19] A further assessment of the charter evidence suggests Æthelbald was still several years from reaching the apex of his authority in the south, but he did begin to gain some traction within Kent, or certainly with the clerical community at Canterbury. After Archbishop Berhtwald's death in January 731, the Mercian king was influential in ensuring that Tatwine, a Mercian-born monk from the monastery at Breedon-on-the-Hill (in present-day Leicestershire) was awarded the archbishop a few months later.[20] Æthelbald appears to have ensured that Tatwine's consecration was a prominent affair, with several bishops attending the ceremony, including Daniel from Winchester.[21] Apart from being the second English-born man to become the figurehead of the English Church, Tatwine is perhaps best remembered for developing the culture of riddle-writing, a skill he attributed to the earlier work of Aldhelm.[22]

If Æthelheard believed that the territorial gains across Berkshire would satisfy the Mercian king he was to be disillusioned. In 733, supporting the argument for Wessex's weakened position, the Mercians launched an attack on Somerset. This was possibly a natural progression of Æthelbald extending his authority, or alternatively the Mercian king was demonstrating his strength as a reminder to Æthelheard, who may have given indications he would deviate from their earlier understanding. Primary sources refer only to the capture of Somerton, the administrative centre and a royal vill, and the regional hub of what would later become the shire of Somerset.[23] Recent archaeology has identified that the settlement had been established by the Celtic British, and was already a major West Saxon site by the 730s. Henry of Huntingdon describes Æthelbald as bringing 'a terrible army' that 'laid siege to Somerton, surrounding it with earthworks', adding that 'there was no one to bring aid to the besieged, or to withstand the besiegers'.[24] Clearly the fyrd system had broken down, or the West Saxon king had left Somerton to its fate.

The Mercian advance had gone deep into Somerset. A broad swathe of territory, including in the region around Wells and Glastonbury, had been captured. Somerton was a further 30 miles south of Glastonbury and was undoubtedly chosen because of its significance as the regional economic and administrative centre. It was perhaps a poignant reminder to Æthelheard and Wessex of Mercia's strength. There is no evidence, for example, that Glastonbury or any settlement nearer to the Mercian–West Saxon border was similarly struck. However, the Mercian army soon went back across the border, and it is unlikely that a permanent military presence was left behind, although there is an argument that after 733 the Mercians were more involved in West Saxon affairs across northern Wiltshire and eastern Somerset. This continued after the demise of Æthelheard, and we see some evidence in the form of Mercian charters from 744 and 746 donating estates to the abbot of Glastonbury and allocating land at Tockenham, near Lyneham in Wiltshire, in 757.[25]

Little is known in terms of Æthelheard's own level of devoutness, but all three of his surviving charters are concerned with donations to the Church, including one for the Old Minster (St Peter and Paul) at Winchester.[26] Another concerned land donated to build a new monastery at Crediton, which in the early tenth century would for a brief period become the primary religious house for Devon and Cornwall before relocating to Exeter. However, some uncertainty surrounds the original charter and its date of 739, as it shows the grant being awarded to Bishop Forthhere, which contradicts other primary source details stating that Forthhere had died two years beforehand. The list of witnesses on this contentious charter included Bishop Daniel of Winchester, but also Cuthred, the man who would succeed Æthelweard in 740. If we accept the document as genuine it suggests Cuthred was already influential; he signs it immediately below the king's signature, perhaps denoting he was being positioned to replace him.[27]

Beyond this meagre charter evidence, the last decade of Æthelweard's reign passes with no further primary source references. The ASC records his death, nevertheless, and depending on which version of the ASC is accepted – it seems the scribes used different calendars for the beginning and end of the year – he died sometime during the last months of 740 or in the early months of 741.[28] He had not reached middle age, but his death appears to have been through natural causes. Where he was buried is unknown.

In recording Æthelheard's death, the ASC also added that his 'relative' Cuthred succeeded to the kingdom. Here, once again, we have within the sources claims of a blood tie between the deceased king and his successor, and the Northumbrian monk and writer Symeon of Durham confirms this by naming Æthelweard and Cuthred as brothers.[29] Symeon's contemporary Henry of Huntingdon calls them kinsmen.[30] Evident from the ASC entry is the contrast to other instances where a full genealogical connection to the Cerdicings is listed. In Cuthred's case no paternal line is offered. We can speculate that in Cuthred's instance the evidence was hard to construct or so weak that even the usually imaginative writers of the late ninth-century versions of the chronicle accepted it was an impossible task. Cuthred attained the throne smoothly, and with no known rival candidate. Æthelweard may have had some awareness of his declining health, and as such all had been prepared in advance for Cuthred's peaceful succession. This is a far cry from the fraught succession processes of the seventh century. Blood ties aside, Cuthred appears to have been linked in some capacity to the royal court for some time, as he is seen low down the witness lists in an undated charter of Ine's.[31]

Following on from what looks to have been the client king role that his predecessor had inhabited relative to Æthelbald of Mercia, we can say with some reliability that Cuthred was initially willing to maintain the status quo between the two kingdoms by accepting vassalage and giving his oath to Æthelbald. However, the ASC perhaps muddies the waters a little, as linked to his entry confirming Cuthred's succession the scribe adds that Cuthred 'boldly made war against King Æthelbald'.[32] There is little evidence that Cuthred initially resisted vassalage to the Mercian king, and the more probable explanation is that the scribe had erred in dating this additional remark. It more reasonably relates instead to Cuthred's 750s push to regain full West Saxon autonomy from Mercian interference, as discussed in due course.

How long the state of vassalage continued during Cuthred's kingship is difficult to assess. For 743–744 the primary sources, including John of Worcester and Henry of Huntingdon, record that Cuthred was called upon by Æthelbald to bring West Saxon troops and accompany him on his military campaign into Wales.[33] This has generally been interpreted as evidence of Æthelbald calling upon Cuthred to meet his oath of vassalage and obligation, whereas some historians have interpreted it as one ally calling for the assistance of another. Henry of Huntingdon elaborated on the military cooperation between the two kings on this campaign, writing effusively that they 'joined forces and fought against an innumerable host of Britons gathered from all parts', whereby 'their illustrious armies split up, and cut through the Britons at different points, overthrowing them eagerly'.[34] This gives the impression of a major conflict, maybe a prominent British incursion rather than a Mercian initiative. Perhaps this was within Gloucestershire – Mercian Hwicce territory – which would better support the involvement of West Saxon forces. Alternately, or perhaps additionally, there was conflict on the Powys–Mercian border, as it has been speculated that it was shortly after this that Æthelbald began construction of the defensive earthwork known as Wat's Dyke, to the west of the later construction of the northern section of Offa's Dyke, running along the border with Powys from Shropshire to the Dee estuary.

Whether as ally or vassal, Cuthred's military involvement in 743–744 appears to have been a turning point in his and Wessex's relationship with Mercia. Some historians point first to a charter from Æthelbald concerning a land transfer to Glastonbury Abbey soon after the campaign which was witnessed by Cuthred, although this looks to be an erroneous link to another individual of the same name.[35] A more appropriate discussion should centre around how Æthelbald had potentially over-committed himself on too many fronts. By the mid to late 740s the Mercians were involved in not just warfare against the Welsh along much of their western border but also in attempts to recover footholds in the south-east. Bede's claim at this point that all of England south of the Humber was 'subject to Æthelbald' still seems exaggerated.[36]

Æthelbald of Mercia had reached the peak of his powers by 748–749. In 746 he had quelled a potential revolt by Essex, killing the East Saxon king Selred (aka Saelred), who had ruled Essex since 709 alongside his brother Swæfberht until the latter's death in 738.[37] Selred was replaced by a Mercian-approved East Saxon client king, Swithred, and it was during this period, as witnessed in Kentish charters, that the transition of London from East Saxon control to Mercian control was completed. However, Mercian successes elsewhere were limited. Contemporary documents suggest that by the mid-740s Kent and Sussex were self-ruling, and for the latter this meant full autonomy also from Wessex.

Beyond politics, the charter evidence indicates that Cuthred had a positive relationship with the Church, unlike Æthelbald of Mercia. News of Æthelbald's vices spread to Boniface in Germany, so much so that in 746 he and several other bishops signed a letter to the Mercian king reproaching him for his behaviour, which apparently included stealing ecclesiastic revenue, violating church privileges, imposing forced labour on the clergy and fornicating with nuns.[38] By all accounts Æthelbald heeded the criticisms. He attended and presided over a council in 747 at Clovesho, the location of which is now lost, where the council focused on relations between the Church and the secular world. The council condemned excesses by the clergy and limited relations between monks and laymen, ruling that secular activities were impermissible for monks.[39] In 749, Æthelbald issued a charter freeing Church lands from all obligations except the requirement to build forts and bridges.[40] This charter was witnessed by Mercian bishops only, but may reflect the situation more widely across the other kingdoms, and could be part of a reform programme agreed at Clovesho.[41]

With Mercia looking in several directions simultaneously, an opportunity was emerging for Cuthred to regain West Saxon independence. However, this looks to have been a slow process. At some stage Cuthred may have formally rejected any oath he may have given to Æthelbald and declared autonomy for Wessex. Mercia's initial response was to recover its dominance by force, and there may have been intermittent fighting into the early 750s. Henry of Huntingdon seems informed on Cuthred's reign, which may infer that he had access at the time to material that other chroniclers had not seen. Huntingdon writes that 'Æthelbald ... often harassed him ... sometimes through rebellions and sometimes by wars', which may describe the Mercian king's immediate actions to pull Cuthred fully back under his authority. The chronicler then adds that 'changeable fortune exalted them by turns in their military engagements', where they would 'agree peace between them which they would maintain for a short time, and then they would wage war afresh'.[42]

The turning tide of power was clear in 752, when Cuthred launched his own invasion into Mercian territory. However, before detailing that campaign we should first look at developments inside Wessex. There is no evidence Cuthred produced an updated version of Ine's law codes, but we should assume they were still in operation. In terms of extant charters there are only four issued in his name during the sixteen years of his reign, two from 745 and two from 749.[43] As expected, they all concern land donations to the Church, much like charters from other kings of the period, further acknowledging the power the Church seems to have held over the monarchy during much of the eighth century.

One of Cuthred's charters from 745 illustrates the typical construction of these documents. As given in William of Malmesbury's *Gesta Regum Anglorum*, this charter gifted land to Glastonbury Abbey, demonstrating the standard interaction between king and Church and the monarch's commitment to it. Written in the king's name, it records that 'confirmed as it is with the subscription of my own hand (i.e. Cuthred) and the sign of the Cross, shall endure for ever approved and ratified, as I hereby decree', and adds, 'The text of this deed of gift was published in the monastery aforesaid in the presence of King Cuthred, and he with his own generous hand laid it upon the high altar.'[44] These sections acknowledge such donations to religious houses were usually if not always made with the king in attendance at a formal signing, with the whole process closely tied to church doctrine and solemn ceremony. Only in later generations is there surviving evidence of royal donations to the senior nobility, but despite lack of evidence, we should assume that grants to the nobility were also enacted by Cuthred and his contemporaries to garner secular support. Perhaps the greater frequency of the survival of charters relating to clerical grants can be understood more clearly when we acknowledge it was often the religious houses or clerics working for the king that were charged with writing them – and, equally importantly, storing them.

While the faces on the thrones came and went, the leading clerics remained in place, detached from all political and military affairs, seemingly safer in their positions than the kings themselves. A case in point was Bishop Daniel of Winchester, who resigned his position to take up retirement at Malmesbury Abbey in 744 after thirty-three years in the role. For the kings of Wessex, only Ine (thirty-eight years, 688–726) and Ecgberht (thirty-seven years, 802–839) can boast similar tenures. In 721, Daniel was among the few who undertook a pilgrimage to Rome. He had also had a hand in appointing and encouraging Boniface to pursue his preaching assignments in Germany and had been one of the correspondents from whom Bede had gathered details of southern events for his *Ecclesiastical History*. Generations later, conflict would arise between Malmesbury and the Old Minster in Winchester over the site of Daniel's tomb. William of Malmesbury backed his own abbey's claim, but could only acknowledge that Daniel was 'said to have been buried there'. Meanwhile, he tries to discredit Winchester's claim when he notes that 'the monks of Winchester claim that his (Daniel) burial place is in their church, but they cannot point to either his real or supposed tomb' – a somewhat disingenuous comment bearing in mind his own abbey's claim rests on a similar shortage of evidence.[45]

Cuthred would experience in 748 and 750 two internal challenges to his rule. We cannot rule out Mercian political or even military involvement in either of them, in much the same way as Æthelbald's probable involvement in the succession of Æthelheard to the West Saxon throne. The first challenge came from an individual named Cynric, whom Henry of Huntingdon describes as 'his (Cuthred's) son ... tender in years but active in war', but who, 'trusting too much in the fortunes of war ... met a violent death in a military uprising, the punishment for his unrestrained character'.[46] The ASC only records that 'Cynric, ætheling of Wessex, was killed'.[47] Whether we should accept, as Huntingdon has done, that Cynric the ætheling was Cuthred's son is perhaps assuming too much. Cuthred's wife is unknown and no primary source names a son. Perhaps Cynric could be a relative of Æthelheard's family.

The second challenge to Cuthred's kingship, and potentially the more serious one, came in 750. It was not from a claim of entitlement but from one of the king's senior nobles, an ealdorman named Æthelhun. The ASC scribe describes him as 'the arrogant ealdorman', while John of Worcester simply calls him 'vigorous'.[48] However, it is Henry of Huntingdon who gives us the most detail, as frequently seen during this period, although the source of his information remains unclear. Huntingdon describes Æthelhun as 'audacious' and says he 'stirred up rebellion ... although in number his troops were far inferior to his lord's'. Despite this, he 'held the field of battle for a long while', with the chronicler adding that Æthelhun's 'high courage was worth thousands of soldiers'.[49] The uprising was quelled only when Æthelhun sustained a serious wound.

The chronicler Æthelweard informs us that the dispute developed 'because of some ill-will in state affairs'.[50] This hints at growing discontent with Cuthred's rule, maybe because he had not taken a strong enough stance against Mercia to that point. More directly, Æthelhun may have represented the original factional support that had gathered behind Cynric's rebellion of two years earlier. Mercian involvement cannot be dismissed. Historians have interpreted the two rebellions in various ways, but the most persuasive thread is dissatisfaction among some of the nobility with Cuthred's continued stance towards Mercia. In hindsight, these internal rebellions may have motivated Cuthred to change direction, committing thereafter to lead his kingdom into direct conflict with Æthelbald.

Whatever Æthelhun's motives in 750, he was, according to the primary sources, allowed back into Cuthred's inner circle soon afterwards and would play a significant part in the important battle that took place two years later between Wessex and Mercia known as Beorhford or Beorgford. The widely accepted view among historians, supported by later archaeology, is that Beorhford relates to Burford in Oxfordshire. Burford is roughly 20 miles north of modern Swindon and overlooks the River Windrush, a tributary of the River Thames about 10 miles north of the larger river, therefore some considerable distance inside Mercia based on the realigned West Saxon–Mercian border as it stood in 752. The location is key. It supports the premise that Cuthred was the aggressor and had taken his army well inside Mercian territory before the Mercians came to challenge him. The numbers involved are uncertain, but probably significant, maybe 2,000 or 3,000 on each side.

Henry of Huntingdon's *Historia Anglorum* provides the most detailed record of events not shared by his contemporaries, again taken from source material otherwise now lost.[51] Huntingdon tells us Æthelbald's Mercian army was supplemented by contingents from Kent, Essex and East Anglia. This raises the question of how the Mercian military system had operated and would continue to do so. Mercian control beyond its own border in vassal states must have involved a degree of military presence, although with manpower at a premium, this was not in the sense of military occupation. Anglo-Saxon vassal kings were often called upon to assist their lord-king on major military campaigns. Given Beorhford's location, it is unrealistic to believe that Mercia could have quickly summoned support from Kent or Essex to confront Cuthred. Taking Henry of Huntingdon's observation that Æthelbald's army had outside conscripts, we should instead contemplate that a system of vassal conscription was already operating in Mercia, whereby detachments of troops from regions under the umbrella of a Mercian alliance or vassal status were already based within Mercia and attached to Mercian units. The effectiveness of these outside troops on the battlefield is questionable.

Present-day Burford lies on a north–south route now known as the Jurassic Way, which runs south on the modern A361 road from Banbury before crossing the River Windrush at Burford and continuing towards the Thames at Lechlade. About 2 miles south of the Windrush it is crossed by the Roman Akeman Street. Cuthred's line of approach to Burford was therefore most probably via a crossing of the Thames at Lechlade, then marching north and then eastward along Akeman Street. The local topography at Beorhford (Burford) seems to have played an important role. Æthelbald likely approached via the Fosse Way before turning south at Stow-on-the-Wold. There is a steep incline south of the Windrush, as the road continues south through Burford, where it rises about 40 metres in less than 400 metres. From what is known it seems that Cuthred positioned his troops some way back from the Windrush to take advantage of the topography and benefit from the rising ground.

The *Historia Anglorum* supplies by far the most detail for the battle. Huntingdon writes that after crossing the river Æthelbald's battle lines marched forward. Æthelhun of Wessex, contrary to some dubious secondary misinterpretations which place him fighting for Mercia, led Cuthred's forces bearing the king's banner, the golden dragon. Huntingdon relates that Æthelhun 'pierced through the enemy standard-bearer's body' with his banner.[52] This reference to a 'golden dragon', or the beast known as a wyvern, is the first mention of a dragon as a central feature of the king of Wessex's standard within the surviving primary sources. It would be referenced again during the reign of Alfred, and later Edmund Ironside (c. 1016), and again as part of Harold Godwinsson's standard at the battle of Hastings in 1066. Some observe, therefore, that the Anglo-Saxon kings' first use of a golden dragon symbol predates the Welsh red dragon by several centuries.[53] The wyvern symbol has resurfaced in more recent times, with a golden wyvern appearing within the idealised flag of Wessex.

Huntingdon, apparently delighting in elaborating on his description of the encounter, tells us the Mercians were 'urged on by swelling passion of pride', with the men of Wessex 'roused up by the horror of servitude'.[54] The main fighting is believed to have occurred at Burford's 'Battle-Edge', according to historians. This site is now occupied by later development but lies south of Sheep Street and east of Tanners Lane on the west side of Burford High Street. Battle Edge sits at the summit of about a 1-in-10 incline 300 metres south of the Windrush. The Mercians and their allies would have been fighting uphill with their backs to the river. As for Æthelbald, he may have ignored this strategic disadvantage in the urgency to oust this major invasion from his kingdom.

Huntingdon writes of Æthelhun and Æthelbald killing all around them before coming to blows and taking injuries. However, as his men fought on Æthelbald was the first to take flight. The outcome was a decisive West Saxon victory, the ASC noting that Cuthred 'put him (Æthelbald) to flight'.[55] Huntingdon goes on to state that the outcome 'would decide whether it would be the Mercians or men of Wessex who would be subject to the victors long into the future'.[56] This was not exactly accurate. Wessex celebrated a famous victory, and there would be no more clashes with Mercia until the 770s. However, the twelfth-century chronicler may have written in anticipation of the known fortunes of Wessex and Mercia in the late ninth century, rather than the eighth-century reality.

The defeat was a significant blow to Æthelbald's prestige, losing him face not only within his vassal kingdoms but more importantly within

Mercia. For Wessex, the victory at Beorhford won back its autonomy and freedom from Mercian influences, the first time perhaps it could fully claim this since Ine's rule. However, Cuthred was not strong enough, militarily or economically, to engage in a protracted war against Mercia, and not all the territory previously lost was recovered. Mercia's grip on parts of northern Wiltshire and parts of Berkshire, for example, although weakened, would remain for now.

In terms of the battle site, a later local tradition expounded first by Victorian historians linked the battle to a stone coffin found by workmen in 1814 a mile to the west of Burford.[57] The coffin was removed and the base of it lies now in the churchyard at St John the Baptist in Burford alongside another stone coffin, with some proposing that either may be related to the tomb of Ealdorman Æthelhun. Unfortunately, archaeologists have convincingly disproved this tradition. The base is Roman, not Anglo-Saxon, and the other coffin is not older than the twelfth century.

After Beorhford, as considered in the following chapter, Wessex would be free of Mercian interference for the next twenty-five years. More immediately, an ASC entry for 753 describes Cuthred then fighting against the Welsh, whom John of Worcester describes as 'Britons'.[58] Whether this was an aggressive campaign or a response to a raiding army is unclear. We can interpret the 'Welsh' or 'Britons' here to be the Dumnonii in the south-west, which contemporaries sometimes called the 'southern Welsh', in contrast to the native tribes and kingdoms in Wales itself, with which Wessex had no direct border.

This was to be Cuthred's last recorded action. In 756 we are told that 'here Cuthred passed away', implying he died of natural causes.[59] Like his predecessor, there is no detail of where he was buried. William of Malmesbury's summed up Cuthred's kingship by writing that he 'devoted great efforts to a prolonged and victorious campaign against the Mercian king Æthelbald and the Britons', which is close enough to the facts.[60] Henry of Huntingdon uses more florid language, noting that 'Cuthred, the great and exalted king, who had enjoyed so much prosperity and victory, ended his earthly joy in the mercy of death'.[61] Like several of his predecessors Cuthred did not, and could not, nominate an heir. There is insufficient detail available, but he either had no legitimate sons eligible as potential successors or was childless. Nevertheless, there is one further caveat. We cannot dismiss the notion that the ætheling Cynric, the leader of the failed rebellion against Cuthred who was killed in 748, was his son, a relationship which was only acknowledged by Henry of Huntingdon among the primary sources.[62]

11
Sigeberht and Cynewulf
756–786

Cuthred's successor was a man named Sigeberht. Versions A and E of the ASC both record that he 'succeeded to the kingdom of Wessex' but notably only version E (the Peterborough text) and not version A (the Winchester text) adds that Sigeberht was 'his (Cuthred's) relative'.[1] However, there are no primary source texts that build a connection between Sigeberht and the Cerdicings. How close a relative he was to Cuthred is undefined. Sigeberht had no antecedence to claim he was a son, brother or nephew of his predecessor, and at best we can extend the idea he may have been a second cousin of Cuthred (sharing a great-grandparent), or possibly a third cousin (sharing a great-great-grandparent).

Sigeberht's nomination appears to have been through witan majority approval, and as noted in a contemporary document he 'received the sceptre of his kingdom'.[2] William of Malmesbury recorded Sigeberht had seized the throne, describing him as 'a monster of cruelty at home and a byword for cowardice abroad'.[3] We might see this entry as giving a general comment on Sigeberht's perceived character (more of which below), rather than a sign he had seized the throne from any unknown rival. There is no obvious evidence of a hostile coup or Sigeberht being a usurper. Presumably he had sufficient backing from within the witan. The etymology of Sigeberht's name, which roughly translates to 'magnificent victory' – in hindsight perhaps an irony – implies an Anglian not Saxon background, more precisely a Mercian or East Anglian association.[4]

Cuthred's death had come only one year before the death of Æthelbald of Mercia, who was to be assassinated in 757 by his own people at his royal estate at Seckington, 4 miles north-east of Tamworth. Æthelbald's murder supports a likely downturn in Mercia's fortunes during his final years that had stemmed from his defeat to Cuthred at Beorhford.[5] Some historians still favour some level of Mercian influence in political events inside Wessex during the brief period between the deaths of the two kings, particularly Sigeberht's direct nomination for the throne of Wessex.[6]

Perhaps the best argument for Mercian involvement in Sigeberht's succession comes from the timing of Æthelbald's removal and Sigeberht's own stint on the throne of Wessex. Is it a coincidence that following regime change in Mercia in 757 the West Saxon witan immediately removed Sigeberht from power? A change of regime in Mercia would have normally given any king of Wessex, particularly a recently appointed one, valuable time to reinforce his political and military standing within his kingdom – on this occasion even more so, because Mercia would be plunged into its own internal struggle upon Æthelbald's murder. However, in Sigeberht's case the opposite looks to have happened.

Within Mercia there was a brief period of civil war. Initially a noble named Beornred took the throne, but only a few months later he was removed and it was seized by Offa, the great-great-great-grandson of Eowa, Penda's brother.[7] The immediate impact was a continued but short-term decline in Mercian power. In that brief period some territory would be recovered by Wessex, and Mercian control in the south-east was lost, with the sub-kingdoms of the Hwicce (Gloucestershire–Worcestershire) and Lindsey (Lincolnshire) also making bids for self-autonomy. Arguably, as already considered, Sigeberht's hold on Wessex may have rested on the parallel fortunes of Æthelbald's, and he would not receive such similar backing from Offa.

Sigeberht's reign lasted little more than a year. Consequently, nothing is known about him. There is only one extant document of his that survives, in which he granted a small parcel of land to the abbot of Glastonbury in exchange for a payment of fifty gold coins (*solidi*).[8] Thereafter, his support and popularity quickly declined. Henry of Huntingdon, taking detail from earlier sources, writes on Sigeberht's character that he was 'puffed up and arrogant ... and intolerable to his own men'. Huntingdon then adds that Sigeberht's noble ealdorman Cumbra had urged him, while he was still king, to change his ways and to 'rule the people according to the laws ... and put away his cruelty', and to 'be seen to be beloved of God and men'.[9] This advice went unheeded.

We are soon informed that in 757 'Cynewulf and the councillors of Wessex', meaning all the witan were in full agreement, deprived Sigeberht of his kingdom 'because of unlawful actions'.[10] John of Worcester, with information taken and extended from the original chronicles, adds without specifics that 'the West Saxon nobles drove their king Sigeberht from the kingdom because of the great number of evil deeds he had committed'.[11] As discussed earlier, Sigeberht's removal came after Offa had seized power in Mercia, supporting the premise his kingship had been closely tied to events there. Continuing this line of debate, we might see Cynewulf as the West Saxon candidate who had been deprived of an earlier chance to stake his own claim, which he was only able to pursue when Sigeberht's Mercian sponsorship had fragmented. Alternately, perhaps matters were much more straightforward, and Sigeberht was simply a poor ruler who needed removing as soon as possible.

Having devoted efforts to linking Sigeberht's fortunes to the former Mercian regime, we might advocate an alternate scenario. We do not know precisely when or how soon Sigeberht was removed from power after Æthelbald's demise and the ongoing Mercian civil war. We could speculate that he was deposed before and not after the Mercian king's murder, and it is plausible that one of Æthelbald's last acts, as the opposite to supporting Sigeberht, was to assist Cynewulf in seizing the West Saxon throne. Similarly, with the timeline of events perhaps flexible, maybe the new Mercian king, Offa, helped to remove Sigeberht and assisted Cynewulf's succession; perhaps *he* was the Mercian-backed candidate. In the end, there is insufficient detail available. All this speculation and hyperbole assumes that Mercia had a level of influence in West Saxon political affairs after Cuthred's death that may stretch beyond the likely reality.

Cynewulf's sudden emergence into power requires its own assessment. The chronicler Æthelweard suggests a military coup took place, and in his *Chronicon Æthelweardi* he writes Cynewulf had 'invaded his (Sigeberht's) realm and took it from him' and 'drew the witan of Wessex with him'.[12] To 'invade' implies outside support, so are we again being drawn towards Mercian involvement? What we know is that Cynewulf appears as a witness entitled 'king of the West Saxons' in Æthelbald of Mercia's last charter before his death. Mercia's involvement in the placements of Sigeberht and Cynewulf in quick succession is a perverse possibility. Alternatively, it may have always been Cynewulf, not Sigeberht, who was preferred from a Mercian standpoint.[13] Potentially we have a fluctuating situation suggesting that Cuthred's last years as king after his victory at Beorhford were not as stable as previously assumed.

One suggestion is that Cynewulf was in one form or another a bloodline descendant of Cenwealh.[14] Any link to the previous West Saxon royal line, or any of the former dynasties, looks unsound. That Cynewulf was to be buried in the Old Minster in Winchester, founded by Cenwealh, where he would be one of only a select handful of West Saxon kings prior to the tenth century to be given that honour, is nevertheless strong support for Cynewulf having some accepted contemporary kinship connection to the line of Cenwealh.

Whether Cynewulf's claim for kingship had been supported by Mercia or not, events within Mercia thereafter would allow Cynewulf the space and time to establish his full authority across Wessex. It would be another twenty years before Mercia, in the shape of Offa, undertook new military action against Wessex. In that period Cynewulf was able to regather territory piecemeal and reestablish the West Saxon–Mercian border along the upper reaches of the River Thames. The problem for Cynewulf was not external but internal. Sigeberht had been deposed from power but not from Wessex. With his nomination and position on the throne secured in 757 Cynewulf sought compromise. His first action, presumably to avoid further conflict, was to cede the deposed Sigeberht control of Hampshire.[15] This is an unusual postscript to Sigeberht's removal, and some historians argue it indicates a weakness in Cynewulf's claim to the throne.[16] Others could argue it was a good political move if Sigeberht still held significant support and remained a potential threat.

A different slant on these events was added by William of Malmesbury. With detail gathered from an unknown contemporary source, he relates that 'the greatness of his (Sigeberht's) fall regained him some supporters', and 'thanks to their valour the region known as Hampshire was not lost to his service'.[17] This claim that Sigeberht kept all of Hampshire is almost certainly misleading, but it implies he held some territory there by strength of arms rather than any gift from Cynewulf. Furthermore, it may also suggest that Cynewulf's original power base had emanated from Berkshire and the Thames Valley. A more fitting appraisal is that Sigeberht preserved some authority of a smaller area, and if we are looking for a specific connection perhaps we can link him to south-east Hampshire and the descendants of the Meonwara Jutes. Our earlier contention that Sigeberht was an Angle not a Saxon could be adapted, with the possibility he was of Jutish extraction.

Sigeberht may have had some cause for grievance that is hidden from us, but whatever support remained to him quickly evaporated. Perhaps showing a character flaw that had prompted his earlier removal from the throne, he is recorded killing Cumbra, the last of the ealdormen to have remained loyal to him.[18] As a consequence Sigeberht was banished by Cynewulf and was driven east into the Andredsweald forest of Sussex. Within weeks he returned to Hampshire to try and gather supporters once more. He was then hunted down by Cynewulf himself, according to John of Worcester. However, before the king had located Sigeberht's whereabouts it was a herdsman avenging the death of ealdorman Cumbra who was to stab the former king to death by a stream at Privett, a village 5 miles north-west of Petersfield.[19] There is no longer a stream at Privett, although the road that runs through the centre of the village is named Merepond Lane, recalling the former watercourse. That a herdsman was Sigeberht's slayer may be true, but its inclusion in the record may also reflect a moral message, one primary source relating that the ex-king had been 'brought to a stand by the lowest of the low'.[20]

Cynewulf now began a long reign of twenty-nine years. The immediate benefit for Wessex was the recovery of territory, with the West Saxon king moving into both east and west Berkshire, recovering West Saxon land that had been under Mercian authority since the reign of Ine. This is evidenced in a charter dated to 760 regarding Cynewulf taking ownership of the monastery at Cookham, lying alongside the Thames to the east of Marlow, which had been under the ownership of Christ Church, Canterbury.[21] This appears to have been followed up by further action along the south bank of the Thames in part of Oxfordshire in which the West Saxons took repossession of the original Gewisse foundation church at Dorchester-on-Thames, plus land in western Oxfordshire.[22]

Offa's strength was to grow during this period but he did not directly confront these issues, choosing instead during the 760s and 770s to recapture Mercian authority in the kingdoms of the south-east that Mercia had held at various times under his predecessors. The death in 762 of Æthelberht II, king of Kent, gave Offa an opening there, and although on the face of it Ecgberht II of Kent (r. 764–779) ruled Kent thereafter it was probably based on some agreement with Offa. A charter from Offa donating land in Kent near Rochester implies inroads had already been made by 764 and evidence from Sussex suggests Mercia was contesting control over the South Saxons again no later than 770.[23] Elsewhere, charter evidence, for example at Pyrton near Watlington and at Wealdstone, shows that Offa had gained control of the north bank of the central reach of the River Thames as far as London.[24] In addition, he would launch a military campaign into East Anglia soon after. In terms of the West Saxon king, all of this ensured that Offa's eye was directed away from Wessex for a considerable period.

In contrast, a new charter from Cynewulf granting land to Bath Abbey on an estate four miles north of Bath shows the West Saxon king had kept or regained some authority within north Somerset.[25] This particular charter, dated to 758, perhaps betrays the political situation between Cynewulf and Offa more clearly during the first full year of both their reigns. Cynewulf's charter bears Offa's name among the witness list, the implication here being that in signing Cynewulf's charter the Mercian king had accepted the fully independent status of Wessex, a situation which looks to have continued into the 770s. As observed by several historians, in general terms there is no evidence that Cynewulf ever acknowledged Offa as his overlord throughout his reign.[26] This is an interesting conclusion if we hold with the potential scenario that he had been originally assisted into power by Offa.

Wessex had previously used periods of peace with its Anglo-Saxon neighbours to expand its strength further westwards into the south-west peninsula, and this time was no different. Although lightly documented among the primary sources, we know Cynewulf conducted more than one major campaign against the Dumnonii and their allies the Cornovii, with the ASC recording that 'Cynewulf often fought great battles against the Britons'.[27] Knowing where these encounters took place is another matter. A charter from Cynewulf from the 760s, a document whose pre-eminence is not completely assured, refers to his remorse for the 'severities (he) inflicted against the Cornish (Cornovii)'.[28] We must assume this took place within eastern Cornwall, even though it is doubtful that any further West Saxon settlement beyond the River Tamar came of it. The timetable of West Saxon control beyond the Tamar continues to pose questions, as we have discussed briefly already. Despite having settled in western Devon in large numbers by the eighth century, they were not yet strong enough to prevent raids from the Dumnonii, which would continue into the early ninth century.

Cynewulf is the subject of curiously few primary source references despite the longevity of his reign. The ASC, as an example, lacks entries for most of his two-decade rule, but what this tells us precisely is unclear. Some have argued that this shows that except for his under-recorded conflict with the Dumnonii, and the passive recovery of territory from Mercia while Offa was occupied elsewhere, Wessex was generally at peace. In terms of Cynewulf's surviving charters, only six are extant and verified as genuine, although we can assume there had been others that have not survived.[29]

Like his royal contemporaries, his charters are dominated by donations to senior clerics or land transfers to religious houses. Cynewulf's commitment to the major religious houses is clear, with grants given to Sherborne, Malmesbury, Wells, Muchelney and Bath, although curiously none have survived for the house at Glastonbury. Only one relates to a land grant to a secular noble, despite this process being an important function which ensured that the king maintained his personal popularity among his senior nobility. We are left to speculate that there may have been more word-of-mouth agreements than presupposed, or that the documents concerning secular grants were in many instances not copied and kept as a matter of course alongside the parallel clerical grants within the religious establishments.

In 772, Cynewulf appeared alongside King Ecgberht II of Kent as witness, not a vassal, in one of Offa's charters transferring land at Bexhill in Sussex to the church at Selsey.[30] An entry from a surprising quarter, the work of Symeon of Durham, refers to a military victory by Mercia over the South Saxons that had taken place the previous year, with the Bexhill charter being formal recognition of Offa's newly established authority in the region.[31] Aside from Cynewulf and Ecgberht, several senior clergy, including Jænberht of Canterbury and the bishops of Rochester, London, Selsey and Leicester, were also witnesses, as were at least five of the Mercian senior nobility. The South Saxons Oswald, Osmund, Oslac and Ælfwald, each of whom may have previously shared the title of joint king during the 760s, also witnessed this charter. But the fact they were named only as '*Dux* (Duke) of the South Saxons' denotes their already reduced position and their vassalage to Offa.[32]

In hindsight, this event would mark the end of Sussex as an independent kingdom. There were to be no more kings of Sussex and the South Saxons thereafter. When Mercia eventually relinquished its authority in the region it would be replaced in the ninth century by a resurgent Wessex. As for Kent, their king Ecgberht II looks to have also ceded territory in some capacity to Offa, but continued to hold Kentish lands east of the River Medway. Ecgberht may have already shared the Kentish throne or assigned regions of influence to a contemporary named Heahberht. It's hard to determine the duration of this arrangement due to unclear sources on Heahberht, but he did issue his own charter in 765.[33]

Further charter evidence confirms that Offa had gained authority west of the Medway by 774.[34] A dispute would break out between him and Ecgberht when the latter granted lands to the Bishop of Rochester without apparently asking the Mercian king's permission. In reality, Offa used this as a pretext to launch a military campaign to remove Ecgberht, something that he had already been planning. However, the sources dispute the timeline of events. The ASC version A dates it to 773, and version E to 774, the year that John of Worcester also accepted. However, in further contrast Henry of Huntingdon places it in 776.[35] Most historians accept Huntingdon's dating in this instance, supported also by Ecgberht's extant charters.

Regarding the campaign itself, the Mercian army reached the River Darent, a Kentish tributary of the River Thames, at Otford, just north of present-day Sevenoaks, before they were challenged. Otford lies about 12 miles south of the Thames, and with the river being much wider in the eighth century than today Otford was the best crossing point of the Darent south of Roman Watling Street (the modern A2). However, Ecgberht's forces, with Heahberht likely alongside, had already covered the ford crossing at Otford before Offa's much larger and slower army arrived. When the Mercians attempted a crossing, the Kentish army won the ensuing battle. Speculation suggests the Mercians numbered over 3,000, with the Kentish army possibly half that size.[36]

Despite Henry of Huntingdon arguing the contrary – declaring that 'Offa emerged victorious', which seems puzzling – the facts in hindsight and the political developments that followed confirm Otford was a Kentish victory.[37] Subsequent charters issued by Ecgberht between 778 and 779 were made without Offa's approval, denoting his continued independence.[38] The Mercian king's conquest of Kent would be delayed until 785, but his later invasion of Kent would bring him into contact with the early career of another Ecgberht, the man who would in 802 take the throne of Wessex.

Following his failed invasion of Kent, Offa returned north and turned his attention to his border with Wales. This period probably saw the major construction phase – although perhaps not the beginnings – of the awesome embankment-and-ditch earthwork project which we now know as Offa's Dyke. This earthwork construction would eventually stretch along the whole length of the defined border between Mercia and the Welsh kingdoms. At the time of its completion it was a physical representation of Offa's power. Over time, agriculture and development have caused the loss of many sections. Long sectors of the dyke still survive today, although large sections of the surviving embankments have been considerably eroded and there has been infill along much of the ditch.

By 779, Offa was able to turn his attention towards Wessex. His initial aim was to recover the territory that the West Saxons had themselves recovered from Mercia along the Upper Thames Valley. This area, once the tribal heartland of the Gewisse, frequently changed hands between Mercia and Wessex. Between the seventh to ninth centuries, control of this region generally determined which of the two kingdoms were dominant, and in the main it was Mercia. Cynewulf appears to have been warned of Offa's impending campaign, but perhaps before he could muster sufficient men to defend his kingdom he was forced into a major battle along the River Thames. According to William of Malmesbury's *Gesta Pontificum Anglorum*, the Mercian attack was directed at the outlying West Saxon royal vill of Bensington, now known as Benson, lying on the Oxfordshire bank of the River Thames 2 miles north of present-day Wallingford.[39] It had been an early settlement of the Atrebates. Malmesbury's *Gesta Regum Anglorum* states that Cynewulf 'suffered heavy losses' there, which we could speculate may have reached several hundred.[40] John of Worcester adds – oddly, since Benson was at that time in West Saxon hands – that the Mercians 'held the town'.[41]

As evidenced by later extant documents, the outcome of the battle would have implications along the whole of the border between the two kingdoms. The later parish connections of Benson with Nettlebed and Henley-on-Thames infers the Mercians thereafter took possession of land towards Reading, although there is no reference either way to know if Offa controlled Reading at this juncture. However, later in that same year Cookham on the River Thames, just north of Maidenhead, also changed hands back to Mercian authority. William of Malmesbury adds that Offa seized a very large area of land from the West Saxons, recording that the Mercians plundered West Saxon territory as far as Purton and Tetbury.[42] Purton lies just to the west of present-day Swindon, about 32 miles in a direct line from Benson, and Tetbury is a further 13 miles west of Purton.

That Tetbury is described as a West Saxon possession being plundered by Offa implies that over the previous two decades Wessex had taken not just Mercian land in Berkshire and part of Oxfordshire but also Hwicce territory, formerly Mercian. This suggests a transference of territory during the 760s and 770s not readily addressed in the primary sources, indicating that Cynewulf might have enjoyed unexpected successes over Offa hitherto hidden from us.

After the battle Offa took an unspecified number of estates from the revised borderland with Wessex, not just former Hwicce territory but also south of the River Avon in Somerset. Offa's campaign reclaimed much of it, stretching from Tetbury in the west to Cookham in the east. This was a much wider landgrab than otherwise implied by reference to Bensington (Benson) alone, so perhaps Offa's army was large enough for him to divide his forces in two as the campaign expanded. His gains also included Bath. During 781, his control around Bath is acknowledged in a charter whereby Heathured, described as the 'bishop of the Hwicce', had to relinquish to Offa the minster at Bath and some land surrounding it in exchange for land at Stratford-on-Avon.[43] The seizure of Bath Minster was symbolic, as the Church had previously purchased the land at Bath from Cynewulf.

Historians have debated whether Offa exercised meaningful overlordship over Wessex soon after these gains.[44] West Saxon territory had been lost, but the evidence suggests not. There is no sign Cynewulf gave vassalage to Mercia, no extant document indicating he submitted to Offa. However, he looks to have been concerned to ensure he suffered no further losses. On the ground, an argument has been put by archaeologists that Cynewulf may have reinforced the Wansdyke earthworks across Somerset and Wiltshire around this period to help prevent further Mercian incursion. There is evidence of late eighth-century work on some sections of the Wansdyke running through the centre of known earlier seventh-century parish boundaries, implying that Cynewulf had felt the need to further underpin these defences.[45]

Historians are satisfied in claiming that Mercia had assumed full control of London by the 780s, although the documentary support for this is limited. However, this would have allowed Offa to look again towards Kent, his focus moving away from London and Wessex towards unfinished business in the south-east. The opening in Kent occurred due to a regime change there. Debate continues over who held power and for how long across east and west Kent after 776, and some historians have also included Sussex in this discussion.[46] The favoured assumption is that Ecgberht II held the kingship but that Heahberht may have acted as sub-king. Whether this extended up to the mid-780s is unclear. His last known dateable charter came in the year 779, although there is another charter donating land to the Bishop of Rochester which cannot be verified beyond it being written sometime between 779 and 784.[47]

It has been presumed that Offa had authority in Sussex during this time, but this does not consider his defeat to Kent in 776. Ecgberht II died sometime before 784, as did Heahberht, and a new king of Kent had emerged in the form of Ealhmund. This gave Offa another opportunity, and Ealhmund's reign in Kent lasted only a year before he was ousted by the Mercian king. During his short rule he issued a single charter, granting land at Reculver, but he did not have the opportunity to mint his own coins.[48] There was no repeat of the Kentish victory at Otford, and Offa may have come with a larger Mercian army behind him. Offa would have then assigned an ealdorman, possibly a Mercian, as sub-king to run affairs. This is where the ealdormanry became critical, as the still primitive forms of government required kings to delegate some responsibility and to rely on ealdormen and senior nobles to implement royal power on their behalf at a regional level.

Offa's first charter relating to Kent came the same year. The following year, another assigned lands to the abbess of Lyminge and her brother around Canterbury and at Ruckinge, 6 miles south of Ashford.[49] The witness lists are striking as they are loaded with important signatories, including Jænberht, archbishop of Canterbury, along with nine other bishops and four Mercian ealdormen. Having been present for the first Sussex charter, Cynewulf of Wessex was not present on this occasion although Cyneberht, the bishop of Winchester, was in attendance. The significance of these two Kentish charters to Offa is evidenced in them being witnessed by his wife Cynethryth and his son Ecgfrith.

Possession of Kent brought with it economic advantages Offa had already experienced upon gaining London. He desired control over Kent and its ports for the valuable trade and income that came with it to expand his empire. Trade with the continent was becoming ever more important, and this is clear in the increased production and distribution of coinage and the further rise of the specialised trading bases known as *wics* along the southern and eastern coasts and along the major rivers.[50] Control of Kent gave Offa even wider access to trade with continental Europe. He had increased silver supplies, and presumably also moneyers around this time, and soon after Ealhmund's expulsion in 785 a new Kentish mint was in operation.[51]

The removal of Ealhmund may not seem exceptionally significant in terms of Wessex, but he would become an important figure in West Saxon history. Most versions of the ASC in 784 are silent, but in version F (the Canterbury manuscript) the scribe notes that 'King Ealhmund was Ecgberht's father'.[52] This refers to none less than the future West Saxon king Ecgberht, the grandfather of Alfred, leaving us with more questions than answers as to how this connection to West Saxon royal genealogy fits into the known history. The version F entry is illuminating in that the father–son link from Ealhmund to Ecgberht was not part of the original entry for that year, but was added instead in the manuscript's margin by another hand sometime later, possibly during the tenth or eleventh century. We should therefore ask whether this later modification was by a Kentish scribe wishing to convey that Ecgberht was of Kentish not West Saxon blood. Also, perhaps more relevantly for the historiography of Wessex, we should wonder whether West Saxon chroniclers involved in justifying Ecgberht's background had instead chosen to augment the entry.

What happened to Ealhmund is unclear, but taking himself into exile in Francia or Flanders seems likely. Ecgberht (the future king of Wessex) probably accompanied his father, although some historians have suggested that he may have first sought sanctuary at the court of Cynewulf. This could go some way towards explaining Ecgberht's future connection to the West Saxon succession, and in parallel, despite his apparent Kentish roots, keeping alive the possibility that Ecgberht's father Ealhmund had blood ties to Wessex, if not through the male line then perhaps through his unknown wife's kinsmen.

Although religion is often seen as a sideshow to the ongoing political power struggles during this period, the papacy in Rome was becoming concerned that constant internal Anglo-Saxon warfare was affecting the further expansion of the Christian message across England. With a remit of assessing the state of Christianity across the kingdoms, and charged with renewing the faith and reporting their findings back to him, Pope Adrian I despatched two envoys to England during 786: George, bishop of Ostia, and Theophylact, bishop of Todi. This shows how deeply aligned the Anglo-Saxon kings and those in power had become with the wider Christian world.

The details of their visit and their findings have survived, although it is sometimes confused with another important synod held the following year.[53] The legates first met with Archbishop Jænberht at Canterbury, before moving on to attend a meeting at Offa's court, possibly at Chelsea, a council which was also attended by Cynewulf.[54] After then visiting the Northumbrian king Ælfwald I, the two bishops returned south and laid out their findings. They listed twenty regulations (canons), concerning both religious and secular affairs, that they expected and required each of the Anglo-Saxon kings to adopt.[55] Both Cynewulf and Offa promised they would make needful reforms, and we can imagine Ælfwald similarly complied. Cynewulf offered to promote the Christian message across Wessex, and Offa additionally vowed that he would donate 365 *mancuses*

(1 *mancus* = 30 pence) each year to Rome in thanksgiving to St Peter. The contribution agreed by Cynewulf is unknown.

Cynewulf's meeting alongside Offa with the papal legates had barely concluded when he faced what seems to be the first real signs of resistance to his reign since he claimed the kingship. Opposition of sorts would appear to have coalesced around Cyneheard, the brother of the former king Sigeberht. William of Malmesbury records that Cynewulf, 'menaced as he was by the growing power of Sigeberht's brother Cyneheard ... compelled him to leave the province', although the chronicler then adds that Cyneheard thought it best to disguise his feelings and 'left as though of his own accord' while planning vengeance on the king.[56] This could be interpreted as the king attempting to force Cyneheard into an oath of allegiance that was met with refusal.

Cyneheard would return soon enough, but before considering subsequent events we should look further into the premise that he was without doubt the former king Sigeberht's brother. If he was, he must either have been considerably younger than his deceased brother or was already past his prime by 786. In contrast, the events described below suggest he was still young enough in 786 to fight hand-to-hand, as was Cynewulf.

John of Worcester refers to Cyneheard as an ætheling, so it is clear Worcester believed he had a right to the throne through his sibling connection to the regnal line.[57] More historians than not consider it out of the question Cyneheard was ever Cynewulf's designated heir.[58] However, if his motivation to remove Cynewulf was feud revenge for his brother Sigeberht, it begs the question what Cyneheard had been doing for the previous twenty years. Some historians have argued, although none of the primary sources follow their argument, that the name association of Cyneheard and Cynewulf suggests Cyneheard was more likely to be the king's younger brother rather than a sibling of his predecessor Sigeberht. This is a persuasive argument, but it is difficult to speculate beyond the primary source detail.

The ASC scribes describe what next took place during 786. The chronicle not only records it but, compared to the normal entries, supplies an inordinate amount of detail. However, rather than finding this detail in the chronology for the year 786, it appears the ASC scribes erred when collating their available information as recognised by historians, erroneously placing their comprehensive entry under 757, the year in which Cynewulf replaced Sigeberht on the throne, rather than in 786.[59] There is no obvious explanation why such an error was made.

Cyneheard's whereabouts during Cynewulf's reign in Wessex are unclear, but it's probable that he was outside the kingdom for most if not all of that period. He may have only just returned when the king made the pre-emptive decision to exile him, which suggests that Cynewulf saw him as a serious potential problem. The ASC fully details what happened next.[60] Cyneheard either sought pardon or instead planned to confront the king. He seized his opportunity when he discovered that the king had gone with an unnamed woman to a hall at a place named Merton, accompanied by only a small retinue of bodyguards. This has usually been further interpreted as an illicit liaison, working on the chronicler Æthelweard's later translation from Old English into Latin, where he interpreted the source entry bluntly as Cynewulf 'staying with a certain loose woman'.[61] Some historians have questioned Æthelweard's original translation, and have proposed instead that the woman in question may have in fact been Cynewulf's own wife.[62]

Locating Merton (aka Merantun) has remained an open debate. One historian has proposed the village of Merton, 3 miles south of modern Bicester, although this lay in what was then Mercia and can be easily dismissed.[63] Henry of Huntingdon names it as being 'Meretun', possibly the village of Marten on the Wiltshire–Hampshire boundary. This is a much more likely spot, and it is also the claimed site of two other battles, including the later clash between King Æthelred I of Wessex and the Vikings in 871.[64]

Æthelweard, John of Worcester and William of Malmesbury provide the greatest detail for what next took place.[65] To summarise and combine their various version of the events, Cyneheard had gathered men and upon arrival immediately laid siege to Cynewulf at the hall at Merton (Meretun). Following a short stand-off, Cynewulf emerged and challenged him. The two men, both presumed to be middle-aged, fought one another, with the king very nearly killing the ætheling. However, Cyneheard's men joined the fight and the king was killed. According to the sources, the outnumbered thegns who comprised the king's retinue refused money from Cyneheard to join him and so were also despatched.[66] In no apparent haste to leave the scene, the ætheling and his men were still at Merton the following morning when news of the king's death reached the nearby ealdorman Osric and his thegn Wigfrith. They arrived in force, killing Cyneheard and, according to the ASC, all eighty-four of his supporters.[67]. Why Cyneheard had not fled the scene after killing Cynewulf is difficult to comprehend.

The West Saxon king would be taken for burial to the Old Minster at Winchester, but perhaps the most intriguing later aspect of this event is what became of Cyneheard's corpse. There are two versions of his later burial based on the research of local historians, although there is no present-day surviving evidence for either claim. The initial claim is for Axminster in Devon. It was at the junction of two significant Roman roads and housed an ancient West Saxon monastery in the eighth century.[68] The second is at Repton Abbey in Derbyshire, where it is claimed from research during the Victorian period that 'Cyneheard, brother of the king of the West Saxons' was buried within the monastery.[69]

The site at Repton would go on to become an important mausoleum for a few Mercian kings in the ninth century. If we accept Cyneheard was Sigeberht's brother and they were both West Saxon, a burial in Devon seems in order. However, if we prefer the claim for Repton it opens up further questions on whether the brothers may have been Mercian or half-Mercian, and beyond that whether Cynewulf also had Mercian connections – after all, the chronicler Æthelweard had noted that Cynewulf 'invaded' Wessex and 'took it from him (Sigeberht)'.

Returning to the original concept of Cynewulf having replaced Sigeberht with putative Mercian support for the latter, we could speculate that Cyneheard had been employed by Offa to kill Cynewulf. The choice of Cynewulf's successor may lend some credence to this scenario. Certainly the West Saxon witan's promotion of Beorhtric to the throne, along with the possibility that Cyneheard's body was brought back to Mercia for burial, suggests that Offa's fingerprints may be found on these events.[70]

However, in terms of the royal succession, on Cynewulf's death the witan may have had even greater limitations than many of their predecessors. There was no royal heir, but there was also no possibility of a bloodline connection via a brother, nephew or cousin of the deceased king available for consideration. Maybe in 786 we finally reach the moment when the thin and stretchy thread to the Cerdicings of the sixth century can no longer be maintained, despite claims made by the ASC scribes of the late ninth century concerning Ecgberht's bloodline connections to Ine's brother Ingeld. Beorhtric's accession came about because, once again, there was no royal heir to be pushed forward as a candidate. We could speculate Offa was fully aware of this, and rather than seek war against Wessex he had looked at other ways of achieving his aims. Beorhtric's reign would be evidence itself that he was closely aligned to Offa and Mercia.

As noted above, Cynewulf was buried at the Old Minster. His remains form part of the collection of bones, along with those of Cynegils, Æthelwulf and Ecgberht, that have been held in mortuary chests within the present-day Norman cathedral at Winchester, where they were transferred after the Old Minster was dismantled in the late eleventh century. The story of Cynewulf and the other remains has been covered in our chapter on Cynegils, and will be revisited briefly in our discussion of Ecgberht.

12
Beorhtric
786–802

Beorhtric (aka Brihtric) succeeded to the throne of Wessex just as King Offa of Mercia was approaching the pinnacle of his power. The involvement of Mercia in West Saxon affairs during Beorhtric's reign will be looked at shortly, but we can claim that, among the Anglo-Saxon kingdoms, by the late 780s only Northumbria appears to have remained free of Mercian interference. However, Northumbria had internal problems of its own making due to the factional interests within its two divisions of Deira and Bernicia. After the murder of King Oswulf in 759, a further seven kings were to rule Northumbria during the fullness of Offa's reign (r. 757–796); of them, one would be murdered and a further four deposed or exiled. Nevertheless, Offa eventually saw an opportunity to entangle himself in the dynastic power struggle of his northern neighbour. In 792 he arranged for his daughter Ælfflaed to marry Æthelred I of Northumbria. The marriage ultimately did not benefit Offa politically in the region as much as he may have hoped, and there is no hint Mercia gained a stronger foothold inside Northumbria.[1]

Some historians have viewed Offa's political machinations – and, to an extent, his military domination – as an early attempt to forge an Anglo-Saxon English nation-state. However, the consensus is that any discussion of a unified England in the eighth century is very premature and not worthwhile.[2] Instead, Offa has been described as emulating the authority that the Frankish king Charlemagne held on continental Europe, although Charlemagne's empire dwarfed the territory Offa controlled. Ultimately, we might conclude Offa had a driven and compulsive personality; why else attempt to involve himself in Northumbrian affairs when he was already influential in every other corner of the Anglo-Saxon kingdoms?

For Wessex, whether the heirless Cynewulf would have named Beorhtric as his successor is perhaps irrelevant. It is unclear how Beorhtric was nominated and approved by the witan. However, there is no obvious evidence of usurpation or hostile takeover, as seen in other power transitions in Wessex. The primary sources do not name any other potential nominees, although one would emerge to challenge Beorhtric in due course. However, in terms of Beorhtric's succession, and in contrast to what we have already discussed, the ASC scribe once again relies on familiar rhetoric, noting on his appointment that his 'direct paternal line goes back to Cerdic'.[3] From all known genealogy links and primary texts, no data can safely support this claim. The chronicle scribes seem to have surpassed even some of their more dubious previously claimed connections to the Cerdicings. William of Malmesbury, not typically a commentator on bloodline connections, is at odds here with the ASC, and perhaps tells the truth of it when remarking that 'Brihtric (Beorhtric) himself and other kings since Ine, although boasting proud lineage as descendants of Cerdic, had diverged considerably from the direct line of the blood royal'.[4]

Beorhtric's name translates as 'magnificent ruler', and in hindsight this was not well chosen. In the end, there is more than a hint of Offa's hand in Beorhtric's succession. From their subsequent dealings, it would appear that the new West Saxon king was very much aligned with Mercia. Wessex's level of autonomy during Beorhtric's reign is therefore debatable, although there is no obvious reference to this within the ASC. It may be reasonable to consider that in return for avoiding any serious military conflict or overarching political interference from Mercia the new king was resigned to the role of a vassal client king under Offa's auspices.

William of Malmesbury gives us a further insight into Beorhtric's character. He describes him as 'a man more devoted to peace than war, an adept at making friends, smooth with foreigners', but then adds that the new king was 'willing to wink at the conduct of his household, at any rate when the force of his rule was not affected'.[5] This conjures up unusual images, but in summary, it would appear that he was perhaps a weaker and more vacillating ruler than most of his illustrious West Saxon predecessors. Certainly, the new West Saxon king appears completely tied into Offa's sphere of influence by 789, when he agreed to a political alliance through marriage to Eadburh, one of Offa's daughters.[6]

Beorhtric may have also been drawn into Offa's attempts to gain greater purchase over Canterbury and its archbishopric in order to advance Mercia's position in its interactions with the Church. An important and 'contentious' council was held at Chelsea in 787 (not to be confused with the council of 786 attended by the papal legates already discussed). At this 787 council, by order of Offa, Archbishop Jænberht of Canterbury was relinquished from his spiritual responsibility for Mercia and a new archbishopric for Mercia was created at Lichfield, with Hygeberht being appointed as its first archbishop.[7] The witness list for this council is not available to us, but due to its significance it was, we assume, attended by all the senior clergy and the key secular nobility. Beorhtric would have been one of the client kings involved in this. The Lichfield archbishopric lasted only until Offa's death. Afterwards, Pope Leo III would reduce Lichfield to its former status. However, the council of 787 was also notable for a ceremony in which Offa's son Ecgfrith was consecrated (by Hygeberht) as king of Mercia.[8] This was not to replace Offa, who did not die until 796, but was rather to guarantee Ecgfrith's succession to the Mercian throne after his father. It is the first known example of the formal consecration of a king in Anglo-Saxon England, a concept that Offa seems to have taken from the Franks.[9]

As for the West Saxons, the primary sources imply that a potential challenger to Beorhtric's throne surfaced in the first twelve months of his reign in the shape of the young ætheling named Ecgberht, perhaps aged only twelve or thirteen. As discussed in the preceding chapter, Ecgberht was the son of Ealhmund, the recently exiled king of Kent. Ecgberht's entitlement to the Wessex throne will be assessed in detail later, but Beorhtric's actions suggest some legitimacy in Ecgberht's claim for Wessex. That he was a serious challenger to replace Beorhtric as early as 787, however, or even that he had anything like sufficient backing to do so, seems difficult to accept.

William of Malmesbury writes that Beorhtric soon forced the young Ecgberht into exile in Francia because it was Ecgberht 'whom he feared as the most effective obstacle to his own advancement'.[10] Malmesbury makes no mention of Offa having been concerned over Ecgberht. In fact he initially casts Offa as Ecgberht's protector, acknowledging that Ecgberht realised Beorhtric had plans to remove him and that Offa had given him sanctuary at the Mercian court. We should perhaps accept this version of events with caution, although Malmesbury does further add that Beorhtric was soon made aware of Ecgberht's location and sent a mission to Offa demanding that the 'fugitive should be handed over for punishment, and tendering the price set on his head'.[11]

Establishing the full truth of what took place is virtually impossible. It is hard to accept that Offa acted as Ecgberht's protector when Beorhtric was already in effect Mercia's vassal sub-king in Wessex. Considering this argument, the Mercian king had no reason to harbour the young pretender. In accepting Malmesbury's version of events is it also logical to argue that Offa would have been more concerned with Ecgberht's potential claims upon the Kentish throne rather than upon already vassaled Wessex. For this reason, Offa may have logically preferred for Ecgberht to be speedily removed. In contrast and contradiction, Beorhtric had no reason to be concerned with a Kentish ætheling challenging his rule of Wessex, and likely only became involved when asked by Offa to help detain Ecgberht. Offa and Beorhtric may have had different reasons to view Ecgberht as a future threat. The key to determining who saw him as a greater threat lies in the reliability of his claimed connections to the thrones of Kent and Wessex.

Ecgberht was able to evade both men. By 789, he was known to have been at Charlemagne's court in Francia. Maybe he initially joined his exiled father, although what became of Ealhmund is unclear. In either scenario, Ecgberht faced a long exile from England. Henry of Huntingdon notes that the ætheling was at Charlemagne's court for only three years, but this timeframe should be regarded with scepticism.[12] A charter issued by Offa in 793 supposedly containing Ecgberht's signature among the witnesses suggests his presence in England that year, but this would seem unlikely in view of earlier events, and we can logically discredit it as a probable forgery.[13]

Talk of Ecgberht being a future threat to Beorhtric would appear to be overblown as things stood around 789–790. However, the relationship the young ætheling was able to establish with Charlemagne during his period of exile would prove more than useful to him when he finally returned to England. Ecgberht had joined several other exiles from Kent who had escaped Offa's clutches, including Eadberht Praen, who would return to England after Offa's death. Hoping to nullify any remaining threat, the Mercian king sought an agreement with Charlemagne to return all the exiles to England, including Ecgberht. However, this request had come at a time when the previously amicable relationship between Offa and Charlemagne was deteriorating.

The cooling of their friendship arose in 789, when the Frankish king proposed the betrothal of his son Charles to one of Offa's daughters.[14] Somewhat surprisingly, the Mercian king refused the proposal unless Charlemagne in turn agreed that his daughter Bertha would marry Offa's own son and heir, Ecgfrith. Perhaps predictably, Charlemagne declined the counter-proposal, and further demonstrated his displeasure by closing off all trade from Francia to the ports across south-east England that were under Offa's authority. Charlemagne refused all further requests from Offa to return the English exiles, and it would be several years before relations between Mercia and Francia returned to normal.

This rift may have been more impactful on a wider scale than is appreciated. Although the cross-movement of goods, culture and ideas with the continent had been flowing for many decades, it has been propounded that during Charlemagne's early reign (768–814) the exchange of goods and ideas gained a new intensity and brought Britain into its closest perennial contact with continental Europe since the fall of the Roman Empire.[15] If trade in the ports of Wessex was similarly impacted by Charlemagne's ban – and the likelihood is it was – this forced Beorhtric for a period to tie himself and Wessex's economy even closer to Offa.

It was during this period that Beorhtric's marriage to Offa's daughter Eadburh took place. Henry of Huntingdon notes the king was 'exalted in pride', although as seen in due course the marriage was not one made in heaven.[16] In any case, 789 would be remembered by later chroniclers for something much more relevant to the future of the Anglo-Saxon kingdoms than a marriage alliance between Wessex and Mercia.

In that year, if the primary sources are accepted, Beorhtric was confronted with the first recorded appearance of Vikings on the shores of England. Version A of the ASC describes how 'there came for the first time three ships', adding with hindsight that 'those were the first ships of the Danish men which sought out the land of the English race'.[17] The assumption they were Danish was followed by John of Worcester, but they could equally have been Norwegian or Frisian rather than Danish.[18] The scribes for versions B to F inclusive described them as 'Northmen', and versions E and F even more specifically as originating from Hordaland, the district in Hardanger Fjord in Norway.[19]

The three ships landed in Wessex near Portland, possibly at Chesil Beach. This location, halfway down the English Channel, implies the small group had perhaps sailed across from Frisia or northern Francia rather than directly from Scandinavia. They were unlikely to have sailed from Normandy, unless as traders or raiders, as during the late eighth century that region was still held by the kings of Francia. It would be another 120 years before the Franks ceded land in present-day Normandy to the Viking leader Rollo. More immediately, it was four years before the more infamous Viking attack on the abbey at Lindisfarne, lying on Holy Island off the coast of Northumbria.

Primary sources offer detailed accounts of the 789 landing in Portland. Having been advised of their arrival, the local reeve, a man named Beaduheard according to the chronicler Æthelweard, rode from Dorchester to meet the Viking party.[20] Not knowing who they were, but assuming they were traders, the reeve attempted to get them to follow him back to Dorchester, but perhaps due to some confusion with his meaning or the language used a fight developed in which the newcomers killed Beaduheard and his men. Strangely, the ASC scribe seems to excuse the actions of the Vikings to some degree, recording that because the reeve assumed 'the arrivals to be merchants ... he spoke to them haughtily'.[21] This almost apologetic explanation, written in the late ninth century, betrays how the clerical scribes would react to later Viking raids. John of Worcester, writing sixty years after the end of the Viking age, uses similar rhetoric, noting that the reeve 'endeavoured to drive them against their will', while William of Malmesbury, also writing in retrospect, adds that they were 'a pirate tribe of Danes, accustomed to live by rapine ... and threw the province into confusion'.[22]

Although disconcerting, the 789 episode was confined to a small part of Dorset. Compared to the historical and ongoing internal warfare the Anglo-Saxon kingdoms had experienced, it barely registered among the West Saxon population at large. It was highlighted by the sources only in the context of future Viking interactions across England. It was also not the immediate prelude to continuous and concerted Viking raids across Wessex, despite the tribulations that the kingdoms – Northumbria in particular – would experience at their hands over the next generation. It took time for the full extent of the Viking threat to become clear.

The first raid with wider significance for Wessex happened in the later years of Ecgberht's reign in 835, when historical records mention a landing in Sheppey, Kent.[23] As seen in the later chapters, these landings would be the prelude to a prolonged series of assaults throughout all the Anglo-Saxon kingdoms by Viking pirates, and then later by Scandinavian armies of invasion, during the ninth century. However, happily for Beorhtric and late eighth-century Wessex there were no more recorded landings during his reign, and across Wessex in general there would be what can best be described as a lull before larger raids developed during the 830s and through into the 850s and beyond.

One way of characterising how much Beorhtric was under his father-in-law's influence is by assessing the coinage in circulation across Wessex during Beorhtric's reign. Finds of coins from this period have been limited but there is widespread evidence that Offa's coins were in wide distribution across Wessex, including in finds as far south as Wareham. This would suggest there were some limitations applied upon the West Saxon king, but a handful of surviving coins minted by Beorhtric have survived, although it is unclear whether these came from the mint at Winchester or Hamtun.[24]

The overall relationship between Beorhtric and Offa was perhaps more nuanced, with some historians arguing for a greater level of independence for Beorhtric than the coinage and other factors would infer. These historians argue we are in danger of viewing all events through the lens of assumed and continuous Mercian pre-eminence, that famed 'Mercian Supremacy'.[25]

One other way of looking into the level of vassalage could be through the extant charters. Here we have a contrast with the evidence inferred from the unearthed coinage. Only three charters issued by Beorhtric are extant; two are for land in Hampshire and one for land in Somerset, the latest of which is dated to 801 and includes the signature of the king's wife, Eadburh.[26] The other two, dated to 794 or earlier, ahead of Offa's death, do not bear the Mercian king's name in the witness lists. This interestingly implies a greater level of independence from Offa's influence than might be assumed. All three concern donations of land to members of the West Saxon nobility and none to the clergy, which is perhaps unexpected but might suggest Beorhtric was more concerned with maintaining his secular support than finding it necessary to placate the Church.

In turning to Offa's own charters and the witness lists we find that of his forty-four extant charters only fourteen can be dated to the period when Beorhtric ruled in Wessex. Of these fourteen, none relate to any estates within the traditional boundaries of Wessex and Beorhtric does not appear as a witness in any of them. This, along with the other detail mentioned earlier, implies Beorhtric's increased independence. On the other hand, though it is a weaker argument, a suggestion can be made that he was so tied within Offa's circle he did not need a reconfirmation of vassalage. It is useful to compare this data to the situation following Offa's death in June 796 and to the brief five-month reign (July–December 796) of Offa's son Ecgfrith as king of Mercia. Beorhtric witnessed two of the four extant charters from Ecgfrith's reign, and both of them were for land along the Mercian–West Saxon border, namely at Bath and at Purton (north-west of modern Swindon).[27] That both these sites were disputed and referred to after Offa's campaign of 779, as discussed in the previous chapter, could imply Beorhtric had recovered some freedom of action. Maybe the young Ecgfrith had transferred some authority back to the West Saxon king in that region after his father's death, showing us a different relationship developed between Beorhtric and Mercia after Offa's death.

Following the deaths of both Offa and Ecgfrith in less than six months, during which time England also experienced a great famine, it took some time for the new Mercian king, Cenwulf (aka Coenwulf), to re-establish Mercian supremacy. In that interlude, Beorhtric looks to have established and exercised a greater level of independence than he had hitherto.[28] Numismatists have assessed that Beorhtric's extant coins, discussed above, are more likely than not to have been minted after Offa's death. In this brief period, it has been further suggested that Beorhtric could have encouraged the rebellion in Kent against Mercia, facilitating the brief reign there of Eadberht Praen.[29] Maybe he saw Eadberht Praen as another way of guaranteeing that the ætheling Ecgberht would find it difficult to reestablish himself if he returned from exile.

However, any involvement in Kentish affairs may have paradoxically worked against Beorhtric. Offa's death not only opened the door for Eadberht Praen and the other Kentish exiles but also the exiled Ecgberht. If anything, Eadberht Praen's return had benefitted the ætheling. They had been closely acquainted at Charlemagne's Aachen court, and one suggestion is that the two exiles were blood-related, possibly cousins.[30] However, Eadberht Praen's period in power was short; he was to survive for just two years before Cenwulf of Mercia recovered Mercian control of Kent.[31]

Ecgberht's position during this period remains obscure. Reviewing the few surviving coins that were minted in Kent during Eadberht Praen's rulership by a moneyer named Babba, who had also produced coins for Offa and would later do the same for Cenwulf, we find a surviving handful that are stamped on the obverse 'Ecgberht Rex'.[32] Numismatists believe this is a reference to the subsequent king of Wessex (post-802), but it is not clear whether we can claim Ecgberht had also gained some authority in Kent as joint king before that alongside Eadberht Praen.

Eadberht Praen's end came when Cenwulf's campaign of 798 recovered Mercian authority across not only Kent but Surrey, Essex and Sussex. Cenwulf's brother Cuthred was installed in Kent as sub-king, and as an example to others Eadberht Praen was paraded in Mercia as a captive and had his eyes put out and his hands cut off.[33] If Ecgberht had been in Kent, which is implied, he was able to escape back to Francia, where he likely remained in exile until surfacing again in 802. For Wessex, Cenwulf may have tried to replicate the arrangement that had existed between the two kingdoms under Offa. However, it is not clear on what level Cenwulf and Beorhtric were to interact.

It is entirely plausible some accord was made between them which has not survived. Some historians claim that a charter from Cenwulf dated from 799 refers to a formal peace agreement between Mercia and Wessex, although this is far from convincing.[34] Nevertheless, there are no instances of Beorhtric witnessing any of Cenwulf's charters. In addition, in terms of a new form of West Saxon–Mercian concord, we should also not discount Beorhtric's wife Eadburh and her status as Offa's daughter, which permitted the former political alliance and connection between the two kingdoms to continue while Beorhtric remained king. Whether she had a greater influence on the political stance of her husband than is evident from the primary sources is unclear, as are her thoughts on Cenwulf succeeding her brother Ecgfrith.

Beorhtric was to die during 802 in unusual circumstances, apparently from poisoning, as considered shortly. However, in the sixteen years that he held the throne of Wessex there is only one reference to him (his marriage to Eadburh) within the ASC prior to the entry regarding his death.[35] The chronicle scribes simply recorded that Beorhtric 'passed away', and some later writers, Henry of Huntingdon for example, also make no mention of it. Lack of detail is more than compensated for by Alfred the Great's biographer Asser in the late ninth century, and Huntingdon's contemporaries, the early twelfth-century chroniclers William of Malmesbury and John of Worcester. They each provide us with good detail of the events that reputedly surround Beorhtric's demise – including the involvement of his wife.[36]

Eadburh was herself an important figure. She is seen witnessing charters issued by her father, brother and husband.[37] Later chroniclers portrayed her as discontented and troublesome, although there is no surviving contemporary primary source which supports this characterisation. She may have disapproved of her husband's approach towards Mercia after her father's death, but the first we hear of her poor character is from Asser, monk and later bishop at Sherborne, nearly a hundred years after Beorhtric's death. Asser writes of Eadburh in his *Life of Alfred* that 'as soon as she had won the king's friendship ... she began to behave like a tyrant after the manner of her father (Offa), to loathe every man whom Beorhtric liked, to do all things hateful to God and men', and to 'denounce all those whom she could before the king'.[38] This portrayal was repeated almost word for word within the works of both William of Malmesbury and John of Worcester.[39]

Asser states that if Eadburh could not remove a person from the king's court by trickery she would resort to poisoning them, and it was this that allegedly led to Beorhtric's death. According to Asser, Eadburh had tried ineffectively to denounce 'a certain young man very dear to the king', and when that had failed she tried to poison him. However, unfortunately, 'King Beorhtric himself is said to have taken some of the poison unawares she had intended to give it not to him ... but the king took it first, and died as a result'.[40]

It is again from Asser that we learn that the West Saxons thereafter, following Eadburh's actions, 'did not allow the queen to sit beside the king, nor indeed did they allow her to be called queen, but rather king's wife'. He then adds in what seems excessive detail that 'this disputed and indeed infamous custom originated on account of a certain grasping wicked queen who did everything she could against her lord and the whole people, so that not only did she earn hatred for herself ... but she also brought the same foul stigma on all the queens who came after her. For as a result of her very great wickedness, all the inhabitants of the land swore that they would never permit any king to reign over them who during his lifetime invited the queen to sit beside him on the royal throne.'[41]

This popularly claimed assertion of the custom of not calling the king's wife 'queen' is very much exaggerated and proved to be short-lived. In reality, it only applied during the reign of Beorhtric's successor Ecgberht. The next in line, Æthelwulf, would himself bypass this edict, and it was only briefly resurrected by Alfred in terms of his wife Ealhswith before being again abandoned by Alfred's son Edward (the Elder). It is interesting that the sources only claim Eadburh poisoned her husband by accident rather than by design. Maybe Eadburh is just a convenient scapegoat here, especially since she was from Mercia. It is possible that Asser's portrayal of her as the villain is too convenient. For him, the possibility of Alfred's grandfather Ecgberht being involved in Beorhtric's death was not open for consideration.

Meanwhile, Asser persists with his views on Eadburh from a distance of a century. He describes her going into exile in Francia, taking with her 'countless treasures', where she reputedly was offered the choice of marriage to either Charlemagne or his son but secured neither, after which she joined a nunnery.[42] She was eventually expelled from the nunnery years later, and finally ended her life in poverty in Pavia, where her tomb was visited by English pilgrims.[43] Should we accept without question Asser's character assassination of Eadburh? Bringing Charlemagne into the story looks to be taking it suspiciously too far. If her tomb in Pavia was later reputedly visited by Anglo-Saxon pilgrims, this hardly sounds like a journey Christians would make for someone of such ill repute.

Returning to the ASC, the death of Beorhtric sits alongside an entry regarding the passing of an ealdorman named Worr, but it is unclear whether the two are connected. The entry is followed with confirmation of Ecgberht's succession to the throne of Wessex, and on the same day there was a battle on the West Saxon–Mercian border. Connecting the pieces leads to some interesting speculation, as all of this seems highly coincidental. We shall speculate further on the potential for Ecgberht's involvement in Beorhtric's removal in the next chapter.

As for Beorhtric's remains, the key primary sources are silent. Tradition has it that his body was taken for burial to the Church of Lady St Mary at Wareham, possibly the area where he grew up and had family connections. It was on what had been a British religious site, with the original Anglo-Saxon church founded by Bishop Anselm in the early eighth century.[44] This first structure was destroyed during a Viking raid in 876, and Beorhtric's tomb with it. Although a new church was built on the same site by Alfred, none of the original Anglo-Saxon structures survive in the present-day Anglo-Norman building.

13
Ecgberht
802–825

Ecgberht succeeded Beorhtric on the throne of Wessex in 802.[1] William of Malmesbury, perhaps revealing his Anglo-Norman views towards the English, writes on Ecgberht's time of exile with the Franks as 'clearing away the rust of indolence, and to acquire a civility of manners very different from the barbarity of his native land'.[2] However, if we accept Ecgberht was the son of the former Kentish king Ealhmund, as considered previously, then an entitlement to the throne of Kent seems more appropriate than being a claimant for the West Saxon throne. His succession to Wessex appears to be so unexpected that it warrants more detailed discussion.

The ASC entry for the year 802 is comprehensive and worthy of a recap. The scribe recorded that 'King Beorhtric and Ealdorman Worr passed away and Ecgberht succeeded to the kingdom of Wessex; and the same day Ealdorman Æthelmund rode from the Hwicce, crossing the Thames at Kempsford, before 'Ealdorman Weohstan met him with the Wiltshire men' and 'there was a big battle ... and the Wiltshire men took the victory'.[3] Bearing in mind this was all on the same day, we need to unpack the information a little further. Regardless of perspective, there was much activity in a brief period. The meeting between the Hwicce and the two Wiltshire ealdormen holds great importance for Ecgberht's succession, beyond what the sources suggest.

Let us look towards Ecgberht. When did his priority switch from Kent to Wessex? Was his arrival back in England the catalyst that led to Beorhtric's death? A growing number of historians advocate that Ecgberht was more involved in these events than first thought. If Kent proved immediately unobtainable, which it may have been, then did he look instead towards Wessex to acquire power? If support was sufficiently strong there against Beorhtric's regime, a coup might have been engineered. He could have been directly involved in a plot to kill the heirless Beorhtric, thus clearing the way to the throne of Wessex. It is equally conceivable that he later originated the story implicating Eadburh – a version of events reinforced by his grandson's biographer Asser – to divert attention away from his involvement.[4]

The military encounter between Wessex and Mercia (Hwicce) on the day Ecgberht assumed the kingship means that the two events must be connected. The ASC entry that Beorhtric and the ealdorman Worr died together on the same day could either suggest that Worr had been poisoned alongside Beorhtric or support the premise that they both died in combat. Maybe there was a palace coup. Furthermore, Ealdorman Æthelmund's appearance with a Mercian fyrd may have been in response to an appeal from Beorhtric's widow to stop Ecgberht's takeover of Wessex. Æthelmund was no minor noble; his family was one of Mercia's most important. Under Offa, he had become the chief authority for the Hwicce and had witnessed charters for Ecgfrith as well as Cenwulf.[5] The West Saxon ealdorman Weohstan, fatally injured during this fight, was reputed by a later source to have been Ecgberht's brother-in-law, married to his sister Alburga.[6] The efficacy of this source is questionable, but if valid it supports the premise that a coup had been planned.

To put all the possible scenarios together, we also need to seriously consider Charlemagne and Francia's involvement in supporting this action, or even in directly helping to secure the West Saxon throne for Ecgberht. Ecgberht, of course, had been in exile in Francia at Charlemagne's court and, as with Eadberht Praen's claim to Kent, had earlier received support from the Frankish king against the hegemony of Mercia. There is already evidence Charlemagne's relationship with Offa and Mercia had turned dramatically sour, partly due to the situation with the Kentish exiles. The Frankish influence in Kent had diminished, and this had not changed when the new Mercian king Cenwulf renewed the kingdom's interests in Kent. There is no evidence of a change in Charlemagne's relationship with Mercia, but his past interference in English domestic politics, not only in Kent but specifically in Northumbria, suggests a strong argument for his involvement during 802.

It is entirely plausible, then, that Ecgberht's return to England was supported from within Francia, and this potentially included financial and military aid alongside diplomatic backing. Support for Ecgberht's regime probably continued beyond the death of Charlemagne in 814 and, as advocated by several historians, Ecgberht continued to receive support from the Franks thereafter until at least the series of events that occurred in 829, which is discussed fully in the following chapter..

Ecgberht's relationship with Francia as a counterpoint to Mercia was vital, and this cannot be discounted as a factor which enabled him to stabilise his regime. In considering the issues surrounding his succession, we have taken speculation to its limit, but there are grounds for valid conjecture. The circumstances look to go beyond the version pushed by his grandson Alfred's biographer Asser. Ecgberht may have forcibly taken the West Saxon throne, which explains why a Kentish ætheling became the king of Wessex, and why Alfred later had to establish for him a West Saxon bloodline back to the time of Ine.

Ecgberht was already father to a son named Æthelwulf, born sometime during the late 790s probably at or near Charlemagne's court at Aachen. However, there is some difficulty in tracing Ecgberht's wife. She is not named in any primary source of the period, although at one time late nineteenth-century historians accepted the idea that she was possibly Redburga, the sister of Charlemagne.[7] If Ecgberht had married Charlemagne's sister, it is hard to imagine contemporary scribes ignoring such a prestigious arrangement, particularly Alfred's scribes compiling the ASC. No other primary sources mention another potential wife, and this is at the time when the identity of the queen in Wessex had lost importance, supposedly due to Beorhtric's wife. This has prompted one historian to suggest that this policy was adopted to reduce conflict and complications over the future line of succession and that of any alternate claimants.[8]

William of Malmesbury asserts Ecgberht had returned to England 'in response to many invitations from his friends'.[9] Who these friends were is not made clear, but he appears to have been welcomed unreservedly. Ecgberht formally received his kingship at either Kingston-upon-Thames, a place later associated with him, or at Winchester. Wilton is another possibility, as it was already the royal administrative centre of Wiltshire, and Ecgberht is known to have ratified an important peace treaty with Northumbria at the royal vill there in 829 alongside other charters at various periods. It would remain an important royal site throughout the ninth century. The remains of the Anglo-Saxon royal residence are said to be buried below Kingsbury Square in the present-day centre of Wilton.[10]

Further ratification of Ecgberht's entitlement to the throne, and that of his sons and grandsons in turn, came in a much later entry added by the ASC scribe towards the end of Ecgberht's son Æthelwulf's reign in 855. The scribe acknowledges Ealhmund of Kent's paternal link to Ecgberht but also that Ealhmund was the great-grandson of Ingeld, brother of Ine of Wessex, a lineage that Asser also supported through Ealhmund via Eafa and Eoppa to Ingeld.[11] This is the first time we see the primary sources acknowledge Ecgberht's father's association with Wessex. This was perhaps a late acknowledgement of his bloodline entitlement, which appears to have been added later to support Æthelwulf's credentials and, by inference, Alfred's as well. Alfred is only referred to as 'Æthelwulf's offspring', and Æthelwulf only as 'Ecgberht's son'.[12]

Further claims Ecgberht's genealogy could be traced back to Cerdic came from the tenth-century chronicler Æthelweard, who refers to 'Cerdic, who was King Ecgberht's tenth ancestor'.[13] However, Æthelweard was not entirely unbiased, as he was descended from another grandson of Ecgberht, Æthelred I of Wessex (r. 865–871). Finally, William of Malmesbury contradicts the ASC genealogy, emphasising that Ecgberht was not a great-grandson of Ingeld but a 'great-great-nephew of King Ine', and that he 'came into prominence in Wessex from his boyhood'.[14]

In terms of Ecgberht's early years as king, it is unfortunate for historians that he disappears from the primary source record thereafter until 815, and beyond that his next reference in the ASC does not appear until 825. Given he is one of Wessex's most successful kings, his absence from the sources during this time is truly remarkable. However, this obscurity was not limited to Ecgberht alone. The ASC version A has only a further five entries between 802 and 815 and then merely five more up to 825, while version E has a total of a dozen for the same period.[15] These primarily concern ecclesiastic events, such as the death of Archbishop Æthelheard of Canterbury and the ordaining of his replacement Wulfred (805–806), the deaths of Pope Leo III (816) and Pope Stephen IV (817), and a synod held at Clovesho (824).[16] Secular matters are given even less space, and all of them concern events relating to Mercia, such as the deaths of Cenwulf's brother Cuthred, the death of Cenwulf himself in 821, and the ousting of Ceolwulf, his successor in Mercia, a year later.[17]

The lack of detail regarding Wessex is disappointing and suggests a broader concern, namely that the scribes had no access to records of activities from Wessex during this period. One response to this among the academic community is that it is easy to imagine Ecgberht reigning unobtrusively in Wessex across these years with nothing to report.[18] This conclusion is unsatisfactory on several levels. As with other periods where there is a dearth of primary source detail, a more likely reason is the later destruction of valuable texts. Annals may have once recorded events from 802 to 825, perhaps lost in a fire or similar disaster, leaving compilers of the ASC versions with no material.

From a Mercian standpoint, Cenwulf would be immersed in his concerns over retaining authority in the south-east, which ran parallel with other problems experienced in his dealings with the Church and its leadership in Canterbury. The Mercian king and Archbishop Wulfred of Canterbury had a long power struggle, resulting in Wulfred's exile twice during Cenwulf's supremacy over Kent. The initial dispute in 808 was so serious that it was referred to in a letter from Pope Leo III to Charlemagne, and the archbishop was exiled for two years. Despite this, charter evidence between 810 and 815 shows that the archbishop and the Mercian king were still conducting land transfers with each other and third parties during that time, with Cenwulf donating several estates to Wulfred.[19]

The difficulties faced by Cenwulf and his successors may have signalled a decline in Mercian authority, particularly in military control over satellite kingdoms. Kent had been on the verge of rebellion against Mercian rule since the 790s, perhaps with some help from Ecgberht, and Essex and East Anglia would push to recover their own autonomy during the 820s. By Cenwulf's death in 821, the period of Mercian supremacy was ending. This was perhaps not fully clear at the time, although Ecgberht's major victory on the battlefield of Ellendun in 825 over the Mercian king Beornwulf, as discussed in detail later, would mark a clear passing of the baton from Mercia to Wessex.

Regarding Ecgberht's activities before 825, the charter evidence proves equally challenging. Only a single extant charter of his has survived from that period, dated to 824, compared to fifteen surviving documents dated during the second half of his reign (825–838).[20] Clearly texts have been lost, as we can surmise that when he was establishing himself as king and thereafter Ecgberht would have been keen to reward his supporters by issuing charters for land grants. He would have acted similarly with the senior clergy. In contrast, for the period of Cenwulf's rule in Mercia (796–821), at least thirty-three of his charters survive. These confirm Ecgberht was never seen as Mercia's vassal; he does not appear as a witness in any capacity, and there is no hint the Mercian king was operating under some formal degree of beneficial friendship. From the day he took the throne, Ecgberht established and maintained full West Saxon independence from any external interference, particularly when it came to Mercia.

During this period of document scarcity, some suggest Ecgberht may have conducted repairs or further strengthened sections of the Wansdyke in foresight of a potential invasion from Mercia that never materialised; although, as propounded by landscape archaeologists, the earthwork was only ever intended to delay and hinder rather than act as a permanent defensible barrier.[21] Excavations have revealed that further reinforcement of some sections of the embankments occurred during the first half of the ninth century, believed to be undertaken during Ecgberht's reign. This makes sense when the threat of a Mercian assault was at its greatest in the early years of Ecgberht's kingship.[22]

As mentioned above, the first entry regarding Ecgberht as king after 802 comes in 815, with the scribe noting that 'in that year King Ecgberht raided in Cornwall from east to west'.[23] There are no other details, but whether a campaign or just a raid it would appear to have been conducted over a large area. The West Saxons had already secured control of the south-west peninsula up to the River Tamar, and had already occupied some estates on the west bank and along its northern reaches in northern Cornwall. It is plausible, therefore, that this 815 action was a West Saxon counter-raid in retaliation for continuous raiding by the Dumnonii and Cornovii against West Saxon settlements in that region. The days when the Cornish-British kings would launch full campaigns to recover lost territory had passed, although they would be emboldened again in 825 and again in 838, the latter event in alliance with a Viking army, to pillage across the Tamar into Devon in large numbers. Ecgberht seems during 815 to have been confident the Mercians would not launch an attack while he was occupied in the south-west, However, in a similar set of circumstances ten years later, as considered below, the Mercian response would be different.

Post-815, there is a subsequent decade of silence regarding events in Wessex from primary sources. Details of Ecgberht's activities re-emerge in 825, although even here he is not mentioned directly by name. The ASC briefly records that 'here there was a battle of Britons and of Devon-men at the Tax Ford'.[24] We can perhaps date this campaign through a charter that suggests Ecgberht was at Crediton in August of that year, which would support the battle at Tax Ford coming at the height of summer.[25]

A few suggestions have been made for the location of the battle site. The given name from the scribes signifies it was at a crossing point of a river where taxes were collected. The Old English word for tax was *gafol*, a word also used when noting tribute or rent, so another name often given for this battle site is Gafol-ford or Galfulford. Based on this detail, a favoured location is next to a farm at a site called Galford Springs in Devon. If Galford Springs was the site for this battle, then the British had already advanced some distance into central Devon. It is an unassuming setting a few hundred metres from the River Lew, a tributary of the River Lyd, which is itself a tributary of the River Tamar. The location lies 9 miles south-west of present-day Okehampton and about 7 miles east of the nearest stretch of the Tamar. Today, the Lew at this location is little more than a stream, but the ford here was presumably significant in Anglo-Saxon times as a tax collection point for trade, possibly between the West Saxons and the Dumnonii.[26]

The other prime candidate for the battlefield, although less favoured, is at Camelford, about 4 miles inland from Tintagel, by the north Cornish coast. This implies the opposite of Galford Springs, with Ecgberht further west than he had ever been beyond the recognised border between the British and the West Saxons. The link to Camelford is again tied to place-name association, with its original name claimed to be Gafolford, 'Camel' being a derivation of 'Gafol'.[27] This may be accurate, but the earliest known record for Camelford is from the early thirteenth century, which implies that the ASC scribes would not have named it as such in the late ninth century. Advocates for this site have attempted to link it to the nearby village of Slaughterbridge a mile to the north, for obvious reasons. Nevertheless, in this case 'slaughter' is derived instead from the Old English word *slothre*, meaning 'muddy' or 'marsh', and does not indicate the scene of a battle.

We have no reasonable way of assessing the numbers that fought at this battle, but we can assume Henry of Huntingdon exaggerates when recording that several thousand died there.[28] Estimates are purely speculative, but if Ecgberht was at the head of this major West Saxon campaign, it is plausible his numbers easily exceeded a thousand and were perhaps well above that figure. Historians generally cannot agree on what constituted a large army during this period, factoring in the time needed to coordinate and consolidate conscription numbers, but given ample time local shire fyrds could have numbered several hundred men or more, and a 'national' fyrd perhaps three or four times that number.

The British would not seriously threaten West Saxon settlement in Devon again until 838, when they allied with a large Viking raiding army to launch a raid into Devon. This tells us two things about the balance of power between the West Saxons and the British in the south-west peninsula as it stood during the early ninth century. First, the West Saxons appear to have been focused on fortifying the settlements across the areas they had already conquered and were only conducting further warfare in response to aggression from the British tribes. As seen by the place-name associations discussed previously, this settlement pattern looks to have included parts of north Cornwall. Second, the British seem to have accepted they would never recover lost territory, and the best achievable thereafter would be the occasional pillaging raid across the Tamar. An uneasy peace was now the norm, and it is possible to argue for there being a regular transfer of trade and goods between the two groups that increased as the ninth century progressed.

In more general terms, historians continue to debate how quickly and how effectively the West Saxons advanced through Devon into Cornwall.

Timeframes vary wildly, with some claiming the West Saxons had crossed the Tamar in the early eighth century while others suggest the Dumnonii still held parts of Devon even up to the early tenth century.[29] This latter date seems wide of the mark by some stretch based on the evidence we have already discussed and the number of known encounters and outcomes in the region before that date. A more rational argument may be that a considerably higher percentage of the population across Devon were still native British. Even at the height of West Saxon settlement in the early tenth century, occasional rebellions were launched by British groups that refused to admit defeat, which explains the continued sporadic fighting noted by some historians.[30]

The peace that finally emerged between the West Saxons and the Dumnonii and Cornovii encapsulates the interactions that had already taken place between the kings of Wessex and the conquered British tribes further east – the Durotriges, Atrebates, Belgae and Dobunni – that had taken place to varying degrees during the previous three centuries. As revealed in the early chapters, once the Anglo-Saxons had acquired control of territory, and settlers had moved in, there was a blending of British and Germanic cultures. Archaeological evidence shows that most of the native British remained *in situ* under the new leadership, assimilating with them.

Wessex was the first Anglo-Saxon kingdom to divide what had been a mix of former tribal areas and sub-kingdoms into administrative regions centred around already established economic hubs, often the former Roman *civitates*, that would be known as shires. Hampshire is widely recognised as the first, evolving from Hamtun to Winchester, although the implementation was gradual. Some historians argue that the shiring of Wessex began during the late eighth century, while others give a more circumspect date of the early ninth century, before the system was in wide operation across all West Saxon-held territory.[31] Devon, deriving from the British name Dumnonia, would become a new shire of Wessex in due course to join the already established shires of Hampshire (including the Isle of Wight), Somerset, Dorset and Wiltshire. Each of their names derived from an extension of either the original British regional tribe or its main economic centre, a case in point being that Hampshire would take its name from its largest trading centre, Hamtun, rather than its royal and religious centre of Winchester. By the mid-ninth century Berkshire, Sussex, Surrey and Kent, and later Essex, would be assimilated into the West Saxon system after the expansion of Wessex under its kings Ecgberht and Æthelwulf.

The gradual movement of Germanic Anglo-Saxon practices further west appears to have been inevitable. Following a quelling of the

Dumnonii military capacity, the religious ideology preached from Canterbury spread westward. By the end of Ecgberht's reign (839) it is argued that new Roman Catholic outposts were already established in Cornwall. The first religious house may have been in Bodmin, with a claim to be the first bishopric in the area, but it ultimately answered to Bishop Ealhstan in Sherborne. Other sites at St Breock (near Wadebridge) and Lawhitton (near Launceston) followed.[32] However, not until the reign of Ecgberht's great-great-grandson Æthelstan in the 920s would Cornwall be granted its own independent bishopric at St Germans, the site of a former Celtic church near the River Lynher west of Saltash.[33]

Ecgberht's 825 campaign in the south-west was cut short by the troubling news that Beornwulf, king of Mercia, was leading an army into Wessex while the West Saxon king was preoccupied elsewhere. If the timing was deliberate, Beornwulf underestimated his opponent's energy and resolve. However, as in many similar scenarios, this decision by the Mercian king was probably also prompted by the internal situation within his own kingdom. He had deposed Ceolwulf only two years earlier, certainly as part of a military coup. Before becoming king he is seen in only two Mercian charters, one for Cenwulf and one for Ceolwulf, and his low position in the witness lists in each infers he was not previously within the highest ranks of the nobility.[34] His antecedents are believed to link him to Beornred, the 'king' of Mercia who ruled for less than a year between the reigns of Æthelbald and Offa. Historians identify this rival dynasty as the B dynastic group, compared to the C dynastic group identifiable through Cenwulf and Ceolwulf.[35] Beorhtwulf and Burgred, two future rulers of Mercia, are also believed to have a kinship connection with Beornwulf.

Beornwulf's motivation for attacking Wessex, as hinted at above, was probably to improve his standing. He had undertaken a series of purges among the nobility upon his succession and soon after that had invaded across Offa's Dyke into Powys in what proved to be an unsuccessful Welsh campaign. He therefore needed to restore some prestige and bolster his position among the Mercian hierarchy that had backed his coup and had so far seen no benefit from it. A further incentive may have been the idea that Ecgberht would soon be strong enough to challenge Mercian authority within Kent (and Sussex), particularly with his Kentish connections, and therefore a pre-emptive strike was perhaps the best way of preventing that. If it had not happened in 825, hindsight tells us that a show of strength between the two kingdoms was likely to happen at some stage when their interests were opposed.

Beornwulf seemingly failed to catch the West Saxon king at a disadvantage, as Ecgberht was able to return quickly to counteract the Mercian invasion. The Mercian king's intelligence gathering was flawed, and he looks to have delayed his advance too long or underestimated Ecgberht's abilities. His army likely crossed the River Thames at the ford at Kempsford, north-east of Cricklade, although by the time Beornwulf had eventually moved all his forces across the border, Ecgberht had already gathered a sufficiently large army to bring Beornwulf to battle.

The battle that ensued was later known as Ellendun, and its outcome would transform the fortunes of Wessex and Mercia irrevocably. 'Ellendun' has been interpreted as meaning 'Elder-bush Down', although this does not assist further in defining the exact site.[36] The ASC record states that 'King Egbert and King Beornwulf fought at Ellendun, and Ecgbert took the victory; and a great slaughter was made'.[37] Historians are reasonably confident that the battle of Ellendun was at one of two possible locations near to modern Swindon, separated by only 3 miles and on opposite sides of the present-day M4 motorway. Depending on our interpretation, these sites may be regarded as part of the same battlefield.

The first suggested location is the village of Wroughton, just south of the M4, which was previously known as Ellingdon, from which comes the name Ellendun. The settlement of Wroughton extended from the present-day village to the west of Swindon, as shown by boundary divisions during the Anglo-Saxon period.[38] The second location, the one most historians consider the centre of most if not all the fighting, is at Lydiard Tregoze, a small village 3 miles from Wroughton and 2 miles west of present-day central Swindon. There is evidence that an ancient trackway existed, an offshoot of the Ridgeway, that is relevant to the favoured field of battle. It ran south to north from Barbury Castle to the west of Wroughton and then through the vicinity of Lydiard Tregoze and on past the adjacent village of Lydiard Millicent before continuing to Cricklade.[39] This trackway served the purpose of both armies, with the Mercians marching down it from Cricklade after crossing the Thames, and the West Saxons approaching from the direction of Barbury Castle.

The twelfth-century *Annals of Winchester* (*Annales de Wintonia*) provides us with much information about the battle, a consequence of the abbey at Winchester having once owned the land around Wroughton/Ellingdon. The text gives a passing reference to dead 'men and horses', implying the use of cavalry. However, its estimate of the combatants involved in the battle is unrealistic, as it notes that Ecgberht was severely outnumbered by as much as ten to one.[40] We can imagine Beornwulf had the larger army, bearing in mind Ecgberht's recent West Country campaign, although a scale of ten to one seems unrealistic. A more reasonable proposal is that Beornwulf had up to 5,000 men versus around 3,000 under Ecgberht.[41]

In trying to narrow down a location for Ellendun, charter evidence refers to the 'brook of Ellandune', which relates to what would have been a stretch of the River Ray that runs through Lydiard Park and today helps form the lake there.[42] Henry of Huntingdon refers to this watercourse in his description of the fighting, noting that 'Ellendune's stream was reddened with blood, was stopped up with the fallen, was filled with stench'.[43] One possibility is that the two armies first assembled astride the old trackway from Wroughton, aligning on what has been defined as two parallel north-east-to-south-west ridges either side of the waterway.[44] Modern development and landscaping have destroyed much of the original topography, although the suggestion is that the rising ground around where Lydiard House now stands was where the Mercians formed ranks, and the ridge on which Ecgberht's West Saxons may have first aligned themselves ran south-westwards from what is now the development at Grange Park.[45]

Ellendun was not the first occasion when a king of Wessex inflicted a heavy defeat on a Mercian army, even when facing greater numbers on the battlefield; the victories of Æscwine over Wulfhere (675) and Cuthred over Æthelbald (752) spring to mind. While the military strategies of individual leaders, the numbers involved and the local landscape all played a part, perhaps there is another factor to consider. It has been proven that the Mercian military system had mercenary recruits from the subservient kingdoms over which it held authority. Maybe there was overreliance on these indentured troops, men who had less desire to fight and were not so committed. The West Saxons' fighting morale may have proved too much for a Mercian leader and his less motivated army. Whatever the truth, Ecgberht's victory at Ellendun would propel Wessex to greater heights during the second phase of his reign, establishing a permanent legacy for his son and grandsons to expand the strength of the kingdom even further.

14
Ecgberht
825–839

The victory over Beornwulf at Ellendun in 825 would give Ecgberht and Wessex an opportunity, perhaps one never before seen, to expand the authority of the kingdom when its old rival Mercia was at a serious political and military disadvantage. For Mercia, the defeat at Ellendun would reopen the cracks within its political hierarchy, ushering in a change of leadership and redirecting military ambitions. Ecgberht may have pondered launching an immediate campaign into Mercia to exploit his newly gained advantage but decided against it. Instead, he used the time instead to build the strength of Wessex further over the following years while observing the widening divisions within the Mercian hierarchy.

The weakened Mercia now had a power vacuum in its vassaled states in the south-east, and Ecgberht was able to exploit it. Mercian authority in Kent had been faltering prior to Ellendun, with numismatic evidence showing a decline in coinage production there compared to a few years earlier. There are surviving examples that Baldred, Beornwulf's appointed client king in Kent, was minting coins at Canterbury by 825 if not beforehand, as was Archbishop Wulfred, which suggests that Baldred may have already reclaimed some independence from Mercia even before hearing of Beornwulf's defeat.[1]

Focusing on advancing his designs in the south-east, Ecgberht appears to have immediately suspended further moves into Cornwall. A lasting peace between the Dumnonii and the West Saxons would emerge in time, and Ecgberht had more significant priorities. According to the ASC record for 825, 'he (Ecgberht) sent his son Æthelwulf from the army, and Ealhstan, his bishop, and Wulfheard, his ealdorman, to Kent with a great troop, and they drove Baldred the king north of the Thames'.[2]

The ASC adds that 'the inhabitants of Kent turned to him (Ecgberht), and the Surrey men and South Saxons and East Saxons – because earlier they were wrongly forced away from his relatives'.[3] This undoubtedly refers to Ecgberht's claimed ties to Kent through his father, although whether they 'turned to him' before or after Baldred had escaped north of the Thames is unclear. This is also the first source reference to Essex being brought into the wider sphere of Wessex, a consequence of its previous connection with Kent.

However, the chronicle's claim that the West Saxons ousted Baldred from Kent within a few months of Ellendun is questionable. The advance into Kent and expulsion of Baldred probably came in the spring or summer of 826, certainly no earlier than April. We know a Kentish charter issued by Archbishop Wulfred at Canterbury acknowledges that Beornwulf and Mercia, through Baldred, still held control there in March 826.[4] The true extent of Beornwulf's continued authority in Kent is uncertain, but this charter at least acknowledges that Baldred had not been removed by the West Saxons as rapidly as the chronicle scribe suggests.

The late ninth-century scribes compiling the chronicle were keen to stress that the West Saxon occupation was not an enforced military takeover in the vein of Mercia's operation under Wulfhere, Offa and others. Overlooking Baldred's forced eviction, they emphasised Ecgberht's peaceful repossession of Kent, highlighting his royal connections and previous right to rule. However, in justifying Ecgberht's entitlement and claim to the Kentish throne through his bloodline and background, the ASC scribe unwillingly reopens the matter of his legitimate claims to the throne of Wessex. Any hereditary claims upon Kent would have the effect of diluting any similar claim made for Wessex. Put simply, Ecgberht cannot have had a legal entitlement to two kingdoms simultaneously, and for this reason the primary source pronouncements remain tenuous.

There is no hint of West Saxon military occupation once the Kentish ties with Mercia were broken. Kent, Sussex and Surrey concurred to the authority of Wessex immediately and Essex was only marginally behind them. Sigered II, the last recorded king of Essex, had already been reduced to a sub-king under Mercia and is last observed in 823, witnessing a Mercian charter donating land in Kent to Archbishop Wulfred.[5] If Sigered had not already been removed by 825, he was certainly removed by Æthelwulf thereafter. As evidenced in an 827 charter, Æthelwulf would be awarded the status of under-king by his father, responsible for the four regions (three former kingdoms) in the south-east.[6]

East Anglia was the next kingdom to break from Mercian overlordship. The last East Anglian independent monarch had been Eadwald, who had briefly held authority between 796 and 800, from after Offa's death up until Cenwulf was able to reestablish Mercian control.[7] Mercia had then held ultimate authority there, but in 826, aware of the developments to its south and the expansion of West Saxon power, the East Angles launched a revolt against Mercia aimed at renewed independence. The ASC records that 'for fear of the Mercians ... the nation of the East Angles sought King Egbert as their guardian and protector'.[8] Ecgberht's response is unknown. We can speculate that he and his son were already fully committed to establishing and securing their authority in their newly gained territories in the south-east. Nevertheless, it is reasonable to expect that Ecgberht was aware of the political advantages that could be gained by further weakening Mercia's position. Perhaps limited military help was sent to encourage the East Anglians to rebel. William of Malmesbury writes that they were 'encouraged by assistance from Ecgberht', and Henry of Huntingdon adds that they 'took King Ecgberht as their defender'.[9]

With or without West Saxon military help, the East Anglians rebelled against Mercian authority in 826. Beornwulf was killed while leading the Mercian army dispatched to quell the revolt.[10] A leader named Æthelstan emerged as the new king of East Anglia, although historians have been unable to identify any clear dynastic link to the previous king, Eadwald. Beornwulf had no known heirs, certainly none old enough to succeed him. He was succeeded instead by a man named Ludeca, whom John of Worcester claims was 'Beornwulf's kinsman', although their precise connection is unknown.[11] He may have been a cousin or nephew, but his unusual name, which does not appear to link him to any of the major Mercian dynastic houses, could suggest Ludeca was a Mercian noble who had seized the throne in a coup in the aftermath of Beornwulf's death.

The following year, Ludeca led a new army into East Anglia to recover Mercia's lost authority. John of Worcester describes him marching 'to avenge his predecessor King Beornwulf', although it is more likely he needed to recover East Anglia to prop up his recently acquired kingship among his supporters.[12] The outcome was a repeat of the previous year. Ludeca was killed on the battlefield alongside five of his senior ealdormen.[13] Independence for East Anglia followed, and in 827 Æthelstan was appointed as its new king, although there is no sign he was connected with the previous East Anglian royal dynasty that had pre-dated vassalage to the Mercian kings.[14] The role of Wessex in securing East Anglian independence from Mercia remains ambiguous, but Æthelstan of East Anglia was producing his own coinage free of outside influence no later than 829–830.[15]

The loss of any direct involvement in the trade that came through the ports of Ipswich, Norwich and Dunwich was a serious blow for the Mercian economy, which had already lost its commercial interest in the trade entering Harwich, Sandwich, Canterbury and Dover. Mercia's hold on the region of Lindsey (Lincolnshire), excluding London, was now its only remaining unfettered access to the east coast. Likewise, with the loss of Surrey and Essex to Wessex, the Mercian hold on London at this period becomes nuanced. Mercia's loss was Wessex's gain. In contrast, with its newly liberated access to the south-east and the Thames Estuary, the economy of Wessex was moving positively and strongly in the opposite direction.

Ecgberht, with his son Æthelwulf acting as the secular authority in the south-east, now held sway over a much larger expanse of territory than Wessex had ever encompassed before. Nevertheless, total authority, morally if not militarily, was still reliant on compromise and resolution with the Church leadership at Canterbury. This meant getting the unequivocal support of Archbishop Wulfred, who was used to working with the Mercian leadership. Theoretically a king did not need Church approval, but it was better for the West Saxon leadership to secure verification and authentication from Canterbury and its archbishop. The Church's approval, though viewed differently today, was an important factor during this period.

From the detail we have, the relationship between the king and the archbishop did not begin smoothly. There are clues that rather than seek to appease the archbishop and give concessions, Ecgberht took measures instead to establish an immediate ascendancy over Canterbury, perhaps knowing that the Mercian secular leadership had previously met unexpected problems with Wulfred. Some estates which had recently been given to Wulfred and Canterbury by Baldred of Kent were seized by Ecgberht and Æthelwulf – one such example being found in an extant charter dated to 830 – and pragmatically redistributed to their local supporters in exchange for money.[16]

The archbishop had been producing his own coinage, apparently with Mercian royal approval, even though it did not bear the king's name, and one of Ecgberht's first acts was to suspend this activity. There are extant examples of Ecgberht's coins being produced from the Kentish mints as soon as Æthelwulf had been installed there.[17] In terms of coin production in general, Ecgberht produced many coinage designs across his full reign. Dependent on where and when the coins were produced, different moneyers adopted varying styles. Extant examples of coins produced by moneyers named Beagmund and Cobba are invariably found without either the king's head or his bust, bearing only his name. Alternately, those produced by the moneyer Dunun have either the head or a bust, usually a head, which was contained in the inner circle. Evidently, there was no standard uniform of design for much of his reign. Ecgberht's name was similarly not uniform, with examples such as 'Æcgbearht' or 'Ecgbearht'. However, as the 830s progressed, there are indications among the extant examples that the engravers at Canterbury were increasingly under the supervision of men from western Wessex to achieve a more uniform production across wider Wessex. Many of these moneyers, including Dunun, can be also found producing coins during Æthelwulf's reign post-839.[18]

A surprising element after 826 is perhaps how easily political control in the south-east was achieved. Ecgberht's claimed kinship ties with Kent played a major role. There is no evidence of attempted insurrection from any of the previous Kentish factions. We also cannot lose sight of the fact that much of his and Æthelwulf's authority could have come from the political – and possibly financial backing – of the regime in Francia. Ecgberht continued to receive support from Louis the Pious following the death of his father Charlemagne, and Kent already enjoyed an established relationship and commercial cooperation with Francia. Frankish influence on political developments in south-east England is often underestimated.

Following the demise of Beornwulf and Ludeca, in 827 the Mercian witan nominated Wiglaf as their new king. Once again, they chose someone without blood ties to the throne, a unifying candidate with no direct link to previous regimes. However, one possible factor suggested by historians is that support for Wiglaf may have come from his wife Cynethryth's claimed kinship connection, through her maternal line, to the earlier Mercian king Æthelbald (r. 716–757).[19] The kingdom that Wiglaf inherited would require time to recover from the setbacks of the previous three years. However, having achieved control of the south-east relatively easily, and having been encouraged by Mercia's inability to prevent East Anglian independence, Ecgberht was soon looking to benefit further from Mercia's weak position.

Whether the king of Wessex had always planned to launch a campaign into Mercia after his victory in 825 is debatable. However, with the emergence of Wiglaf, he must have sensed that his opportunity to severely damage his kingdom's old rival would never be so strong again. In 829, Ecgberht marched his West Saxon army into Mercia. The military response from its new regime was negligible; perhaps Ecgberht had known it would be. He was apparently able to march deep into Mercia without serious opposition. The absence among the primary sources of any recorded resistance or countermeasures by Wiglaf and the Mercian leadership to an event of such magnitude is perhaps hard to grasp, and demonstrates just how quickly they succumbed. Mercia had a long history of armed invasions of the other Anglo-Saxon kingdoms, but not since Penda's seventh-century wars with Northumbria had it been invaded so comprehensively. In terms of West Saxon achievements, before 829 the furthest push into Mercian home territory had been Cuthred's advance to Burford in 752.

Wiglaf's regime capitulated, with the ASC recording that 'King Egbert conquered the kingdom of Mercia and all that was south of the Humber'.[20] Henry of Huntingdon noted briefly that 'Ecgberht drove out Wiglaf ... and acquired the kingdom (Mercia) for himself'.[21] His contemporary William of Malmesbury simply adds that Wiglaf 'was at first driven from his kingdom, then accepted as tributary'.[22] While it is appreciated these extant primary source entries were written sometime long after these events, they all seem to underplay what was a seismic shift of power across Anglo-Saxon England. Yet the depth of West Saxon control is hard to determine. When considering Ecgberht and Wessex's conquest of the kingdom of Mercia within twelve months, like other similar primary source texts documenting similar events, it may be more appropriate to interpret it in a figurative rather than literal sense. One piece of evidence of Mercia's capitulation, around London at least, can be seen in Ecgberht's coinage, with coins from the London mint calling him 'king in Mercia'.[23]

We can imagine that Ecgberht's army may have undertaken a route of pillage across the breadth and depth of Mercia. What remains unclear is whether he believed he could successfully hold on to any political control there and replace the Mercian hierarchy. The suspicion is he would have known that such an undertaking was beyond his capabilities at every level – militarily, financially and politically. In brief, Wessex could not indefinitely sustain a large-scale military campaign or permanent occupation comparable to that achieved by the Mercians in other regions during their heyday. The best achievable option would have been to agree to receive significant tribute payments. Wiglaf looks to have initially taken voluntary exile, giving Ecgberht a brief period of complete dominance south of the River Humber. However, we can speculate that with Wiglaf exiled, there was no Mercian leadership for the West Saxon king to negotiate with or force into vassalage.

This could explain why Ecgberht continued to march his army northwards, presumably pillaging as he went. Sometime towards the end of 829, the West Saxons arrived at the border between Mercia and Northumbria, then a few miles south of present-day Sheffield. The edge of Mercian territory at this period was marked by several tributaries of the River Don that fed into it from the south, and it was at Dore – a derivation of the Old English word 'door', in this case referring to the passage between Northumbrian Deira and Mercia – that Ecgberht halted his advance.[24] Today, the village of Dore is less than 5 miles south-west of the centre of present-day Sheffield. It lies next to the River Sheaf and its tributary, the Limb Brook, which, along with the nearby Meers Brook, formed the kingdom's boundary markers. Here Ecgberht met Eanred, who had been the king of Northumbria since 810, and 'there they offered him (Ecgberht) submission and concord; and on that they parted'.[25] William of Malmesbury writes that the Northumbrians 'submitted hostages, and decided to give in'; and then turns to general summary by adding that 'having thus become master of the whole of Britain, Ecgberht passed the last nine years of his life in tranquillity' – a pleasant but not exactly accurate assessment.[26]

The thirteenth-century chronicler Roger of Wendover, taking his details from earlier Northumbrian annals, gives a different scenario, claiming that Ecgberht marched his army into Northumbria and pillaged the kingdom before forcing Eanred to pay tribute.[27] Realistically, it is probable that the West Saxons had threatened to move into Northumbria next, although whether they did is debatable. The brokered peace agreement and the lack of any details of further fighting within the sources would suggest otherwise. However, how Ecgberht would have fared had he continued his military campaign further north is difficult to evaluate. The comparative military capacity of the two kingdoms needs also to consider Ecgberht's distance from home soil. It is doubtful if he could have sustained anything beyond limited pillaging before having to retire south again. He had just conquered Mercia and was in danger of over-extending his military capacity for a prolonged war. The agreement at Dore was therefore a pragmatic deal that probably entitled Ecgberht to receive tribute from Eanred but not necessarily, as the ASC infers, vassalage. From Eanred's perspective, his kingdom was already in prolonged conflict with the Scots of Alba and Strathclyde. Furthermore, although the southern-based chronicles omit reference to it, he was already dealing at this time with increased Viking raiding.

In 1968, a metre-high stone commemorating the treaty between Ecgberht and Eanred was placed on Dore village green, close to the corner of Vicarage Lane and Savage Lane. The stone contains a plaque with an image of Wessex's wyvern and names Ecgberht as the 'overlord of all England', thereby echoing the primary source claims of his title of Bretwalda and acknowledging Wessex's war emblem, the wyvern. However, the assertion by William of Malmesbury that Ecgberht had become master of all Britain, which copied the original ASC claim, is inappropriate. It was more symbolic, a declaration of Ecgberht's standing among his contemporaries rather than a statement of fact. Nevertheless, for a very brief period, the West Saxon king was technically, if not militarily, the dominant political force south of the River Humber.

Having received tribute from Northumbria, in 830 Ecgberht moved back across northern Mercia into north Wales. Leading his army 'among the Welsh ... he reduced them to humble submission'.[28] This was less a campaign of subjugation and more an opportunity to extensively pillage the kingdoms of Powys and Gwynedd.

In the same year that the ASC describes Ecgberht's army moving into Wales, the previous entry records the reappearance of Wiglaf of Mercia: 'Here Wiglaf obtained the kingdom of Mercia again.'[29] Some historians have reasoned this implies that the king of Wessex was driven out of Mercia by a resurgent Wiglaf, who had retaken his kingdom by force.[30] There is some support for this scenario, but it would have meant that a complete *volte-face* in fortunes had occurred, and from what we know of the relative strengths of Wessex and Mercia in 830, this is unlikely.

Ecgberht had indeed probably overstretched his resources after continuing his campaign across Wales, but so far there had been no need to commit his forces to a shield-wall battle either, so we can conclude he had not been forced to retreat hastily back to Wessex. Henry of Huntingdon describes, mischievously, how the king of Wessex 'moved by pity, conceded to Wiglaf that he should hold the kingdom of Mercia under him'.[31] Ecgberht therefore, if we accept it, seemingly obtained Wiglaf's vassalage and allowed him to remain in Mercia as his vassal king. Some historians have interpreted Huntingdon's text and the scenario completely differently, decoding the 'moved by pity' wording as a face-saving explanation, suggesting instead that Wiglaf returned to power in Mercia without giving vassalage to Ecgberht.

This scenario may be the better interpretation. The ASC entry for 830 notes that 'here Wiglaf obtained the kingdom of Mercia again', which is hardly an acknowledgement that Ecgberht's withdrawal back to Wessex was in complete triumph.[32] The sources are unhelpful by their silence, but reading between the lines Wiglaf resumed his position on the throne of Mercia remarkably quickly following Ecgberht's withdrawal. The power Ecgberht held over Mercia seems to have dissipated rapidly, almost as quickly as his successes had come the previous year. There is no obvious reasoning behind this. However, a possible clue may be to look at the parallel developments taking place in Francia that might explain Ecgberht's rapid change of fortune. One argument we can expand upon is Ecgberht's long relationship with the kingdom of Francia, initially through Charlemagne and then for several years before 830 through Louis the Pious, and how events in that kingdom unfolded at the same time.

Historians are uncertain as to Louis' involvement in West Saxon politics but a reconfiguration of Frankish influence may have had a real and theoretical impact upon Ecgberht's designs for West Saxon expansion. It is plausible that his Mercian campaign in 829 was supported by Louis materially and financially, although presumably not in manpower. Under Charlemagne, it appeared that the Franks did not wish a particular Anglo-Saxon kingdom to become too powerful within England. This may still have been a factor in 829–830 under Louis.

1. A section of the Wansdyke defensive earthwork. (Courtesy of Alan Harris, CC BY-ND 2.0)

2. A section of the River Avon near Charford in Hampshire. The probable early border between the British and West Saxons and close to the possible location of the battle of Cerdic's Ford in 508. (Author's collection)

3. Badbury Rings Hillfort in Dorset. Strong contender for the site of the British victory over the Anglo-Saxons at the battle of Mount Badon in the early sixth century. (Courtesy of Simaron, CC BY-SA 2.0)

4. Old Sarum Hillfort just north of Salisbury. Seized by King Cynric of Wessex after his victory there over the British in 552. (Author's collection)

5. Barbury Castle Hillfort, lying on the Ridgeway in Wiltshire. Site of king Cynric and king Ceawlin's victory over the British in 556. (Author's collection)

6. Walkers Hill, on the Ridgeway just north of Alton Priors in Wiltshire. The location of the battles of 592 between kings Ceawlin and Ceol and 715 between kings Ine and Ceolred. (Author's collection)

7. River Itchen at Southampton. Looking across to the west bank and the district of St Mary's, site of the original Saxon twin settlement and port of Hamtun and Hamwic. (Author's collection)

8. View looking south of part of the 577 battlefield of Dyrham adjacent to Hinton Hill, Gloucestershire, a victory by King Ceawlin and Cuthwine over the British. (Author's collection)

9. The Shrine for Bishop Birinus at the abbey at Dorchester-on-Thames, which details the depiction of Birinus baptising King Cynegils in 635 (right). (Author's collection)

10. Marked footprint of the original seventh-century site of the Old Minster (St Peter & St Paul) at Winchester lying alongside the later Norman Cathedral. (Author's collection)

Above: 11. The Anglo-Saxon church of St Laurence at Bradford-on-Avon, the original building of which was founded by Abbot Aldhelm *c.* 700.(Author's collection)

Left: 12. Detail of King Ine depicted in the Transfiguration Window at Wells Cathedral. Recognition that he founded the first church there at Wells in the early eighth century. (Courtesy of Greenshed, CC0)

13. The River Camel at Egloshayle in Cornwall. A favoured location for the battle of Hehil which saw a British victory over King Ine in 722. (Author's collection)

14. Somerton, formerly the chief administrative capital of the shire of Somerset, which was besieged by King Æthelbald of Mercia in 733. (Author's collection)

15. Tanner's Lane in Burford in Oxfordshire. Looking north down the hill towards the site of Battle Edge, the location for King Cuthred's victory over the Mercians in 752. (Author's collection)

16. The Golden Dragon (Wyvern) flag of Wessex. Traditionally credited as the banner of the kings of Wessex from the eight century onwards. (Derived from work by Hogweard, CC BY-SA 3.0)

17. The village of Privett in Hampshire. Near the site of the murder of King Sigeberht in 757. (Author's collection)

18. River Thames at Benson in Oxfordshire. The border between Wessex and Mercia in 779 and adjacent to the Mercian victory over the West Saxons at the battle of Bensington. (Author's collection)

19. The Church of Lady St Mary at Wareham in Dorset, where the original Saxon building was the claimed burial place of King Beorhtric. (Author's collection)

20. River Lew at Galford Springs in Devon, close to the probable site for the battle of Galfulford in 825 between King Ecgberht and the British. (Author's collection)

Above: 21. Lydiard Park near Swindon. Favoured location near Lydiard Tregoze for King Ecgberht's famous victory over the Mercians at the battle of Ellendun in 825. (Author's collection)

Right: 22. Stone and plaque at village of Dore in Yorkshire, denoting where King Ecgberht took the submission of the Northumbrian king in 829. (Courtesy of Andy Scott, CC BY-SA 4.0)

23. View from the east bank of the River Tamar at Calstock at the Devon–Cornwall border. Probable landing site in 838 of the Viking fleet that allied with the British ahead of the battle of Hingston Down. (Author's collection)

24. Silver pennies of Ecgberht and Æthelwulf. (A) Struck *c.* 828-39 at Canterbury mint; obverse reads 'ECGBEΛR HT REX' (King Ecgberht) and reverse 'OBΛ MONETΛ' (Oba, moneyer). (B) Struck *c.* 854–58 at Canterbury mint; obverse reads 'ΛEÐELVVLF REX' (King Æthelwulf) and reverse 'VERMV ND MO N E T Λ' (Wærmund, moneyer). (Courtesy of Classic Numismatic Group, www.cngcoins.com)

Right: 25. Stone lid standing near the porch at the Church of St Andrew and St Cuthman in Steyning, West Sussex, claimed to be from the original tomb of King Æthelwulf. (Author's collection)

Below: 26. Bones located and preserved in the floor of Sherborne Abbey, reputedly part of the surviving remains from the original burials of kings Æthelbald and Æthelberht. (Author's collection)

Above: 27. View of part of the favoured site for the battle of Ashdown in 871 between the West Saxons and the Vikings, looking south-east from Lowbury Hill north of the village of Aldworth in Berkshire. (Author's collection)

Left: 28. Stone monument and plaque at Swanborough Tump near Pewsey, Wiltshire, commemorating the meeting and agreement in 871 between King Æthelred I and his brother Alfred during the Danish wars. (Author's collection)

29. Brass and plaque at Wimborne Minster, Dorset. Memorial to King Æthelred I near the site of his known burial in the original church. (Author's collection)

30. Estuary of the River Parrett, Somerset, into which the Viking fleet sailed in 878 ahead of their defeat to the West Saxons at nearby Cannington. (Author's collection)

Above: 31. The Sarsen stone and plaque at Bratton Camp Hillfort near Westbury, Wiltshire, commemorating King Alfred's famous victory there in 878 over the Dane Guthrum at the battle of Edington (aka Ethandun). (Author's collection)

Right: 32. Statue of King Alfred the Great in the Broadway, Winchester, commissioned in 1899 and erected in 1901. (Author's collection)

It would seem that support from Francia for Wessex suddenly stopped at the height of Ecgberht's power, and nothing else comes close to explaining the sudden reversal of his fortunes.[33] In 829, Louis I had suffered a rift with his eldest son, Lothair, which led the following year to what effectively became a Frankish civil war, the first of three over the next decade, involving not just Louis and each of his three sons but all the regions of Francia and a potential partition of the Frankish empire.

Support for Ecgberht at the height of his 829–830 campaign may have stopped for one of three reasons or a combination of them. First, the domestic turmoil within Francia may have forced Louis to withdraw support for Ecgberht and direct it towards more critical issues at home. Second, he may have decided to deliberately withhold support due to concerns about Ecgberht's rapidly expanding power relative to the other Anglo-Saxon kingdoms. However, a third reason could have been something beyond Louis's control. The Frankish civil war was impacting trade, both internally and across the English Channel and the North Sea, and Ecgberht's campaign against Mercia may have further compounded these difficulties. Such lulls in European trade could affect his own commercial network and deprive him of the supplies necessary for an extended and expensive campaign in the vast Mercian territory, leaving him no option but to take his army back to Wessex.

Wiglaf is named as beginning his second spell as king of Mercia in 830; he would thereafter reestablish Mercian vassalage over at least one Welsh kingdom.[34] In 831 he issued one of his two surviving charters, for a land donation at Hayes in Middlesex to Archbishop Wulfred, with no required counter-witness from Ecgberht.[35] This opposes our previous assumptions that Wessex had already seized full control of London. It may indicate a fresh agreement between Ecgberht and Wiglaf to share authority over London and its trade routes at a period when trade with the continent was impacted. It also looks to have been part of a greater peace treaty between them. There was to be no further direct conflict between the two kingdoms. Perhaps we are looking at a compromise, with Mercia acknowledging Wessex's domination across the south and south-east on the understanding that Wessex would not interfere in Mercian affairs. However, the lack of any surviving Mercian coinage from the London mint dateable to Wiglaf's reign clouds the issue of how authority was divided there, leading to speculation that Ecgberht also denied permission for Wiglaf to produce his own coinage at the London mint.

The evidence is contradictory when assessing the balance of power from 831 onwards. During the 830s, Wiglaf and Mercia successfully regained control of Berkshire, which was confirmed as Mercian territory by the time of Ecgberht's death in 839. In addition, the ongoing cooperation between Wiglaf and the Church headquarters at Canterbury perhaps symbolises the extent to which Mercia during the 830s recovered some portion of its previous influence. Extant charters acknowledge that the Canterbury clergy were still open to Mercian influences, in fact, they continued to deal directly with Wiglaf rather than Ecgberht.

The situation regarding the relationship between the West Saxon and Mercian kings in terms of Canterbury was still unchanged by 836. We have an extant charter of that year detailing a council held near Leominster presided over by Wiglaf, which was attended by Ceolnoth, archbishop of Canterbury.[36] However, the interesting aspect of this charter can be found in the witness lists. This was clearly an important meeting, though this is not evident from the text itself. Apart from Ceolnoth and Wiglaf, no fewer than nine bishops are among the signatories, including those from the West Saxon-controlled houses of Sherborne, Selsey and Rochester. The only notable senior cleric missing from south of the Humber is Bishop Eadhun of Winchester. His absence, and that of Ecgberht and Æthelwulf, perhaps tells us much about the continued problematic relationship between the Wessex leadership and Ceolnoth.

While the situation between Wessex and Mercia had stabilised, there had been a fundamental change to the status quo. The accepted order among the remaining Anglo-Saxon kingdoms had changed in the turbulent five years between 825 and 830, with Wessex emerging as the dominant kingdom, taking the baton from Mercia and holding it firmly.

The continued truce between Wessex and Mercia allowed the West Saxon administration in the south-east the opportunity to turn to other matters, and the pursuit of a harmonious relationship with the Church at Canterbury and its archbishop finally drifted to the top of the agenda in the last years of Ecgberht's reign. However, we should first briefly review developments between Ecgberht and Ceolnoth's predecessor, Archbishop Wulfred. Ecgberht seems to have encountered the same difficulties with him that some Mercian kings had previously faced. Wulfred had held his position as head of the Church since 804 and seems to have been free to produce his own coinage while Kent was under Mercian client kings. However, there is a gap shortly before Wulfred's death where coinage in his name was suspended, presumably on Ecgberht's orders, and this situation prevailed until the archbishop's death on 21 March 832. There then followed a disagreement as to Wulfred's successor, probably caused by Canterbury's refusal to deal with either the king of Wessex or his son Æthelwulf in his role as 'king' of Kent. In consequence, Wulfred was succeeded briefly by either Feologild or Swithred, with confusion brought about by the Canterbury clergy refusing to accept the candidate nominated by Ecgberht.[37]

The ASC records Feologild's death in 832 but entitles him 'abbot', not archbishop, reflecting the ongoing contention ahead of his long-term successor

Ceolnoth's appointment.[38] However, the relationship with Canterbury did not improve. As seen in the above referenced charter of 836, there was still impasse between them for the first six years of Ceolnoth's archbishopric. He would continue to work in concert with the Mercian king, implying that Canterbury had persisted with a policy of non-cooperation with the West Saxons, stemming from a refusal to acknowledge their legal occupation of Kent. This dispute between Ecgberht and the archbishop of Canterbury could not go on indefinitely, and they would reach a resolution in 838. However, it would not be ratified until the following year after Æthelwulf had succeeded his father, which might lead us to speculate that it was Ecgberht's death that resolved the situation to Ceolnoth's satisfaction.

Just over a dozen charters have survived from Ecgberht's reign between 825 and 839, and the majority were issued either soon after his famous victory in 825 or during the last two years of his rule. These later charters were part of the move to establish greater West Saxon authority in the south-east and ensure an acceptance by the senior secular and ecclesiastic figures that his son Æthelwulf would automatically succeed and be accepted as king of Wessex. Of these later charters most relate, not unexpectedly, to land donations to the Church, primarily at Winchester or in Kent, rather than to his secular support.

Similarly, most of the surviving coins from Ecgberht's reign are shown to have been minted at either Canterbury or Rochester or, after 830, at Southampton (Hamtun), which seems in many ways to match the extant charter distribution. While Hamtun remained the larger of the two main Hampshire settlements, Winchester was experiencing a new level of urbanisation as a flourishing centre of trade with a growing population of several thousand. The Anglo-Saxon royal courts were of course itinerant, with Ecgberht moving his court from shire to shire, but it is reasonable to accept that Winchester may also have become the location for the primary royal residence by the mid-ninth century. Unfortunately, nothing survives of the former royal palace, although some historians have advocated that any such residence would have been near the Old Minster, with a suggested location perhaps having been to the north-west of the minster, underneath part of the area now occupied by Winchester Museum.

Beyond Mercia and the Church, from the mid-830s onwards, Wessex and Ecgberht had to respond to a new surge of Viking attacks along the extended Wessex shorelines. The first raid came in 834 at Sheppey in Kent, the first to be recorded by the ASC within Wessex since the landing at Portland in 793.[39] The next came in 836, a much larger affair in which the ASC notes that 'King Ecgberht fought against 35 ship-loads at Carhampton, and great slaughter was made there, and the Danish had possession of the place of slaughter'.[40] Carhampton was a West Saxon royal vill a mile inland from the north Somerset coast near Porlock Bay, and its location shows that the raiders had likely sailed from Scandinavian settlements across the Irish Sea. This was also the first instance of the chronicle scribe calling the raiders 'Danish', a description used thereafter for most Viking raids and landings. This even applies to those raids which historians have identified as being by Norsemen or other undefined groups, including those from Ireland and northern Britain. This association with 'Danes' acknowledges the conception of the chronicle in the 890s, as scribes of that period focused on England's ongoing fight against Danish invasion.

The most significant Viking-Danish incursion during Ecgberht's reign came in 838, a year before his death, and once again it came in the south-west. However, this raid was distinctive because the Vikings allied themselves with the native British before launching their attack. The presumption of a prior agreement between the groups is unclear, as is the speed of the allies' advance after the arrival of the Viking fleet. The British may have seen this as an attempt to permanently recover occupied territory, whereas the Vikings viewed it as nothing more than an opportunity for plunder.

The ASC has it that 'here a great raiding ship-army (Danes) came to Cornwall, and they turned into one (i.e. joined the Cornovii British), and were fighting against Egbert'.[41] In response to news of the Vikings having landed in force, the king, approaching his mid-sixties, led the West Saxon fyrd himself to confront them. The ASC version A notes that he 'travelled (version E states 'campaigned') with the army and fought against them'.[42] Ecgberht advanced his forces quickly and the battle was joined at a site named Hingston Down, which John of Worcester alternately names Hengist's Down.[43] By association there are two locations with the place name Hingston that historians have identified for the battle site, one in Cornwall and one in Devon.

The Devon location is a sloping hill less than a mile east of present-day Moretonhampstead, where the B3212 road bends around it to its north, about 25 miles east of the River Tamar and 10 miles west of Exeter. It is some distance from any significant waterway, so we must wonder where the Vikings beached their ships. Historians who favour this site argue the allies had the time to march some distance east before Ecgberht could assemble his army to meet them and that their logical intention was to pillage Exeter, at that time the largest Anglo-Saxon settlement in the south-west.[44] However, the hill suggests a prepared defensive position, which implies that the West Saxons had already established themselves there to block the road to Exeter ahead of the allies.

The alternate Hingston location is close to the Devon–Cornwall border. More historians support this location, as it was closer to a wide waterway along which the Viking ships would have sailed inland before linking with the British.[45] This Hingston Down is situated a mile and a half west of the River Tamar where it passes through Gunnislake. It is half a mile north of the modern A390 road to Callington, which was at that time the main route from and into Cornwall. The down is now dominated by the Hingston Down Quarry, but its topography suggests it was once a strategic defensive position. Because it is further west than the other Hingston option, the likelihood is that the British–Viking allies established themselves there after having received news of Ecgberht's fast-approaching army.

The most interesting aspect of this latter location is perhaps the suggested approach routes of both armies ahead of the battle. Local folklore tells us that the Viking force marched north towards Hingston to join the assembled British force via the Danescombe Valley, which later took its name from this incident, after having first sailed their ships up the Tamar to beach them along the stretch of the river near Calstock. The allies had expected the West Saxons to approach them via the main route from the east, fording the Tamar at the crossing point at Gunnislake. However, provincial military historians, combining their knowledge of the local landscape, have speculated that Ecgberht did not take the obvious route and caught them unawares. Bypassing Gunnislake, his army crossed the river instead at Latchley, 2 miles to the north-west, and approached the allies at Hingston from the north, not the east.[46] We have no further details, but if we accept Ecgberht's clever strategy it appears to have worked. The ASC notes that he 'put to flight both the British and the Danish', and Henry of Huntingdon describes them being 'shattered ... in a crushing defeat'.[47] Hingston Down would prove to be the last recorded major conflict involving the British tribes against the West Saxons.

As noted above, 838 saw a resolution of the ongoing row between the head of the English Church and the secular leadership of Wessex. At a council held at Kingston-upon-Thames, a location representing what we could describe as a neutral zone for all parties, their new accord survives within an extant charter, which neither Ecgberht nor Ceolnoth appears to have issued. Instead, to continue the theme of neutrality, the document declares itself as 'Confirmation by Southumbrian bishops of the agreement made at Kingston'.[48] The text confirms that Ecgberht and Æthelwulf acknowledged restoring to Ceolnoth and Canterbury an estate at Malling in Sussex which had been granted to Christ Church Canterbury by Baldred when he was briefly king in Kent during the 820s. Evidently, this estate had been taken from Canterbury by Ecgberht or Æthelwulf when they had assumed control of Kent and Sussex. As part of this agreement, ratified in a charter at Wilton the following year, Ceolnoth ceded to Ecgberht the right to influence electing abbots and abbesses within the Kentish minsters and gave the king control of the free minsters under Canterbury's authority.

It is hard to imagine the twelve-year dispute between the West Saxon kings and Christ Church had begun because of these issues. The agreement achieved a formal acceptance from Canterbury of the West Saxon right to rule over Kent, with Ceolnoth and the Christ Church community and their successors promising loyalty to the West Saxon kings and their heirs.[49] The reason why the Church finally gave these concessions in 838 may be easily explained. As part of this agreement, Ecgberht confirmed he would protect all Church property in the south-east from Viking raiders. Presumably, raids on Church property in the region had already increased, and as Wiglaf and Mercia were unable to assist militarily Ceolnoth therefore chose pragmatism. The archbishop had recognised that the military protection provided by Wessex was important, and the recent large raid at Sheppey earlier in the year had probably underlined his concerns.

Ecgberht, now in his mid-sixties, died in 839. The ASC recorded he had ruled for '37 years and 7 months', and as he had assumed the throne in 802 we can conclude he died during the last few months of the year.[50] An unverified Frankish source claimed Ecgberht was in contact with Louis the Pious no later than Easter 839 to discuss safe passage for a pilgrimage to Rome. This may have been brought on by a recognition that his health was failing. However, he does not appear to have made the trip, which suggests his health suffered a rapid decline. He left the kingdom in a much better position than he had first found it. It is from Alfred's own will in the late ninth century that some insight is gained into his grandfather's will. Ecgberht left land only to his male descendants to ensure that royal estates would not be lost through marriage to other West Saxon nobility – or, more importantly perhaps, through marriages to the nobility within any other Anglo-Saxon kingdom.

Like his predecessors Cynegils and Cynewulf, Ecgberht was buried within the Old Minster at Winchester. His and their remains, plus also the remains of Wine, the first bishop of Winchester during the 660s, and those of several other monarchs and senior clerics who had also been buried there prior to and following the Norman Conquest, were placed into nine mortuary chests and moved into the new Norman-designed cathedral built in the late eleventh century to replace the Old Minster. The footprint of the present-day Norman cathedral was slightly to the south of and overlapping the south-west corner of the earlier Anglo-Saxon building. The floor layout of the smaller Anglo-Saxon minster is today marked out by tiles on the grass enclosure close to the north of the cathedral. The later story of the remains previously buried in the Old Minster, as discussed in the chapter on Cynegils, is both perturbing and fascinating.[51]

15
Æthelwulf
839–856/8

Ecgberht had already put everything in place to ensure that his son Æthelwulf took the throne of Wessex unchallenged in 839.[1] Unlike many previous transfers of the throne, this transition saw no confusion or debate. This was before the age of primogeniture – the right of succession belonging to the firstborn child – but it was a clear marker for the future. Ecgberht's dynasty would survive through successive kings of Wessex, one after the other, through his son and four grandsons and beyond. Æthelwulf was Ecgberht's only son, although there are claims he had a sister or half-sister named Æthelburh (aka Alburga). She may have been Ecgberht's half-sister, not his daughter;[2] there is an Æthelburh who later became the abbess at Wilton Abbey, which suggests a strong connection to the West Saxon royal court.

Likely born in Francia during his father's exile, and now in his early forties, Æthelwulf's first action appears to have been an arrangement to devolve some authority to his eldest son, Æthelstan. This was to continue the arrangement that had been in place between him and his father. Æthelwulf held overall control, but he assigned to Æthelstan responsibility to administer eastern Wessex, the region that comprised Kent, Sussex, Surrey and Essex. The ASC proclaimed Æthelwulf had 'succeeded to the kingdom of Wessex' but immediately granted his eldest son, the ætheling Æthelstan, 'the kingdom of the inhabitants of Kent and to Surrey and to the kingdom of Sussex'.[3] Essex is notably excluded by the scribe. However, the East Saxons were already closely tied to events in Kent, long before Wessex took control of the south-east, so we are safe in including Essex within Æthelstan's remit. Sources describe him as a 'king' in his own right, not just a sub-king of Wessex, despite being no older than twenty. Without doubt, he would have also acted as his father's deputy.

Based on the estimated age of Æthelstan, historians have concluded that Æthelwulf had married his wife, Osburh, no later than 820. According to Alfred's biographer Asser, she was of noble birth, the daughter of an official at the royal court named Oslac.[4] Her lineage through Oslac was noted as being Jutish from origins in Kent or otherwise traceable back to the sixth-century warlord brothers Stuf and Wihtgar.[5] However, her father does not appear as a witness in any of Ecgberht's or Æthelwulf's charters and is described in a contemporary text as a '*pincerna*', which means butler to the king. This would suggest Æthelwulf's marriage was not, after all, an ideal political arrangement and that perhaps the social status of his wife was exaggerated by some later sources.

Osburh is normally accepted by historians as being the mother to all Æthelwulf's six children: Æthelstan, Æthelbald, Æthelswith, Æthelberht, Æthelred and Alfred. Even acknowledging that she was much younger than her husband when they married, and speculating that she gave birth to Æthelstan while still only fifteen or sixteen (no later than 822 perhaps), we need to tally against this that her last child Alfred was not born until 849. We therefore have an estimated period of around twenty-seven years between her first and last child, so she was apparently into her mid-forties by the time of Alfred's birth.

While the longevity of Osburh's fertility is absolutely plausible, her potential age has caused some historians to question the assumption she was mother to all Æthelwulf's children. It has been proposed that she was not Æthelwulf's first wife but his second (of three), and that another unnamed woman, unmentioned in the primary sources, was the mother of Æthelstan.[6] Support for this comes when it is realised that there is an approximate fifteen-year gap between Æthelstan's birth and that of the next eldest child, Æthelbald, meaning that Osburh's second child was not born until she had passed the age of thirty. This large gap between pregnancies contrasts with the later sequence of births, wherein from Æthelbald to Æthelswith to Æthelberht we have three births in about three or four years. All of this casts doubt on Osburh having been Æthelstan's mother, and suggests instead that she was much younger than her husband and was nearly the same age as the ætheling Æthelstan.

When Æthelwulf became king, four of his six children had already been born. Osburh does not appear in any of his charters, and she is scarcely referred to in contemporary documents. She seems, unlike Æthelwulf's later spouse Judith of Flanders, to have been a victim of the short-lived West Saxon custom of excluding the king's wife from a position at court.[7] However, Æthelwulf would ignore it when he remarried after Osburh's death, naming his new wife Judith as his queen during the 850s. His fourth son, later king Æthelred (I), would also entitle his own wife, Wulfthryth, as queen in his charter of 868.[8] Why, then, did Asser emphasise the matter of whether the king's wife should be named 'queen' or not? Perhaps it is possible Alfred was disillusioned by his father's marriage to Judith, and this had some effect on his approach to the functional title of a king's consort.

Æthelwulf's administration revolved around responsibility for tax collecting and upholding the law through regional officials and regular sessions of the hundreds and the shires. Ealdormen represented the king regionally, with reeves providing local support in financial and judicial affairs. The role of the reeve would change over time. At some stage, perhaps during Æthelwulf's reign, the station of high reeve was beginning to appear, deputising for the ealdorman and, if need be, commanding the local fyrd.[9]

Government officials were supported by the senior clergy, who themselves were very much part of the nobility. In most cases, the clergy were the only literate class to record and distribute court pronouncements. Overriding all of this in upholding the link between central and regional government was Æthelwulf's itinerant court. Æthelwulf's administration was typical of the period, with court activities often conducted through a circuit of royal estates and shire centres so that the king and his court, the scribes, royal officials and senior nobles would criss-cross the kingdom regularly to deal at a local level with the regional nobility and wider populace. This was the primary method of relaying the directives of central government throughout the kingdom. It was an important political consideration that there was a clear societal link between the king and his people. A review of a selection of charters issued by Æthelwulf or any of his predecessors and successors up to the twelfth century shows that the king and his court travelled extensively to conduct royal councils.

In terms of Æthelwulf's extant charters, there are around forty. This is a much better document survival rate than witnessed by any of his predecessors, including the much longer reign of his father. Three-quarters of them relate to donations to churches or to individual clergy. Among them are grants for land for all the major religious houses within Wessex, including Christ Church Canterbury, St Augustine's Canterbury, Glastonbury, Malmesbury, Sherborne and Winchester. Most went to Malmsbury and Winchester, which have eleven between them.[10] The charters donating estates to Christ Church are undoubtedly proof that Æthelwulf was intent on maintaining the new accord with Archbishop Ceolnoth that had taken him and his father several years to achieve. Ceolnoth was to remain as archbishop until his death in 870.

One document that stands out as exceptional during Æthelwulf's reign is a charter from 857 to the church of Saint-Denis in Paris, donating an estate at Rotherfield near Pevensey in Sussex.[11] This implies that Æthelwulf continued to maintain a good relationship with his Frankish connections, and the donation may have been at the suggestion of his Frankish wife Judith, coming as it did a year after their marriage. This is proof of the ongoing West Saxon alliance with the Frankish court that dated back to Ecgberht's exile. Æthelwulf's own acknowledged ties with Francia had held thereafter throughout his lifetime. During the 840s, as an example, he appointed a personal Frankish secretary named Felix to the royal court.[12]

During Aethelwulf's first decade on the throne, the frequency of Viking raids continued unabated. The Vikings may have been exploiting a change in the kingdom's monarch after Ecgberht's long rule. The first such raid came in 840, when Ealdorman Wulfheard of Wiltshire fought and defeated a raiding army of thirty-three ships, comprising maybe a thousand warriors, that had landed in the Solent. However, elsewhere the Vikings fared better. The same year Ealdorman Æthelhelm of Dorset fought but lost a battle against a large Danish raiding army in Portland and was killed.[13] The following year another group landed at Romney Marsh, killing Ealdorman Hereberht of Kent, and other raids were reported that same year within Kent and further north in East Anglia and Lindsey (Lincolnshire).[14]

In 842 Rochester was raided, although the invaders concentrated their major effort that year on Mercian-controlled London, and in 843 the Irish Vikings returned to attack Carhampton in Devon, landing in Blue Anchor Bay. This repeated the 836 raid against Carhampton, and the outcome was replicated also, with the Danes having 'possession of the place of slaughter'.[15] The ASC entry infers Æthelwulf fought there in person, similar to his father being present during the earlier encounter, which could imply the raiders had prior knowledge that the king would be visiting the royal vill with perhaps a reduced retinue.

There was a lull after 843, at least according to the primary sources, although we can assume that not all raids were recorded, including other Viking raids along the East Anglian and Northumbrian coasts. Sometime before 845 in Northumbria, the relics of St Cuthbert were removed from Lindisfarne for safety on what would be the first of two separate necessary occasions, and translated inland to the church at Norham-on-Tweed.[16] Elsewhere, excavations at Beverley, next to the River Hull, have located a hoard of coins buried around 851, linked to the pillaging of the monastery there by Vikings that year.

Viking raids resumed in 848 across greater Wessex. Now incorporating the coasts and rivers of Kent, Sussex and Essex, there was a much more extended mileage of West Saxon coastline to cover than twenty years earlier. However, it would seem from the outcome of these new encounters that the

West Saxons had used the intervening period to adjust their strategy and tactics to more successfully counteract raiders. The 848 raids involved a large Viking fleet sailing into the Bristol Channel. However, the West Saxons, led by ealdormen Eanwulf of Somerset and Osric of Dorset, with Bishop Ealhstan of Sherborne alongside them, challenged them as they landed at the mouth of the River Parret in Somerset, and 'made a great slaughter there and took the victory'.[17] The speed of this response, alongside the noted involvement of the Dorset fyrd fighting near the Bristol Channel, would suggest a new level of coordinated resistance. We can only speculate – the primary sources provide no clues – but Aethelwulf may have instigated and implemented a better system for summoning the local fyrds, or possibly a rudimentary system of regional standing armies on rotational service to respond to major raids, preceding the later changes made by Alfred in the 880s.

There were another two attacks in 850. The first involved the Devonshire fyrd under Ealdorman Ceorl defeating the invaders at a place the ASC named 'Wicga's stronghold', which Henry of Huntingdon later renamed Wicganbeorg.[18] This location remains the subject of debate. Some have suggested Wigborough, a small village in south Somerset 6 miles west of present-day Yeovil.[19] Another potential location is around the former hamlets named Lower and Higher Weekaborough in Devon, 3 miles north-east of Totnes.[20] The landscape around Wigborough gives us no clues, but the Weekaboroughs are situated in a rolling landscape a few miles from the River Dart, which may imply the river had been the Vikings' access point.

The second attack of that year came at the other end of Wessex, where Æthelstan, in his role as king of Kent, with the aid of Ealdorman Ealhhere, defeated a raiding army at Sandwich. Sandwich was on the River Stour in the Wantsum Channel, which separated the Isle of Thanet from mainland Kent. It seems to have been specifically targeted, as it was the site of the Anglo-Saxon naval base with the dual responsibility for guarding the Dover Straits and the Thames Estuary. The ASC records Æthelstan and Ealhhere captured nine ships and 'put the others to flight'.[21] Henry of Huntingdon describes it as a naval battle, but whether the Anglo-Saxon navy was already proficient enough at this point to defeat the more experienced sailors within the Viking fleets is highly debatable.[22] The inference we might take is that the Vikings were challenged soon after they had landed, implying the ships were captured while they were anchored on the River Stour. However, the Vikings stayed in camp on this side of the Channel for the first time during the following winter. John of Worcester names their base as Sheppey.[23]

These raids were a prelude to what would in 851 be the arrival of the largest Viking (or Danish) fleet to that date to invade English shores. They sailed from several bases not only in Denmark but nearer to hand in Frisia,

Francia and Normandy. The ASC scribe recorded that 'three and a half hundred ships came into the mouth of the Thames and stormed Canterbury and London'.[24] This was a problem not just for Wessex but perhaps more so for the Mercian king Beorhtwulf at London. On the size of this fleet we should perhaps take the recorded number of vessels with caution, because, as observed by many historians, contemporary scribes were prone to exaggeration.[25] However, even if we downgrade the fleet to around only 200 vessels with a conservative estimate of twenty-five to thirty men per vessel the fighting strength of this army would have still exceeded anything else seen before across all the Anglo-Saxon kingdoms. It could have numbered at least 5,000 fighting men. Æthelstan was unable to counteract such a large fighting force with the *Kentish* fyrd, and Canterbury was sacked. The raiding army then sailed up the Thames to London and 'put to flight Beorhtwulf king of Mercia with his army'.[26] Beorhtwulf's loss of London led soon afterwards to his loss of the throne. The last two charters in his name are dated to 851, but even here historians suspect them of being forgeries by the clergy at Worcester.[27] His successor, Burgred, first appears in a charter dated to July 852.[28]

Having sacked London, the Viking army, purportedly led by a warlord named Roric, left their ships on the south bank of the Thames and moved into Surrey. It should be noted there was no bridge crossing between London and Southwark; the Roman bridge had fallen into disrepair and collapsed generations earlier, and the Anglo-Saxons did not build a replacement until the late ninth century. From the primary sources, we know that Æthelwulf and his second son, Æthelbald, challenged and fought the invaders soon afterwards.

The absence of any mention of Æthelwulf's eldest son, Æthelstan, raises questions. He may have been seriously injured during or after the fighting at Sandwich months earlier, possibly even mortally. His last valid appearance in a charter had come in 850. He was to also appear in 855 as a witness in one of his father's charters, but that document is considered spurious.[29] We know he died no later than 852.[30] In recent times excavations around the former site of the Old Minster at Winchester revealed the remains of a mid-ninth-century burial of a man aged between twenty-five and thirty-five. It was discovered at what would have been a prestigious location in the former nave, with the individual showing evidence of having worn distinctive headgear, indicating royal status. As all other obvious elite burials at Winchester between 840 to 870 have been accounted for, some have concluded that Æthelstan is the likeliest putative candidate for these remains.[31]

On encountering the Danish army, the king and his son Æthelbald, 'with the West Saxon army fought against them (Danes) at Oak Field (aka

Aclea) ... and there took the victory', with 'the greatest slaughter of a heathen raiding army that we have ever heard tell of'.[32] As this account was written after the subsequent Danish wars during the 860s to 890s, it was reportedly more decisive than even the two more famous later West Saxon victories at Ashdown and Edington. Similar detail of the battle is given by Asser, and later in John of Worcester's *Chronicon*.[33] Conjecture on the numbers involved is guesswork. By this period the West Saxon king was able to muster potentially a maximum of 5,000 men, working on the system of one conscripted man per 5 hides of land, with twenty men coming from each of the estimated 250 Wessex hundreds, with a hundred, as it sounds, being 100 hides of land.

Considering time and location, Æthelwulf likely had a maximum of 3,500 men at Aclea. Even with fewer than 350 ships, with some troops remaining with the fleet, and the losses received at London and Canterbury, the Vikings still likely numbered over 4,000 men. Notwithstanding the claimed Viking losses, Aclea therefore involved the largest number of combatants in a single battle between Anglo-Saxons and Vikings across the ninth and tenth centuries. The location of the battlefield of Aclea/Oak Field remains under debate. Based on a mix of place-name association, the perceived goals of the invading army and the timespan and direction of Æthelwulf's response, there are three primary sites.[34] Taking the name Aclea (from Old English), which the ASC calls Oak Field and John of Worcester 'the field of the oak', historians have narrowed the possibilities to Oakleigh, Ockley and Oakley.

Oakleigh lies in Kent north of the village of Higham, less than 2 miles from the south bank of the River Thames opposite Tilbury. Historians favour its proximity to where the Danish fleet may have anchored. However, it is hard to imagine Æthelwulf had been able to assemble a force sufficiently large enough to challenge the Viking army that far east in the time available. Asser's reference to the Vikings moving into Surrey might suggest Oakleigh as a starting point, but his reference is also misleading, in that 'Surrey' in the tenth century was defined by him as 'a district situated ... to the west of Kent', which could possibly incorporate the whole region as far as northern Hampshire.[35]

The second option, Ockley, lies a few miles from both Dorking and Horsham, and sits on the modern A29, on what was the route of Stane Street, the Roman road from London to Chichester. Oak trees still surround the present-day village. Potentially, the Danish army may have been pillaging down Stane Street towards the south coast, with their ships already moving out of the Thames Estuary into the English Channel to meet them at Chichester (Bosham harbour) or Pevensey in a pre-planned action. However, in terms of place-name association support for Ockley is weak. Further research has found that the Old English for Ockley was not Aclea but rather 'Okele' or 'Okalee' instead.[36]

The last major place-name candidate is Oakley in Hampshire, just west of modern Basingstoke, although like Ockley it also presupposes the Danes had carried out a significant march away from London, in this instance a much greater distance. The area around Oakley today contains areas of oak woodland, although we should not overplay this in terms of its original name of 'field of oaks'. Oakley has more potential if we accept the proposal by some historians that the Vikings had, after sacking London, conducted a wide arc of pillage through Surrey and across Berkshire, perhaps being shadowed by their fleet, before choosing to return east via the more open country of north Hampshire, perhaps via the ancient track of Harrow Way.[37]

The choice of Oakley seems, for some, too far west in terms of potential Viking movements, but it would have allowed Æthelwulf more time to muster the largest West Saxon fyrd he could. By challenging them in central Wessex he was able to call on additional troops from Wiltshire, Somerset and Dorset to supplement the men mustered from Surrey, Hampshire and Sussex. Time was a crucial factor in assembling a force strong enough to counteract such a large Viking army. Closer locations to London would have limited his time to gather enough men. Oakley lay less than a mile and a half west from where the Roman road from Winchester to Silchester bisected the track known as the Harrow Way, which on this stretch is now known as Pack Lane, about 2 miles south-west from the centre of modern Basingstoke. In terms of an extended area of pillage by the Vikings, these were routes that allowed easy access into central Wessex but also a fast route back to London or to the River Thames in Berkshire.

Proponents for this location have identified the potential battlefield as being east of Oakley within the aptly named area of Battle Down Farm and the Battle Down Junction of the Salisbury and Southampton railway lines.[38] These names purport to come from the 851 battle, although this cannot be verified. However, we can imagine a scenario where the West Saxon army had approached via the Roman road from Winchester and then blocked the Danish army as it returned east along the Harrow Way.

After Aclea, only two more major raids within Wessex are recorded before 860, although Frankish sources refer to further attacks on England elsewhere.[39] Francia had also experienced several large Viking attacks during this period and some historians have suggested there may have been dialogue between Æthelwulf and Charles the Bald of Francia for combined operations against the Vikings.[40] Possibly, Charles had given Æthelwulf advance notice of significant Viking movements, but this did not prevent raids on religious houses in eastern Wessex. Lyminge, Sheppey, Thanet, Folkestone, Hoo and Dover were all plundered and forced to close, illustrating that minor raids continued unabated.

Æthelwulf's fifth child, Æthelred, had been born sometime before 847, possibly in Winchester, and the last and youngest was Alfred, born in Wantage in Berkshire in 848 or 849. Most if not all of Berkshire had been ceded from Mercian to West Saxon authority sometime during the mid-840s following the transition of the Mercian throne from Wigstan to Beorhtwulf. The Mercian king is seen issuing charters involving estates at Pangbourne in 844 for his ealdorman Æthelwulf, perhaps a final attempt by Beorhtwulf to keep this man and the region within Mercian authority.[41] However, the administrative and military control of Berkshire transferred soon afterwards, along with Ealdorman Æthelwulf's allegiance. Osburh giving birth in Wantage acknowledges the earlier peaceful transfer of control from Mercia to Wessex.

Despite not being universally acknowledged, signs point to a peace agreement between the two kingdoms stretching back to the 830s. One indication could come from a review of the coinage. Beorhtwulf of Mercia had resumed coin production around 841, the first in Mercia since Ecgberht and the Mercian king Wiglaf had come to terms. However, there were no longer enough skilled die-cutters in Mercia and Beorhtwulf was probably forced to employ moneyers in Wessex. We have evidence therefore of Mercian coins possibly being produced at Rochester before transferring to Mercian-controlled London, where it appears based on the moneyers' marks that Æthelwulf was able to mint some of his own coinage in parallel.[42]

In 853 the ASC recorded that Burgred, the new king of Mercia, requested help from Æthelwulf's Wessex to subdue the Welsh of Powys who had been raiding across Offa's Dyke. Æthelwulf agreed to help and a combined Mercian and West Saxon army marched into Wales and 'made them all subject to them'.[43] That Wessex was able to commit forces to aid Mercia well beyond its own borders tells us that the immediate Viking threat from the continent had faded after Aclea. More relevantly, we see a new level of cooperation emerging between old adversaries. A key part of this detente was the marriage of Æthelwulf's only daughter, the twenty-something Æthelswith, to Mercia's Burgred. The ceremony took place just after Easter in early April 853 at the West Saxon royal vill at Chippenham.

Æthelswith was given a prominent position in Mercian court politics in the same way other Mercian queens enjoyed a higher profile than their contemporary West Saxon equivalents. The marriage did not produce any known heirs. Of the eight surviving charters issued by Burgred Æthelswith signs six, and in two – one dated 864 and the other 869 – she signs with equal prominence.[44] In 868 she also issued in her name as 'Queen of the Mercians' a charter regarding an estate in what was already then West Saxon-controlled Berkshire.[45] William of Malmesbury adds that by this marriage alliance Burgred 'found relief both from the payment of tribute and from the depredations of the enemy'.[46] This entry is a little puzzling. We could presume the 'enemy' refers to either the Welsh or Vikings, but it remains unclear to whom Burgred was already paying tribute. If it relates to Æthelwulf's Wessex, we cannot imagine what other advantage the West Saxon king gained as recompense other than perhaps the larger part of the plunder taken from the Welsh campaign. It is plausible it was already known, for whatever reason, that the couple could not have children, but that their union was arranged to cement a closer political alliance without concerns to the future succession within Mercia.

The year 853 saw another raiding army land at Thanet in Kent, where they were met by ealdormen Ealhhere of Kent and Huda of Surrey. Although the Vikings were defeated both ealdormen died, with many from both sides either killed or drowned in the fighting.[47]

Asser's writings prevent us from disregarding another reputedly significant event that year. According to Asser, the king of Wessex sent his youngest son Alfred to Rome, then aged no more than four, accompanied by 'a great number of both nobles and commoners', where, on his arrival, Pope Leo IV 'anointed the child Alfred as king, ordaining him properly, received him as an adoptive son, and confirmed him'.[48] Alfred would make another trip to Rome, accompanied by his father Æthelwulf, two years after the first visit. However, some historians have recently argued that perhaps Asser was mistaken, and that Alfred's first and only visit to Rome was the 855 journey, and it was then that he met the pope alongside his father. The 'anointing as king' affair has been much debated. However, the question of a child, still only aged six in 855, being anointed as a future king of Anglo-Saxon England by the pope is as unlikely as it sounds. The papacy demonstrably had no jurisdiction to appoint anyone as heir to any English kingdom, whatever their age. In addition, during 853 or 855 Alfred still had three older brothers very much alive who were in line to succeed ahead of him, and it was plausible any one of them could have male heirs of their own, pushing Alfred even further down the line of succession.

Perhaps we can interpret this story instead as Asser creating retrospective history in the light of Alfred's later achievements. The 'kingly' anointment was central to the aura Asser later wished to create around Alfred's reputation, aimed at promoting the inevitability of the king's destiny after he had saved Wessex from the Danes in the 870s and 880s.[49] There is no denial that Alfred visited Rome and met Pope Leo IV. We know from his writings how his time in Rome had a profound effect on his later approach to kingship and his ideological viewpoint. However, there is a more rational explanation as to what likely took place in an audience with the pope. Alfred was not 'anointed' as a future king. As now accepted by many academics, the child was presented instead with the insignia of a Roman consul, which historians now agree was part of a formal ceremony during confirmation and baptism rather than a bold pronouncement on Alfred's future fate.[50]

Other kings before Æthelwulf had travelled to Rome – Ine and Caedwalla spring to mind – but they had plans of a peaceful retirement or a formal absolution before their approaching deaths. This was not the case for Æthelwulf. He seems, from assessing his final actions before departing for Rome, to have undertaken the trip after a personal epiphany. From contemporary writings, the death of Æthelwulf's wife Osburh is understood to have taken place while Alfred was still a boy. Perhaps this had been during 855, and her death after a marriage of over thirty years may have prompted his pilgrimage.

The king's eldest surviving son, Æthelbald, having acted as king or under-king of Kent since the death of his brother Æthelstan, was appointed as regent for the whole of Wessex in his father's absence. As a consequence, the next eldest son, Æthelberht, was appointed to replace Æthelbald in Kent. Æthelbald's assigned responsibilities are not known, nor the intended duration of his tenure. Æthelwulf was away from his kingdom for more than a year. When he returned, circumstances had changed.

Before he departed, as noted by the ASC and Asser, Æthelwulf granted a 'tenth part of his land over all his kingdom to the praise of God and his own eternal salvation'.[51] Bishop Swithin of Winchester, *in situ* since October 852, has been credited with persuading the king to undertake this generous act. Asser liked to claim that this act of decimation transferred land directly to the Church. In any case, for a king to grant away a tenth of his estates in the context of ninth-century practices was particularly generous, and the charter has been described as one of the most controversial documents of its time.[52]. A charter from 855 issued to a thegn named Dunn may better illustrate Æthelwulf's intent.[53] All land could be regarded as the king's land, and Æthelwulf's act of decimation conveyed a tenth of the royal demesne – in other words the lands of the crown – to the Church, as opposed to a tenth of his own personal estates. As noted by historians, Asser's interpretation that this transfer of land was a pious or virtuous act by the king is therefore a false assessment.[54] We can hypothesise that rather than donating land to the Church the West Saxon king was instead transferring estates to his senior thegns, who in turn could do what they wished with it.[55] The probability therefore is that Æthelwulf's act may have been implemented not to appease the Church but to appease the nobility, in the hopes of relieving the pressure upon his appointed regent, Æthelbald, during his planned absence from England.

Pope Leo IV died in July 855 and was succeeded by Benedict III while Æthelwulf was still on his way to Italy, so it was Benedict, not Leo, upon whom the West Saxon king lavished his gifts, and it was Benedict who baptised Alfred and presented him with his insignia. The West Saxon king's gifts included a gold crown weighing 4 pounds, a sword bound with fine gold, four silver-gilt Saxon bowls, two gold goblets, and additional donations of gold and silver to the clergy.[56] After remaining in Rome for almost twelve months Æthelwulf began his return journey, but stopped en route at the court of Charles II the Bald, ruler of Francia. As mentioned previously, the two rulers may have adopted a joint strategy against ongoing Viking attacks some years earlier and were already on good terms. Charles's father, Louis the Pious, had known Æthelwulf's father Ecgberht well.

The meeting was obviously pre-arranged. It was announced that Æthelwulf was to marry Charles's twelve-year-old daughter, Judith, giving the West Saxon king added status. But it is unclear at what stage the news reached the acting regent, Æthelbald. On his return Æthelwulf had to face down what one historian has called potential 'filial resentment'.[57] It is unclear how the king imagined Æthelbald and his other sons and the senior nobility would react to the news, but it is hard to believe that Æthelbald was overjoyed, and events on Æthelwulf's return suggest the same.

The marriage ceremony took place in Paris on 1 October 856.[58] Judith was young, but in the social and religious practices of the period girls were deemed to reach the age of lawful consent and sexual maturity by the age of twelve, and it was possible to be betrothed as young as seven. In a medieval context, the realities of life were significantly different from our own, and modern morals look on this practice as objectionable and abusive. Daughters were frequently used to form political marriage alliances. Those aged twelve or over were able to marry immediately, with younger girls being betrothed until they achieved the age of consent. As part of the alliance the Frankish king insisted his daughter Judith was consecrated as queen before she left for England, the first wife of any Anglo-Saxon king to be anointed queen in more than just name.[59]

Æthelwulf's motives for the marriage seem obvious: a closer union with Francia, and, combined with his recent visit to the papacy, a more central role in European affairs. As Judith was also the great-granddaughter of the Holy Roman Emperor and Frankish king Charlemagne, the prestige involved in marrying her was enormous. Charles the Bald had less to gain from the arrangement, although he must have seen Æthelwulf as a useful ally. He had encountered problems after the breakdown of his original amicable agreement for control of the Frankish kingdom, where he had held power in western Francia while his brothers Louis the German (of East Francia) and Lothair I (of Middle Francia) held the rest. However, Lothair had recently died, and redistributing Middle Francia had become an issue, with Charles's own position under pressure from Louis and Lothair's son Louis II (the Younger). Charles himself, unforeseen, would be exiled to Burgundy the following year, but was reinstated in 858.

While the king was away, acting regent Æthelbald and his brother Æthelberht in Kent had to deal with a new Viking fleet that had overwintered at Sheppey between 855 and 856.[60] The primary sources are silent on what became of these Vikings, but we have evidence that religious houses in Kent were targeted during this period. Æthelwulf and his new queen, with the young Alfred, returned to England in the last weeks of 856. With Æthelbald having dealt well with all issues as regent during Æthelwulf's extended absence, to then be presented with the news of his father's remarriage was presumably a shock.

As he stepped ashore in England, Æthelwulf was purportedly faced with a crisis. In view of the recent development this is perhaps unsurprising. Asser points all blame towards Æthelbald as perpetrating unrest, but interestingly, the ASC omits mention of it, recording that Æthelwulf 'came home in good health' and 'came to his people and they were glad of it'.[61] Reference to the king's 'people' being 'glad' for his return may be the scribe's subtle sign that not all had been well beforehand. Meanwhile, Asser bluntly writes of there being a 'disgraceful episode – contrary to the practice of all Christian men' regarding Æthelbald, which he states was told to him from Alfred's own recollections.[62] Asser records that Æthelbald, in alliance with several members of the witan from Somerset and Dorset, particularly Bishop Ealhstan of Sherborne and Ealdorman Eanwulf of Somerset, became what he describes as 'co-conspirators' and plotted to usurp the throne.[63] The level of political backing for Æthelbald over his father cannot be known, although support existed for Æthelbald within Somerset, Dorset and Wiltshire. Presented with the *fait accompli* of Æthelwulf's marriage seems to have sparked the tension. Æthelbald likely did not anticipate his father marrying Judith, which could see him replaced as heir to the throne if they were to have a son.

Asser's viewpoint on the scandal endured. By the time John of Worcester was writing his *Chronicon*, Ealhstan and Eanwulf were portrayed as 'false advisers' to Æthelbald, the perpetrators behind a scheme to 'drive out the king (Æthelwulf) from his own realm'.[64] His contemporary William of Malmesbury further describes Æthelbald in serious terms as 'worthless and disloyal to his father'.[65] It is clear Æthelbald is portrayed as the villain of the piece, but beyond these entries it is difficult to unravel what happened. Ultimately, conflict was avoided, according to Asser due only to Æthelwulf's forbearance. There are no indications that the temporary factional divide extended to violence.

However, another issue looks to have arisen on Æthelwulf's return and further inflamed the situation. Based on the limited detail gathered from his later will, Æthelwulf appears to have intended to permanently split the kingdom of Wessex in two, dividing it between his two eldest sons. For Æthelbald and his supporters, this may have been a larger concern even than his father's sudden marriage. The timing of Æthelwulf's transfer of authority to Æthelbald remains uncertain, but it created a complication for Æthelbald as to his expected role when his father resumed authority. Æthelberht was already holding the position of sub-king/king in Kent. Perhaps Æthelbald had expected his father to abdicate, and when it became clear that this would not occur he feared being left with even less power than his younger brother.[66]

We know Æthelwulf arranged a compromise with Æthelbald soon after his return, one in which they apparently shared power across the kingdom. The arrangement saw Æthelbald given full authority in western Wessex (from Hampshire westwards) and Æthelwulf accepting a reduced role replacing the acquiescent Æthelberht in eastern Wessex (Kent, Sussex, Surrey and Essex). William of Malmesbury noted Æthelwulf responded mildly to avert potential civil war, stating that 'it was not a fair division', with Æthelbald receiving 'the better half to the westward'.[67] One historian has further suggested that the division was not at the Sussex–Hampshire border, but perhaps further west at Selwood Forest near the border between Wiltshire and Somerset, thereby also bringing Hampshire under Æthelwulf's aegis.[68]

A 'reduced role' is subjective when we are discussing Æthelwulf. Control of just the eastern half of Wessex may well have suited him considering his father's claimed Kentish origins and his desire to divide the kingdom, and his will is evidence that he was preparing to do so on a more permanent basis, sharing it between Æthelbald and Æthelberht after his death. Why he wished to do this is unclear. Certainly Æthelbald saw the arrangement as him losing half of his kingdom to his younger brother, and he looks to have been determined that it would not happen.

Æthelwulf died on 13 January 858, with the *Annals of St Neots* informing us he was buried at the minster church at Steyning in Sussex.[69] His association with Steyning is not clear; maybe he had a kinship connection to it or had died in the vicinity. The reputed original stone lid to his tomb at Steyning can be seen just inside the entry porch at the present church of St Cuthman. However, his remains were later removed on the instructions of his son Alfred and taken for reburial alongside his father, Ecgberht, at the Old Minster in Winchester sometime during the 870s.[70] His remains, along with those of Ecgberht and the other kings and clerics that had been buried in the Old Minster, were later desecrated and defiled, as discussed earlier, during the civil war of the seventeenth century.

Historians have devoted much attention to assessing Æthelwulf's reign, certainly more than is paid to his father and his first three successors, on the basis of the greater library of primary sources during his time as king. Despite this, some argue that he has 'not always been accorded the attention (he) might be thought to deserve' as he not only secured Wessex politically but, more than any other ninth-century king, was responsible for opening up channels with the Holy Roman Empire and the papacy.[71] He has been described as 'one of the great underrated among Anglo-Saxons', laying the foundations for Alfred's later success.[72]

More negative assessments describe Æthelwulf as 'a religious and unambitious man, for whom engagement in war and politics was an unwelcome consequence of rank'.[73] His legacy is said to be 'clouded by accusations of excessive piety which, to modern sensibilities at least, has seemed at odds with the demands of early medieval kingship'.[74] His pilgrimage to Rome has been attributed to 'the unpractical piety which had led him to desert his kingdom at a time of great danger', while his marriage to Judith is described as 'the folly of a man senile before his time'.[75] These criticisms seem a little harsh. He was a devoted and pious Christian, but from our knowledge of his military involvements he was assured when protecting West Saxon interests. These differences could be explained if we accept Æthelwulf underwent a personal epiphany during 855. Others before him had done the same when approaching their final years.

Æthelwulf's reign is clouded by two issues: his plan to divide the kingdom among his sons and his prolonged absence on the continent. Had he succeeded in the first of these, Wessex might have been permanently divided into separate eastern and western regions.[76]

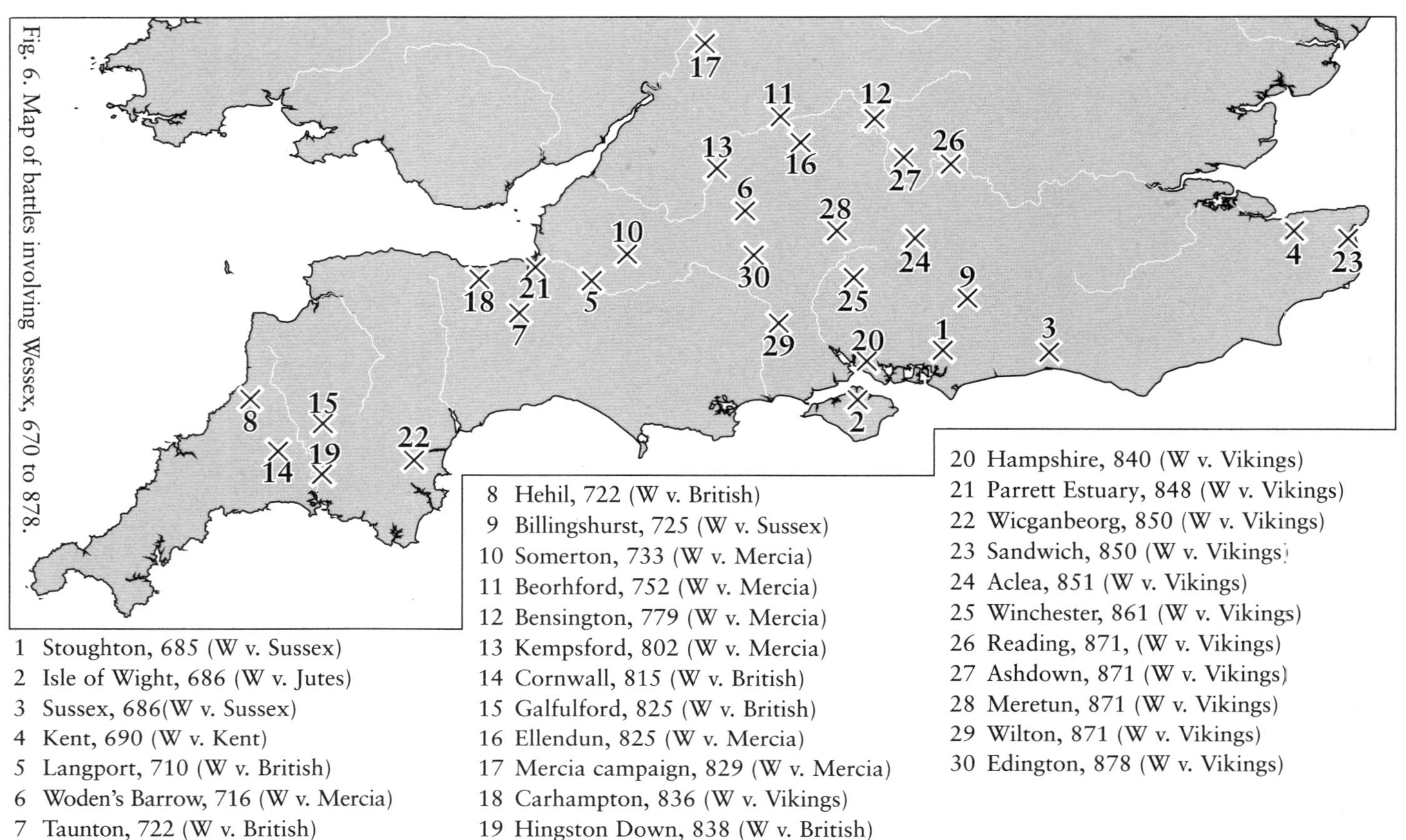

Fig. 6. Map of battles involving Wessex, 670 to 878.

16
Æthelbald and Æthelberht
856/8–865

Following the partition of authority into east and west after Æthelwulf's return to England, historians may be left pondering who held the greater power across Wessex in the fourteen months from November 856 to his death in January 858. The general assumption in most secondary sources is that Æthelwulf retained overall control, but this is difficult to determine. There is no incident recorded in which Æthelwulf's and Æthelbald's separate spheres of influence seem to clash during this period.

However, in his life of Alfred, Asser refers to a document that was drawn up by Æthelwulf, making it clear that he and not Æthelbald held the overall authority to make arrangements for both the eastern and western parts of the kingdom during their period of joint rule.[1] On the premise that 'his sons should not quarrel unnecessarily among themselves', this document, part of which acted as his will, committed to the formal division of the kingdom between his two eldest surviving sons.[2] He was perhaps taking his cue from the provisions which Charlemagne had previously made for the division of the Frankish kingdom among his own sons.

The primary sources cannot agree on when the throne was transferred from father to son. The ASC version A is clear that Æthelbald, when recording his death in 860, had ruled for five years, effectively dating his succession from the moment his father left the country in 855 and he became regent.[3] William of Malmesbury meanwhile writes that Æthelbald replaced his father in 857, while elsewhere Æthelwulf is recorded in some secondary sources as retaining the kingship of all the kingdom until the day of his death.[4] Æthelwulf was certainly producing his own coinage in Kent during 857. We see greater royal control over production and a programme of recoinage from the moneyers employed in Kent, resulting in higher-quality coins and greater standardisation of design.

This programme bypassed the years of Æthelbald's kingship, but was continued on the succession of Æthelberht in 860.[5]

Had the division of power continued for longer there is no knowing what may have developed, but Æthelwulf's death prevented that scenario. Who held final authority prior to that seems to have confused the chronicle scribes. Version A of the ASC contradicts itself when noting that Æthelbald ruled for five years while also adding that his father had ruled before him for 'eighteen and a half years'.[6] This meets the criteria that Æthelwulf was king from 839 to 858 but is incompatible with Æthelbald having ruled from 855. Adding to the primary source confusion, the same scribe adds that on Æthelwulf's death his two eldest sons succeeded to the kingdom, Æthelbald to Wessex and Æthelberht to the south-east region.

Ultimately, Æthelwulf's wishes were not honoured. On his death, Æthelbald was sworn in as king across all of Wessex with his brother Æthelberht accepting the role of king/sub-king in Kent. An 858 charter from Æthelberht transferring land in Kent identifies him as 'king of Kent, East Saxons, Surrey and South Saxons'.[7] However, this was acknowledged as a subservient role to Æthelbald's overall kingship and not a position with equal footing, effectively returning the power balance across greater Wessex to how it had been during the early reign of their father.

We can perhaps see Æthelberht's position here as being the sub-king to his brother's kingship. Their father's wish to divide the kingdom between them was not supported by either brother, most significantly by Æthelberht. He did not contest the throne at his father's death, instead allowing Æthelbald to hold the primary position. Æthelbald's reign as the undisputed sole king of Wessex, if we accept that he shared power with his father in the earlier period, was nevertheless limited from January 858 to his known date of death on 20 December 860, a reign of thirty-five months.

The coronation of Æthelbald, whose Old English name translates as 'noble and bold', took place either at the Old Minster in Winchester or at Sherborne Abbey. One of his first actions as king was to marry the young widow of his father, his stepmother Judith of Flanders, daughter of the Frankish king Charles the Bald. Judith was younger than him, about fifteen or sixteen while Æthelbald was in his mid-twenties. As with his father's union to Judith, the marriage was deemed advantageous for Æthelbald, as her status as a Frankish princess and descendant of Charlemagne enhanced his status among the other Anglo-Saxon kingdoms and the continental nobility. The marriage received a blessing from Judith's father and an entry in the *Annals of St Bertin* at Saint-Omer in Judith's home region.[8]

Æthelbald had appeared in the witness lists of several of his father's charters prior to his period as regent. However, no extant charters issued by him have been found during his own regency in Wessex, and there is only one surviving charter issued by him for his period as king, dated to 860.[9] Æthelbald also countersigned a charter transferring land from Bishop Swithin, with the provision that the estate would return to the ownership of the Old Minster on his death.[10] We can assume others were raised but have not survived. The single extant document, which donated land to a minister named Osmund, contains an interesting list of absent witnesses. Among them are the king's brother Æthelberht, as expected, but not his younger brothers Æthelred and Alfred. They were young, but that would not have prevented their witnessing.

Does this imply some level of family disagreement because Æthelbald had not divided the kingdom? Asser's text on their father's wishes suggests that Alfred may have seen Æthelbald in a negative light. Other witnesses included Bishop Swithin of the Old Minster, and Bishop Ealhstan of Sherborne, who had been named by Asser as one of Æthelbald's chief supporters during the claimed plot to usurp the throne.[11] More surprising on this charter is the signature of Judith of Flanders, who witnesses as the 'queen of the West Saxons'.

From a Church perspective, the union of stepson and stepmother would have been frowned upon, being incestuous under canon law. Condemnation came again from Asser, who wrote that it was 'against God's prohibition and Christian dignity ... and incurred great disgrace from all who heard it'.[12] The ASC avoids mention of the marriage, but William of Malmesbury added to Asser's disapproval by noting that the new king had 'sank so low as to marry his stepmother' and to have 'defiled his father's marriage-bed'.[13] Moving back to Asser, he further betrays his apparent disdain for Æthelbald by commenting that the new king controlled Wessex and the West Saxons 'for two and a half lawless years after his father'.[14] As he had never known Æthelbald, perhaps we should assume that his negativity originated from Alfred himself; maybe as a child the young Alfred had recollections of the dispute between his brother and father and had formed his opinions from that.

Asser and John of Worcester, and to a lesser extent William of Malmesbury, were to comment on Judith and her position as queen. Their texts contain almost identical entries, but it is interesting that Asser limits his comments to her marriage to Æthelwulf and Worcester limits his to her marriage to Æthelbald. There was a change of policy in how the king's wife was to be addressed. It appears Æthelbald was more than happy to abandon his grandfather's edict and espouse the noble pedigree of his new wife, Charlemagne's great-granddaughter. She could sit beside the king as his queen 'without any disagreement or ill-feeling', which contrasted with the earlier pronouncements that denied 'or even allow(ed) her to be called the queen but rather the king's wife'.[15] It is difficult to conclude whether or not Asser is criticising the re-introduction of the title of queen for the consort; possibly it was necessary to be vague because to criticise Æthelbald for naming Judith as his queen would also be to criticise Æthelwulf before him.

There is a distinct lack of evidence for Æthelbald having minted coinage. Whereas there is plenty of evidence that his father minted coins in Kent after 856, and that his brother Æthelberht did likewise after 860, numismatists and archaeologists have so far drawn a blank on finding any extant coinage produced across Wessex during Æthelbald's reign. It is plausible none were produced, and this brings us back briefly to the putative power-sharing arrangement with his father.

It is conceivable that the only coinage in circulation during his time on the throne of Wessex was that previously produced by his father's moneyers, and perhaps he had not been able to mint his own coinage until at least January 858 if at all.

Beyond his marriage, there is precious little detail to illuminate Æthelbald's thirty-five-month reign. Some historians have suggested that, under pressure from the Church, he was forced at some stage to annul his marriage to Judith. However, there is no contemporary evidence to confirm that argument. His reputation remains mixed. Because we have little to go on from the primary sources, his earlier dispute with his father stands out as the primary recorded event. However, not all subsequent writers had negative opinions of him. Unlike other contemporary chroniclers Henry of Huntingdon praised Æthelbald, describing both him and his brother and successor Æthelberht as 'young men of superlative natural quality'.[16]

Æthelbald died on 20 December 860, still only in his twenties, but whether it was by disease or from an injury in battle is uncertain. His death might be related to the Viking raid on Winchester in 860. He was taken to Sherborne Abbey for burial. This was ostensibly an unusual choice, beyond his known friendship with Bishop Ealhstan of Sherborne. However, it is plausible that Æthelbald may have already moved his primary court to Sherborne, where he traditionally had greater support. It should be remembered that when Wessex was divided in 857 Hampshire was assigned to his father's half of the kingdom.

Æthelbald's tomb at Sherborne would be disturbed at some later stage, as would his brother Æthelberht's, and we will consider this in due course. As there is no proof that his marriage to Judith had been annulled, she was probably alongside him until his death but soon returned to her father's court in Francia where she was welcomed back warmly. Judith was placed into the monastery at Senlis, north-east of Paris, by her father until another suitable husband was found. However, with the aid of her brother Louis she eloped with the Flemish prince Baldwin, later to be Baldwin I of Flanders, and married him in 862.[17] She was a founding part of a new Anglo-Flemish connection decades later when her son Baldwin II took Alfred's youngest daughter, Ælfthryth, as his wife.

The ASC scribe, presumably working with a year-ending calendar date of late March 861, records that 'Æthelberht ... succeeded to the entire kingdom, and he ruled it in good concord and great tranquillity'.[18] Æthelbald's brief reign had witnessed a lull in major Viking activity, at least in terms of raids on Wessex, but a major attack upon Winchester would take place, unusually, over the winter months of 860–861. A large Viking Danish fleet arrived in the Solent, the largest to land in Wessex since 851, a sign that an increased threat to the Anglo-Saxon kingdom was materialising. Viking attacks now posed a different longer-term threat, not just to the Anglo-Saxons but to much of western Europe. The source of this change came from the Danish Viking homelands, which had, up to 854, kept the Viking warlords in check through their king Horik I. However, in that year Horik I was himself killed and replaced by his namesake Horik II (aka Erik Barn). The restraining influence had gone, and the Danish warlords were free to conduct new and more expansive campaigns of pillage overseas.

According to *The Annals of St Bertin*, the Vikings in the 860 raid had sailed from their base in the River Somme, comprising by all accounts almost 200 ships.[19] Based on a conservative estimate of only 150 ships and twenty fighting men per vessel, that would still equate to a minimum of 3,000 fighting men. Perhaps up to 10 per cent of these men were ordered to stay and guard the fleet as the main force moved towards Winchester. William of Malmesbury records the settlement was 'sacked'.[20] The ASC expands on this, adding that a 'great raiding-ship army came up and destroyed Winchester'.[21] Use of the word 'destroyed' in this context should not be underestimated; it is used only sparingly throughout the chronicle.

Winchester had been the political centre of Wessex for some time, growing into an important administrative and religious centre, but by the mid-ninth century it had also become a major commercial hub. At this stage it was beginning to eclipse the settlement at Hamwic/Hamtun (Southampton) in economic importance. Although not mentioned, it can be assumed that Hamwic, due to its location at the mouth of the

River Itchen, was also raided in advance of the move against Winchester. This is the only reference within such primary sources to a successful Viking assault on the recognised capital and royal centre of Wessex, but also an acknowledgement that the walls were breached. There is some evidence from fragments of stained glass, identified as originating from the ninth century, that the Old Minster suffered in this raid. According to archaeologists, the destruction was also responsible for subsequent changes to the street layout within Winchester that preceded the further defensive changes undertaken by Alfred in the late ninth century.

It appears the Vikings did not hold the city for long. While returning to their ships in the Solent, carrying what Asser describes as 'immense booty', they were intercepted by two West Saxon fyrds led by Ealdorman Osric of Hampshire and Ealdorman Æthelwulf, the former Mercian nobleman of Berkshire.[22] Æthelberht is not mentioned. The inference is the Hampshire fyrd had been unable to muster in time to help defend the settlement but had formed shortly after to combine with the Berkshire force and match the Danes in numbers. Asser recorded 'the Vikings were cut down everywhere', and then followed with an ideological footnote, adding that the enemy 'took to flight like women, and the Christians were masters of the battlefield'.[23] The inability to defend Winchester is perhaps an issue, but the speed of the West Saxon response thereafter suggests that the system within Wessex – certainly the assembly of the levies – was already effective even prior to the reforms Alfred was to implement in later decades.

While the primary sources all relate this event to Æthelberht's early rule, it is perhaps worthwhile approaching this from a different angle. Some historians have speculated that if the attack had come earlier than the ASC presupposes, around the time of Æthelbald's death, it would explain not only why he died young but also why he was taken to Sherborne and not buried in Winchester.[24] Did the later scribes misdate the entry, and can we ponder the possibility that Æthelbald received a fatal injury during the fighting at Winchester, or perhaps a wound that led to his death some weeks after his brother had assumed command? His transfer to Sherborne may be attributed to this, but it requires a dating error in the ASC.

Despite a lack of confirmed dates, Æthelberht became king during the Christmas period of 860. He was a few years younger than Æthelbald, perhaps aged around twenty-four when succeeding to the throne. The location for Æthelberht's formal crowning is uncertain. Maybe Viking damage to the Old Minster prevented it being available. He appears, because of his earlier role, to have naturally held stronger ties with Kent and eastern Wessex, so maybe the ceremony was held at Canterbury or Rochester. In contrast, Sherborne was also a possibility, for no better reason than it would become his chosen place of burial, alongside his brother, when he died in 865.

Æthelberht had already appeared as a signatory in several of his father's charters, as did his younger brothers Æthelred and Alfred. He is also seen in the witness list on Æthelbald's only known extant charter of 860.[25] His succession may have come with provisos relating to Æthelwulf's recent expectations for the division of power within Wessex after 858. As gathered from Alfred's recollections in his will, it would seem both Alfred and Æthelred had previously entrusted their share of the kingdom singularly to Æthelberht on the condition that the one who survived the longest of the three of them would at some point inherit the whole.[26] This went against Æthelwulf's dying wishes but it ensured that Wessex remained united and strong. This arrangement might explain why there is no record of Æthelberht marrying or having any children. If an agreement between him and his younger brothers was in place, it would have complicated matters if or when Æthelberht died. Therefore, perhaps Æthelberht purposely remained unmarried.

On becoming king it is assumed Æthelberht took immediate responsibility for the entire kingdom. Because of the formal division of the regions that had existed between him and his brother, some historians have theorised that Æthelberht quickly annexed what had been Æthelbald's Wessex – the old shires of Wessex – not the other way round.[27] The sub-king role for the south-east was suspended indefinitely. In any case, the next immediate heir, Æthelred, was probably still too young for such duties, aged only around fourteen or fifteen in 861. Æthelred's status before 865 remains uncertain. He is believed to have issued a charter in his own right in 862, which is when the king assigned him some level of responsibility for Kent. However, it is difficult to identify the individual, as a Kentish ealdorman with the same name appears in various charters during this period.[28]

In terms of ongoing Viking activity in Wessex, we find William of Malmesbury linking a movement of the Viking survivors from the Winchester raid and those who had lost to ealdormen Osric and Æthelwulf to a subsequent landing at Thanet, where he writes that the Vikings took winter quarters.[29] However, both the ASC and Malmesbury's contemporary Henry of Huntingdon place the Thanet landing not at the beginning of Æthelberht's reign but at the end.[30] We are therefore certainly looking at a different Viking fleet to that involved in the Solent landing of 860. The ASC notes that the inhabitants of Kent promised the 865 Viking raiders 'money in return for peace', although the Vikings were to renege on the deal and later 'raided across all eastern Kent'.[31] Huntingdon adds more detail but repeats the chronicle entry. This group may have joined the Viking fleet that arrived in East Anglia a few months later, the Viking invasion force later known as the 'Great Danish Army'.

The programme of recoinage begun by his father continued under Æthelberht, with extant examples of coins that were minted at both Canterbury and Rochester, but no similar surviving examples from the mints in western Wessex.[32] This follows an earlier perceived precedent, where in this period most coins produced in Wessex, as evidenced by finds, were being produced by Kentish moneyers. Coin discoveries also support proof of ongoing cooperation between Wessex and Mercia, with evidence emerging of the commencement of a monetary alliance under Æthelberht and his Mercian brother-in-law Burgred, a practice that continued through into the reign of Æthelred, by which coinage of similar design was used and interchanged between the two kingdoms.

It is noticeable that of the seven extant charters issued by Æthelberht during his reign five of them concern donations to Rochester and other estates in Kent, which tells us that the strength of his connections in the region surpassed those he had with Hampshire and the shires further west.[33] This supports the initial argument, as also seen with his father, that the family dynastic ties were closely linked to Kent. Of the two charters that relate to central Wessex neither is associated with Winchester or the Old Minster.[34] The second and more significant of these, witnessed by both of his surviving brothers, relates to Sherborne Abbey, where the document declares Æthelberht placed his charter of privileges – something that denoted a special grant of exemptions – on the high altar at the abbey on Good Friday 865.

There are several possible motivations for this practically ritualistic act. We know his brother Æthelbald was already buried there. But it may also have been a display of friendship towards Bishop Ealhstan, his brother's closest ally among the nobility in the earlier crisis with their father, denoting perhaps Æthelberht's readiness to form closer ties with the western half of the kingdom. If that had been Æthelberht's intention, fate would intervene sooner than he may have imagined. His act at Sherborne may be significant, as it took place only four or five months before his death. Perhaps rather than a display of closer union with western Wessex, this was the act of a man who knew he was dying and wished to be buried alongside his brother.

It was during Æthelberht's reign that version F of the ASC (the Canterbury version) records the death of Bishop Swithin of Winchester.[35] The date has variously been given as either 861 or 863 on 2 July, but interestingly it was the Canterbury version not the Winchester version of the chronicle that recorded his death.[36] Swithin was buried as per his wishes outside the entry porch of the Old Minster, to ensure that people visiting the Minster would have to cross over his grave as they entered the building. Thereafter, through the testaments of monks and pilgrims, he was credited with performing miracles and was given a sainthood. However, 110 years later in 971 his remains were moved to an indoor shrine. The reinterment reputedly took place on 15 July, today known as St Swithin's Day, on which day folklore dictates that the weather will be repeated for the following forty days. The origin of this folklore may come from the fact that transferring his grave inside the Minster was against his distinct wishes. In subsequent centuries the Church distributed some of his relics to other shrines, including his head to Christ Church Canterbury, and an arm to Peterborough Abbey.

In terms of Æthelberht's entries in the ASC, his almost five-year period as the king of Wessex is regrettably limited to just two. He is named as succeeding his brother as king in 860 and being succeeded by another brother in 865. Once again there is no obvious reason for this lack of detail, beyond the fact that documents marking his reign may have been destroyed during the Danish wars that would follow. We know his five-year reign was bracketed by the large Viking raid on Winchester and the arrival of the Great Danish Army into East Anglia, so it is plausible there were other, unrecorded Viking raids into Wessex during that period.

It is perhaps surprising Æthelberht remained unmarried, although he was not the first king of Wessex to die without an heir. It is possible he had an illegitimate son called Oswald or Osweald, one who is known to have attested later charters in 868 and 875, where he is described as '*filius regis*' (king's son).[37] As put forward earlier, perhaps his bachelordom revolves around the will of his father and the arrangement made with Æthelred and Alfred whereby Æthelberht deliberately stayed unmarried so as not to complicate the future succession.[38]

The ASC does not confirm Æthelberht's death but in its normal fashion states who replaced him, in this case his brother Æthelred.[39] The chronicle entry was recorded as 866, but as observed by academics the scribe here was working on a calendar year change coming on 24 September, meaning that we can reliably accept that Æthelberht died sometime after 25 September in 865. Asser observed of Æthelberht that 'after governing in peace, love and honour for five years, Æthelberht went the way of all flesh, to the great sorrow of his people; and he lies buried honourably beside his brother, at Sherborne'.[40] William of Malmesbury briefly added that he was 'a vigorous but kindly ruler'.[41] These entries are in marked contrast to comments on Æthelbald from the same writers.

Æthelberht's early death is comparable with those of his brothers Æthelstan and Æthelbald, with all three of them dying before they reached thirty years of age. We have presumed that Æthelstan and Æthelbald either died as a result of fighting the Vikings or from disease. However, when we have the additional early death of Æthelberht, which was apparently unconnected with battle injuries, then maybe we need to ask whether there was a genetic problem they all shared. We can never know beyond speculation. Their other brother Æthelred would die while fighting the Danes in 871 while still under thirty, and although the youngest brother, Alfred, lived to fifty, we know he suffered from what has been identified as Crohn's disease for most of his life.

Æthelberht was taken for burial alongside his brother Æthelbald at Sherborne.[42] Nothing now remains of the original West Saxon church as it stood in the ninth century, which was to the west of the nave of the present abbey church. Surviving Anglo-Saxon sections of the rebuilt abbey are from the eleventh century. The remains of the two West Saxon kings were moved into the new Norman building close to the altar. But as noted by the sixteenth-century antiquarian John Leland, there was no evidence of their tombs still being there during his day.[43] There is a plaque in the present-day abbey marking the approximate location of their tombs. Nearby, beneath a section of glass floor, can be seen several human bones which are claimed and revered by some as belonging to Æthelbald and/or Æthelberht, although it is impossible to verify this assertion.

17
Æthelred I
865–871

For 865, the ASC records, 'Here Æthelred, brother of Æthelberht, succeeded to the kingdom of Wessex.'[1] He became the third son of Æthelwulf to do so, continuing the dynasty of his grandfather Ecgberht, with the family having held the throne for sixty-three years thus far. This continuity played a strong part in the kingdom enjoying a steady development during the ninth century while other kingdoms faltered.

Æthelred was about nineteen or twenty when he came to the throne. His name in Old English translates as either 'noble counsel' or 'well-advised'. He would later be designated as King Æthelred I by historians, due to another, Æthelred (II), emerging to become king of England in the late tenth century. The second Æthelred was a fourth-generation descendant through Alfred's bloodline and is more usually recognised by his epithet of 'the Unready', coming from the Old English word '*unræd*' meaning 'poorly advised', a pun on his name.[2]

Henry of Huntingdon writes that Æthelred (I) 'received the insignia of kingship', although whether the ceremony took place at the Old Minster at Winchester or elsewhere is unknown.[3] Based on the evidence already considered he had held the sub-kingship in the south-east under Æthelberht for a minimum of two years, but on his succession to Wessex, unlike previous transfers of power, the youngest brother Alfred did not replace him in that role. This confirms that their father's wish for a permanent partition of Wessex was not shared by his youngest sons, and it follows what seems to have been the agreement made between the three youngest brothers at the time of Æthelberht's accession.[4]

Æthelred's period as king, alongside his contemporaries within Mercia, Northumbria and East Anglia, would be dominated by a new threat to England from the Vikings more potent than anything that had come

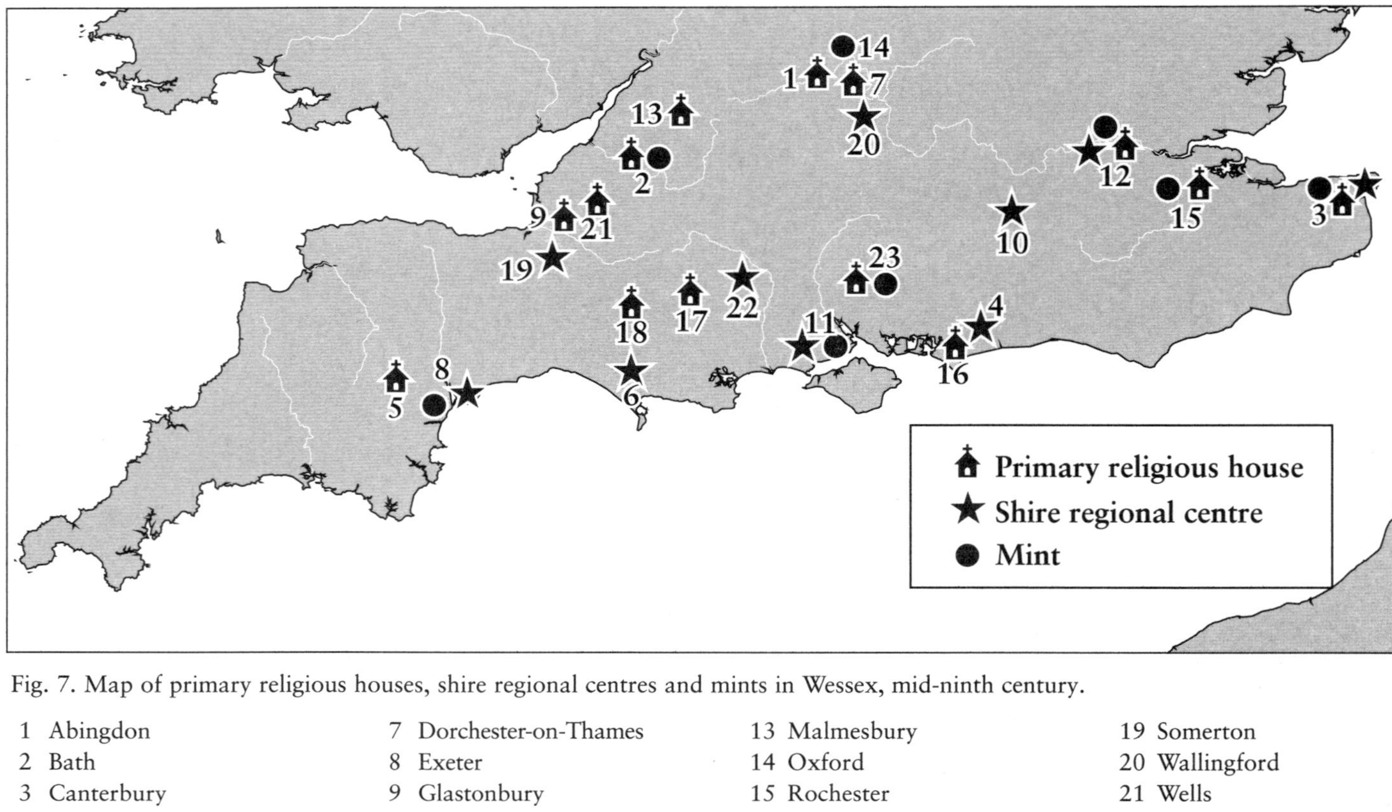

Fig. 7. Map of primary religious houses, shire regional centres and mints in Wessex, mid-ninth century.

1 Abingdon
2 Bath
3 Canterbury
4 Chichester
5 Crediton
6 Dorchester
7 Dorchester-on-Thames
8 Exeter
9 Glastonbury
10 Guildford
11 Hamtun (Southampton)
12 London
13 Malmesbury
14 Oxford
15 Rochester
16 Selsey
17 Shaftesbury
18 Sherborne
19 Somerton
20 Wallingford
21 Wells
22 Wilton
23 Winchester

before. The chronicle scribe, following his entry on Æthelred's succession, immediately added that 'a great raiding army came to the land of the English'.[5] This large Viking fleet first landed in East Anglia, and it would later also be known as the Great Heathen Army. Although Wessex was initially spared attack while the Vikings pillaged across the other Anglo-Saxon kingdoms, this would prove a mere reprieve for Æthelred and Wessex.

The invaders had come from Denmark and from Danish and Norse groups already settled in the coastal regions of Francia, Flanders and Frisia. It quickly became apparent that this was more than just a raid for plunder; indeed, their arrival marked the beginning of a long-term strategy of conquest and settlement. Primary sources lack evidence regarding numbers of ships and men, but it seems to have been a well-planned invasion with numerous longships. Historians have put forward various estimates as to the size of this 'great' army, from as many as 10,000 down to just 2,000 or 3,000.[6] We could imagine there were at least several thousand in the first wave, and that others, on hearing of the initial success of their contemporaries within East Anglia and Mercia, came afterwards to add their strength to the Danish army in the months and years that followed.

There had been other large raids before, but nothing on this scale. The causes behind it appear to be related to political and economic changes in Scandinavia which had become more acute by the 860s. Expanding populations and land shortages had already seen Danes and Norse sail to find settlements along the coasts of mainland Europe, or in northern Britain and Ireland. Many had raided and settled in West Francia from the 840s, corresponding with similar Viking attacks on the English kingdoms, and following the sacking of Paris in 845 and other attacks thereafter had been given land as tribute in exchange for peace by the Frankish king Charles (II) the Bald.

However, the catalyst behind the Viking invasion of England in 865 appears to have arisen from a recent change of strategy in Francia by Charles.[7] From 862 onwards the Frankish king had adopted improved methods to frustrate major Viking incursions, including fortifying major towns, enlisting permanent standing armies, and constructing new fortified bridges across the major rivers, which had up to that point had been the Viking method of gaining easy access to the hinterland. It would be the same system that would later successfully be adopted by Alfred the Great in Wessex during the 880s, of fortified burhs and permanent garrisons to counteract newly arrived Danish armies. As things stood in 865, Charles the Bald's changes had significantly reduced Viking chances of gaining plunder or tribute across Francia, so, with newly arrived Vikings vying for land and riches, their attention moved to England.

The only immediate concern for Æthelred and Wessex during 865 was the Viking group that had previously overwintered in Thanet. Asser writes that the men of Kent concluded a peace treaty with the Vikings in return for giving them money, but the Vikings, 'like crafty foxes ... broke the treaty and laid waste the entire eastern district of Kent'.[8] He further adds that the invaders had spurned the offer of money, 'for they knew they could get more money from the pillaged booty than from peace'. Asser's text on this Viking practice marks him as the first contemporary writer to acknowledge what would later be recognised and known as Danegeld, the payments given by various Anglo-Saxon leaders in exchange for the Vikings promising peace. This would be a policy used frequently during the wars against subsequent Danish invaders up to the early eleventh century, particularly associated with King Æthelred (II) the Unready (r. 978–1016). More often than not Danegeld proved defective, as the Vikings liberally broke such agreements, having alighted on a profitable combination of coercion and pillage.

Before relating the progress of the 865 Viking invasion and the subsequent details, it is useful to understand the mindset of the Anglo-Saxon establishment as the invasion unfolded. In general terms it is revealing to witness the response from the Anglo-Saxon Church leaders to the arrival of the Great Heathen Army and the destruction that followed. Without exception contemporary ecclesiastic leaders and later clerical scribes saw it as a penance or atonement, a sign that the Anglo-Saxons had angered their God. Several chroniclers, all dedicated adherents to religious principles, supported this deeply profound ideological approach. Henry of Huntingdon was vigorous in claiming that the English had brought their tribulations (i.e. the Vikings) down on their heads by their own immoral acts. He wrote of an earlier time, a more religiously devout period within England that had somehow, in his twelfth-century opinion, declined by the mid-ninth century when 'all goodness so withered away in them (the English), that no other nation was their equal for treachery and wickedness'.[9] It reminds us perhaps of the situation during the fifth century, when contemporaries and later chroniclers berated the British leadership for bringing down divine retribution on themselves in the shape of the Germanic invaders.

Rebuke, sermons and ideology aside, the Viking invasion of 865 had not been a divine judgement upon the English, but was more the hard reality of an Anglo-Saxon military system and its leadership being totally unprepared for such a concerted and continuous assault on its resources. The Anglo-Saxon response to the Viking invasion between 865 and 870 was weak and uncoordinated. Wessex and Æthelred would benefit from the Viking army's preoccupation with the other kingdoms until 870.

To appreciate the situation in which Wessex would find itself in due course we can follow the progress of the Vikings in the intervening period. Having first landed in East Anglia in 865, the Danes sacked the religious houses of Crowland, Ramsey and Huntingdon. Ely monastery was then burned to the ground and the monks slaughtered at Medeshamstede. Valuable East Anglian texts stored in these religious houses, holding much of the kingdom's recorded historical and cultural legacy, was lost.

By the ninth century East Anglia was recognised as the prominent horse-breeding kingdom in England, and the Vikings were able to commandeer East Anglian warhorses on a large scale, allowing them to move rapidly across the country in numbers. The Vikings capitalised on the Anglo-Saxons' failure to anticipate this crucial aspect, using it to their advantage in warfare against other kingdoms. It would lead on a wider scale to a diminishing stock of horses suitable for mounted warfare, and in the longer term some historians have identified this as the root cause of the English failure to develop cavalry tactics in parallel with the military advances taking place in continental Europe.[10]

While the Viking Danes established themselves, the East Anglians received no aid from Mercia or Wessex. This is perhaps more surprising from Æthelred's aspect as Wessex held overlordship over Essex, which had a common border with East Anglia. However, it should be remembered that the recent pact between Wessex and Mercia was the exception rather than the rule. The independent Anglo-Saxon kingdoms had a long history of non-cooperation, particularly when it came to military alliances. Initially, the West Saxons possibly underestimated the future threat of the Great Heathen Army. After all, none of the previous Viking invasions had led to a permanent occupation.

Having subdued East Anglia and its king, Edmund, the Vikings, led by the Danish warlords Ivar, Ubba and Halfdan, moved northward during 866, pillaging through eastern Mercia. Mercia's king, Burgred, took no action to prevent it, although the suspicion must be that he had given the Danish leaders tribute payments to keep them moving north. In the late autumn the Danes crossed into Northumbria, and on 1 November, in what might have been a surprise attack, they were able to take control of York, the former Roman *civitas* and the main royal, administrative and trade centre in Deira (southern Northumbria). They had been fortunate – or perhaps they were already aware – that support for the Northumbria king, Osberht, had fractured. A Northumbrian challenger to the throne named Ælla had emerged, weakening the kingdom's resistance to an external threat.[11]

The Vikings overwintered in York before, as recorded by Symeon of Durham, Osberht and Ælla united their forces and attacked the walls of

York on 21 March 867.[12] But the Viking leadership had devised a plan in expectation. They allowed the Northumbrians to enter York as a feint, and once inside the walls the Northumbrians were trapped and ambushed by Vikings, who attacked them from within the city and from the rear, with both Osberht and Ælla killed during the fighting or soon after. As had happened in East Anglia, much of the earlier historiography of the Northumbrian kingdom of Deira and its legacy was destroyed at this time, with one historian referring to the destruction across the kingdoms as negating all the significant advances that had been made during the ninth century to that date.[13] Eastern Mercia was soon to experience the same, and in time so would part of Wessex, although it would appear from the level of survival of primary source texts that Wessex was able to preserve more than most of its Anglo-Saxon neighbours.

In due course the Viking army headed back south into Mercia and was able to move unmolested to occupy Nottingham over the winter of 867–868. To devise a plan to evict the Vikings, in the spring of 868 Burgred of Mercia invoked the standing alliance agreement between Mercia and Wessex. According to the ASC, he requested 'Æthelred, king of Wessex, and his brother Alfred to help them fight against the raiding army'.[14] Whether this went beyond the terms of their previous understanding is unclear, but Æthelred responded positively, and with Alfred alongside him marched a West Saxon fyrd to join Burgred's Mercians outside the walls of Nottingham.

The fyrd system had barely changed from the time of Ine (r. 689–726), and we know this from Alfred's own laws, which he issued in the late ninth century, wherein he attached to his edicts many of the same clauses that Ine had produced within his own set of codes. In terms of military conscription, the fyrd's full muster was one man for each 5 hides of land, meaning about 20 per cent of the adult male population in a widespread call-up.[15] However, although the obligations were clear enough the system fell short when it came to mobility. Asser claims that Æthelred took an 'immense army' into Mercia, although from what soon transpired this seems an exaggerated assessment of the West Saxon fyrd that accompanied the king.[16]

Nottingham witnessed Æthelred and Wessex's first encounter with the Great Heathen Army, but there was no battle. The ASC scribe writes that they 'met the raiding army there in the fortification, and no heavy fight occurred there, and the Mercians made peace with the raiding army'.[17] This looks like something of an anti-climax, particularly as the West Saxons had marched over 125 miles from Winchester to aid Burgred. Asser provides detail to explain the reasons behind the peaceful conclusion, noting that 'since the Vikings, protected by the defences of the stronghold, refused to give battle, and since the Christians were unable to breach the wall, peace was established'.[18]

Methods of siege warfare were still unpractised in England, and we must assume Burgred had negotiated for a peace resolution, but this, nonetheless, seems weak reasoning. In hindsight his weakness – and Æthelred cannot be excluded from this – likely encouraged the Viking leadership to expand their campaign even wider. During the apparent period of inactivity outside Nottingham, the kings of Wessex and Mercia reinforced their ties further, ironically perhaps in view of subsequent events. An agreement between them was made whereby the ætheling Alfred was betrothed to Ealhswith, the young daughter of a regional Mercian ealdorman named Æthelred Mucel, and it is believed that they married on her father's estate only days later. The peace treaty then agreed between Burgred and the Viking leadership involved the Viking army moving back into Northumbrian Deira, having been given tributes from Burgred to do so. From Burgred's perspective it proved to be a temporary solution, although it would keep the Vikings out of Mercia for the next two years. Meanwhile, Æthelred and his West Saxon army returned to Wessex intact and untried.

In 869 the Viking army returned to East Anglia and took winter quarters at Thetford. This time, unlike four years earlier, King Edmund sought battle, but 'the Danish took the victory and killed the king'.[19] His death is recorded as happening on 20 November. The story of how Edmund died at the hands of the pagans Ivar and Ubba, shot by many arrows for refusing to denounce his Christianity, would later lead to his martyrdom and subsequent canonisation by the Church almost fifty years later.[20] Having then overwintered in East Anglia, in the spring of 870 the Vikings divided their forces, with Ivar and Ubba moving back to Northumbria, where new Danish reinforcements gathered at York between 870 and 871. A large part of this army then re-entered and campaigned across eastern Mercia between 871 and 872, establishing themselves in the long term around Repton, most notably in a large camp at Torksey next to the River Trent.[21]

Repton looks to have been a symbolic choice for the pagan Vikings. Once a crucial Mercian royal centre, it hosted an abbey with a mausoleum. Notable tombs in the mausoleum include that of Æthelbald, the king who battled Cuthred of Wessex in 756, and Wiglaf, the king of Mercia during Ecgberht's reign. Today, the former royal mausoleum, with origins going back to the eighth century, can be found within the crypt of the church of St Wystan. Later, Ivar and Ubba would lead their followers further north into the kingdom of Strathclyde and thereafter, at least in the case of Ivar, reputedly joined up with other Viking forces on a major campaign into Ireland.

Now under the leadership of Halfdan, the rest of the Viking army made its way south during 870 to occupy sites close to the Thames Estuary, and from his later movements we can assume Halfdan was able to seize London soon afterwards. We know that by the autumn of 870 Halfdan was able to sail his fleet down the Thames towards Reading in Berkshire, which lay within West Saxon territory. Æthelred, having had news of the Viking successes elsewhere, would have been aware that the Viking leadership was undoubtedly now looking towards his kingdom, the only one to have yet escaped serious attention. He may have requested reciprocal military help from his new brother-in-law Burgred, but the Mercian king looks to have been occupied in dealing with his own problems and no help was forthcoming.

For Æthelred and Wessex, the last months of 870 would be the final peaceful days of his regime. Now is the time, then, to review his existing charters and other aspects of his reign. As considered beforehand, he had issued two charters while in the role of sub-king/king of Kent and the south-east during the reign of his brother Æthelberht, although one of them concerns granting a nobleman an estate in Berkshire and is seen by some historians as bogus.[22] Of the seven extant documents issued during his kingship of Wessex they are all, unsurprisingly, dated before the autumn of 870, ahead of the Vikings reaching Reading. Only two concern grants issued to the clergy, two of the first three issued during his reign. One was awarded to Bishop Cuthwulf at Rochester and the other to a clergyman at St Martin's Church at Canterbury.[23] This again perhaps reveals the family link to Kent, and also Æthelred's earlier position there as sub-king to his brother Æthelberht. The remaining charters are to members of the secular nobility, in contrast to most of his predecessors wherein their charters were mainly grants made to religious houses or individual clergy.[24] This may suggest that Æthelred was already stabilising and tightening his support among the nobility, planning for what he knew would be an imminent Viking invasion of Wessex.

Another charter issued by Æthelred's sister Æthelswith, as the wife of King Burgred of Mercia, also includes the signatures of both her brothers Æthelred and Alfred.[25] Perhaps the most interesting two aspects of this document are that it illustrates that Mercian queens were still being given more power than their equivalents in Wessex and that it relates to an estate near Wantage in Berkshire, which, as already considered, had passed from Mercian to West Saxon control during the 840s.

Historians concur that Æthelred's wife Wulfthryth, whom he had married just before or after his succession, was probably Mercian. It tells us that the familial ties between Wessex and Mercia forged over the previous twenty years held some significance. This was in keeping with the previous prominent West Saxon–Mercian unions of Æthelred's sister Æthelswith and Burgred, Alfred marrying the Mercian noblewoman Ealhswith and, a few years later during the 880s, Alfred's daughter Æthelflaed marrying the Mercian lord Æthelred.[26] King Æthelred and Wulfthryth would have two children, the brothers Æthelhelm and Æthelwold, both born between 865 and 869. Wulfthryth also witnessed one of her husband's charters. Her appearance in the witness list argues for her having a high status in the West Saxon royal court similar to the previous position of Judith of Flanders. Her standing can be seen from a charter now lost but contemporarily referred to in the medieval *Codex Wintoniensis*, a cartulary of Winchester cathedral priory, whereby she is referred to as '*regina*' (queen).[27]

While his father Æthelwulf and his brother Æthelberht had made reforms of the coinage, it is during Æthelred's six-year reign that we see the beginnings of serious reforms.[28] As noted by numismatists, from the many examples of coins discovered from Æthelred's period as king he is seen changing the coin production from across the Wessex mints to adopt and match existing Mercian coin designs, perhaps with encouragement from his wife, prefiguring unify coinage style and interchangeability between the two kingdoms.[29]

Reading, lying on the River Thames, was a suitable starting point for Halfdan's invasion of Wessex. We cannot be certain, but a mounted Viking contingent probably moved cross-country to Reading via the Icknield Way and the Ridgeway, while the main force sailed up the Thames.[30] It was the regional administrative centre and royal vill, lying where the River Kennett met the Thames. The settlement seems to have fallen without great difficulty; the Vikings might have struck at the beginning of the twelve-day Christmas festival, when it would have been well stocked with winter supplies and 'food rents' already gathered from the surrounding area.[31]

The defence of Berkshire was still under the control of Æthelwulf, an ealdorman born in Mercia. One of the two ealdormen who had played a significant part in repulsing the Vikings from Winchester in 860,[32] Æthelwulf had switched his loyalty to the West Saxons when Berkshire was handed over to Wessex. His primary estate was at Pangbourne, less than 6 miles upriver from Reading. Upon seizing Reading, Halfdan set to reinforcing its existing defences, adding further earth embankments and a ditch between the Thames and the Kennet. A nineteenth-century historian identified part of the original Danish fortifications that united the rivers, known as the Plummery Ditch. It was still a watercourse in the early nineteenth century but has since disappeared. This ditch formerly passed next to the later site of the twelfth-century abbey and the area now occupied by Fosbury Gardens, before adjoining the Thames near where King's Meadow Road in Reading is located today.[33]

With Reading already taken, much of Ealdorman Æthelwulf's Berkshire fyrd – perhaps half of the twenty Berkshire hundreds – was nullified.

Nevertheless, he assembled a force at Pangbourne while sending word to the king.[34] Before Æthelred could respond, Halfdan's jarls reconnoitred west of Reading, and the first clash of arms came on 31 December 871, with the ASC scribe adding that it took place only three days after the Vikings had taken Reading.[35] Æthelwulf moved his west Berkshire levies to what is now the village of Englefield, next to marshland between Pangbourne and Theale, while the Danes marched out of Reading along a track that followed the line of Tilehurst ridge.[36] Englefield takes its name from the subsequent encounter, the name meaning 'the field of the English', the site being close to where the Tilehurst track crossed the old Roman road from Silchester. West of the local school at Theale runs Deadman's Lane, the name possibly associated with the battle.[37]

The ealdorman's defensively aligned army possibly numbered a maximum of several hundred, and the Viking reconnaissance force probably much less. The ASC recorded that 'Æthelwulf opposed them at Englefield and fought against them and won the victory; and one of the jarls, named Sidroc, was slain there'.[38] In context the victory proved nothing, but it may have encouraged the West Saxons into an overconfidence that led to Æthelred's decision soon afterwards to attack Halfdan's forces at Reading without further delay. On 4 January 871, with Alfred and Ealdorman Æthelwulf alongside him, the West Saxon king and his hastily gathered army of perhaps a few thousand, presumably comprising men from Hampshire and Wiltshire, launched an attack on the Danish defences.[39] Additional detail from the twelfth-century writer Geoffrey Gaimar infers the West Saxon attack came from the south across the River Kennett, pushing back the Danes' outer defensive ring but then failing to breach the inner defences.[40] The main fighting was alongside the Plummery Ditch, where, according to the ASC, 'great slaughter was made on either side'.[41]

With hindsight, perhaps Æthelred should have delayed his attack until more of his fyrd had assembled, as the West Saxon attack was forced back over the Kennett, with the remnants wheeling eastward towards Sonning or Woodley. Local tradition has stories of ongoing skirmishes east of Reading at Whistley Green and on towards Twyford, with Ealdorman Æthelwulf being killed near the River Loddon. The tenth-century chronicler Æthelweard recorded that the Berkshire ealdorman's body was later recovered and returned north for burial at Derby, the seat of his Mercian kinsmen.[42]

The writer Gaimar also places Æthelred and Alfred at Twyford, only avoiding capture by their knowledge of the local terrain before they were able to regroup 12 miles away at Windsor.[43] Taking advantage of his victory, Halfdan marched the bulk of his army westward four days later along the valley of the Kennett. With the Hampshire, Berkshire and Wiltshire fyrds now depleted, Æthelred regrouped and summoned new levies from further afield in Somerset and Dorset. If a call was made to Burgred for Mercian help he did not respond, although Burgred may have still held Æthelred accountable for the failure to engage the Vikings at Nottingham three years earlier.[44]

By the morning of 8 January 871, Æthelred and Alfred had assembled a new fyrd on the slopes of the Berkshire Downs just west of the Thames at Goring to deter Halfdan from following the Ridgeway into the heartland of central Wessex. Knowing the landscape was an advantage, but the Vikings had also likely gleaned information from Saxon locals. The two forces encountered each other at a site known as Ashdown, a name meaning 'mount ash'.[45] We know more about this battle from various primary sources than most other contemporary clashes. Several sites for the battleground have been suggested. The one most favoured by Victorian historians interested in Alfred's story was White Horse Hill, 6 miles west of Wantage. This forms part of the escarpment of Uffington Hill Fort and has on its northern slopes the oldest turf-cut equine figure on the southern downs. The West Saxons are said to have gathered at Alfred's Castle, an Iron Age enclosure 3 miles to the south at nearby Compton Beauchamp.[46]

An alternate battle site with limited support is a further mile or two west of Uffington, by name connotation just north of Ashdown House, close to where the modern B4000 crosses the Ridgeway track. Associated with this and the Uffington site is the legend of Alfred and the blowing stone, a small sarsen stone lying alongside the B4507 near Kingston Lisle east of Uffington, containing holes through which Alfred is reputed to have blown to summon the West Saxon army. Myths aside, both Uffington and Ashdown/Ridgeway are unpromising options. Many historians consider them too far west of Reading (28–30 miles) to be viable sites, knowing that the Viking survivors reputedly returned to Reading on the evening of the battle.

A more rational argument would be a location perhaps no more than 10 miles from Reading close to either the Ridgeway or the Icknield Way. If Æthelred positioned his army on the assumption Halfdan would follow the Ridgeway, he needed to allow his fyrd the opportunity to move laterally to prevent a flanking movement while also protecting moves towards Wallingford and the abbey at Abingdon.[47] To enable this, the West Saxon fyrd needed to hold a position to the west of Goring, to observe and counteract any movements along either the Thames or the Ridgeway.[48]

Given these criteria, there are two outstanding sites for the battlefield of Ashdown. The first is west of Moulsford on the Cholsey Downs, specifically a prominent point alongside the modern A417 road (Streatley to Wantage) called Kingstanding Hill, which was allegedly named after this battle.[49] This hill commands a view of the lower course of the Icknield Way and the Ridgeway to the south where it crosses the Thames at Goring Gap. However, the approach from the south of Kingstanding Hill is steep enough that it should have dissuaded Halfdan and his senior warlord Bagsecg from risking an uphill attack. In such a situation Æthelred only needed to hold the high ground, but risked his army being outflanked. The other, adjacent site, which is accepted by most historians and acknowledged by the Battlefields Trust, as indicated on many modern maps, is a point on the Ridgeway where three other ancient tracks converge and cross it between Louse Hill and Lowbury Hill just over 3 miles north-west of Aldworth, a village 3 miles west of Streatley and the Thames.[50] It has none of the strategic difficulties associated with Kingstanding Hill. The location can be reached by following a lane northward from Aldworth to where it meets the Ridgeway.

William of Malmesbury observed that the two armies arrived on the afternoon of 7 January but delayed the battle until the following day as darkness was encroaching.[51] The West Saxons had probably camped at Roden Down, to the east of Compton, and the Danes perhaps in Streatley. On the morning of 8 January 871, based on the Ridgeway site discussed above, West Saxon battle lines were formed on a crest stretching across the Ridgeway just south of Lowbury Hill. As they advanced the Vikings would have seen the West Saxons had left the more easterly and nearer Louse Hill unoccupied, prompting them to seize it. Cavalry contingents were likely present on both sides, but they were not used at Ashdown. The preferred method of fighting was shield-wall and hand-to-hand combat.

What took place has been gathered from several primary sources, including the ASC and the work of Alfred's biographer Asser, reiterated later by William of Malmesbury and others.[52] They record both armies split into two divisions, the Danish Vikings dividing first and the West Saxons following suit, with Æthelred facing Halfdan and Bagsecg, and Alfred's division facing the other senior Danish jarls. However, the Vikings on Louse Hill instantly negated their high-ground advantage and came down to attack up the slope of Lowbury Hill. Asser tells us that Æthelred was still in the rear praying when the Vikings launched their first assault, and he describes Alfred's division taking the full brunt of the attack, with Alfred then charging into the enemy 'like a wild boar'.[53] This reference may refer not to Alfred's attack being reckless or bold, but rather to a wedge formation of shields and spears known at the time as a 'boars head'.[54]

The West Saxon king, according to Asser, allegedly refused to leave his prayers early despite being aware that his brother's forces were already under heavy assault.[55] This may be an unfair criticism of Æthelred, although several historians have counter-argued that withholding his contingent behind Lowbury Hill and releasing it at a critical moment was part of his overarching strategy for the battle.[56] Malmesbury records that the arrival of the king's division at the precise moment when Alfred's division was in difficulties turned the tide, as Æthelred 'with the Holy Cross as his standard unexpectedly charged ... throwing the enemy into confusion'.[57] Amid heavy fighting the brothers slowly pushed both Viking divisions back past the junction of the five tracks, up Louse Hill and down its eastern slope, forcing the Vikings back into the boggy turf at the foot of the hill, and killing many before those who had horses could reach them. The Viking survivors fled eastward, the fight lasting only a few hours as dusk approached.

The number of participants and casualties at Ashdown can only be estimated, as none of the primary sources provide any reliable figures. The West Saxons may have numbered at the beginning between 2,000 to 3,000 men after the losses at Reading, with the Viking army perhaps slightly larger. It is possible Halfdan had not waited for reinforcements before marching west. The ASC noted that 'many thousands' of Danes died at Ashdown, which is clearly an exaggeration, but the scribe recorded the deaths of the warlord Bagsecg and five senior jarls, Sidroc the Old, Sidroc the Young, Osbern, Fræna and Harold, which supports the Vikings having significant numbers.[58] Ashdown was a famous West Saxon victory, but from the evidence of coming events it scarcely stemmed the tide, as within a few weeks Halfdan, with new reinforcements, was ready to move out once more.

The next clash, a minor battle in contrast to Ashdown, came on 22 January at Basing, the site of a royal vill just east of modern-day Basingstoke. Possibly the Danes had advanced via the Harrow Way track hoping to plunder the vill before perhaps striking towards Winchester. The West Saxons look to have been at Basing in suitable numbers, perhaps several hundred, but 'the Danes won the victory'.[59] A probable site for the battle at Basing is the area known locally as Daneshill, on the north-east outskirts of Basingstoke, although the battle was more widespread, involving a series of disjointed fights that continued along the River Loddon and southward next to the Harrow Way. Despite their minor victory the Danes withdrew to regroup. There was now a lull in the fighting, during which Asser confirms that Halfdan's forces were joined by another Danish army, possibly led by the warlord Guthrum.[60] A major push deeper into Wessex would begin in March.

However, before the next phase of fighting began Æthelred assembled an important Witan war council at Swinbeorg in Wiltshire, better known today as Swanborough Tump, 2 miles west of Pewsey, the meeting place of the local hundred some distance from the recent area of conflict. The tump (mound) is marked today by a sarsen stone and another recently added stone and brass plaque recording the meeting and the agreement made there. in which Æthelred and Alfred made a joint pledge. Detail of the Swinbeorg council comes from Alfred's recollections within his will, written before 888, and the major item for discussion beyond the state of the war was the West Saxon succession, reflecting Æthelred's and Alfred's concerns about the course of the war and the potential for them being fatally injured in the fighting ahead.

Æthelred, approximately twenty-four or twenty-five, and Alfred, three years younger, were both still young. Alfred had a history of illness and his constitution was a concern, and it is also possible that Æthelred may have been ill or wounded prior to Swinbeorg, which prompted him to clarify the question of the succession. In 871 both of Æthelred's sons, Æthelhelm and Æthelwold, were under ten years of age and too young to succeed him directly. The witan at Swinbeorg therefore concluded and agreed that if one of the brothers died the survivor would inherit all the other's possessions, and, more relevantly, should Æthelred be killed Alfred would immediately succeed him as king of Wessex. We do not know, but can imagine, that Æthelred had foreseen his eldest son replacing Alfred in due course upon reaching his maturity. However, the only reference we have, in the absence of other contemporary evidence, is Alfred's later version of events written within his will.[61]

He recalled that 'when we assembled at Swinbeorg we agreed, with the cognisance of the West Saxon Council, that whichever of us survived the other was to give the other's children the lands which we had ourselves acquired, and the lands which King Æthelwulf gave us'.[62] There may have been discussion over Wessex's royal ties with Mercia in terms of the West Saxon succession. Both brothers had married Mercian wives, and while Alfred and Ealhswith's daughter Æthelflaed was born around this time, Æthelred and Wulfthryth already had their two young sons. If the king and his brother died in quick succession there would be complications. Alfred's later provision for his nephews once he became king proved less than edifying, as in the fullness of time by the 890s Æthelred's sons were essentially side-lined from the succession in favour of Alfred's.

Around mid-March 871, two months after Basing, the Danes resumed their campaign. However, following the encounters at Reading and Ashdown, and to a lesser extent Basing, the West Saxons were to become reactive rather than proactive. The lack of troops appears to have forced a withdrawal of the front line deeper into central Wessex. The Danes in contrast had received reinforcements, new warriors eager to gain wealth through pillaging, one characteristic of which was the targeting of key royal estates. This strategy provided several benefits, not least the richest monetary rewards and access to the regional food renders accumulated within those estates, which seriously disrupted the West Saxon command structure.

The next encounter took place on 22 March close to the important royal estate of Great Bedwyn, about 4 miles south-west of present-day Hungerford.[63] The battle was named by the ASC as Merton, and by John of Worcester as Meretun.[64] The place name of Meretun/Merton has featured previously – it was where Cynewulf of Wessex was ambushed and killed by Cyneheard in 786 as described in a previous chapter. Historians have identified the favoured site for the 871 Meretun as the village of Marten, lying only 2 miles south of Great Bedwyn next to the modern A338 road from Hungerford to Burbage, although two other potential locations have been suggested, and these will be considered.

Taking the favoured location of Marten for Meretun, we can assume the Danes were making for Great Bedwyn, which at one time had its own mint, marching via the Port Way track from Silchester, and then the Inkpen track past Walbury Hill Camp towards Shalbourne.[65] Assessing the local landscape here, Æthelred probably positioned his army defensively along the slopes west or south of Shalbourne. Of the battle itself little is known. The ASC tells us the Viking Danes were in two divisions and that the Anglo-Saxons 'put both to flight and for a long time during the day were victorious', but that 'the Danes had possession of the place of slaughter'.[66] Henry of Huntingdon acknowledges the West Saxon defeat, stating that the Danes 'were victorious in the end'.[67] A noted West Saxon fatality at Meretun was Bishop Heahmund of Sherborne, indicating part if not all the Dorset fyrd, alongside the men of Wiltshire and/or Hampshire. However, a far more relevant fatality in due course would be the king himself, as discussed below.

Of the other two suggested sites for the battle, the first of these is Martin. It is situated on the downs to the south of the modern A354 road between Salisbury and Blandford Forum. The second is Merritown, in heathland to the north of present-day Bournemouth south of Hurn Airport. One argument put forward for both Martin and Merritown is that Wimborne Minster, the final resting place of Æthelred – if we accept he died in the fighting and his body was carried there immediately – is only 13 miles from the former and 6 from the latter, whereas the preferred battle site at Marten is over 40 miles from Wimborne.[68]

However, geographically and strategically, both Martin and Merritown look to be too far south to be reasonable claimants for Meretun. To support this argument the next encounter would take place a month later at Wilton, an important royal vill just south-west of Old Sarum, further north than either of them. We cannot credit the Danes as already making a significant breakthrough towards Dorset at this stage. We know east Dorset remained in West Saxon hands, as Wimborne would not have been chosen for Æthelred's burial site if it was under serious and immediate threat. We also know he did not die during the battle, but must have received wounds that were eventually fatal. Asser informs us that 'after Easter in the same year' (mid-April), more than three weeks after the battle, 'King Æthelred went the way of all flesh' and was buried at Wimborne Minster.[69]

There is no known earlier personal association of Æthelred with Wimborne, but the minster there was connected with his ancestry, as it was originally founded by Cuthburh, the sister of Ine and Ingeld.[70] The choice of Wimborne might also imply that the Old Minster and Winchester were considered too vulnerable to contemporary or future Viking attack for him to be buried there alongside his grandfather. His father had chosen burial at Steyning in Sussex (although Alfred would later move his remains to Winchester) and his brothers Æthelbald and Æthelberht had chosen Sherborne. All trace of the original Saxon minster at Wimborne, and the building in which Æthelred was buried, was to be destroyed in a Viking raid early in the eleventh century, and during that raid Æthelred's tomb was devastated. Today, in the present-day twelfth-century Norman minster, with later additions, the memory of King Æthelred I of Wessex is commemorated by a fifteenth-century brass tablet, purportedly dated to 1440, on the wall near the altar.

18
Alfred
871–886

Alfred became the king of Wessex at the age of twenty-two during 871. It was a role he neither sought nor craved, and being the youngest of five ætheling brothers he would not have expected to succeed to the throne. Three of his brothers had died before the age of thirty; the only exception was Æthelstan, the first and eldest, who may have reached the age of thirty or thirty-one. Without further evidence it is possible that two of them, Æthelbald and Æthelberht, had died naturally while still in their mid-twenties from non-traumatic circumstances. This might imply a familial genetic disorder.

Alfred had his own health issues. According to the work of Asser, he was regularly afflicted with 'all kinds of illnesses unknown to the physicians' from a young age and throughout his life, including a bout of severe abdominal pain while at the feast marking his marriage to the Mercian noblewoman Ealhswith in 868.[1] In recent times historians have reasoned that from all that is known Alfred was suffering from Crohn's disease, an ailment that his contemporaries would have been unable to diagnose.[2] Research identifies that Crohn's disease shares many of its symptoms with ulcerative colitis, and it is acknowledged that both these afflictions begin in late adolescence and continue to recur spasmodically into and beyond middle age.[3]

Alfred was to be the last king of Wessex, or more precisely he was the last man to have used or been accredited with that title. Although he would remain king until his death in 899, it was Alfred himself who consigned the title of 'King of Wessex' to history mid-way through his reign. In alignment with the book's theme, we'll conclude this history at that same point: the moment around 886 when the King of Wessex retitled himself 'King of the Angles and Saxons' or 'King of the Anglo-Saxons', thereby making the former role of 'King of Wessex' a redundant designation.[4]

A month after becoming king, and seven weeks after the defeat at Meretun, Alfred was faced with defending the important royal vill and administration centre at Wilton from a new Danish advance under the leadership of Halfdan. This once again confirms that the Viking strategy was centred on pillaging these royal vills. They were profitable in both money and produce, and their importance to the West Saxons is evident in their efforts to defend them, such as at Great Bedwyn. Wilton was equally important. Alfred's need to defend it is confirmed by the ASC, which notes that he fought there 'with a small troop ... against the whole raiding army'.[5]

From this comment we envisage the West Saxons had already suffered significant losses after the string of battles they had been forced to fight during 871. According to the ASC, including Wilton, they experienced 'nine national fights' within Wessex against the raiding army that year.[6] Asser's count is 'eight battles', but he confirms the manpower problem when noting that at Wilton 'nor should it seem extraordinary to anyone that the Christians had a small number of men in the battle; for the Saxons were virtually annihilated to a man in this single year in eight battles against the Vikings'.[7]

Of the battle itself, access to Wilton proved more difficult for the Vikings than just a direct assault across the River Wylye, which flowed around the northern edge of the settlement. The river crossing was defended, but how the defences stood in 871 is difficult to determine. Evidence of ninth-century fortifications at Wilton found by archaeologists, near the northern end of West Street, are likely to be those ordered by Alfred at a later period during the 880s or 890s.[8] John of Worcester records the main battle of 871 was fought on a hill on the south bank of the river 'Guilou' (the Wylye), but there is no suitable feature directly adjacent between the river and the town which meets this description.[9] The supposition therefore is that the Vikings, having approached from Old Sarum, were unable to cross the Wylye due to strong West Saxon resistance, and were forced instead to seek another crossing point of the river further north between Stoford and Great Wishford. On assessing the local topography, Worcester's reference to a 'hill' must refer therefore to either Hadden Hill or Heath Hill, either of which the Vikings would have needed to bypass to enter Wilton after crossing the Wylye near Stoford. To support this scenario Alfred must have taken men from the river defences and placed them on one of the two hills to counteract the second Viking approach towards Wilton.

After holding off the Vikings for some time, Alfred was forced to withdraw his beaten force, allowing the Vikings to enter Wilton. The

West Saxon numbers defending Wilton were perhaps less than a thousand, but it seems that the Vikings had also not attacked in full force. The Vikings may already have divided their forces once again. However, they were to receive additional men that summer as previously hinted,, as there is a reference to the arrival in 871 of a new 'Great Summer Army'. Led by warlords Guthrum, Osketel and Anwend, these men were undoubtedly aware of their compatriots' earlier successes. Guthrum would be prominent in the later campaign against Wessex, although we do not know the power dynamics at play among the Danish leadership.

At some stage after the Wilton defeat, Alfred sued for peace.[10] The West Saxon resources appear to have run dry, and their remaining men had been fought to a standstill. Unlike the Vikings, they had no war-ready recruits to replace previous casualties. Tribute was given to the Viking leadership to withdraw their forces from Wessex, or at least central Wessex, although the primary sources do not refer to what must have been the equivalent of Danegeld payments. Halfdan and Guthrum withdrew to Reading and then back to London. Some historians have suggested that the Vikings, like the West Saxons, may have grown tired of the fighting.[11] This is perhaps only half of the story. They presumably used the lull to consolidate their hold on the regions north of the Thames, with many of the warriors who had arrived in or soon after 865 choosing to lay down their arms and settle on farmland at this stage.

The Danegeld payments gave Wessex peace for three years. In the interim, the Vikings established a permanent presence in East Anglia and much of eastern Mercia. The ASC records that in 872 the Vikings settled permanent winter quarters at Torksey in Lindsey (Lincolnshire), lying on the River Trent several miles north-west of Lincoln, linking their land force with their fleet.[12] Archaeologists had originally found artifacts and coinage to the south of the camp during the 1990s, and the main Viking camp at Torksey was located and excavated during the 2000s just north of the modern village. The size of the Viking presence is confirmed by the findings which reveal that the camp covered an area of around 64 acres (about 26 hectares or the equivalent of forty-three football pitches) on the eastern bank of the river. Among the finds over 300 coins have been discovered, including examples from Francia and a high number of tiny copper-alloy coins known as *stycas* minted only in Northumbria, the concentration of which at Torksey implies that the Viking army had pillaged Northumbria extensively ahead of settling at Torksey.[13]

In 873 the Great Army, or much of it, moved down the Trent to establish itself at the major Mercian royal site of Repton, but the following year there was a significant and final division of its forces. As noted by the

ASC and other primary sources, Halfdan went north to camp at the River Tyne, pillaging northern Northumbria and then moving into Strathclyde. Guthrum, Osketel and Anwend meanwhile moved south to conquer Mercia, driving Burgred to seek exile and retirement in Rome, before marching and/or sailing south-east (the River Cam was a tributary of the River Great Ouse) to over-winter at Cambridge.[14] In place of Burgred, the Viking leadership appointed a puppet king named Ceolwulf to rule Mercia on their behalf. It is unclear, but historians speculate it was at this point if not earlier that Ivar and his followers separated from Guthrum and joined Halfdan on campaign in Strathclyde. Ivar would later move across to Ireland and vie for territory against the native Irish kings and other Scandinavian warlords.

By 875, Alfred and Ealhswith's first child, their daughter Aethelflaed, would have been about five, and it was in 875, give or take a year, that their first son, Edward (later to become King Edward the Elder), was born.[15] As noted previously, Æthelred had two known sons, Æthelhelm and Æthelwold, who were probably still both under seven years old. To preserve his future position, and with one eye to favour the throne passing to his son Edward in due course, Alfred in later life would ensure that his nephews were excluded from the succession. Edward's own succession was not assured, and there was no established right of primogeniture for the kingship.

Furthermore, although it was not a serious concern for the future succession, some historians have debated that Æthelred, or even one of his previously deceased brothers, may have had two illegitimate sons named Beorhtfrith and Oswald. Beorhtfrith appears in only a single surviving charter list, from the year 868, where he is identified as the 'son of the king'.[16] Which of the brothers was his father is unclear. Evidence of Oswald is more clear cut, and he appears within four separate charters dated between 863 and 875, two during Æthelberht's kingship and one each under Æthelred and Alfred, where he witnesses as the 'son of king Æthelred'.[17] Their illegitimacy barred both Beorhtfrith and Oswald from any entitlement to the throne, but in Oswald's case, from the earliest of these charters, it appears he was born ahead of Æthelred's two legitimate sons.

Oswald may have produced his own son who remained linked to the royal court decades later. An entry in Alfred's will left property to a kinsman named Osfrith (aka Osferth), whose relationship to Alfred is unknown, but he may have been his grand-nephew, the child of Oswald and therefore grandchild of Æthelred.[18] Osfrith consistently witnessed charters – over thirty still survive – from 898 onwards through Edward the Elder's reign to the second half of the reign of Æthelstan in 934. In most them he is titled '*dux*', a member of the nobility, but he is described as 'king's brother' from some of Edward's charters onwards. The implication, as put forward by several historians, is that Osfrith was probably an illegitimate son of Alfred.[19]

During 875 the primary sources record Alfred fighting and defeating at sea a small Viking fleet of seven vessels somewhere along the south coast.[20] Some historians have emphasised this incident, and other naval engagements that followed it during the rest of his reign, to describe Alfred as the 'father' or founder of the English navy. This is a hard claim to substantiate. Primary texts, including the action involving his brother Æthelstan in 850, acknowledge that the Anglo-Saxons had already been involved in seaborne fighting before Alfred's tenure as king.[21] With this in mind, the best that we can accept is that Alfred carried our innovations to the design of English warships and to seaborne tactics against Viking longships, which improved the Anglo-Saxons' ability to fight the Vikings at sea.

The naval encounter suggests Viking intentions were again moving towards Wessex, leading to Guthrum's 875 campaign against the West Saxons. As recorded by the ASC, towards the end of that year 'the raiding army stole away from the West Saxon army into Wareham'.[22] The inference is that Alfred had been tracking Viking activity prior to this sudden advance, but it also implies that Guthrum was trying a different strategy than that employed by the Vikings during the initial 871 campaign into Wessex. We can speculate Guthrum had taken a significant cavalry force by the fastest route possible from the Thames Valley, perhaps via the Portway, a track that had been in use even before the Roman arrival, which took a course from Silchester to Old Sarum and then on via Badbury Rings Hillfort towards Wareham in Dorset.

Guthrum's aim was unquestionably to capture a settlement deep inside Wessex that he could reinforce directly from the sea. Wareham was ideal in that it lay on the River Frome, which flowed a few miles further east into the large expanse of Poole Harbour, which was then and remains today Europe's largest natural harbour. Thereafter, Guthrum would wait to be joined by his fleet of ships, the vast majority of his force, which he had planned would sail down the English Channel and join him in Dorset, utilising the large harbour at Poole ahead of an enlarged campaign during 876.

After hearing the initial news that Guthrum had seized Wareham, Alfred assembled the West Saxon fyrd and laid siege to the settlement over the winter of 875–876. He may still have been oblivious to the impending arrival of the Danish fleet.

Guthrum's winter manoeuvre into Dorset had caught the West Saxons unawares, but directing his fleet to move at that time of year down the Channel was also a risk. The whereabouts and prompt appearance of the fleet carrying the bulk of his army was critical. However, something went wrong. At some stage, before the arrival of his fleet, Guthrum was forced to agree to a peace treaty with Alfred. He transferred some of his senior men as hostages, and oaths were sworn on sacred Viking rings, a significant symbolic gesture for Scandinavians, which the chronicler Æthelweard records 'they had never done to the kings of the other districts', adding that in return Alfred gave Guthrum money.[23]

In hindsight, the modifying of Guthrum's plans must have been forced on him through a lack of news on the whereabouts of his fleet. Regardless, he broke with the promises made to Alfred and stole away westward from Wareham overnight, making for Exeter. His fleet had meanwhile made progress down the English Channel, but it was still the early months of 876 and the weather was unreliable. As recorded by the ASC, 'the raiding ship-army sailed around west, and then they met a great storm at sea, and 120 ships were lost at Swanage'.[24] In other words, the whole of Guthrum's fleet had been sunk, with the loss of perhaps several thousand men.

There is still some confusion on the timing of events. Historians differ in their interpretation of whether the fleet was wrecked en route to Poole Harbour, or was later lost after Guthrum had left Wareham as it sailed out from Poole Harbour into the Channel.[25] One historian has proposed that the Viking fleet had already reached the harbour but Alfred's forces had stopped them from entering the River Frome and liaising with Guthrum to relieve the siege, forcing the compromise.[26] This is plausible, and it may explain why the arrival of the fleet did not immediately change the situation. It would certainly explain why Guthrum needed to sue for peace and escape Wareham overnight and overland even though his fleet was located nearby.

Giving chase, Alfred's forces followed Guthrum to Exeter and settled in for a siege. Guthrum's own force had been able to take the city unawares after his 70-mile dash from Wareham.[27] The estuary of the River Exe at Exeter was the next most suitable location along the Channel to accommodate and relocate Guthrum's large Viking fleet, but he was unaware that disaster had already befallen his ships after they had set sail from Poole Harbour to join him; only later would he learn that they would not be coming. With no other alternative left open to him, Guthrum sued for peace and offered Alfred as many hostages as he wanted. This time the agreement held.

Nevertheless, something which the primary sources do not dwell on is that it was only during harvest time in 877 that the Vikings finally left West Saxon territory and made their way into Mercia. What took place over that prolonged period after the agreement at Exeter is unclear. We should question why Alfred appears so lenient, and open to peace at any cost. Specifically, why did he let Guthrum stay in Wessex for eighteen months? It would be this misplaced trust in Guthrum that nearly cost him and all his family their lives in January 878.

Guthrum was still able to command a substantial Danish army on settling in Mercia, and within months he had forced Ceolwulf II of Mercia, already subjugated by previous Danish warlords and effectively acting as a puppet-king, to cede him and his supporters territory, most of it in Gloucestershire and Gloucester itself. Thereafter, before the onset of winter 877–878, Guthrum moved his main army 20 miles south of Gloucester to Cirencester in Wiltshire. This transpired to be the prelude to a renewed campaign against Wessex.

Meanwhile, in late December 877, Alfred took his family to celebrate the Christmas feast in Chippenham, a district controlled by the West Saxon ealdorman Wulfhere. The settlement was an important centre. It was where Alfred's sister Æthelswith had married the Mercian king Burgred in 853 and would later, in 884–885, be the site of Alfred's daughter Æthelflaed's wedding to Lord Æthelred of Mercia. Chippenham lay scarcely a dozen miles from the Mercian Danish-controlled territory, and about 20 miles from Cirencester. This infers that, despite there being safer locations for his family, Alfred was not overly worried the Danes were about to launch a new military offensive into his kingdom, even less so at him directly. Æthelflaed was by now a child aged around seven, and Edward was perhaps three. Ealhswith had also since given birth to Æthelgifu, another daughter, possibly several months old, and had perhaps recently become pregnant with what would be her fourth child, Ælfthryth.

In hindsight, Alfred's decision to visit Chippenham was ill founded. Once more the Vikings broke their peace agreement, and on 6 January 878, the last and twelfth night of the Christmas festivities, they launched a surprise night-time assault on Chippenham.[28] Guthrum's forces were complimented by new Danish recruits led by Osketel and Anwend.[29] It was not a known element of Viking warfare for them to attack at night, and the ease with which the Danes got into Chippenham suggests the gates were unguarded and open and there were Anglo-Saxon accomplices.[30] Primary source evidence would point to several possible suspects, particularly those nobles who had grudgingly financed the earlier Danegeld payments Alfred had made to keep the peace. However, suspicion falls chiefly on ealdorman Wulfhere of Wiltshire, Alfred's host that Christmas. Chippenham was Wulfhere's principal residence. It is speculated he was linked by kinship to Æthelred's widow Wulfthryth, and therefore to her sons Æthelhelm and Æthelwold. Some argue that Wulfhere may therefore have been disillusioned that Alfred had already barred Æthelhelm and Æthelwold from any genuine authority after the death of their father. That he later fell afoul of Alfred can be found in a charter from Edward (the Elder) of 901, which shows that sometime after 878 Wulfhere had been relieved of his estates, accused of treason and of deserting his king.[31]

Alfred and his family barely escaped with their lives, presumably saved by the king's retinue of bodyguards, and made for the Somerset marshes at Athelney. His flight from Chippenham to the marshes of Athelney in the Somerset Levels has become almost mythical, a story familiar to nearly everyone. This is further mixed with the allegorical and ethically charged account of Alfred burning the cakes while sheltering in the marshes. Athelney takes its name from the Old English 'Æthelinga' meaning 'Isle of Princes', which may denote earlier royal connections or was so named because of the events of January 878. Tradition says that Alfred's plight was serious to the point of imminent disaster.

However, the marshland of the Somerset Levels was hard for Guthrum's Danes to penetrate in sufficient numbers, even if he had been able to locate the king and his remaining supporters. At Athelney Alfred established a large fortified camp, accessible only by a narrow causeway at its southern end, where a long, low ridge of ground above the flood levels gave him the time to recover, assemble what resources and men he could, and plan a way back to power. Archaeologists have detected traces of possible ninth-century fortifications and iron smelting activity at Athelney associated with Alfred. In 888, years after the crisis, Alfred had an abbey built on the eastern end of Athelney to offer thanks to God in memory of his tribulations. The abbey was demolished during the sixteenth century, and a stone monument, which can still be seen today, was erected in 1801 at the spot where the abbey once stood.

While Alfred was at Athelney, the rest of Wessex may have remained unaware of his survival, perhaps even for weeks. The ASC tells us that the Danes 'over-rode and occupied the land of Wessex, and drove many of the people across the sea'.[32] This is not exactly as it sounds. The reference to the 'sea' probably refers to the Solent across to the Isle of Wight. Having perhaps pillaged initially to the south coast, the Danes would not have been able to occupy Wessex indefinitely with the manpower available to them. Initially Guthrum would have occupied the royal vills, where the winter stores would have been plentiful. However, once these were depleted there was no tactical benefit in occupying them while Alfred and other prominent West Saxon nobles were at large and able to raise resistance. In reality, in the early weeks of 878, Danish control of West Saxon territory in the west was at best limited to Wiltshire and perhaps swathes of Dorset and Somerset.

Historians have posed the question why Guthrum did not make greater efforts to locate Alfred. He was unable or reluctant to attempt penetration of the Somerset Levels and marshes, but it is plausible that he first believed Alfred to be dead or at least deprived of any relevant support. Furthermore, in Alfred's absence, he may simply have expected the senior West Saxon nobles to accept the reality of the situation and accept him as their new king. However, as long as Alfred remained alive and on the English side of the Channel, Guthrum was merely a king in waiting. In the spring, word spread that the king of Wessex was alive and ready to reclaim his throne. The news undoubtedly reached Guthrum too, and he summoned help to find and finish Alfred. The Danes knew Alfred was hiding in the Levels, and Ubba, the brother of Ivar and Halfdan, took up the challenge of finding him. Ubba sailed his fleet of twenty-three ships into the Bristol Channel up to the mouth of the River Parrett, the major waterway that entered the Somerset Levels, intending to seek Alfred.

However, the Vikings had perhaps been overconfident. Support for Alfred had already coalesced, certainly across Somerset and Devon. Ubba's fleet had been monitored by Ealdorman Odda, who had assembled his Devon fyrd on a strategic hill site overlooking the Bristol Channel. Several potential locations for this hill have been proposed, including Clovelly Dykes, Castle Hill near Beaford and Countisbury Head near Lynmouth, the latter site being supported by Asser.[33] Nevertheless, in studying the maps, all of these are too far west to have effectively blocked access to the mouth of the River Parrett, which was the major waterborne gateway to the Levels.[34]

As a better alternative, the Iron Age hillfort of Cannington Hill (aka Cynwit Hill), 4 miles north-west of modern Bridgwater, seems the most straightforward choice, as it permitted Odda a perfect view of the Parrett estuary 5 miles away and was only a mile from the nearest stretch of the river. To access the Parrett, Ubba had first to deal with Odda, but against the Danish leader's expectations Odda did not wait to be challenged but charged his troops down to engage Ubba's forces. The ASC scribe noted that Ubba and 840 of his men were slain, while Asser and John of Worcester numbered the Viking dead at 1,200, which is too many for twenty-three ships unless every Dane was killed.[35]

Seven weeks after Easter, in early to mid-May 878, having earlier sent out a summons for men to be mustered to join his new army, Alfred and his followers left Athelney and moved eastward. A meeting point was arranged at Ecgberht's stone to the east of Selwood, which in the medieval period was a huge forest stretching from mid-Dorset and Somerset across to the Wiltshire Downs, comprising an area of 100,000 to 130,000 acres. The assembly point at Ecgberht's stone was symbolic, as it was named after Alfred's grandfather. There are two conflicting sites for the location, and both have reasonable claims. The first is a stone just north of the village of Bourton, west of Mere, where the three shires of Dorset, Somerset and Wiltshire converge, and the other site contains three stones next to the Church of St Mary's at Kingston Deverill, 4 miles south of Warminster.

Alfred was joined at this assembly point by those who had responded to his summons from the fyrds of Somerset and Wiltshire, together with Hampshire levies from west of Southampton Water.[36] Based on assessments of the possible fighting strength available from these areas, Alfred's force could have numbered over 3,000. The following day the army advanced to Iley Oak (aka Iglea or Island Wood), now thought to be present-day Eastleigh Wood or Southleigh Wood just south of Warminster and south of the River Wylye.[37] Historians prefer Eastleigh Wood as it has been identified as a former meeting place of the local hundred, and contains the remains of an Iron Age camp known as Robin Hood Bower, now hidden by plantation woodland, which could be associated with the name 'Island Wood'.

John of Worcester tells us that Alfred remained at Iley Oak for a further day to allow more men to join him.[38] The West Saxons then headed north in the direction of Guthrum's base at Chippenham as a direct challenge to him. The Danish leader counteracted by marching his forces south to confront Alfred's army in the field, and they were to meet in battle at the site that various sources have named as either Ethandun or Edington.[39] Like many Anglo-Saxon battle sites, the location for Edington is contested. One such location is Battlebury Hill, but as it lies only 2 miles from where Alfred had rested his army at Iley Oak (Eastleigh Wood), we can probably dismiss this option.[40]

The site favoured by virtually all the academic fraternity is the Iron Age hillfort of Bratton Camp in Wiltshire. It overlooks the north-facing slope that would later accommodate the Westbury White Horse and is a couple miles west of the village of Edington, from which the battle takes its popular name. It is also a logical location on the basis it lies between Warminster and Chippenham, a meeting point as the two armies converged. Guthrum must have acted on first hearing Alfred was gathering men, and his men had covered three-quarters of the distance between them to reach Bratton ahead of Alfred's forces. The Vikings had probably already formed defensive lines inside the earthworks of Bratton. However, the strongest defensive section at Bratton was the northern slope, and the rise on the southern slope did not offer a significant advantage.

Details of the battle of Edington are imprecise, as is the date, which is thought to be between 7 and 14 May 878.[41] Alfred may have had upward of 4,000 men at this point, it is difficult to say, and Guthrum's numbers are even more difficult to determine but were perhaps several hundred fewer. On the approach of the West Saxon army, Guthrum most likely left his position behind the southern earthworks and formed his army into a shield-wall to its south. Asser's attempt to describe events is sadly unhelpful, but the general assumption is that after fighting for hours the West Saxons were able to force the Danish shield-wall slowly backwards, down the northern slope of Bratton Hill towards their encampment and horses.[42]

Many of the Danes may have fled the scene on horseback to escape death or capture. Their initial losses were more modest than previously considered, as it is understood that much of Guthrum's army was able to make it back to Chippenham.[43] This might explain why the ASC and other contemporary primary sources did not enthuse about the battle of Edington to the extent we night expect, given its later relevance. Only in hindsight was the victory appreciated in the full context of the survival of Wessex, and in turn Anglo-Saxon England. A monument to the battle, a small sarsen stone taken from the group of stones at Kingston Deverill associated with Ecgberht, was erected on Bratton Camp above the White Horse in 2000. It bears two inscriptions, one commemorating the battle of 878 and Alfred's victory, and the other denoting its connection with Kingston Deverill. Nothing of note concerning the Saxon royal vill or the battle can be seen today at Edington village, but in the tenth century King Edgar gave the royal estate to Romsey Abbey and a priory was established there, a few fragments of which can be viewed today in the parish church and surrounding grounds.

Soon after the fighting had ended, Alfred's forces pursued the Danes and besieged them within their Chippenham fortification, and they were prevented from venturing out and securing new provisions for two weeks.[44] That no other Danish force came to assist Guthrum counteracts those who argue he controlled all of Wessex while Alfred was at Athelney. This was principally an illusion. Wessex had been without its king, leaderless and uncoordinated for several weeks, but there is no evidence the Danes seriously developed a wider authority across the kingdom. At Chippenham, Guthrum was forced to negotiate a truce before his men starved to death, and in Asser's words 'the Vikings, thoroughly terrified by hunger, cold and fear', sought peace.[45]

Shortly after the Danish surrender, Guthrum was baptised by Alfred with great ceremony at the church at Aller, a few miles to the east of Athelney, along with thirty of his senior men. At the end of the process, Guthrum was given the Christian name of Æthelstan. After the baptism, Alfred and Guthrum agreed to what has been called the Peace of Wedmore. The text for this treaty has not endured, but it likely agreed similar terms to the document signed between them several years later known as the Treaty of Alfred and Guthrum. Whatever was settled at Wedmore did not require the prompt exit of Guthrum's forces from Wessex. Only in autumn 879, at the earliest, did the Danes finally leave Chippenham and re-enter Mercia. Once again, some historians have questioned the timescale and why this process took so long. Does it imply that Alfred's position was not as strong as assumed in the months after Edington, or does it acknowledge and affirm his renewed and obvious faith in the newly baptised Guthrum?[46] By 880, Guthrum would move his army and followers from Gloucestershire across to East Anglia, where he established himself as the region's new king.

For several years after 880 there were intermittent Viking incursions into eastern Wessex along the Thames Estuary and north Kent, possibly encouraged by, or at least overlooked by, Guthrum. Raids had taken place on Rochester and other sites south of the River Thames, and battles between Vikings and Alfred's new navy had taken place in 885 in the Thames Estuary. The Wedmore treaty was fracturing. To resolve this, Alfred renegotiated with Guthrum, who was by then the main Danish figurehead in lowland Britain, and the agreement of Wedmore was updated as the Treaty of Alfred and Guthrum, formalising the earlier understanding between them.

This treaty re-established and reconfirmed the peace, and introduced several clauses on the legal rights of Anglo-Saxons and Danes and the trade permitted between them. However, most significantly, it recognised the separation of the regions north of the River Thames into English and Danish spheres of influence.[47] The Danish-controlled territory would later be identified as the Danelaw, and England was split between Anglo-Saxon and Dane at a line running from the Thames Estuary, then northward up the River Lea. The Lea was a major tributary of the Thames, joining it near Bow Creek. From the Lea, the new border ran to Bedford and then followed the River Great Ouse south-west until it met Roman Watling

Street. The agreed border then extended along Watling Street (essentially the route of the modern A5) north-west to Tamworth, the former capital of Mercia. Whether it continued beyond Tamworth is unclear. However, we can speculate that it probably did not continue along the line of Watling Street to its original Roman terminus at Wroxeter near the Welsh border, but more likely extended along an unrecorded route north beyond the western edge of the Peak District, marking in that area a divide between Mercia and Viking-controlled Northumbria.[48]

Ceolwulf II, the nominal Mercian puppet king appointed by the Vikings several years earlier, died a year after the Wedmore agreement. With him, the line of Mercian kings ended. After 879, Lord Æthelred, husband of Alfred's daughter Æthelflaed, had become the senior Anglo-Saxon inside Mercia, but although Wessex had not formally held authority in Mercia beforehand this all changed in 886. Æthelred was forced to recognise vassalage to Alfred as the king of their new union. More significant to the Mercians was the loss of half of their pre-878 territory, which now lay in the Viking-controlled Danelaw. Historians have found no evidence of any Mercian involvement in the negotiations in which Alfred formally divided Mercian territory in 886.

The agreement coincided with the West Saxon occupation of London, the principal trading centre in England. London was integral to the Anglo-Saxon economy, but it was also strategically important to secure it and to deny the Scandinavians future hostile access into the centre of Wessex via the Thames. London had been Mercian, but it is unclear what recent Danish involvement there had been in the area before we hear of Alfred seizing control of it for Wessex.[49] In the 886 treaty not a single hide or acre of West Saxon territory south of the River Thames was lost, but on the other side of the coin Alfred had conceded the loss of West Saxon-controlled Essex to the Danelaw. By the agreement with Guthrum, Alfred had gained ultimate authority over Mercia and London, even though as a concession he would allow his son-in-law Æthelred of Mercia to nominally control London for a period. Finally, it was after this treaty that Alfred dropped his title as King of Wessex and took on a title reflecting his greater role in shaping England's future.

19
From Wessex to England

If we include Creoda and Cwichelm, the monarchs with disputed claims to having ruled in their own rights, and add the reign of its single woman monarch, Queen Seaxburh, Alfred the Great was the twenty-fifth and final ruler of the independent kingdom of Wessex. Its separate and distinct kingship was the last to disappear among the seven original Anglo-Saxon kingdoms, known as the heptarchy, which had comprised Wessex, East Anglia, Essex, Kent, Mercia, Northumbria and Sussex. Beyond Wessex, the other six kingdoms had all relinquished their independence by the mid-ninth century, with some having done so much earlier.

In and around 886, after the Treaty of Alfred and Guthrum, the detached independence of Wessex would follow. But it was not forced by warfare or political upheaval as the others had been, rather its change of circumstance reflected a rise in its status as a kingdom and that of its king. Before the ink was dry on Alfred's treaty with the Dane Guthrum to divide England into Anglo-Saxon and Danish spheres of authority, he was consigning his old title of 'King of Wessex' to history. He now became the first king in the history of the Anglo-Saxon kingdoms to give himself the distinctive title of 'King of the Anglo-Saxons'.

This new and enhanced role is first witnessed in the prologue of his treaty with Guthrum, wherein the text infers he regarded himself as the leader of more than the West Saxons alone.[1] The ASC noted rather grandly that after his occupation of London 'all the English race turned to him, except what was in captivity to Danish men'.[2] However, this was not as grand as it may initially sound. Half of England was under Danish control in the 880s. It would be left to Alfred's son Edward the Elder and his grandson Æthelstan to recover and restore that Danish-held land during the tenth century.

Alfred was to successfully defeat further Danish raiding armies during the 890s by implementing a network of permanently garrisoned burh forts across Wessex, each no more than 20 miles from the next, along with instigating changes to the fyrd system to provide a permanent standing army. However, his last decade also saw him devote time to expanding the Christian message as he saw it, and to initiatives to develop learning, including the translation of major texts from Latin into Old English and prompting the inauguration of the *Anglo-Saxon Chronicle*.[3] His many achievements during his reign go beyond the remit of this book. However, his later given designation of 'the Great', a singularly distinctive appellation among all the Anglo-Saxon kings, aptly demonstrates the importance of Alfred and his reign in the history of England.

Something often overlooked in Alfred and Wessex's story is the part the Viking Danes played in the late ninth-century fortunes of Wessex. From the arrival of the Great Heathen Army in 865 to the 880s, a sequence of events and warfare led to the collapse of all the Anglo-Saxon kingdoms except Wessex. It had endured its own crisis period between 871 and 878, but it had survived. Wessex's final triumph over Mercia was ironically due to the changes caused by the Viking invasion. It is difficult to envisage Wessex acquiring permanent, durable power across Mercia, and then later across England, without the Viking wars of the ninth century.

From his twenty-eight-year reign, from 871 to 899, only fifteen of Alfred's charters are extant. Given the extensive information on him and the events of his reign, this number is unexpectedly low. The evocative watershed of 886 and Alfred's change of title, as noted above, is acknowledged and confirmed within his charters. In texts before that date, he signs documents as 'King of the West Saxons'.[4] It is in the lists of two charters from the mid-880s that he is first found using his new title 'King of the Anglo-Saxons' or 'King of the English and the Saxons'.[5]

Alfred is often credited as the first king of England because he governed territories beyond Wessex prior to his demise. This, some argue, can be supported by the knowledge that his bloodline would form the roots of the newly created English line of kings.[6] There is some sympathy for this viewpoint. However, naming Alfred as the first 'King of England' seems a title too far, an augmentation beyond his actual power. The more valid counter-argument is that during the rest of his reign, after he had signed his agreement with Guthrum and between 886 and 899, Alfred still only ruled only half of the country. Northumbria, East Anglia and the Danelaw half of Mercia remained beyond his jurisdiction during his lifetime, and England as a concept did not exist until mid-way through the tenth century.[7] The transition from Wessex to England came in stages. Beyond

Alfred, it would take several successful campaigns by his son Edward the Elder to recover the southern Danelaw territories, and after Edward's death in 924 his son Æthelstan would take up the challenge. Æthelstan may have a valid claim to be considered the first 'king of England', after his famous victory in the north at Brunanburh in 937 against a combination of Norse and Scots that finally united all the regions of England under a single ruler. However, it was not until the reigns of Alfred's grandsons Edmund and Eadred that England's union was fully recognised.

As expressed above, the title of the king of Wessex passed into history when Alfred took upon himself his greater role. However, the concept of Wessex as a defined territory and identified geographical region would live on through his descendants and in other ways. The kingship had ended. But more than a century after Alfred's death, the new title of earl of Wessex was created in 1019 by King Cnut and awarded to an Anglo-Saxon noble with origins along the Hampshire–Sussex border named Godwin. He first appears as 'earl' in a charter issued by Cnut that year.[8] His jurisdiction covered what had formerly been the extended territory of greater Wessex south of the River Thames, similar to how it had stood after the reign of Ecgberht. At Godwin's death in 1053, his eldest surviving son, Harold Godwinson, succeeded to the earldom. Harold became king of England in 1066 (as Harold II), and, as everyone will surely know, was the English king who died at the Battle of Hastings. On his death, his former title of earl of Wessex died with him.

The wider view of Wessex today is perhaps best captured through its original regional identity, which was the territory that the West Saxons and the Gewisse first conquered. It is still centred on those regions: Hampshire, Berkshire, Dorset, Somerset and Wiltshire. However, Wessex survives as much more than just an abstract concept. The name has lived on in diverse ways within the names of regional authorities, public utilities and organisations, army regiments and many private companies. The title of earl of Wessex was also to resurface the best part of a millennium after Harold Godwinson's death when Prince Edward became the first royal in centuries to receive an earldom instead of a dukedom, being given the earldom of Wessex at the time of his marriage in 1999 by his mother, Queen Elizabeth II.

In seeking a single symbol to represent the identity of Wessex today, perhaps it can be best distinguished through the golden dragon war emblem of its former kings. It still appears as part of the design of the county council coats of arms for Dorset and Hampshire. The dragon was a popular symbol throughout Europe, but the Wessex dragon – actually a wyvern, a winged non-avian beast with two feet – is believed to precede even the Welsh red dragon.[9] It was repopularised during the Victorian era but has its roots as the ancient standard of the West Saxons. The chronicler Henry of Huntingdon noted the connection when writing that Cuthred went into battle 'bearing the banner of the king of Wessex, that is, the golden dragon'.[10] It is the dragon banner under which Alfred defeated the Danes at Edington, the dragon banner that was carried by Athelstan when he defeated the Norse–Scots alliance at Brunanburh, and the dragon banner that was raised by Edmund Ironside when he fought against Cnut. It was also with Harold II at Stamford Bridge – and, as shown in the Bayeux Tapestry, the wyvern banner of Wessex was with him at Hastings.[11]

Notes

The following abbreviations have been used for frequently referenced primary works in the endnotes.

ASC	*Anglo-Saxon Chronicle*
ALA	Asser's *Life of King Alfred*
BEH	The Venerable Bede's *Ecclesiastical History of the English People*
CA	*Chronicon Æthelweardi*
CJW	Chronicle of John of Worcester
EHD	English Historical Documents
GPA	William of Malmesbury's *Gesta Pontificum Anglorum*
GRA	William of Malmesbury's *Gesta Regum Anglorum*
HA	Henry of Huntingdon's *Historia Anglorum*
SMO	Symeon of Durham's *Symeonis Monachi Opera Omnia*
WSGRL	West Saxon Genealogical Regnal List

Note: Charter numbers have the prefix 'S', a system of charter identification taken from the catalogue system first adopted by Professor Peter Sawyer in 1968.

Introduction

1. T. E. Mommsen, 'Petrarch's Conception of the Dark Ages', in *Medieval and Renaissance Studies* (Cornell University Press, 1959), pp. 106-129; A. Williams, A. Smyth, & D. P. Kirby, *A Biographical Dictionary of Dark Age Britain c.500-1050* (London, 1991)
2. K. Verdun, 'Medievalism', in C. W. Jordan (ed.), *Dictionary of the Middle Ages*, Vol. 1 (New York, 2004), pp. 389-397.
3. R. Naismith, *Early Medieval Britain c.500-1000* (Cambridge, 2021), pp. 67-8
4. T. Williamson, *Environment, Society and Landscape in Early Medieval England: Time and Topography* (Woodbridge, revd edn, 2015), p. 7
5. Williamson, p. 6
6. *The Anglo-Saxon Chronicles*, ed. and trans. M. Swanton (London: revd edn, 2000)

7. A. Williams, *Kingship and Government in Pre-Conquest England, c.500–1066* (Basingstoke, 1999), p. 2
8. D. N. Dumville, 'The West Saxon Genealogical Regnal List and the Chronology of Early Wessex', *Peritia: Journal of the Medieval Academy of Ireland*, Vol. 4 (1985), pp. 21-36
9. *Bede's Ecclesiastical History of the English People*, eds J. McClure and R. Collins (Oxford: New York, revd edn, 2008)
10. BEH, pp. 3-4
11. Gildas, *De Excidio et Conquestu Britanniae (The Ruin of Britain, and Other Works)*, ed. and trans. M. Winterbottom, *Arthurian Period Sources*, Vol. 7 (London, 1978); Naismith, p. 181
12. K. George, 'Gildas's De Excidio Britonum and the Early British Church', *Studies in Celtic History*, Vol. 26 (Woodbridge, 2009), p. 125; G Halsall, 2013, *Worlds of Arthur: Facts & Fictions of the Dark Ages* (Oxford, 2013), p. 54
13. Nennius, *Historia Brittonum (The History of the Britons, in Six Old English Chronicles)*, trans. J. A. Giles (London, 1847); D. N. Dumville, 'Nennius and the "Historia Brittonum",' *Studia Celtica*, Vol. 10/11 (1975), pp. 78-95
14. N. Wright, *The Historia Regum Britannie of Geoffrey of Monmouth* (Woodbridge, 1984), p. xvii
15. D. N. Dumville (ed.), 'Annales Cambriae, A.D. 682-954: Texts A-C in Parallel' (Cambridge, 2002)
16. *Asser's Life of King Alfred & Other Contemporary Sources*, trans. & intro S. Keynes & M. Lapidge (London, repr. 2004)
17. *Chronicon Æthelweardi* (Chronicle of Æthelweard), ed. and trans. A. Campbell (London, 1962)
18. William of Malmesbury, *Gesta Regum Anglorum: The History of the English Kings*, Vol. 1, ed. and trans. R. A. B. Mynors, R. M. Thomson and M. Winterbottom (Oxford; New York, 1998); William of Malmesbury, *Gesta Pontificum Anglorum, The History of the English Bishops*, trans. M. Winterbottom and R. M. Thomson (London; New York, 2007); John of Worcester, *The Chronicle of John of Worcester*, Vol. 3, ed. and trans. P. McGurk (Oxford: New York, 1998); Henry of Huntingdon, *Historia Anglorum: The History of the English People*, ed. and trans. D. E. Greenway (Oxford, 1996)
19. *Prosopography of Anglo-Saxon England* (PASE website), History Faculty at the University of Oxford. Authors & eds J. L. Nelson, S. Keynes, S. Baxter, A. Burghart, A. Bell, N. Hodgson, J. Dresvina, B. Snook; author & design: J. Bradley, H. Short, P. Vetch, T. Hill, P. Rose & M. Jessop; D. Whitelock (ed.), *English Historical Documents, 500-1042* (London: 2nd edn, 1996)

1 The Germanic Migrations

1. S. S. Frere, *Britannia: A History of Roman Britain* (Oxford, 1987), p. 354
2. C. A. Snyder, *An Age of Tyrants: Britain and the Britons AD400-600* (Pennsylvania, 1998), p. 18

3. A. R. Birley, *The Roman Government of Britain* (Oxford, 2005), pp. 461-3
4. *The Anglo-Saxon Chronicles*, trans. M. Swanton (London: revd edn, 2000), p. 10
5. *ASC*, v. A & E, pp. 10-11
6. B. Eagles, *From Roman Civitas to Anglo-Saxon Shire: Topographical Studies on the Formation of Wessex* (Oxbow, 2018), p. 15
7. Nennius, *Historia Brittonum*, ch. 49, trans. J. A. Giles (London, 1847)
8. R. Naismith, *Early Medieval Britain c.500-1000* (Cambridge, 2021), pp. 67-8
9. Bede, *The Ecclesiastical History of the English People* (Oxford: rev edn, 2008) bk I, ch. 15-16, pp. 26-8
10. ASC, v. A & E, pp. 12-13
11. ASC, v. A & E, p. 12
12. Gildas, *De Excidio et Conquestu Britanniae (The Ruin of Britain, and Other Works)*, ed. and trans. Michael Winterbottom (London, 1978) ch. 23.1
13. Gildas, ch. 23.1; Bede, bk I, ch. 15-16, pp. 26-8
14. D. N. Dumville, 'Nennius and the "Historia Brittonum",' *Studia Celtica*, Vol. 10/11 (1975), pp. 78-95; BEH, bk I, ch. 15, p. 27
15. Gildas, ch. 7
16. Nennius
17. Gildas
18. Eagles, p. xiv
19. R. Matthews, *Ceawlin: The Man who Created England* (Barnsley, 2012), p. 124
20. T. Sullivan, *The Early Anglo-Saxon Kings* (Barnsley, 2023), p. 21
21. Sullivan, *The Early Anglo-Saxon Kings*, p. 22
22. S. Schiffels, W. Haak, P. Paajanen, *et al.*, 'Iron Age and Anglo-Saxon genomes from East England reveal British migration history', *Nat Commun*, Vol. 7, 10408 (2016)
23. Matthews, *Ceawlin: The Man who Created England*, p. 48
24. Gildas, ch. 23
25. B. Cunliffe, *Britain Begins* (Oxford, 2013), p. 242
26. K. Dark, 'Civitas to Kingdom: British Political Continuity 300-800', in *Studies in the Early History of Britain* (Leicester, 1994), pp. 78-9; S. Laycock, *Warlords: The Struggle for Power in Post-Roman Britain* (Stroud, 2009), p. 64
27. M. Ashley, *British Monarchs* (London, 1998), p. 113
28. Laycock, p. 87
29. Eagles, p. 8
30. A. Woolf, 'Apartheid and Economics in Anglo-Saxon England', in *Britons in Anglo-Saxon England* (Woodbridge: Boydell Press, 2007), pp. 127-9
31. Naismith, *Early Medieval Britain c.500-1000*, pp. 110, 158
32. T. M. Charles-Edwards, 'Language and Society among the insular Celts AD400-1000', in M. Green (ed.), *The Celtic World* (London, 1995), pp. 730-33
33. Eagles, p. xvii
34. Eagles, pp. 111, 138

2 West Saxon Origins and the Gewisse

1. BEH, bk I, ch. 15, p. 27
2. *Shorter Oxford English Dictionary* (Oxford, 2007)
3. BEH, bk I, ch. 15, p. 27
4. Whittock, Martyn. J., *The Origins of England: 410 to 600* (Totowa, 1986), pp. 186-191
5. H. Hamerow, C. Ferguson, J. Naylor, 'The Origins of Wessex Pilot Project', *Oxoniensa*, Vol. 78 (2013), pp. 49-69
6. www.reading.ac.uk/news-and-events/releases/PR848532.aspx
7. BEH, bk II, ch. 5, p. 80; bk III, ch. 7, p. 119; bk IV, ch. 15, p. 197
8. BEH, bk III, ch. 7, p. 119
9. A. Williams, *Kingship and Government in Pre-Conquest England, c.500–1066.* (Basingstoke, 1999), p. 10
10. Matthews, p. 101
11. Laycock, p. 61
12. Eagles, p. 186
13. ASC, v. A & E, pp. 14-15
14. ASC, v. A, p. 20
15. B. Yorke, *Wessex in the Early Middle Ages* (Leicester, 1995), p. 34
16. H. E. Walker, 'Bede and the Gewissae', *Cambridge Historical Journal*, Vol. xii (1956), pp. 54-8
17. D. P. Kirby, *The Earliest English Kings* (London: revd edn, 2000), pp. 44-5
18. Sullivan, p. 14
19. Eagles, p. xxx

3 Cerdic and Cynric, c. 500–534

1. GRA, p. 39; Frank M. Stenton, *Anglo-Saxon England* (Oxford: 3rd edn, 1971), p. 19
2. *Chronicon Æthelweardi*, ed. and trans. Alistair Campbell (London, 1962)
3. Matthews, p. 99
4. ASC, v. A, p. 16
5. B. Yorke, *Kings and Kingdoms of Early Anglo-Saxon England* (London, 1990), p. 155
6. Laycock, p. 123
7. J. N. L. Myres, *The English Settlements* (Oxford, 1986), pp. 146-48
8. ASC, v. A & E, pp. 14-15
9. Stenton, p. 20
10. ASC, v. A & E, pp. 14-17
11. CA, p. 11
12. Henry of Huntingdon, *Historia Anglorum: The History of the English People*, ed. and trans. D. E. Greenway, *Oxford Medieval Texts* (Oxford, 1996), p. 97; ASC, v. A & E, pp. 14-15
13. Matthews, p. 116
14. ASC, v. A & E, pp. 14-15
15. HA, p. 95

16. ASC, v. A & E, pp. 16-17
17. HA, p. 99; BEH, bk I, ch. 15, p. 28
18. HA, p. lix
19. ASC, v. A & E, pp. 16-17
20. BEH, bk II, ch. 5, p. 78
21. D. Dumville, 'The West Saxon Genealogical Regnal List and the Chronology of Early Wessex', *Peritia: Journal of the Medieval Academy of Ireland*, Vol. 4, pp. 21-36
22. Yorke, *Kings and Kingdoms of Early Anglo-Saxon England*, p. 131
23. Ashley, p. 299
24. ASC, v. A, p. 66
25. Kirby, p. 41
26. HA, p. 97
27. ASC, v. A & E, pp. 14-15
28. BEH, bk II, ch. 5, p. 78
29. Sullivan, p. x
30. G. Halsall, *Worlds of Arthur: Facts & Fictions of the Dark Ages* (Oxford, 2013), p. 71
31. C. J. Arnold, *An Archaeology of the Early Anglo-Saxon Kingdoms* (London, 1997)
32. Stenton, pp. 7-8
33. ASC, v. A & E, pp. 16-17; HA, p. 99
34. *Domesday Book: A Complete Translation* (London: New York; 2003); Matthews, p. 119
35. ASC, v. A & E, pp. 16-17
36. A. F. Major, *Early Wars of Wessex: being studies from England's school of arms in the west*, Vol. 3 (Cambridge, 1913), pp. 18-19
37. Ashley, p. 112
38. Geoffrey of Monmouth, *Historia regum Britanniae*, trans. S. Evans (2021)
39. S. Blake, & S. Lloyd, *Pendragon: The Definitive Account of the Origins of Arthur* (2004), p. 161
40. Gildas, ch. 26; BEH, bk I, ch. 16, p. 29
41. D. Dumville (ed.), 'Annales Cambriae, A.D. 682-954: Texts A-C in Parallel' (2002)
42. G. Phillips, & M. Keatman, *King Arthur: The True Story* (London, 1993)
43. S. Hirst *et al.*, 'Liddington Castle and the battle of Badon: Excavations and research 1976', *Archaeological Journal*, Vol. 153 (1996), pp. 1–59; T. Burkitt & A. Burkitt, 'The Frontier Zone and the Siege of Mount Badon: A Review of the Evidence for their Location', *Proceedings of the Somerset Archaeological and Natural History Society*, Vol. 134 (1990), pp. 81-93
44. A. Breeze, *British Battles 493-937: Mount Badon to Brunanburh* (2020), pp. 6-7; D. Cooper, *Badon and the Early Wars of Wessex c.500 to 710* (Barnsley, 2018), pp. 107-132; K. H. Jackson, 'The Site of Mount Badon', *Journal of Celtic Studies*, Vol. 2 (1953-8), pp. 152-5
45. M. Papworth, *The Search for the Durotriges: Dorset and the West Country in the Late Iron Age* (Stroud, 2011), p. 178

46. Eagles, p. 129
47. ASC, v. A & E, pp. 16-17
48. P. Harper, *Cerdic: Mysterious Dark Age king who founded England* (Barnsley, 2024)

4 Cerdic, Cynric and Creoda, 534–560

1. B. Yorke, 'The Jutes of Hampshire and Wight and the origins of Wessex', in S. R. Bassett (ed.), *The Origins of Anglo-Saxon Kingdoms* (Leicester: LUP, 1989), pp. 84-96.
2. Yorke, *Kings and Kingdoms of Early Anglo-Saxon England*, p. 133; Kirby, pp. 50-1
3. Whittock, p. 193
4. P. Clemoes, S. Keynes, M. Lapidge, *Anglo-Saxon England*, Vol. 17 (Cambridge, 1981)
5. T. P. Newfield, 'The Climate Downturn of 536-50', in S. White, C. Pfister & F. Mauelhagen (eds), *The Palgrave Handbook of Climate History* (2018), pp. 447-93
6. ASC, v. A & E, pp. 16-17; BEH, bk V, ch. 24, p. 291
7. Britton, C. E., 'A Meteorological Chronology to AD 1450', *Meteorological Office Geophysical Memoirs*, Vol. VIII (70) (London, 1937)
8. Newfield, pp. 447-93
9. Eagles, pp. xiii-xiv
10. A. J. Clark, 'The nature of Wansdyke', *Antiquity*, Vol. 32 (1958), pp. 89-96
11. J. N. L. Myres, 'Wansdyke and the origins of Wessex', in H. Trevor-Roper (ed.), *Essays in British History presented to Sir Keith Feiling* (1964), pp. 1-28
12. ASC, v. A, p. 16
13. ASC, p. 66 n.3
14. *Asser's Life of King Alfred & other Contemporary Sources*, trans. & intro S. Keynes & M. Lapidge (London, 2004), p. 67
15. D. Dumville, 'The Anglian collection of royal genealogies and regnal lists', in Clemoes (ed.), *Anglo-Saxon England*, No. 5 (1976), pp. 23-50
16. ASC, v. A & E, pp. 16-17
17. D. P. Kirby, 'Problems of Early West Saxon History', *The English Historical Review*, Vol. 80, No. 314 (Oxford, 1965), p. 22
18. ASC, v. A & E, pp. 16-17
19. L. V. Grinsell, *The Archaeology of Wessex: An account of Wessex Antiquities from the Earliest Times to the End of the Pagan Saxon Period, with Special reference to Existing Field Monuments* (London, 1958), p. 278
20. ASC, v. A & E, pp. 16-17
21. H. Hamerow, *et al.*, 'The Origins of Wessex Pilot Project', *Oxoniensa*, Vol. 78 (2013), pp. 49-69
22. S. Oosthuizen, *The Emergence of the English* (Leeds, 2019)
23. K. E. Dinwiddy, 'An Anglo-Saxon Cemetery at Twyford, Near Winchester', *Proceedings of the Hampshire Field Club Archaeological Society*, Vol. 66 (Hampshire Studies, 2011), pp. 75-126
24. ASC, v. A & E, pp. 16-17

25. *The Chronicle of John of Worcester*, Vol. 2, ed. R. R. Darlington and P. McGurk, trans. J. Bray and P. McGurk, *Oxford Medieval Texts* (Oxford; New York: Clarendon Press, 1995), p. 59
26. H. W. Timperley & Edith Brill, *Ancient Trackways of Wessex* (Stroud: revd edn, 2005), pp. 55-6
27. HA, p. 105
28. Laycock, p. 157
29. ASC, v. A & E, pp. 18-19
30. WSGRL
31. BEH, bk III, ch. 7, pp. 119-21

5 Ceawlin and Ceol, 560–597

1. ASC, v. A & E, pp. 18-19; CJW, p. 61
2. WSGRL
3. Yorke, *Kings and Kingdoms of Early Anglo-Saxon England*, p. 133
4. ASC, v. A & E, pp. 18-19
5. ASC, v. A & E, pp. 18-19
6. ASC, v. F, n. p.18; HA, p. 107
7. William of Malmesbury, *Gesta Regum Anglorum: The History of the English Kings*, Vol. 1, ed. and trans. R. A. B. Mynors, R. M. Thomson and M. Winterbottom (Oxford, 1998), pp. 41, 47
8. CJW, p. 63
9. ASC, v. A, E, F, pp. 18-22, 38, 66
10. Matthews, p. 139
11. Matthews, p. 139
12. ASC, v. A & E, pp. 22-3
13. ASC, v. A & F, pp. 26, 28
14. BEH, bk II, ch. 5, p. 78
15. Kirby, *The Earliest English Kings* (London: revd edn, 2000), p. 44
16. K. Dark, *Britain and the End of the Roman Empire* (Stroud, 2002), p. 97
17. ASC, v. A & E, pp. 18-19
18. GRA, pp. 39-41
19. ASC, v. A, p. 18
20. Cooper, pp. 168-71
21. HA, p. 107
22. CA
23. Cooper, pp. 168-71
24. E. W. Brayley, *et al.*, *The History of Surrey*, Vol. 2, Part 1 (Dorking, 1842), p. 27; J. Morris, 'A Gazetteer of Anglo-Saxon Surrey', *Surrey Archaeological Collections*, Vol. 56, pp. 132–58 (1959), p. 156
25. H. E. Malden (ed.), *The Victoria History of the County of Surrey*, Vol. 1 (London, 1902), p. 257
26. Brayley, p. 46
27. BEH, bk I, ch. 25, p. 39
28. Cooper, pp. 168-71

29. ASC, v. E, p. 19; BEH, bk II, ch. 5, p. 77
30. Matthews, p. 176
31. Kirby, *The Earliest English Kings* (London: revd edn, 2000), pp. 31-33
32. Roger of Wendover, *Flowers of History, Comprising the History of England from the descent of the Saxons to AD1235*, trans. J. A. Giles, 2 vols (London: Bohn, 1849)
33. ASC, v. A & E, pp. 18-19
34. HA, p. 107
35. ASC, v. A & E, pp. 18-19; CJW, p. 63
36. J. N. L. Myres, *The English Settlements* (Oxford, 1986)
37. P. Marren, *Battles of the Dark Ages: British Battlefields AD410-1065* (Barnsley: revd edn, 2011), p. 37
38. Matthews, p. 179
39. ASC, v. A & E, pp. 18-19; CJW, p. 65
40. J. Wacher, *The Towns of Roman Britain* (London, 1995)
41. HA, p. 109
42. R. Brooks, *Cassell's Battlefields of Britain and Ireland* (London, 2005), pp. 38-9; Marren, p. 38
43. A. H. Burne, *The Battlefields of England* (Barnsley: revd edn, 2005), p. 29
44. ASC, v. A & E, pp. 18-19
45. Cooper, p. 173
46. Eagles, p. 143
47. Sullivan, p. 11
48. ASC, v. A & E, pp. 20-1
49. CJW, p. 67; HA, p. 109
50. Stenton, p. 29
51. Brooks, p. 39
52. ASC, v. A & E, pp. 20-1
53. Stenton, p. 30
54. ASC, v. A, pp. 20-1
55. Marren, p. 42
56. ASC, v. A & E, pp. 20-1
57. GRA, pp. 39-41
58. G. B. Grundy, 'The Ancient Highways and Tracks of Wiltshire, Berkshire, Hampshire, and the Saxon Battlefields of Wiltshire', *Archaeological Journal*, No. 75 (1918), pp. 69-194
59. Timperley, p. 28
60. ASC, v. A & E, pp. 20-1
61. BEH, bk II, ch. 5, p. 78
62. Stenton, p. 30
63. GRA, p. 41
64. CJW, p. 69
65. Ashley, p. 392
66. Yorke, *Kings and Kingdoms of Early Anglo-Saxon England*, p. 135
67. S227
68. Kirby, *The Earliest English Kings*, p. 46

6 *Ceolwulf, Cynegils and Cwichelm, 597–642*

1. ASC, v. A, p. 20
2. ASC, v. A, p. 20
3. BEH, bk III, ch. 8, p. 122
4. Yorke, *Kings and Kingdoms of Early Anglo-Saxon England*
5. ASC, v. A, p. 40
6. CJW, p. 79
7. D. N. Dumville & M. Lapidge (eds), *Anglo-Saxon Chronicle 17: The Annals of St Neots with Vita Prima Sancti Neoti* (Cambridge, 1984)
8. ASC, v. A & E, pp. 22-3; WSGRL
9. ASC, v. A, p. 38
10. A. Roberts, *Buried: An alternative history of the first millennium in Britain* (London, 2022), p. 253
11. WSGRL
12. ASC, v. E, p. 25
13. WSGRL; HA, p. 113
14. Yorke, *Kings and Kingdoms of Early Anglo-Saxon England*, p. 137
15. Ashley, p. 303; Kirby, *The Earliest English Kings*, pp. 48-9
16. ASC, v. A, p. 28; CJW, p. 81
17. Kirby, *The Earliest English Kings*, pp. 48-9; Yorke, *Kings and Kingdoms of Early Anglo-Saxon England*, pp. 133-36, 143-44
18. ASC, v. A & E, pp. 22-3
19. Cooper, p. 194
20. T. Venning, *An Alternative History of Britain: The Anglo-Saxon Age* (Barnsley, 2013), p. 47
21. R. Matthews, *Battlefield Walks: Devon* (London, 2008), pp. 9-21; J. Morris, *The Age of Arthur: A History of the British Isles from 350 to 650* (London, 1995), p. 307
22. ASC, v. A & E, pp. 22-3
23. CJW, p. 81; HA, p. 113
24. R. Matthews, *Battlefield Walks: Devon*
25. Eagles, p. 73
26. BEH, bk II, ch. 5, p. 78
27. Kirby, *The Earliest English Kings*, pp. 61-2
28. Yorke, *Kings and Kingdoms of Early Anglo-Saxon England*, p. 60
29. BEH, bk II, ch. 5, p. 80
30. Ashley, p. 303
31. ASC, v. E, p. 25; BEH, bk II, ch. 9, pp. 85-6; CJW, pp. 85-7
32. BEH, bk II, ch. 9, pp. 85-6; CJW, p85-7
33. ASC, v. E, p. 25
34. BEH, bk II, ch. 9, p. 86
35. ASC, v. E, p. 25
36. Kirby, *The Earliest English Kings*, p. 9
37. N. J. Higham, *An English Empire: Bede and the early Anglo-Saxon Kings* (Manchester, 1995), p. 74
38. ASC, v. E, p. 25

39. CJW, p. 87; HA, p. 117
40. GRA, p. 41
41. Yorke, *Kings and Kingdoms of Early Anglo-Saxon England*, p. 136; C. Heighway, *Anglo-Saxon Gloucestershire* (Gloucester, 1987), pp. 22-31
42. Cooper, p. 195
43. ASC, v. E, p. 25; BEH, bk II, ch. 20, p. 105
44. Kirby, *The Earliest English Kings*, p. 36
45. ASC, v. A, p. 28
46. ASC, v. A, p. 28; BEH, bk III, ch. 24, p. 150
47. C. Cubitt, 'Pastoral Care and Religious Beliefs', in P. Stafford (ed.), *A Companion to the Early Middle Ages: Britain and Ireland c.500-c.1100* (Chichester, 2013), pp. 395-413
48. Stenton, p. 110
49. BEH, bk III, ch. 7, p. 118; GPA, p. 103
50. F. M. Powicke and E. B. Fryde, *Handbook of British Chronology* (London: Royal Historical Society, 2nd edn, 1961), p. 219
51. R. J. Coles, *Southampton's Historic Buildings* (City of Southampton Society, 1981)
52. ASC, v. A & E, pp. 26-7
53. BEH, bk III, ch. 7. p.120; GPA, p. 104
54. F. L. Attenborough (ed.), *The Laws of the Earliest English Kings* (Cambridge, 1922), pp. 60-61
55. ASC, v. A & E, pp. 26-7
56. T. Venning, *An Alternative History of Britain: The Anglo-Saxon Age* (Barnsley, 2013), p. 82
57. Yorke, *Kings and Kingdoms of Early Anglo-Saxon England*, p. 132
58. ASC, v. B, C, F, pp. 26-8
59. BEH, bk III, ch. 9, p. 124; S. Bassett (ed.), 'The Formation of the Mercian Kingdom', in *The Origins of Anglo-Saxon Kingdoms* (Leicester, 1989)
60. *Annales Cambriae (Annals of Wales)*, ed. J. Williams ab Ethel (London, 1866)
61. Kirby, *The Earliest English Kings*, p. 54
62. T. Clarkson, 'Oswald, King and Saint: His Britain and Beyond', *The Heroic Age: A Journal of Early Medieval Northwestern Europe*, Vol. 9 (2006)
63. A. D. Mills, *A Dictionary of English Place Names* (Oxford, 2011)
64. ASC, v. A & E, pp. 26-7
65. *Current Archaeology*, No. 353 (July 2019); Cat Jarman, *The Bone Chests: Unlocking the Secrets of the Anglo-Saxons* (London, 2023)

7 Cenwealh and Seaxburh, 642–674

1. ASC, v. A & E, pp. 26-7
2. C. Hills, *Origins of the English* (London, 2003), p. 105
3. Laycock, p. 119, 155
4. BEH, bk III, ch. 7, p. 120
5. ASC, v. A, B, C, E, pp. 26-7
6. ASC, v. F, p. 26

7. Kirby, *The Earliest English Kings*, p. 48
8. CJW, p. 99
9. BEH, bk III, ch. 7, p. 120
10. CJW, p. 97
11. ASC, v. A, p. 26; HA, p. 119
12. CJW, p. 99
13. Kirby, *The Earliest English Kings*, p. 48
14. HA, p. 119
15. Yorke, *Kings and Kingdoms of Early Anglo-Saxon England*, p. 143
16. BEH, bk III, ch. 21, p. 144
17. P. Warner, *The Origins of Suffolk* (Manchester & New York, 1996), pp. 110–13
18. BEH, bk III, ch. 24, p. 150
19. A. Breeze, 'The Battle of the Uinued and the River Went, Yorkshire', *Northern History*, Vol. 41 (2) (2004), pp. 377–83
20. ASC, v. E, p. 29
21. BEH, bk III, ch. 24, p. 152
22. GPA, p. 104; F. M. Powicke & E. B. Fryde, p. 219
23. Kirby, *The Earliest English Kings*, p. 49
24. BEH, bk III, ch. 7, p. 120
25. N. Brooks, 'The formation of the Mercian kingdom', p. 168, in Bassett, Steven (ed.), *The origins of Anglo-Saxon kingdoms, Studies in the Early History of Britain* (Leicester, 1989), pp. 159–170
26. ASC, v. A, p. 28
27. CA, p. 19
28. GRA, p. 43
29. ASC, v. A, p. 32; GRA, p. 43
30. HA, p. 123
31. W. G. Hoskins, *The Westward Expansion of Wessex* (Leicester, 1960), pp. 15-16
32. Cooper, pp. 204-7
33. ASC, v. A & E, pp. 32-3
34. N. R. Mann, *The Isle of Avalon: Sacred Mysteries of Arthur and Glastonbury* (2001), pp. 16–17
35. Hoskins, p. 14
36. Yorke, 'The Foundation of the Old Minster and the Status of Winchester in the Seventh and Eighth Centuries', *Proceedings of the Hampshire Field Club Archaeological Society*, Vol. 38 (1982), p. 75
37. BEH, bk III, ch. 7, p. 121
38. N. J. Higham, *The Convert Kings: Power and religious affiliation in early Anglo-Saxon England* (Manchester, 1997), p. 255
39. ASC, v. A & E, pp. 32-3
40. CA, p. 19
41. HA, p. 123
42. ASC, v. A & E, pp. 32-3
43. Charter S68

44. N. Brooks, *The Early History of the Church of Canterbury: Christ Church from 597 to 1066* (London, 1984), pp. 67-69
45. A. Williams, *Kingship and Government in Pre-Conquest England c.500-1066* (1999), p. 21
46. Kirby, *The Earliest English Kings*, p. 43
47. ASC, v. A & E, pp. 34-5
48. Charters S227, S228, S229
49. CJW, p. 117
50. E. B. Fryde, *et al.*, *Handbook of British Chronology* (Cambridge, 1996), p. 223
51. BEH, bk III, ch. 7, p. 121
52. N. Doggett, *The Anglo-Saxon See and Cathedral of Dorchester-on-Thames: the Evidence Reconsidered* (1983), p. 50
53. BEH, bk III, ch. 7, p. 121
54. ASC, v. A & E, pp. 34-5
55. R. Abels, 'The Council of Whitby: A Study in Early Anglo-Saxon Politics', *Journal of British Studies*, Vol. 23, No. 1 (Cambridge, Autumn 1983), pp. 1-25
56. BEH, bk III, ch. 25, pp. 153-55
57. R. Naismith, *Early Medieval Britain c.500-1000* (Cambridge, 2021), p. 46
58. BEH, bk III, ch. 25, p. 153
59. Naismith, pp. 46-7
60. ASC, v. A, p. 34
61. C. H. Talbot (ed.), *The Anglo-Saxon Missionaries in Germany: Being the Lives of S.S. Willibrord, Boniface, Strum, Leoba and Lebuin, together with the Hodoeporicon of St. Willibald and a Selection from the Correspondence of St. Boniface* (New York, 1954), p. 28
62. C. Hart, 'The Tribal Hidage', *Transactions of the Royal Historical Society*, 5th series, Vol. 21 (1971)
63. W. Davies & H. Vierck, 'The contexts of Tribal Hidages: social aggregates and settlement patterns', *Fruhmittelalterliche Studien*, Vol. 8 (1974), pp. 223-93
64. *Annales Cambriae*; T. Venning, *An Alternative History of Britain: The Anglo-Saxon Age* (Barnsley, 2013), p. 218
65. Yorke, *Kings and Kingdoms of Early Anglo-Saxon England*, p. 136
66. ASC, v. A, p. 34
67. P. Grierson, Philip, *Medieval European Coinage: With a Catalogue of the Coins in the Fitzwilliam Museum, Cambridge, 1: Earlier Middle Ages (400-900)* (Cambridge, 1986), p. 157
68. H. P. R. Finberg, 'Sherborne, Glastonbury, and the Expansion of Wessex', *Transactions of the Royal Historical Society*, Vol. 3 (1953), pp. 101-24
69. GRA, p. 43
70. GRA, p. 43
71. M. Lapidge & M. Rosier (eds), *Aldhelm: The Poetic Works* (Cambridge, 1985), pp. 46–60
72. ASC, v. A, p. 32; WSGRL
73. BEH, bk IV, ch. 12, p. 190

74. Yorke, *Kings and Kingdoms of Early Anglo-Saxon England*, pp. 133-4
75. Kirby, *The Earliest English Kings*, p. 52
76. WSGRL
77. GRA, p. 47
78. ASC, v. A & E, pp. 34-5; WSGRL
79. GRA, p. 47

8 Æscwine, Centwine and Caedwalla, 676–688

1. Kirby, *The Earliest English Kings*, p. 42
2. BEH, bk IV, ch. 12, pp. 190-1
3. ASC, v. A & E, pp. 34-5; WSGRL
4. Roger of Wendover, *Flowers of History, Comprising the History of England from the descent of the Saxons to AD1235* (London, 1849)
5. GRA, p. 47
6. ASC, v. A, p. 34
7. Charter S1164
8. Charters S236, S1170
9. Charter S231; *Chronicon Monasterii de Abingdon*, ed. J. Stevenson (London, 1858)
10. ASC, v. A & E, pp. 34-5
11. HA, p. 125
12. Kirby, *The Earliest English Kings*, p. 52
13. Cooper, p. 221
14. Burne
15. *Vita Sancti Wilfrithi* (Life of St Wilfrid), trans. Bernard J. Muir & Andrew J. Turner (Exeter, 1998); J. F. Webb & D. H. Farmer (eds), *The Age of Bede: Bede – Life of Cuthbert* (London, 1998); *Vita Sancti Wilfrithi* (Life of St Wilfrid)
16. HA, p. 127
17. GPA, p. 113
18. GRA, p. 45
19. Charter S1245
20. ASC, v. A & E, pp. 36-7
21. ASC, v. A, p. 38
22. T. Venning, *Kings and Queens of Anglo-Saxon England* (Stroud, 2013), p. 66
23. M. Lapidge & M. Rosier (eds), *Aldhelm: The Poetic Works* (Cambridge, 1985), pp. 47-8
24. Yorke, *Kings and Kingdoms of Early Anglo-Saxon England*, pp. 145-6
25. *Vita Sancti Wilfrithi* (Life of St Wilfrid)
26. BEH, bk IV, ch. 12, p. 191
27. BEH, bk IV, ch. 21, p. 207
28. GPA, p. 136
29. J. Munby & J. Haslam (eds), *Anglo-Saxon Towns in Southern England :Saxon Chichester and its Predecessors* (Chichester, 1984), pp. 317–20
30. *Vita Sancti Wilfrithi* (Life of St Wilfrid), pp. 148-9
31. F. Mee, *A History of Selsey* (Chichester, 1988), pp. 11–12

32. ASC, v. A & E, pp. 38-9
33. *Aldhelm: The Poetic Works* (Cambridge, 1985), pp. 47-9
34. GPA, p. 246
35. Finberg, p. 109
36. Charter S237
37. *Aldhelm: The Poetic Works* (Cambridge, 1985), pp. 47-9
38. Charters S71, S73
39. Charter S1166
40. M. Morris, *The Anglo-Saxons: A History of the Beginnings of England* (London, 2021), p. 115
41. *Aldhelm: The Poetic Works* (Cambridge, 1985), pp. 47-9
42. ASC, v. A, p. 38
43. GRA, pp. 47, 49
44. Ashley, p. 306
45. *Vita Sancti Wilfrithi* (Life of St Wilfrid); Kirby, *The Earliest English Kings*, p. 100
46. ASC, v. A, p. 38
47. GRA, p. 47
48. Ashley, p. 307
49. Yorke, *Kings and Kingdoms of Early Anglo-Saxon England*, pp. 145-6
50. CJW, p. 143
51. BEH, bk IV, ch. 26, p. 222
52. A. Barr-Hamilton, *In Saxon Sussex* (1953), p. 21
53. HA, p. 207
54. Charter S230
55. *Vita Sancti Wilfrithi* (Life of St Wilfrid
56. BEH, bk IV, ch. 15, p. 197; GRA, p. 49
57. D. Kirby, 'Bede's Native Sources for the Historia Ecclesiastica', *Bulletin of the John Rylands Library*, No. 48 (1966), pp. 364-6
58. BEH, bk IV, ch. 16, p. 197
59. ASC, v. A, p. 38
60. BEH, bk IV, ch. 16, p. 197
61. GRA, p. 49
62. HA, p. 215
63. *Vita Sancti Wilfrithi* (Life of St Wilfrid)
64. BEH, bk IV, ch. 16, p. 198; HA, p. 209
65. BEH, bk IV, ch. 15, p. 197
66. HA, p. 209
67. GRA, p. 35
68. EHD, No.58; Charters S235, S1248
69. Charter S1171; Kirby, *The Earliest English Kings*, p. 102
70. Yorke, *Kings and Kingdoms of Early Anglo-Saxon England*, p. 30
71. HA, p. 215
72. S. Kelly & M. Hobbs (eds), *Chichester Cathedral: An Historic Survey* (Chichester, 1994), p. 14
73. Charter S233

74. HA, p. 217
75. GRA, p. 35
76. HA, p. 217; R. Hodges, *The Anglo-Saxon Achievement: Archaeology and the Beginnings of English Society* (London, 1989), p. 76
77. BEH, bk IV, ch. 12, p. 191
78. Stenton, p. 70
79. BEH, bj.V, ch. 7, p. 244
80. BEH, bk V, ch. 7, p. 245
81. Kirby, *The Earliest English Kings*, p. 119
82. N. Wright, *The Historia Regum Britannie of Geoffrey of Monmouth* (Woodbridge, 1984)
83. Charters S230 to S235 inc.
84. Charter S234; GPA, p. 240
85. *Aldhelm: The Poetic Works*, p. 15
86. GRA, p. 49

9 Ine, 688–726

1. Kirby, *The Earliest English Kings*, p. 101; Yorke, *Kings and Kingdoms of Early Anglo-Saxon England*, pp. 145-6
2. ASC, v. A & E, pp. 40-1
3. Charters S15, S18; Kirby, *The Earliest English Kings*, pp. 103-4
4. Charters S45, S1164
5. Stenton, p. 72
6. CJW, p. 149
7. GRA, p. 49
8. Charter S238
9. Ashley, p. 308
10. CJW, p. 175
11. ASC, v. A & E, pp. 42-3
12. ASC, v. A, p. 42; Charter S1164
13. Kirby, *The Earliest English Kings*, p. 124
14. ASC, v. A & E, pp. 40-1; GRA, pp. 49-51
15. CJW, p. 157
16. E. A. Freeman, 'King Ine', *Proceedings of the Somersetshire Archaeological and Natural History Society*, Vol. 18, Pt 2 (1872) pp. 1–59, p. 15
17. EHD, p. 357; F. L. Attenborough (ed.), *The Laws of the Earliest English Kings* (Cambridge, 1922), pp. 4-17
18. Fryde *et al.*, p. 219
19. EHD, pp. 339-407
20. A. Williams, *Kingship and Government in Pre-Conquest England c.500-1066* (Basingstoke, 1999), p. 58
21. Attenborough
22. Eagles, p. xvi
23. G. Williams, 'The Circulation and Function of Coinage in Conversion-Period England, c. AD 580–675', in *Coinage and History in the North*

Sea World, c. 500 – 1250: Essays in Honour of Marion Archibald (Leiden, 2006), pp. 145–92
24. Attenborough; Naismith, p. 394
25. GPA, pp. 35-36
26. Kirby, *The Earliest English Kings*, p. 39
27. Cubitt, p. 405
28. Naismith, p. 293
29. H. Ridgeway, 'The History of the Abbey Church' (Sherborne Abbey, 2014), pp. 4-5
30. ASC, v. A & E, pp. 40-1
31. ASC, v. A & E, pp. 40-1; BEH, bk V, ch. 18, p. 266
32. GPA, p. 116
33. D. Whitelock, *Some Anglo-Saxon Bishops of London* (London, 1975), pp. 10-11
34. GPA, p. 255
35. M. Lapidge, 'The Career of Aldhelm', *Anglo-Saxon England*, Vol. 36 (2007), pp. 15–69
36. GPA, pp. 235-6
37. GRA, p. 51; Fryde, *et al.*, *Handbook of British Chronology*, p. 222
38. GPA, p. 223
39. Stenton, p. 71
40. GPA, p. 241
41. Charter S245
42. D. Farmer (ed.), *The Oxford Dictionary of Saints* (Oxford, 2011), p. 378
43. Talbot, p. 121
44. Charters S238-9, S241-3, S245, S247-52
45. ASC, v. E, p. 43; CJW, p. 169
46. HA, pp. 223-5
47. T. Venning, *Kings & Queens of Anglo-Saxon England* (Stroud, 2013), p. 82
48. Finberg, p. 109
49. Talbot, p. 125
50. Kirby, *The Earliest English Kings*, p. 109
51. Grundy, pp. 69-194
52. ASC, v. A & E, pp. 42-3; Kirby, *The Earliest English Kings*, p. 109
53. HA, p. 225
54. EHD, p. 820
55. ASC, v. A & E, pp. 42-3; CJW, p. 175
56. ASC, v. A, p. 66; CA, p. 33
57. ASC, v. E, p. 43
58. R. Dunning, *Somerset Castles* (Tiverton: 1995), pp. 47–51
59. ASC, v. A & E, pp. 42-3; CJW, p. 177
60. Charter S250
61. *Annales Cambriae* (Annals of Wales)
62. *Annales Cambriae* (Annals of Wales)
63. M. Todd, *The South West to AD 1000* (London, 1987), pp. 272–73

64. R. Higham, *Making Anglo-Saxon Devon* (Exeter, 2008), p. 30; L. Alcock, *Economy, Society, and Warfare among the Britons and Saxons* (Cardiff, 1987), p. 231
65. Finberg, p. 113
66. Charter S42
67. ASC, v. E, pp. 42-3; HA, p. 227
68. Ashby, p. 309
69. ASC, v. A & E, pp. 42-3
70. GRA, p. 53
71. ASC, v. F, p. 43
72. CJW, p. 179
73. Roger of Wendover, *Flowers of History, Comprising the History of England from the descent of the Saxons to AD1235* (London, 1849); *Asser's Life of King Alfred & Other Contemporary Sources* (London, 2004), p. 244

10 *Æthelheard and Cuthred, 726–756*

1. ASC, v. E, p. 43
2. GRA, p. 55; HA, p. 227
3. CJW, p. 179
4. *Proceedings of the Somersetshire Archaeological and Natural History Society*, Vol. 18, Pt 2 (1871–2), p. 15
5. Charters S238, S241, S252
6. ASC, v. A, p. 42
7. Yorke, *Kings and Kingdoms of Early Anglo-Saxon England*, p. 142
8. ASC, v. A, p. 42; WSGRL
9. GRA, p. 55
10. ASC, v. A & E, pp. 44-5
11. A. Williams, *Kingship and Government in Pre-Conquest England c.500-1066* (Basingstoke, 1999), p. 24
12. Ashley, p. 310
13. Kirby, *The Earliest English Kings*, p. 96; T. Venning, *Kings & Queens of Anglo-Saxon England* (Stroud, 2013), p. 83
14. Charter S253
15. ASC, v. A & E, pp. 44-5
16. T. Venning, *Kings & Queens of Anglo-Saxon England* (Stroud, 2013), p. 83
17. Charter S93
18. BEH, bk V, ch. 23, p. 289
19. Kirby, *The Earliest English Kings*, p. 111; Stenton, pp. 203-5
20. N. Brooks, *The Early History of the Church of Canterbury: Christ Church from 597 to 1066* (London, 1984), p. 80; E. B. Fryde, *et al.*, p. 213
21. BEH, bk V, ch. 23, p. 289; HA, p. 231
22. *Aldhelm: The Poetic Works* (Cambridge, 1985), p. 66
23. ASC, v. A & E, pp. 44-5
24. HA, p. 231
25. Charters S96, S1410, S1679; H. Edwards, *The Charters of the Early West Saxon Kingdom* (1985), pp. 41-5

26. Charters S253, S254, S255
27. Charter S255
28. ASC, v. A & E, pp. 44-5
29. *Symeonis Monachi Opera Omnia* of Symeon of Durham, Vol. II, p. 32
30. HA, p. 235
31. Charter S742
32. ASC, v. A, p. 44
33. CJW, p. 193; HA, p. 239
34. HA, p. 239
35. Charter S1410; Kirby, *The Earliest English Kings*, p. 113
36. BEH, bk V, ch. 23, p. 289
37. ASC, v. A & E, pp. 46-7
38. *The Letters of St. Boniface: With a New Introduction and Bibliography*, trans. E. Emerton (New York, 2000), p. 105
39. J. Campbell, E. John, P. Wormald, *The Anglo-Saxons* (London, 1991), p. 78
40. Charter S92
41. Campbell, *et al.*, p. 100
42. HA, p. 239
43. Charters S256 to S259
44. GRA, pp. 819-21
45. GPA, p. 105
46. HA, p. 241
47. ASC, v. A & E, pp. 46-7
48. ASC, v. A & E, pp. 46-7; CJW, p. 197
49. HA, p. 241
50. CA, p. 21
51. HA, p. 241
52. HA, pp. 241-3
53. J. S. P. Tatlock, 'The Dragons of Wessex and Wales', *Speculum*, Vol. 8, No. 2 (April 1933), pp. 225, 231
54. HA, p. 243
55. ASC, v. E, p. 47
56. HA, p. 243
57. J. W. Monk, *The History of Burford* (Burford & London, 1891)
58. ASC, v. A & E, pp. 46-7; CJW, p. 197
59. ASC, v. A & E, pp. 46-7
60. GRA, p. 55
61. HA, p. 245
62. HA, p. 241

11 Sigeberht and Cynewulf, 756–786

1. ASC, v. A & E, pp. 46-7
2. EHD, pp. 263-76
3. GRA, p. 55
4. T. Venning, *Kings & Queens of Anglo-Saxon England* (Stroud, 2013), p. 84
5. BEH, Continuations, p. 297

6. Kirby, *The Earliest English Kings*, p. 114
7. HA, p. 247
8. Charter S1680
9. HA, p. 245
10. ASC, v. A & E, pp. 46-7
11. CJW, p. 199
12. CA, p. 22
13. Charter S96
14. Yorke, *Kings and Kingdoms of Early Anglo-Saxon England*, p. 142
15. ASC, v. A, p. 46
16. T. Venning, *Kings & Queens of Anglo-Saxon England* (Stroud, 2013), p. 94
17. GRA, pp. 55-7
18. ASC, v. A & E, p. 47
19. ASC, v. A & E, pp. 46-7; CJW, p. 199
20. GRA, p. 57
21. Charter S1258
22. Kirby, *The Earliest English Kings*, p. 139
23. Charters S105, S108
24. Charters S106, S107
25. Charter S265
26. A. Williams, *Kingship and Government in Pre-Conquest England, c.500–1066* (Basingstoke, 1999), p. 27; Stenton, p. 209
27. ASC, v. A & E, pp. 46-7
28. Finberg, p. 111
29. Charters S260 to S265 incl.
30. Charter S108
31. SMO, p. 44
32. Stenton, pp. 206-9; Charter S108
33. Charter S34
34. Charters S34, S110, S111
35. ASC, v. A & E, pp. 50-1; CJW, p. 211; HA, p. 251
36. R. Matthews, *The Battle of Otford 776* (2017)
37. HA, p. 251
38. Charters S35, S36, S37
39. GPA, p. 264
40. GRA, p. 57
41. CJW, p. 211
42. GPA, p. 264
43. EHD, pp. 466-7; Charter S1257; A. Williams, *Kingship and Government in Pre-Conquest England, c.500–1066* (Basingstoke, 1999), p. 28
44. N. J. Higham & M. J. Ryan (eds), *The Anglo-Saxon World* (New Haven, 2013), p. 187
45. A. Shaw Mellor, 'Parish boundaries in relation to Wansdyke', *Wiltshire Archaeological and Natural History Magazine*, Vol. 51, No. 182 (June 1945), pp. 24-7
46. Kirby, *The Earliest English Kings*, p. 136

47. Charters S36, S37
48. Charter S38
49. Charters S123, S125
50. Yorke, *Kings and Kingdoms of Early Anglo-Saxon England*, p. 166
51. R. Naismith, 'The Coinage of Offa Revisited', in *British Numismatic Journal*, No. 80 (2010), pp. 77-9
52. ASC, v. F, p. 52
53. EHD, pp. 836-40
54. C. Cubitt, *Anglo-Saxon Church Councils c.650–c.850* (London, 1995), p. 270
55. A. Williams, *Kingship and Government in Pre-Conquest England, c.500–1066* (Basingstoke, 1999), p. 59
56. GRA, p. 57
57. CJW, p. 215
58. D. N. Dumville, 'The Aetheling: A Study in Anglo-Saxon Constitutional History', *Anglo-Saxon England*, Vol. 8 (Cambridge, 1979), p. 15
59. ASC, v. A & E, pp. 48-9
60. ASC, v. A & E, pp. 46-7
61. CA, p. 23
62. D. Scragg, '*Wifcyþþe* and the Morality of the Cynewulf and Cyneheard Episode in the Anglo-Saxon Chronicle', in *Alfred the Wise: Studies in honour of Janet Bately* (Cambridge: 1997), pp. 179-85.
63. S. Zaluckyj, *Mercia: The Anglo-Saxon kingdom of central England* (2013), p. 149
64. HA, p. 253
65. CA, pp. 23-4; CJW, pp. 215-19: GRA, p. 57
66. EHD, p. 23
67. ASC, v. A & E, pp. 52-3
68. W. G. Hoskins, *Devon* (London, 1954), pp. 43-4
69. F. C. Hipkins, *Repton and its Neighbourhood: A Descriptive Guide of the Archaeology and of the District* (Repton, 1849), p. 9
70. Zaluckyj, p. 149

12 Beorhtric, 786–802

1. M. Lapidge, Michael (ed.), *The Blackwell Encyclopaedia of Anglo-Saxon England* (Oxford, 1999), p. 340
2. Higham & Ryan, p. 187
3. ASC, v. A, p. 52
4. GRA, p. 59
5. GRA, p. 59
6. ASC, v. A, p. 54
7. ASC, v. E, p. 53; N. Brooks, *The Early History of the Church of Canterbury: Christ Church from 597 to 1066* (London, 1984)
8. A. Williams, 'Ecgfrith king of Mercia' in Ann Williams, Alfred P. Smyth, D. P. Kirby (eds), *A Biographical Dictionary of Dark Age Britain* (London, 1991)

9. ASC, v. A & F, pp. 52-5; M J Swanton, *Crisis and Development in Germanic Society 700-800* (Goppingen, 1982), pp. 55-60
10. GRA, p. 59
11. GRA, p. 153
12. HA, p. 261
13. Charter S136
14. Stenton, p. 220
15. J. M. H. Smith, *Europe after Rome: A New Cultural History 500-1000* (Oxford, 2005), p. 268
16. HA, p. 255
17. ASC, v. A, p. 54
18. CJW, p. 219
19. ASC, v. A, n.4, p. 54
20. CA, p. 27
21. ASC, v. A, p. 54
22. CJW, p. 219; GRA, p. 59
23. ASC, v. E, p. 63
24. M. Dolley, 'Proceedings for the Year 1970; the Location of the Pre-Alfredian Mints of Wessex', *British Numismatic Journal*, Vol. XXVIII, pp. 57-61
25. Higham & Ryan, p. 181
26. Charters S267, S268, S269
27. Charters S148, S149
28. HA, p. 257
29. T. Venning, *Kings & Queens of Anglo-Saxon England* (Stroud, 2013), p. 95
30. A. Williams, *Kingship and Government in Pre-Conquest England, c.500–1066* (Basingstoke, 1999), p. 30
31. ASC, v. A & E, pp. 56-7
32. H. H. Howorth, 'Ecgberht, King of the West Saxons and the Kent men, and his coins', *The Numismatic Chronicle and Journal of the Numismatic Society*, 3rd Series, Vol. 20 (1900), pp. 66-87
33. ASC, v. F, p56
34. Charter S154; Kirby, *The Earliest English Kings*, p. 150
35. ASC, v. A & E, pp. 58-9
36. CJW, p. 271; GRA, p. 173
37. Charters S127, S149, S268
38. ALA, p. 71
39. CJW, pp. 271-3; GRA, p. 173
40. ALA, p. 72
41. ALA, p. 71
42. ASC, v. A & E, pp. 58-9
43. ALA, p. 72; CJW, p. 273; T. Venning, *Kings & Queens of Anglo-Saxon England* (Stroud, 2013), p. 95
44. R. Cramp, *Corpus of Anglo-Saxon stone sculpture in England*, Vol. 7 (Oxford, 2006), p. 65

13 Ecgberht, 802–825

1. ASC, v. A & E, pp. 58-9
2. GRA, p. 153
3. ASC, v. A & E, pp. 58-9
4. ALA, p. 72
5. Charter S59
6. B. Yorke, 'Edward as Aetheling', in Higham and Hill (eds), *Edward the Elder 899-924* (London, 2001), p. 36
7. W. G. Searle, *Onomasticon Anglo-Saxonicum* (Cambridge, 1897)
8. P. Stafford, 'The King's Wife in Wessex 800-1066', *Past & Present,* No. 91 (Oxford, May 1981), pp. 3-27
9. GRA, p. 153
10. E. Crittall (ed.), 'Wilton: Early History', *A History of the County of Wiltshire*, Vol. 6 (London, 1962)
11. ASC, v. A, p. 66; ALA, p. 67
12. ASC, v. A & E, pp. 62-3, 72-3
13. CA, p. 28
14. GRA, p. 153
15. ASC, v. A & E, pp. 58-61
16. C. Cubitt, *Anglo-Saxon Church Councils c.650–c.850* (London, 1995), pp. 99-124
17. ASC, v. A & E, pp. 58-61
18. Kirby, *The Earliest English Kings*, p. 155
19. Kirby, *The Earliest English Kings*, pp. 185-7
20. Charter S283
21. J. N. L, Myres, 'Wansdyke and the origins of Wessex', in H. Trevor-Roper (ed.), *Essays in British History presented to Sir Keith Feiling* (1964), pp. 1-28
22. A. J. Clark, 'The nature of Wansdyke', *Antiquity*, Vol. 32 (1958), pp. 89-96
23. ASC, v. A & E, pp. 58-9
24. ASC, v. A & E, pp. 60-1
25. J. J. Alexander, *'When the Saxons Came to Devon; Part IV': Report & Transactions of the Devonshire Association* (1922), p. 193
26. R. Higham, *Making Anglo-Saxon Devon* (Exeter, 2008), p. 33
27. R. Whitlock, *The Warrior Kings of Saxon England* (New York, 1991), p. 41
28. HA, p. 263
29. H. R. Loyn, *Anglo-Saxon England and the Norman Conquest* (London: 2nd edn, 1991)
30. P. Payton, *Cornwall* (Fowey, 1996)
31. P. H. Blair, *An Introduction to Anglo-Saxon England* (Cambridge, 2003)
32. J. R. Davies, 'Wales and West Britian', in P. Stafford (ed.), *A Companion to the Middle Ages: Britain and Ireland c.500-c.1100* (Chichester, 2013), p. 349
33. N. Orme, *Cornwall and the Cross: Christianity 500-1560* (Chichester, 2007), p. 8
34. Stenton, p. 231
35. Zaluckyj, p. 136

36. J. E. B. Gover, 'The Place-Names of Wiltshire', *English Place-Name Society*, Vol. XVI (Cambridge, 1939), p. 279
37. ASC, v. A & E, pp. 60-1
38. C. Oman, *A History of England before the Norman Conquest* (London: 3rd edn, 1913) ch. xix, p. 392
39. Timperley & Brill, p. 55
40. *Annales de Wintonia in Annales Monastici*, ed. H. R. Luard, Vol. II (Rolls Series, 1865)
41. G. Halsall, 'The Battle of Ellendun AD825', *Miniature Wargames* (February 1985), pp. 38-42
42. Marren, pp. 99-100
43. HA, p. 263
44. Burne, p. 42
45. T. Spicer, 'The Battle of Ellandun and Lydiard Tregoze', *Friends of Lydiard Tregoze Report*, No. 34 (May 2001)

14 Ecgberht, 825–839

1. S. E. Kelly, 'Baldred (fl. c.823–827)', *Oxford Dictionary of National Biography* (Oxford, 2004) Online edn, accessed 26 March 2024
2. ASC, v. A & E, pp. 60-1
3. ASC, v. A & E, pp. 60-1
4. Charter S1267
5. Charter S187
6. Charter S285
7. R. McKitterick (ed.), *The New Cambridge Medieval History*, Vol. 4, Part 2 (Cambridge, 1995), p. 555
8. ASC, v. A & E, pp. 60-1
9. GRA, p. 155; HA, p. 263
10. Yorke, *Kings and Kingdoms of Early Anglo-Saxon England*, p. 122
11. CJW, p. 243
12. CJW, p. 245
13. ASC, v. A & E, pp. 60-1
14. M. P. Brown & C. A. Farr, *Mercia: An Anglo-Saxon Kingdom in Europe* (London; New York, 2001), p. 222
15. H. E. Pagan, 'The Coinage of the East Anglian kingdom', *British Numismatic Journal*, Vol. 52 (1982), p. 43
16. Charter S282
17. C. E. Blunt, 'The Coinage of Ecgbeorht, King of Wessex, 802-39', *British Numismatic Journal*, Vol. 28 (3) (1957), pp. 467-476
18. Blunt, pp. 467-76
19. Kirby, *The Earliest English Kings*, p. 157
20. ASC, v. A & E, pp. 60-1
21. HA, p. 263
22. GRA, p. 155
23. Zaluckyj, p. 237

24. J. E. Vickers, 'Dore, In Old Sheffield Town', in *An Historical Miscellany* (2nd edn, 1999), pp. 64-71
25. ASC, v. A & E, pp. 60-1
26. GRA, p. 155
27. Roger of Wendover, *Flowers of History, Comprising the History of England from the descent of the Saxons to AD1235* (London, 1849)
28. ASC, v. A & E, pp. 62-3
29. ASC, v. A & E, pp. 62-3
30. Stenton, p. 233
31. HA, p. 263
32. ASC, v. A & E, pp. 62-3
33. Kirby, *The Earliest English Kings*, p. 159
34. Kirby, *The Earliest English Kings*, p. 161
35. ASC, v. A, p. 62; Charter S188
36. Charter S190
37. S. Keynes, 'Ceolnoth', in *Blackwell Encyclopedia of Anglo-Saxon England* (London, 2001); N. Brooks, *Early History of the Church of Canterbury*, p. 129
38. ASC, v. A, p. 62
39. ASC, v. A & E, pp. 62-3
40. ASC, v. A & E, pp. 62-3
41. ASC, v. A & E, pp. 62-3
42. ASC, v. A & E, pp. 62-3
43. CJW, p. 253
44. J. Fletcher, *The Western Kingdom* (Stroud, 2022), pp. 88–90; C. Weatherill, *Cornish World Magazine* (October 2007)
45. T. M. Charles-Edwards, *Wales and the Britons 350-1064* (Oxford, 2013), p. 431; D. Hadley, 'Viking Raids and Conquest', in Pauline Stafford (ed.), *A Companion to the Early Middle Ages: Britain and Ireland c. 500–c. 1100* (Chichester, 2013), pp. 195–211
46. P. E. Coleman, *The last battle for Cornwall*, Online website: Cornwallyesteryear.com
47. ASC, v. A, p. 62; HA, p. 265
48. Charter S1438
49. N. Brooks, *Early History of the Church of Canterbury*
50. ASC, v. A & E, pp. 62-3
51. C. Jarman, *The Bone Chests: Unlocking the Secrets of the Anglo-Saxons* (London, 2023)

15 Æthelwulf, 839–856/8

1. ASC, v. A & E, pp. 62-3
2. D. Farmer, *The Oxford Dictionary of Saints* (Oxford: 5th revd edn, 2011), p. 11
3. ASC, v. A, p. 62
4. ALA, p. 68
5. J. Peddie, *Alfred: Warrior King* (Stroud, 2005), p. 3

6. S. Miller, 'Æthelbald', *Oxford Dictionary of National Biography* (Oxford, 2004) Online edn. Accessed 7 June 2024
7. ALA, p. 71
8. Charter S340
9. A. Williams, *Aethelred the Unready: The Ill-counselled King* (London, 2003), p. 64
10. Charters; for Malmesbury: S294b, S301, S305, S306, S320; for Winchester: S307, S309 to S313 incl.
11. Charter S318
12. S. Keynes, 'The West Saxon Charters of King Æthelwulf and his sons', *English Historical Review*, Vol. 109 (Oxford, November 1994), pp. 1109–49
13. ASC, v. A & E, pp. 62-3; CA, p. 30
14. ASC, v. A & E, pp. 62-5
15. ASC, v. A & E, pp. 64-5
16. M. Whittock, & H. Whittock, *The Viking Blitzkrieg AD789-1098* (Stroud, 2013), p. 21
17. ASC, v. A & E, pp. 64-5
18. ASC, v. A & E, pp. 64-5; HA, p. 279
19. D. Gore, *The Vikings and Devon* (Exeter, 2001), pp. 35-6
20. J. E. B. Glover, A. Mawer & F. M. Stenton, *Place Names of Devon* (Cambridge, 1932), p. 506
21. ASC, v. B & C, p. 64
22. HA, p. 279
23. CJW, p. 265
24. ASC, v. A, p. 64
25. Marren, p. 106
26. ASC, v. A & E, pp. 64-5
27. Charters S200, S201
28. Kirby, *The Earliest English Kings*, p. 194
29. Charters S300, S320
30. A P. Smyth, *King Alfred the Great* (Oxford, 1995), p. 11
31. B. Yorke, 'Royal Burial in Winchester: Context and Significance', in R. Lavelle *et al.* (eds), *Early Medieval Winchester: Communities, Authority and Power in an Urban Space, c.800-c.1200* (Oxford, 2021), p. 65
32. ASC, v. A & E, pp. 64-5
33. ALA, p. 68; CJW, p. 265
34. R. Brooks, *Cassell's Battlefields of Britain & Ireland* (London, 2005), p. 57
35. ALA, p. 68
36. Marren, p. 107
37. C. F. Cooksey, 'On the site of the Battle of Aclea AD851', *Hampshire Field Club & Archaeological Society*, Vol. 5 (1905), pp. 26-35
38. Cooksey, pp. 26-35
39. ASC, v. A & E, pp. 64-7
40. P. Stafford, 'Charles the Bald, Judith and England', in M. Gibson & J. L. Nelson (eds), *Charles the Bald, Court and Kingdom* (British Archaeological Reports, 1981), pp. 137–51

41. Ian Walker, *Mercia and the Making of England* (Stroud, 2000), p. 38
42. M. Blackburn, & P. Grierson, *Medieval European Coinage* (Cambridge, 2006), pp. 292-3
43. ASC, v. A, p. 64
44. Charters S210, S214
45. Charter S1210
46. GRA, p. 141
47. ASC, v. E, pp. 65-7
48. ALA, p. 69
49. ALA, p. 232
50. ASC, note, pp. 64-5; J. L. Nelson, 'Problem of King Alfred's Royal Anointing', in *Journal of Ecclesiastical History 18* (1967), pp. 161-2
51. ALA, pp. 69-70; ASC, v. A, p. 66
52. S. Kelly, *Charters of Malmesbury Abbey* (Oxford, 2005), p. 65
53. Charter S315
54. S. Keynes, 'The West Saxon Charters of King Æthelwulf and his sons', *English Historical Review*, Vol. 109 (Oxford, 1994), pp. 1119–20
55. ALA, pp. 232-3
56. J. Story, *Carolingian Connections: Anglo-Saxon England and Carolingian Francia, c. 750–870.* (Aldershot, 2003), pp. 238–39
57. J. L. Nelson, 'Britain, Ireland and Europe c.750-c.900', in P. Stafford (ed.), *A Companion to the Early Middle Ages c.500-c.1100* (Oxford, 2013), pp. 231–47
58. *Annals of St Bertin*, trans. J. Nelson, in *Ninth-Century Histories: the Annals of St Bertin* (Manchester, 1991)
59. P. Stafford, 'The King's Wife in Wessex 800-1066', *Past & Present,* No. 91 (Oxford, May 1981), pp. 3-27
60. ASC, v. A & E, p. 66
61. ASC, v. A & E, pp. 66–7
62. ALA, p. 70
63. ALA, p. 70
64. CJW, p. 271
65. GRA, p. 177
66. R. Abels, *Alfred the Great: War, Kingship and Culture in Anglo-Saxon England* (London, 1998), pp. 80-1
67. GRA, p. 171
68. J. L. Nelson, 'Æthelwulf', *Oxford Dictionary of National Biography* (Oxford, 2004)
69. CJW, p. 275; D. N. Dumville & M. Lapdige (eds), *Annals of St Neots with Vita Prima Sancti Neoti* (Cambridge: CUP, 1984)
70. Smyth, p. 674
71. S. Keynes, 'Introduction' in P. H. Blair, *An Introduction to Anglo-Saxon England* (Cambridge, 2003), p. xxxiii
72. J. L. Nelson, 'England and the Continent in the Ninth Century: III, Rights and Rituals', *Transactions of the Royal Historical Society*, Vol. 14 (Cambridge, 2004), pp. 1–24

73. Stenton, p. 245
74. Story, pp. 218-28
75. R. H. Hodgkin, *A History of the Anglo-Saxons*, Vol. 2 (Oxford, 1935), pp. 514–15
76. R. Abels, *Alfred the Great: War, Kingship and Culture in Anglo-Saxon England* (London, 1998), p. 87

16 Æthelbald and Æthelberht, 856/8–865

1. ALA, p. 237
2. ALA, pp. 72-3
3. ASC, v. A & E, pp. 66-7
4. GRA, p. 177
5. Naismith, *Money and Power in Anglo-Saxon England: The Southern English Kingdoms, 757–965*. (Cambridge, 2012), pp. 65, 110-12
6. ASC, v. A, p. 66
7. Charter S328
8. EHD, Doc. No.23
9. Charter S326
10. Charters S326, S1274
11. ALA, p. 70
12. ALA, p. 73
13. GRA, p. 177
14. ALA, p. 73
15. ALA, p. 71; CJW, p. 271; GRA, p. 171
16. HA, p. 281
17. P. J. Geary, *Women at the Beginning: Origin Myths from the Amazons to the Virgin Mary* (Princeton, 2009), pp. 52-3
18. ASC, v. A, pp. 67-8
19. *The Annals of St Bertin*, trans. J. L. Nelson (Manchester, 1991)
20. GRA, p. 177
21. ASC, v. A & E, pp. 66-9
22. ALA, p. 68
23. ALA, p. 74
24. Peddie, p. 13
25. Charter S326
26. Charter S1507
27. ALA, n.41, p. 238
28. Charter S335
29. GRA, p. 177
30. HA, p. 281
31. ASC, v. A & E, pp. 68-9
32. Naismith, *Money and Power in Anglo-Saxon England: The Southern English Kingdoms, 757–965*, pp. 110, 125-6
33. Charters S266, S327, S328, S331, S332
34. Charters S329, S333
35. ASC, v. F, p. 69

36. S. Keynes, 'Archbishops and Bishops', in 'Appendix II: Archbishops and Bishops 597–1066', in M. Lapidge, *et al.* (eds), *The Wiley Blackwell Encyclopedia of Anglo-Saxon England* (Chichester: 2nd edn, 2014), p. 549
37. D. N. Dumville, 'The Ætheling: A Study in Anglo-Saxon Constitutional History', in *Anglo-Saxon England, Vol. 8* (1979), pp. 1-33
38. D. N. Dumville, 'The Ætheling: A Study in Anglo-Saxon Constitutional History', in *Anglo-Saxon England, Vol. 8* (1979), pp. 21-24
39. ASC, v. A & E, pp. 68-9
40. ALA, p. 74
41. GRA, p. 179
42. CJW, p. 277
43. *The Itinerary of John Leland in or about the years 1535–1543*, ed. L. Toulmin Smith, Vol. I, pt.2, p. 153

17 Æthelred I, 865–871

1. ASC, v. A & E, pp. 68-9
2. L. Roach, *Æthelred the Unready* (New Haven & London, 2016), pp. 6-7
3. HA, p. 281
4. D. N. Dumville, 'The Ætheling: A Study in Anglo-Saxon Constitutional History', *Anglo-Saxon England*, Vol. 8 (1979), pp. 21-24
5. ASC, v. A & E, p. 68
6. R. Abels, *Alfred the Great: War, Kingship and Culture in Anglo-Saxon England* (London, 1998), p. 113; G. Halsall, *Warfare and Society in the Barbarian West 450-900* (London, 2003), pp. 119-33; P. H. Sawyer, *Age of the Vikings* (London: 2nd edn, 1975), pp. 124-25
7. J. L. Nelson, *Charles the Bald* (London, 1992)
8. ALA, p. 74
9. HA, p. 275
10. P. Hill, *The Age of Aethelstan* (Stroud, 2004), p. 116
11. N. J. Higham, *The Kingdom of Northumbria AD 350-1100* (Stroud, 1993) pp. 178–79
12. SMO, p. 74
13. Peddie, p. 19
14. ASC, v. A & E, pp. 68-9
15. EHD, pp. 364-72
16. ALA, p. 77
17. ASC, v. A & E, pp. 70-1
18. ALA, p. 77
19. ASC, v. A & E, pp. 70-1
20. CJW, p. 287
21. D. Hadley, 'The Winter Camp of the Viking Great Army, AD 872–3, Torksey, Lincolnshire', *Antiquaries Journal*, Vol. 96 (2016), pp. 23–67
22. Charters S335, S336
23. Charters S338, S339
24. Charters S334, S338a, S340, S341, S342
25. Charter S1201

26. S. Hollis, *Anglo-Saxon Women and the Church* (Woodbridge, 1992), p. 215
27. A. R. Rumble, 'The purposes of the *Codex Wintoniensis*', in R. A. Brown, *Proceedings of the Battle Conference on Anglo-Norman Studies*, Vol. IV (Woodbridge, 1982), pp. 153-66 & 224-32; J. L. Nelson, 'Reconstructing a royal family: reflections on Alfred', in *People and Places in Northern Europe 500-1600: essays in honour of Peter Hayes Sawyer* (Woodbridge, 1991), p. 55
28. Naismith, *Money and Power in Anglo-Saxon England: The Southern English Kingdoms, 757–965*, p. 11
29. Lyons, & Mackay, pp. 71-2, 77, 98-99
30. Smyth, p. 30; Timperley, p. 22
31. P. Sawyer, 'The royal tun in pre-conquest England', in P. Wormald (ed.), *Ideal and Reality in Frankish and Anglo-Saxon Society, studies presented by J M Wallace-Hadrill* (Oxford, 1983), pp. 280-84
32. ASC, v. A, p. 68
33. J. Man, *History and Antiques, ancient and modern, of the borough of Reading, in the county of Berkshire* (orig 1816, repr. 2010)
34. R. Brooks, p. 58
35. ASC, v. A & E, pp. 70-1
36. G. B. Grundy, 'The Ancient Highways and Tracks of Wiltshire, Berkshire, Hampshire, and the Saxon Battlefields of Wiltshire', in *Archaeological Journal*, No. 7
37. Marren, p. 114
38. ASC, v. E, p. 71
39. ASC, v. A & E, pp. 70-1
40. G. Gaimar, *Estoire des Engleis*, ed. A. Bell (Anglo-Norman Text Society, 1960), v. 2963-72
41. ASC, v. A & E, pp. 70-1
42. CA, p. 37
43. Gaimar, *Estoire des Engleis*; R. Abels, *Alfred the Great: War, Kingship and Culture in Anglo-Saxon England* (London, 1998), pp. 127
44. Walker, p. 209
45. CJW, p. 289
46. Marren, p. 119
47. J. Peddie, *Alfred the Good Soldier: His Life and Campaigns* (Bath, 1994), p. 97
48. Timperley & Brill, p. 76
49. Peddie, *Alfred: Warrior King* (Stroud, 2005), p. 100
50. Burne, pp. 50-1; battlefieldstrust.com, Online (accessed 22 Aug 2024)
51. GRA, p. 179
52. ASC, v. A & E, pp. 70-1; ALA, pp. 79-80
53. ALA, p. 79
54. Marren, p. 117
55. ALA, p. 79; GRA, p. 179
56. Abels, *Alfred the Great: War, Kingship and Culture in Anglo-Saxon England*, p. 131
57. GRA, p. 179

58. ASC, v. A & E, pp. 70-1
59. ASC, v. A, p. 70
60. ALA, p. 80
61. ALA, pp. 173-5
62. EHD, p. 493
63. J. Pollard, *Alfred the Great: The man who made England* (London, 2005), p. 127
64. ASC, v. A & E, p. 71; CJW, p. 291; HA, p. 285
65. Timperley & Brill, p. 97
66. ASC, v. A & E, pp. 72-3
67. HA, p. 285
68. Marren, p. 122
69. ALA, p. 80
70. B. Yorke, *Wessex in the Early Middle Ages* (London, 1995), p. 187

18 Alfred, 871–886

1. ALA, pp. 76, 88
2. P. Wormald, 'Alfred the Great', *Oxford Dictionary of National Biography* (Oxford, 2004), Online edn, Accessed 19 May 2024
3. G. Craig, 'Alfred the Great: A diagnosis', *Journal of the Royal Society of Medicine*, Vol. 84 (1991), pp. 303-305.
4. Abels, *Alfred the Great: War, Kingship and Culture in Anglo-Saxon England*, pp. 184-5
5. ASC, v. A & E, pp. 72-3
6. ASC, v. A & E, pp. 72-3
7. ALA, p. 81
8. J. Haslam, 'The towns of Wiltshire', in *Anglo-Saxon towns in Southern England* (1984), pp. 126-27
9. CJW, p. 299
10. ASC, v. A, p. 72
11. Abels, *Alfred the Great: War, Kingship and Culture in Anglo-Saxon England*, p. 142
12. ASC, v. A & E, pp. 72-3
13. *Current Archaeology*, No. 281 (August 2013)
14. ASC, v. A & E, pp. 74-5
15. M. J. Key, *Edward the Elder: King of the Anglo-Saxons* (Stroud, 2019), p. 39
16. Charter S338a
17. Charters S332, S340, S1201, S1203
18. ALA, p. 322
19. J. L. Nelson, 'Reconstructing a Royal Family: Reflections on Alfred', in *People and Places in Northern Europe 500-1600: Essays in honour of Peter Hayes Sawyer* (Woodbridge, 1991), pp. 47-66
20. ASC, v. A & E, pp. 74-5
21. M. Firth & E. Sabo, 'Kingship and Maritime Power in 10th-Century England', *International Journal of Nautical Archaeology*, Vol. 49, No. 2 (July 2020), pp. 329-340

22. ASC, v. A & E, pp. 74-5
23. CA, p. 40; CJW, p. 307
24. ASC, v. A & E, pp. 74-5
25. Peddie, *Alfred: Warrior King* (Stroud, 2005), p. 124
26. Pollard, pp. 150-2
27. ASC, v. A, p. 74
28. HA, p. 289
29. Marren, p. 124
30. P. Stafford, *Queen Emma and Queen Edith: Queenship and Women's Power in Eleventh-century England* (Oxford, 2004), p. 324; Yorke, 'Edward the aetheling', in *Edward the Elder 899-924* (London, 2001), p. 31
31. Charter S362
32. ASC, v. E, p. 75
33. ALA, p. 84
34. R. Brooks, p. 65
35. ASC, v. A & E, pp. 76-7; ALA, p. 84; CJW, p. 309
36. ASC, v. A, E, pp. 76-7
37. Marren, p. 126; Pollard, p. 184
38. CJW, p. 311
39. ASC, v. A & E, pp. 76-7
40. Burne, pp. 56-7
41. Smyth, p. 75
42. ALA, pp. 84-5
43. R. Brooks, p. 67
44. ALA, pp. 84-5
45. ALA, p. 85
46. Peddie, *Alfred: Warrior King* (Stroud, 2005), p. 156
47. ALA, pp. 171-2
48. P. Hill, *The Age of Aethelstan* (Stroud, 2004), p. 164
49. Stenton, pp. 258-9

19 From Wessex to England

1. ALA, pp. 38-9, 50
2. ASC, v. A & E, pp. 80-1
3. ALA; ASC
4. Charters S342a, S343, S344
5. Charters S346, S347
6. Ashley
7. N. P. Brooks, 'England in the Ninth Century: The Crucible of Defeat', *Transactions of the Royal Historical Society*, Fifth Series, Vol. 29 (1979), p. 1
8. M. J. Key, *The House of Godwin: The Rise and Fall of an Anglo-Saxon Dynasty* (Stroud, 2022), p. 46; Charter S956
9. Tatlock, pp. 223-35
10. HA, p. 243
11. M. J. Lewis, '"Incipient Armory" in the Bayeux Tapestry?', *The Coat of Arms: The Journal of the Heraldry Society*, Vol. VIII, pt.1, No. 223 (2012), p. 8

Bibliography

Primary Sources

Aldhelm: The Poetic Works, ed. and trans. Michael Lapidge and Michael Rosier (Cambridge: Brewer, 1985)

Annales Cambriae (Annals of Wales), ed. J. Williams ab Ethel (London; Rolls Series XX, 1866)

Annales de Wintonia in Annales Monastici, ed. H. R. Luard, Vol. ii (Rolls Series, 1865)

Annals of St Bertin, eds F. Grat, J. Vielliard & S. Clemencet (Paris, 1964), trans. J. Nelson, in *Ninth-Century Histories: The Annals of St Bertin* (Manchester, 1991)

Annals of St Neots with Vita Prima Sancti Neoti, eds D. N. Dumville & M. Lapidge, *Anglo-Saxon Chronicle 17* (Cambridge: CUP, 1984)

Asser's *Life of King Alfred* & other Contemporary Sources, trans. & intro S. Keynes & M. Lapidge (London: Penguin, repr. 2004)

Bede's Ecclesiastical History of the English People, eds, J. McClure and R. Collins (Oxford, New York: Oxford University Press, revd edn, 2008)

Chronicon Æthelweardi (Chronicle of Æthelweard), ed. and trans. Alistair Campbell (London: Nelson, 1962)

Chronicon Monasterii de Abingdon, ed. J. Stevenson (London: Longman, 1858)

Domesday Book: A Complete Translation (London: New York; Penguin, 2003)

Dumville, David N. (ed.), 'Annales Cambriae, A.D. 682-954: Texts A-C in Parallel' (Cambridge: CUP, 2002)

Dumville, David N., 'Nennius and the "Historia Brittonum"', *Studia Celtica*, 10/11 (1975)

Dumville, David N., 'The West Saxon Genealogical Regnal List and the Chronology of Early Wessex', in *Peritia: Journal of the Medieval Academy of Ireland 4* (1985), pp. 21-36

G. Gaimar, *Estoire des Engleis*, ed. A. Bell (Anglo-Norman Text Society, 1960)

Geoffrey of Monmouth, *Historia regum Britanniae* (The History of the Kings of Britain), trans. Sebastian Evans (2021)

George, Karen, *Gildas's De Excidio Britonum and the Early British Church*, Studies in Celtic History 26 (Woodbridge: Boydell Press, 2009)

Gildas, *De Excidio et Conquestu Britanniae* (*The Ruin of Britain, and Other Works)*, ed. and trans. Michael Winterbottom, Arthurian Period Sources, 7 (London: Phillimore, 1978)

Henry of Huntingdon, *Historia Anglorum: The History of the English People*, ed. and trans. D. E. Greenway, Oxford Medieval Texts (Oxford: Clarendon Press, 1996)

John of Worcester, *The Chronicle of John of Worcester, Vol. 2*, ed. R. R. Darlington and P. McGurk, trans. J. Bray and P. McGurk, Oxford Medieval Texts (Oxford; New York: Clarendon Press, 1995)

John of Worcester, *The Chronicle of John of Worcester, Vol 3*, ed. and trans P. McGurk, Oxford Medieval Texts (New York; Oxford University Press, 1998)

Nennius, *Historia Brittonum* (The History of the Britons, in Six Old English Chronicles), trans. J. A. Giles (London: George Bell, 1847)

Prosopography of Anglo-Saxon England (PASE website), authors & eds: Janet L. Nelson, Simon Keynes, Stephen Baxter, Alex Burghart, Andrew Bell, Natasha Hodgson, Juliana Dresvina, Ben Snook; author & design: John Bradley, Harold Short, Paul Vetch, Timothy Hill, Peter Rose and Martyn Jessop.

Roger of Wendover, *Flowers of History, Comprising the History of England from the descent of the Saxons to AD1235*, trans. J. A. Giles, 2 vols (London; Bohn, 1849)

Smith, Toulmin Lucy ed, *The Itinerary of John Leland in or about the years 1535–1543, Vol. I, part* 2 (Palala Press, 2016)

Symeon of Durham, Symeonis Monachi Opera Omnia: Vol. 1, Historia Ecclesiae Dunelmensis, ed. T. Arnold (New York: Cambridge University Press, revd edn, 2012)

The Anglo-Saxon Chronicles, ed. and trans. M. Swanton (London: Phoenix Press, revd edn, 2000)

The Bayeux Tapestry, intro D. M. Wilson (London: Thames and Hudson, revd edn, 2004)

The Letters of St. Boniface: With a New Introduction and Bibliography, tran. Ephraim Emerton, ed. Thomas. F. X. Noble (New York: Columbia University Press, 2000)

Vita Sancti Wilfrithi (Life of St Wilfrid), trans. Bernard J. Muir & Andrew J. Turner (Exeter, 1998)

Whitelock, D. (ed.), *English Historical Documents, 500-1042* (London: Eyre Methuen, 2nd edn, 1996)

William of Malmesbury, *Gesta Regum Anglorum: The History of the English Kings, Vol. 1*, ed. & trans. R. A. B. Mynors, R. M. Thomson and M.

Winterbottom, Oxford Medieval Texts (Oxford; New York: Clarendon Press, 1998)

William of Malmesbury, *Gesta Regvm Anglorvm: The History of the English Kings. Vol. 2: General Introduction and Commentary*, ed. R. M. Thomson, Oxford Medieval Texts, repr. (Oxford; New York, Clarendon Press, 2003)

William of Malmesbury, *Gesta Pontificum Anglorum, The History of the English Bishops*, trans. M. Winterbottom and R. M. Thomson (London; New York: Oxford University Press, 2007)

William of Malmesbury, *Gesta Pontificum Anglorum, The Deeds of the Bishops of England*, trans. D. Preest (Woodbridge: Boydell Press, 2002)

Wright, Neil (1984); *The Historia Regum Britannie of Geoffrey of Monmouth* (Woodbridge: Boydell and Brewer, 1984)

Secondary Sources

Abels, Richard, *Alfred the Great: War, Kingship and Culture in Anglo-Saxon England* (London: Routledge, 1998)

Abels, Richard, 'The Council of Whitby: A Study in Early Anglo-Saxon Politics', *Journal of British Studies*, Vol. 23, No. 1 (Cambridge: CUP, Autumn 1983)

Abels, Richard, 'Royal Succession and the Growth of Political Stability in Ninth-century Wessex', *The Haskins Society Journal: Studies in Medieval History*, Vol. 12 (Woodbridge: Boydell & Brewer, 2002), pp. 83–97

Adams, Max, *The King in the North: The Life and Times of Oswald of Northumbria* (Apollo, revd edn, 2014)

Alcock, Leslie, *Economy, Society, and Warfare among the Britons and Saxons* (Cardiff: Univ. of Wales Press, 1987)

Alexander, J. J., *'When the Saxons Came to Devon; Part IV': Report & Transactions of the Devonshire Association.* (1922)

Arnold, C. J., *An Archaeology of the Early Anglo-Saxon Kingdoms* (London: Routledge, 2nd edn, 1997)

Ashley, Mike, *British Monarchs* (London: Robinson Publishing, 1998)

Attenborough, F. L. (ed.), *The Laws of the Earliest English Kings* (Cambridge, 1922)

Barr-Hamilton, Alec, *In Saxon Sussex* (Arundel Press, 1953)

Bassett, S. (ed.), *The Origins of the Anglo-Saxon Kingdoms* (Leicester, LUP, 1989), pp. 75-83

Bassett, S. (ed.), 'The Formation of the Mercian Kingdom', in *The Origins of Anglo-Saxon Kingdoms* (Leicester, LUP, 1989)

Battlefieldstrust.com, Online (accessed 22 Aug 2024)

Birley, A. R., *The Roman Government of Britain* (Oxford: OUP, 2005)

Blackburn, Mark, & Grierson, Philip, *Medieval European Coinage.* (Cambridge: CUP, repr. 2006)

Blair, Peter Hunter, *An Introduction to Anglo-Saxon England* (Cambridge: CUP, 2003)

Blake, Steve, & Lloyd, Scott, *Pendragon: The Definitive Account of the Origins of Arthur* (Lyons Press, 2004)

Blunt, C. E., The Coinage of Ecgbeorht, King of Wessex, 802-39. *British Numismatic Journal*, Vol. 28 (3) (1957), pp. 467-476

Brayley, Edward Wedlake, et al., *The History of Surrey, Volume 2, Part 1* (Dorking, R. B. Ede, 1842)

Breeze, Andrew, *British Battles 493-937: Mount Badon to Brunanburh* (Anthem, 2020)

Breeze, Andrew, 'The Battle of the Uinued and the River Went, Yorkshire', *Northern History, 41:2* (2004)

Britton, C. E., 'A Meteorological Chronology to AD 1450', *Meteorological Office Geophysical Memoirs*, Vol. VIII (70) (London, 1937)

Brooks, N., *The Early History of the Church of Canterbury: Christ Church from 597 to 1066* (London: LUP, 1984)

Brooks, N, 'England in the Ninth Century: The Crucible of Defeat', *Transactions of the Royal Historical Society*, Fifth Series, Vol. 29 (1979)

Brooks, Nicholas, 'The formation of the Mercian kingdom' in S. Bassett (ed.), *The origins of Anglo-Saxon kingdoms, Studies in the Early History of Britain* (Leicester: LUP, 1989), pp. 159-170

Brooks, Richard, *Cassell's Battlefields of Britain & Ireland* (London: Weidenfeld & Nicolson, 2005)

Brown, Michelle P; Farr, Carol Ann, *Mercia: An Anglo-Saxon Kingdom in Europe* (London, New York: Leicester University Press, 2001)

Burkitt, Tim & Burkitt, Annette, 'The Frontier Zone and the Siege of Mount Badon: A Review of the Evidence for their Location', *Proceedings of the Somerset Archaeological and Natural History Society*, Vol. 134 (1990), pp. 81-93

Burne, A. H., *The Battlefields of England* (Barnsley: Pen & Sword, revd edn, 2005)

Campbell, James; John, Eric; Wormald, Patrick, *The Anglo-Saxons* (London: Penguin Books, 1991)

Cavill, Paul, *Anglo-Saxon Christianity* (London: Harper Collins, 1999)

Charles-Edwards, T. M., 'Language and Society among the insular Celts AD400-1000', in M. Green (ed.), *The Celtic World* (London, 1995), pp. 703-36

Charles-Edwards, T. M., *Wales and the Britons 350-1064* (Oxford: OUP, 2013)

Clark, A. J., 'The nature of Wansdyke', *Antiquity*, Vol. 32 (1958), pp. 89-96

Clarkson, T., 'Oswald, King and Saint: His Britain and Beyond', *The Heroic Age: A Journal of Early Medieval Northwestern Europe*, Vol. 9 (2006)

Clemoes, Peter; Keynes, Simon; Lapidge, Michael, *Anglo-Saxon England*, vol. 17 (CUP, 1981)

Coleman, Patrick. E., *The last battle for Cornwall*, in Cornwallyesteryear.com, Online website (accessed 7 June 2024)

Coles, R. J., *Southampton's Historic Buildings*, City of Southampton Society (1981)

Cooksey, C. F., 'On the site of the Battle of Aclea AD851', *Hampshire Field Club & Archaeological Society*, Vol. 5 (1905), pp. 26-35

Cooper, D., *Badon and the Early Wars of Wessex c.500 to 710* (Barnsley: Pen & Sword, 2018)

Craig, G., 'Alfred the Great: A diagnosis', *Journal of the Royal Society of Medicine*, Vol. 84 (1991)

Cramp, Rosemary, *Corpus of Anglo-Saxon stone sculpture in England, Volume 7* (Oxford OUP, 2006)

Crittall, Elizabeth (ed.), 'Wilton: Early History', in *A History of the County of Wiltshire*, Vol. 6 (London, 1962)

Cubitt, Catherine, *Anglo-Saxon Church Councils c.650–c.850.* (London: LUP, 1995)

Cubitt, C., Pastoral Care and Religious Beliefs, in P. Stafford (ed.), *A Companion to the Early Middle Ages: Britain and Ireland c.500-c.1100* (Chichester, 2013)

Cunliffe, Barry, *Britain Begins* (Oxford: OUP, 2013)

Cunliffe, Barry, *Wessex to 1000AD* (London: Routledge, 1993)

Current Archaeology, Issue 281 (Aug 2013)

Current Archaeology, Issue 353 (July 2019)

D'Amato, Raffaele, & Pollington, Stephen, *Anglo-Saxon Kings and Warlords AD400-1070* (Oxford: Osprey Publishing, 2023)

Dark, K., *Britain and the End of the Roman Empire* (Stroud: The History Press, 2002)

Dark, K., *Civitas to Kingdom: British Political Continuity 300-800* (Studies in the Early History of Britain) (Leicester, LUP, 1994)

Davies, J. R., 'Wales and West Britian', in P. Stafford (ed.), *A Companion to the Middle Ages: Britain and Ireland c.500-c.1100* (Chichester: Wiley-Blackwell, 2013), pp. 341-57

Davies, W & Vierck, H., 'The contexts of Tribal Hidages: social aggregates and settlement patterns', *Fruhmittelalterliche Studien*, Vol. 8 (1974)

Dinwiddy, K. E., 'An Anglo-Saxon Cemetery at Twyford, Near Winchester', *Proceedings of the Hampshire Field Club Archaeological Society*, Vol. 66 (Hampshire Studies, 2011), pp. 75-126

Doggett, N., *The Anglo-Saxon See and Cathedral of Dorchester-on-Thames: the Evidence Reconsidered* (1983)

Dolley, Michael, 'Proceedings for the Year 1970; the Location of the Pre-Alfredian Mints of Wessex', *British Numismatic Journal*, Vol. XXVIII, pp. 57-61

Dumville, David N., 'The Ætheling: A Study in Anglo-Saxon Constitutional History', in *Anglo-Saxon England*, Vol. 8 (1979), pp. 1-33

Dumville, David, 'The Anglian collection of royal genealogies and regnal lists', in P. Clemoes (ed.), *Anglo-Saxon England*, No. 5 (1976), pp. 23–50

Dunning, Robert, *Somerset Castles* (Tiverton: Somerset Books, 1995)

Eagles, Bruce, *From Roman Civitas to Anglo-Saxon Shire: Topographical Studies on the Formation of Wessex* (Oxbow, 2018)

Edwards, Heather, 'The charters of the early West Saxon Kingdoms' (unpublished thesis, 1985)

Enright, Michael J., 'Charles the Bald and Æthelwulf of Wessex: Alliance of 856 and Strategies of Royal Succession', *Journal of Medieval History*, Vol. 5 (1) (1979)

Farmer, David (ed.), 'Richard (d. 720)', in *The Oxford Dictionary of Saints* (Oxford: OUP, 5th edn, 2011)

Finberg, H. P. R, 'Sherborne, Glastonbury, and the Expansion of Wessex', *Transactions of the Royal Historical Society*, Vol. 3 (1953), pp. 101-124

Firth, M, & Sabo, E., 'Kingship and Maritime Power in 10th-Century England', *International Journal of Nautical Archaeology*, Vol. 49 (2) (July 2020), pp. 329–340

Fleming, Robin, *Britain after Rome: The Fall and Rise 400 to 1070* (London: Penguin, 2011)

Fletcher, John, *The Western Kingdom.* (Stroud: The History Press, 2022)

Foot, Sarah, *Monastic Life in Anglo-Saxon England c.600-900* (Cambridge: CUP, 2009)

Freeman, Edward A., 'King Ine', *Proceedings of the Somersetshire Archaeological and Natural History Society*, Vol. 18, Pt 2 (1872), pp. 1–59

Frere, S.S., *Britannia: A History of Roman Britain* (London: Routledge & Kegan Paul, 3rd revd edn, 1987)

Fryde, E. B., Greenway, D. E; Porter, S; Roy, I., *Handbook of British Chronology* (Cambridge: CUP, 3rd revd edn, 1996)

Geary, Patrick J., *Women at the Beginning: Origin Myths from the Amazons to the Virgin Mary* (Princeton University Press, 2009)

Gore, D., *The Vikings and Devon* (Exeter: Mint Press, 2001)

Glover, J. E. B., *The Place-Names of Wiltshire*, English Place-Name Society XVI (Cambridge, 1939)

Glover, J. E. B; Mawer, A. & Stenton, F. M., *Place Names of Devon* (Cambridge, 1932)

Grierson, Philip (1986). *Medieval European Coinage: With a Catalogue of the Coins in the Fitzwilliam Museum, Cambridge, 1: Earlier Middle Ages (400-900)* (Cambridge: CUP, 1986) p. 157

Grinsell, L. V., *The Archaeology of Wessex: An account of Wessex Antiquities from the Earliest Times To the End of the Pagan Saxon Period, with Special reference to Existing Field* Monuments (London: Methuen, 1958)

Grundy, G. B., 'The Ancient Highways and Tracks of Wiltshire, Berkshire, Hampshire, and the Saxon Battlefields of Wiltshire', *Archaeological Journal*, No. 75 (1918), pp. 69–194

Hadley, Dawn, 'The Winter Camp of the Viking Great Army, AD 872–3, Torksey, Lincolnshire', *Antiquaries Journal*, Vol. 96 (2016), pp. 23–67

Hadley, Dawn, 'Viking Raids and Conquest', in Pauline Stafford (ed.), *A Companion to the Early Middle Ages: Britain and Ireland c. 500–c.1100* (Chichester: Wiley-Blackwell, 2013), pp. 195–211

Halsall, Guy, 'The Battle of Ellendun AD825', *Miniature Wargames*, Feb 1985, pp. 38-42

Halsall, Guy, *Warfare and Society in the Barbarian West 450-900* (London: Routledge, 2003)

Halsall, Guy, *Worlds of Arthur: Facts & Fictions of the Dark Ages* (Oxford: OUP, 2013)

Hamerow, Helena, *Rural Settlements and Society in Anglo-Saxon England* (Oxford: OUP, 2012)

Hamerow, H; Ferguson, C; Naylor, J; The Origins of Wessex Pilot Project, *Oxoniensa*, Vol. 78 (2013), pp. 49-69

Harper, P., *Cerdic: Mysterious Dark Age king who founded England* (Barnsley: Pen & Sword, 2024)

Harrington, Sue, & Martin Welch, *The Early Anglo-Saxon Kingdoms of Southern Britain AD 450-650: Beneath the Tribal Hidage* (Oxbow Books, 2018)

Hart, Cyril., 'The Tribal Hidage', *Transactions of the Royal Historical Society*, 5th Ser., Vol. 21 (1971)

Haslam, Jeremy, 'The towns of Wiltshire', in *Anglo-Saxon towns in Southern England* (Phillimore, 1984)

Heighway, C., *Anglo-Saxon Gloucestershire* (Gloucester, 1987)

Higham, N. J., *An English Empire: Bede and the early Anglo-Saxon Kings* (Manchester, MUP, 1995)

Higham, N. J. & Hill, D. H., *Edward the Elder 899-924* (London: Routledge, 2001)

Higham, N. J., *The Convert Kings: Power and religious affiliation in early Anglo-Saxon England.* (Manchester: MUP, 1997)

Higham, N. J., *The Kingdom of Northumbria AD 350-1100.* (Stroud: Sutton, 1993)

Higham, Nicholas J.; Ryan, Martin J. (eds), *The Anglo-Saxon World.* (New Haven, Connecticut: Yale University Press, 2013)

Higham, Robert, *Making Anglo-Saxon Devon* (Exeter, Mint Press, 2008)

Hill, David, *An Atlas of Anglo-Saxon England* (Oxford: Blackwell, 1981)

Hill, Paul, *The Age of Aethelstan* (Stroud: The History Press, 2004)

Hill, Paul, *The Anglo-Saxons at War* (Barnsley: Pen & Sword, 2012)

Hills, Catherine, *Origins of the English* (Duckworth Debates in Archaeology) (London: Bloomsbury, 2003)

Hindley, Geoffrey, *A Brief History of the Anglo-Saxons* (London: Constable & Robinson, 2006)

Hipkins, F. C., *Repton and its Neighbourhood: A Descriptive Guide of the Archaeology and of the District* (Repton: A. J. Lawrence, 2nd edn, 1899)

Hirst, S, et al, 'Liddington Castle and the battle of Badon : Excavations and research 1976', *Archaeological Journal*, vol. 153 (1996), pp. 1–59

Hodges, R., *The Anglo-Saxon Achievement: Archaeology and the Beginnings of English Society.* (London, 1989)

Hodgkin, R. H., *A History of the Anglo-Saxons, Vol. 2.* (Oxford: OUP, 1935)

Hollis, Stephanie, *Anglo-Saxon Women and the Church* (Woodbridge: Boydell & Brewer, 1992)

Hoskins, W. G., *Devon* (Collins, London, 1954)

Hoskins, W. G., *The Westward Expansion of Wessex* (Leicester, LUP, 1960)

Howorth, H. H., 'Ecgberht, King of the West Saxons and the Kent Men, and his coins', *The Numismatic Chronicle and Journal of the Numismatic Society*, 3rd series, Vol. 20 (1990), pp. 66–87

Huscroft, Richard, *Making England, 796–1042* (Abingdon: Routledge, 2019)

Jackson, K. H., 'The Site of Mount Badon', *Journal of Celtic Studies*, Vol. 2 (1953–8)

Jarman, Cat, *The Bone Chests: Unlocking the Secrets of the Anglo-Saxons* (London: William Collins, 2023)

Kelly, S. E., 'Baldred (fl. c.823–827)' in *Oxford Dictionary of National Biography* (Oxford: OPU, 2004) online edn, accessed 26 March 2024

Kelly, Susan, *Charters of Malmesbury Abbey* (Oxford: OUP, 2005)

Kelly, Susan, & Hobbs, Mary (ed.), *Chichester Cathedral: An Historic* Survey (Chichester: Phillimore, 1994)

Key, M. J., *Edward the Elder: King of the Anglo-Saxons* (Stroud: Amberley, 2019)

Key, M. J., The House of Godwin: The Rise and Fall of an Anglo-Saxon Dynasty (Stroud: Amberley, 2022)

Keynes, Simon, 'Archbishops and Bishops', in 'Appendix II: Archbishops and Bishops 597–1066', in M. Lapidge, *et al.* (eds), *The Wiley Blackwell Encyclopedia of Anglo-Saxon England* (Chichester: 2nd edn, 2014)

Keynes, Simon, 'Intro to Peter Hunter Blair; An Introduction to Anglo-Saxon England' (Cambridge: CUP, 2003) p. xxxiii

Keynes, Simon, 'Ceolnoth' in Lapidge, M. *et al.*, *Blackwell Encyclopedia of Anglo-Saxon England* (Oxford: Blackwell Publishing, revd edn, 2001)

Keynes, Simon, 'The Control of Kent in the Ninth Century' in *Early Medieval Europe*, Vol. 2 (1993)

Keynes, Simon, 'England, 700–900', in Rosamond McKitterick (ed.), *The New Cambridge Medieval History, Volume 2, c.700–c.900* (Cambridge: CUP, 1995). pp. 18–42

Keynes, Simon, 'The West Saxon Charters of King Æthelwulf and his sons', *English Historical Review*, Vol. 109 (Oxford: OUP, Nov 1994), pp. 1109-49

Kirby, D. P., 'Bede's Native Sources for the Historia Ecclesiastica', *Bulletin of the John Rylands Library*, No. 48 (1966), pp. 341–71

Kirby, D. P., *The Earliest English Kings* (London: Routledge, revd edn, 2000)

Kirby, D. P., 'Problems of Early West Saxon History', *The English Historical Review*, Vol. 80, No. 314 (Oxford: OUP, Jan 1965), pp. 10–29

Lapidge, Michael, 'The Career of Aldhelm', *Anglo-Saxon England*, Vol. 36 (2007), pp. 15–69

Lapidge, Michael; Blair, John; Keynes, Simon, & Scragg, Donald (eds), *The Blackwell Encyclopaedia of Anglo-Saxon England* (Oxford: Blackwell Publishing, revd edn, 2001)

Laycock, Stuart, *Warlords: The Struggle for Power in Post-Roman Britain* (Stroud: The History Press, 2009)

Lewis, Michael, J., '"Incipient Armory" in the Bayeux Tapestry?', *The Coat of Arms: The Journal of the Heraldry Society*, Vol. VIII, pt.1, No. 223 (2012)

Line, Philip, *The Vikings and their Enemies: Warfare in Northern Europe 750-1100* (Barnsley: Pen & Sword, 2014)

Loyn, H. R., *Anglo-Saxon England and the Norman Conquest* (London: Routledge, 2nd edn, 1991)

Loyn, H. R. *The Governance of Anglo-Saxon England 500-1087* (Hodder Arnold, 1984)

Lyons, Adrian W. & Mackay, William A., 'The Coinage of Æthelred I (865–871)', *British Numismatic Journal*, Vol. 77 (2007), pp. 71–118

McKitterick, Rosamond (ed.), *The New Cambridge Medieval History*, Vol. 2 (Cambridge: CUP, 1995)

Major, Albany F., *Early Wars of Wessex* (Cambridge: CUP, 1913)

Malden, H. E. (ed.), *The Victoria History of the County of Surrey*, Vol. 1, pp. 255–73 (London: Archibald Constable, 1902)

Man, J., *History and Antiques, ancient and modern, of the borough of Reading, in the county of Berkshire* (Snare & Man, General Books LLC, orig. 1816 repr. 2010)

Mann, Nicholas R., *The Isle of Avalon: Sacred Mysteries of Arthur and Glastonbury* (Green Magic, 2001)

Marren, Peter, *Battles of the Dark Ages: British Battlefields AD410-1065* (Barnsley: Pen & Sword, revd edn, 2011)

Matthews, Rupert, *Battlefield Walks: Devon* (London: Frances Lincoln, 2008)

Matthews, Rupert, *Ceawlin: The Man who Created England* (Barnsley: Pen & Sword, 2012)

Matthews, Rupert, *The Battle of Otford 776* (Bretwalda Books, 2017)

Mee, Frances, *A History of Selsey* (Chichester: Philimore, 1988)

Mellor, A. Shaw, 'Parish boundaries in relation to Wansdyke', *Wiltshire Archaeological and Natural History Magazine*, Vol. 51, no. 182 (June 1945), pp. 24–7

Miller, Sean, 'Æthelbald', *Oxford Dictionary of National Biography* (Oxford: OUP, 2004) Online edn. Accessed 7 June 2024

Mills, A. D., *A Dictionary of English Place Names* (Oxford: OUP, 2011)

Mommsen, T. E., 'Petrarch's Conception of the Dark Ages', in *Medieval and Renaissance Studies* (Cornell University Press, 1959), pp. 106–29

Monk, William John, *The History of Burford* (Burford & London, 1891)

Morris, John, *The Age of Arthur: A History of the British Isles from 350 to 650* (London: Phoenix, 1995)

Morris, John, 'A Gazetteer of Anglo-Saxon Surrey', *Surrey Archaeological Collections*, Vol. 56 (1959), pp. 132–58

Morris, Marc, *The Anglo-Saxons: A History of the Beginnings of England* (London: Hutchinson, 2021)

Munby, Julian, Jeremy Haslam (ed.). *Anglo-Saxon Towns in Southern England: Saxon Chichester and its Predecessors* (Chichester: Philimore, 1984)

Myres, J. N. L., *The English Settlements* (Oxford: OUP, 1986)

Myres, J. N. L., 'Wansdyke and the origins of Wessex', in H. Trevor-Roper (ed.), *Essays in British History presented to Sir Keith Feiling* (1964), pp. 1-28

Naismith, Rory, 'The Coinage of Offa Revisited', *British Numismatic Journal*, 80 (2010), pp. 77-9

Naismith, Rory, 'The Origins of the Line of Egbert, King of the West Saxons, 802 – 839', *English Historical Review*, Vol. 518 (Oxford: OUP, 2011), pp. 1–16

Naismith, Rory, *Money and Power in Anglo-Saxon England: The Southern English Kingdoms, 757–965* (Cambridge: CUP, 2012)

Naismith, Rory, *Early Medieval Britain c.500 – 1000*, Cambridge History of Britain, Series No.1 (Cambridge: CUP, 2021)

Nelson, Janet. L., 'Æthelwulf', *Oxford Dictionary of National Biography* (Oxford, 2004), Online edn, Accessed 6 June 2024

Nelson, Janet. L., *Charles the Bald* (London: Longman, 1992)

Nelson, Janet L., 'Problem of King Alfred's Royal Anointing', *Journal of Ecclesiastical History*, Vol. 18 (1967), pp. 145–63

Nelson, Janet L., 'Reconstructing a royal family: reflections on Alfred', in I. N. Wood & N. Lund (eds), *People and Places in Northern Europe 500-1600: essays in honour of Peter Hayes Sawyer* (Woodbridge, 1991)

Nelson, Janet L., 'The Queen in Ninth-century Wessex', in S. Keynes & Alfred P. Smyth (eds), *Anglo-Saxons: Studies Presented to Cyril Roy Hart* (Dublin: Four Courts Press, 2006), pp. 69–77

Nelson, Janet L., 'Britain, Ireland, and Europe, c. 750–c.900', in Pauline Stafford (ed.), *A Companion to the Early Middle Ages: Britain and Ireland c.500–c.1100* (Chichester: Wiley-Blackwell, 2013), pp. 231–47

Nelson, Janet L., 'England and the Continent in the Ninth Century: III, Rights and Rituals', *Transactions of the Royal Historical Society*, Vol. 14 (Cambridge: CUP, 2004), pp. 1–24

Newfield, T. P., 'The Climate Downturn of 536-50', in S. White, C. Pfister & F. Mauelhagen (eds), *The Palgrave Handbook of Climate History* (2018), pp. 447-493

Oman, Charles, *A History of England before the Norman Conquest* (London: Methuen, 3rd edn, 1913)

Oosthuizen, Susan, *The Emergence of the English* (Leeds: Arc Humanities Press, revd edn, 2019)

Orme, Nicholas, *Cornwall and the Cross: Christianity 500-1560* (Chichester: Phillimore, 2007)

Pagan, Hugh, 'Coinage in Southern England, 796–874', in M. A. S. Blackburn (ed.), *Anglo-Saxon Monetary History* (Leicester: LUP, 1986), pp. 45–65

Pagan, H. E., 'The Coinage of the East Anglian kingdom', *British Numismatic Journal*, Vol. 52 (1982), pp. 41-83

Papworth, Martin, *The Search for the Durotriges: Dorset and the West Country in the Late Iron Age* (Stroud: The History Press, 2011)
Payton, Philip, *Cornwall* (Fowey: Alexander Associates, 1996)
Peddie, John, *Alfred the Good Soldier: His Life and Campaigns* (Bath, 1994)
Peddie, John, *Alfred: Warrior King* (Stroud: Sutton Publishing, 2005)
Peers, Chris, *Offa and the Mercian Wars: The Rise and Fall of the First Great English Kingdom*, Barnsley, Pen & Sword, 2012)
Phillips, Graham & Keatman, Martin, *King Arthur: The True Story* (Arrow Books, London, 1993)
Pollard, J., *Alfred the Great: The man who made England* (London, 2005)
Powicke, F. M, & Fryde, E. B., *Handbook of British Chronology* (London: Royal Historical Society, 2nd edn, 1961)
Proceedings of the Somersetshire Archaeological and Natural History Society, Vol. 18, Pt 2 (1871-2), pp. 1–59
Redgate, A. E., *Religion, Politics and Society in Britain, 800-1066*, Abingdon, Routledge, 2014)
Richards, Julian D, *Viking Age England* (Stroud: The History Press, repr 2012)
Ridgeway, H., '*The History of the Abbey Church*' (Sherborne Abbey, 2014)
Roach, L., *Æthelred the Unready* (New Haven & London, Yale Univ Press, 2016)
Roberts, Alice, *Buried: An alternative history of the first millennium in* Britain (London: Simon and Schuster, 2022)
Rumble, A. R., 'The purposes of the Codex Wintoniensis', in R. A. Brown (ed.), *Proceedings of the Battle Conference on Anglo-Norman Studies*, Vol. IV (Woodbridge, 1982), pp. 153–66 & 224–32
Ryan, Martin J., 'The Anglo-Saxons and the Vikings, c. 825–900', in Nicholas J. Higham & Martin J. Ryan (eds), *The Anglo-Saxon World* (New Haven, Connecticut: Yale UP, 2013)
Saul, Nigel (ed.), *The Oxford Illustrated History of Medieval England* (Oxford: OUP, 1997)
Sawyer, P. H., *Age of the Vikings* (London: Hodder & Stoughton, 2nd ed, 1975)
Sawyer, P. H., 'The royal tun in pre-conquest England', in P. Wormald (ed.), *Ideal and Reality in Frankish and Anglo-Saxon Society, studies presented by J M Wallace-Hadrill* (Oxford, 1983), pp. 280–84
Schiffels, S., Haak, W., Paajanen, P. *et al.*, 'Iron Age and Anglo-Saxon genomes from East England reveal British migration history', *Nat Commun*, Vol. 7, 10408 (2016)
Scragg, D., 'Wifcyþþe and the Morality of the Cynewulf and Cyneheard Episode in the Anglo-Saxon Chronicle', in *Alfred the Wise: Studies in Honour of Janet Bately* (Cambridge, 1997), pp. 179-85
Searle, W. G., *Onomasticon Anglo-Saxonicum* (Cambridge, 1897)
Shorter Oxford English Dictionary (Oxford: OUP, 2006)
Smith, J. M. H., *Europe after Rome: A New Cultural History 500-1000* (Oxford, 2005)
Smyth, A. P., *King Alfred the Great* (Oxford: OUP, 1995)

Snyder, C. A., *An Age of Tyrants: Britain and the Britons AD400-600* (Pennsylvania, PSUP, 1998)

Spicer, Tony, 'The Battle of Ellandun and Lydiard Tregoze', *Friends of Lydiard Tregoze Report*, No. 34 (May 2001)

Stafford, Pauline, *Queen Emma and Queen Edith: Queenship and Women's Power in Eleventh-century England* (Oxford: Blackwell, 2004)

Stafford, Pauline, 'The King's Wife in Wessex 800-1066', *Past & Present*, No. 91 (Oxford: OUP, 1981), pp. 3-27

Stafford, Pauline, 'Charles the Bald, Judith and England', in Margaret Gibson & Janet L. Nelson (eds), *Charles the Bald: Court and Kingdom* (Oxford: British Archaeological Reports, 1981), pp. 137–51

Stafford, Pauline (ed.), *A Companion to the Early Middle Ages: Britain and Ireland c.500-c.1100* (Chichester: Wiley-Blackwell, 2013)

Stenton, Frank M., *Anglo-Saxon England* (Oxford: OUP, 3rd edn, 1971)

Story, Joanna, *Carolingian Connections: Anglo-Saxon England and Carolingian Francia, c. 750–870* (Aldershot: Ashgate, 2003)

Sullivan, Tony, *The Early Anglo-Saxon Kings* (Barnsley: Pen & Sword, 2023)

Swanton, M. J., *Crisis and Development in Germanic Society 700-800* (Goppingen, 1982)

Talbot, C. H. (ed.), *The Anglo-Saxon Missionaries in Germany: Being the Lives of S.S. Willibrord, Boniface, Strum, Leoba and Lebuin, together with the Hodoeporicon of St. Willibald and a Selection from the Correspondence of St. Boniface* (New York: Sheed and Ward, 1954)

Tatlock, J. S. P., 'The Dragons of Wessex and Wales', *Speculum*, Vol. 8 (2) (April 1933), pp. 223-235

Timperley, H. W. & Brill, Edith, *Ancient Trackways of Wessex* (Stroud: Nonsuch Publishing, revd edn, 2005)

Todd, Malcolm, *The South West to AD 1000, in Series A Regional History of England* (London: Longman, 1987)

Venning, Timothy, *An Alternative History of Britain: The Anglo-Saxon Age* (Barnsley: Pen & Sword, 2013)

Venning, Timothy, *Kings & Queens of Anglo-Saxon England* (Stroud: Amberley, 2013)

Verdun, Kathleen, 'Medievalism', in C. W. Jordan & J. R. Strayer (eds), *Dictionary of the Middle Ages, Vol. 1* (New York: Scribner, 2004), pp. 389-397

Vickers, J. E., 'Dore, In Old Sheffield Town', in *An Historical Miscellany* (2nd edn, 1999), pp. 64–71

Wacher, John, *The Towns of Roman Britain* (London: Batsford, 1995)

Walker, Ian, *Mercia and the Making of England* (Stroud: Sutton Publishing, 2000)

Walker, H. E., 'Bede and the Gewissae', *Cambridge Historical Journal*, Vol. xii (1956), pp. 54-8

Warner, Peter, *The Origins of Suffolk*. (Manchester and New York: MUP, 1996)

Weatherill, Craig, *Cornish World Magazine* (Oct 2007)

Webb, J. F. & Farmer, D. H. (eds), *The Age of Bede: Bede — Life of Cuthbert* (London: Penguin, 1998)

Whitehead, Annie, *Mercia: The Rise and Fall of a Kingdom* (Stroud: Amberley, 2018)

Whitehead, Annie, *Women of Power in Anglo-Saxon England* (Barnsley: Pen & Sword, 2020)

Whitelock, Dorothy, *English Historical Documents vol I, c.500–1042.* (London: Eyre & Spottiswoode, 1968)

Whitelock, Dorothy, *Some Anglo-Saxon Bishops of London* (London: 1975)

Whitlock, Ralph, *The Warrior kings of Saxon England* (New York, Barnes & Noble, 1991)

Whittock, Martyn. J., *The Origins of England: 410 to 600* (Totowa, Barnes & Noble, 1986)

Whittock, Martyn & Whittock, Hannah, *The Viking Blitzkrieg AD789-1098* (Stroud: The History Press, 2013)

Williams, Ann, *Æthelred the Unready: The Ill-counselled King* (London, 2003)

Williams, Ann, 'Æthelwulf King of Wessex 839-58', in Ann Williams, Alfred P. Smyth & D. P. Kirby (eds), *A Biographical Dictionary of Dark Age Britain* (London: Seaby, 1991), pp. 35–36

Williams, Ann, 'Ecgfrith king of Mercia', in Ann Williams, Alfred P. Smyth & D. P. Kirby (eds), *A Biographical Dictionary of Dark Age Britain* (London: Seaby, 1991)

Williams, Ann, *Kingship and Government in Pre-Conquest England, c. 500–1066.* (Basingstoke, Palgrave MacMillan Press, 1999)

Williams, G., 'The Circulation and Function of Coinage in Conversion-Period England, c. AD 580 – 675', in B. Cook & G. Williams (ed.), *Coinage and History in the North Sea World, c. 500 – 1250: Essays in Honour of Marion Archibald* (Leiden, 2006)

Williamson, Tom, *Environment, Society and Landscape in Early Medieval England: Time and Topography* (Woodbridge: Boydell Press, revd edn, 2015)

Woolf, A., 'Apartheid and Economics in Anglo-Saxon England', in N. J. Higham (ed.), *Britons in Anglo-Saxon England* (Woodbridge: Boydell Press, 2007), pp. 115-29

P. Wormald, 'Alfred the Great', *Oxford Dictionary of National Biography* (Oxford: OUP, 2004), Online edn, Accessed 19 May 2024

Wormald, Patrick, 'Kingship and Royal Property from Æthelwulf to Edward the Elder', in N. J. Higham & D. H. Hill (eds), *Edward the Elder 899–924* (Abingdon, Routledge, 2001), pp. 264–79.

Wright, Neil, *The Historia Regum Britannie of Geoffrey of Monmouth* (Woodbridge, Boydell and Brewer, 1984)

Yorke, Barbara, 'Edward as Aetheling', in N. J. Higham & D. H. Hill (eds), *Edward the Elder 899–924* (Abingdon, Routledge, 2001)

Yorke, Barbara, 'The Jutes of Hampshire and Wight and the origins of Wessex', in Bassett, S. (ed.), *The Origins of the Anglo-Saxon Kingdoms*, pp.75-83, Leicester, 1989)

Yorke, Barbara, *Kings and Kingdoms of Early Anglo-Saxon England* (London: Routledge, 1990)

Yorke, Barbara, 'Royal Burial in Winchester: Context and Significance', in Ryan Lavelle, Simon Roffey, & Katherine Weikert (eds), *Early Medieval Winchester: Communities, Authority and Power in an Urban Space, c.800-c.1200* (Oxford: Oxbow Books, 2021)

Yorke, Barbara, *Wessex in the Early Middle Ages.* (Leicester, LUP, 1995)

Yorke, Barbara, *The Conversion of Britain: Religion, Politics and Society in Britain, 600-800* (London: Routledge, 2014)

Yorke, Barbara, 'The Foundation of the Old Minster and the Status of Winchester in the Seventh and Eighth Centuries', *Proceedings of the Hampshire Field Club Archaeological Society*, Vol. 38 (1982)

Zaluckyj, Sarah, *Mercia: The Anglo-Saxon kingdom of central England* (Gaston Press, revd ed, 2013)

Index